The School of Charity

Books by Thomas Merton
available in Harvest/HBJ paperback editions
from Harcourt Brace Jovanovich, Publishers

THE SCHOOL OF CHARITY

The Letters of

THOMAS MERTON

on Religious Renewal
and Spiritual Direction
selected and edited by
Brother Patrick Hart

A Harvest/HBJ Book
Harcourt Brace Jovanovich, Publishers
SAN DIEGO   NEW YORK   LONDON

First published 1990 by Farrar, Straus & Giroux, Inc.

*Library of Congress Cataloging-in-Publication Data
Merton, Thomas, 1915–1968.
The school of charity: the letters of Thomas Merton on religious
renewal and spiritual direction/selected and edited by
Patrick Hart.—1st Harvest/HBJ ed.
p.   cm.
Includes index.
ISBN 0-15-679515-9
1. Merton, Thomas, 1915–1968—Correspondence.
2. Trappists—United States—Correspondence.
3. Church renewal—Catholic Church.
4. Catholic Church—History—20th century.
5. Spiritual direction.
I. Hart, Patrick.   II. Title.
[BX4705.M542A4   1993]
271'.12502—dc20   92-33541*

Printed in the United States of America

First Harvest/HBJ edition 1993

A B C D E

Contents

Preface

The School of Charity is the third volume of the projected five-volume series of the letters of Thomas Merton. It is appropriate that this volume of letters on religious renewal and spiritual direction should be placed at the center of the series. The monastic life—the particular form of religious life which Merton had embraced—and its renewal were very much at the center of his thought and activities. If in his writing he often moved from that center to discuss other issues, invariably he saw these issues from a monastic perspective and through the eyes of a monk.

It is true that Merton had questions about the monastic life—some of them radical, even disturbing—but they came from the heart of a monk. When he writes of the monastic life, it is his own way of living the Christian vocation that is at stake; when he talks about monastic renewal, it is about something happening in his own experience. Disillusioned at times, but never despairing, bitingly critical (especially in his later years), yet always (or almost always) creatively so, he was able to combine a lively idealism with a practical realism. He blended both into that love for the monastic life which first captured his heart when he originally visited Gethsemani and which, despite serious testing and a good deal of rethinking, never left him.

On a number of occasions when I visited the Abbey of Gethsemani, I had the pleasure of speaking with the late Dom James Fox, Merton's Abbot through most of the crucial years of his life in the monastery. On more than one occasion Dom James said to me: "I never knew a more humble or more obedient monk than Father Louis." These words were not intended as an after-the-fact "canonization" of a recalcitrant monk by a forgiving Abbot. They are his Abbot's final summing-up of the life of a monk who, though sometimes disagreeing with him, knew at the deepest level what it meant to be a monk. If some find it difficult to perceive the qualities of humility and obedience in Thomas Merton, the reason may be that they are looking only on the surface of what was deep in his heart.

We are fortunate to have Brother Patrick Hart as our mentor through the joys and frustrations of Merton's letters on monastic life and renewal. Brother Patrick was Merton's disciple and, later, secretary; he was also his friend and brother in the monastic family of Gethsemani. Multitudes of people have found in the person of Brother Patrick the same qualities of deep monastic commitment and a genuine desire to serve people that emerge from the writings of Thomas Merton. Helping us make our way through these letters is part of the ongoing service to Merton scholars and readers which Brother Patrick has offered for more than two decades, and continues to offer.

WILLIAM H. SHANNON
General Editor

Introduction

St. Bernard of Clairvaux expanded and implemented the thought of St. Benedict when he called the monastery a school of charity. The main object of monastic discipline, according to St. Bernard, was to restore man's nature created in the image and likeness of God—that is to say, created for love and for self-surrender.

THOMAS MERTON IN *Monastic Peace*

In the mid-forties Thomas Merton had tentatively titled one of his pamphlets *The School of Charity*, a projected work on the common life of Cistercians and especially the place and function of fraternal charity in the life of union with God. Although it was never published as he had planned, "The School of Charity" became a subtitle in a small book, *Monastic Peace*, which was subsequently included in the posthumous collection *The Monastic Journey*.

The Merton letters included here are concerned with renewal in the Church at large as well as religious and monastic *aggiornamento*. When I began to gather letters that would fit into this category nearly ten years ago, I found that the subjects of renewal and spiritual direction were often intertwined. Merton was sometimes seeking counsel, as in the case of the letters addressed to his Abbots, or to the Abbot General in Rome, or to some trusted friend. But more often he was simply responding to another person's written request for a word of advice and direction during a difficult period.

Although the editorial policy adopted in the two previous volumes of Merton letters has been generally followed, I have arranged these letters in chronological order throughout, for a number of reasons. First, by reading the letters in sequence one can more readily observe the development of Merton's monastic maturing over the years. It is also possible, when comparing letters written at the same time to different persons, to appreciate how often Merton adjusted his language to the sensibilities of the recipient. Salutations and closings have been omitted from the letters for the sake of space, unless something of significance warrants retaining them. It was decided to use brackets for editorial notes and clarifications, rather than to clutter the book with footnotes. Also when a short Latin or French phrase appears, a translation in English has been given in brackets. All the letters were written at the Abbey of Gethsemani unless otherwise indicated.

Many letters are addressed to religious men and women of various congregations and orders during a period of extraordinary changes in the life of the Church, as well as the updating of religious communities. When letters deal with a spiritual or moral problem, the recipients are identified with an initial, such as "Sister A." or "Brother B.," in order to preserve their anonymity; the intrinsic value of Merton's advice is evident without any need to reveal identities.

There are a considerable number of letters written to well-known people, like Father Barnabas M. Ahern, Nora Chadwick, Etienne Gilson, Dom Aelred Graham, Father Bruno Scott James, Dom Jean Leclercq, Father M. Basil Pennington, Colman McCarthy, Archbishop Paul Philippe, Father Aelred Squire, Sister Mary Luke Tobin, Dom Hubert Van Zeller, Dom Damasus Winzen, and Father (later Cardinal) Hans Urs von Balthasar, among others. Of course, there were many more less well-known monks and nuns from the United States and other countries who corresponded with Merton in regard to renewal and at the same time brought up questions of spiritual direction. The majority of the letters were written to monks and nuns who follow the Rule of St. Benedict, mainly Benedictine and Cistercian, but also some Camaldolese and Carthusian hermits. Women and men from active religious communities, such as the Dominicans and Franciscans, also availed themselves of Merton's counsel during the troubled times following Vatican II.

It seemed convenient to divide this volume into three parts, which can be seen as the major segments of Merton's monastic years. The very first letter was written by a youthful Tom Merton from Olean, New York, where he was teaching English at St. Bonaventure College (later a university). He had made a retreat at Gethsemani on the recommendation of Dr. Daniel C. Walsh, his former teacher at Columbia University. Merton was deeply impressed by the experience and wrote enthusiastically to the Abbot, Frederic Dunne, expressing his appreciation of the contemplative life as lived at Gethsemani, and enclosing a stipend for several Masses to be offered "for my particular intention." By the end of the same year he would return to Gethsemani, arriving on December 10, 1941. He entered the novitiate on December 13, the Feast of St. Lucy, given the new name of Frater M. Louis, and a white woolen postulant's robe and cloak.

The next letter, which was unearthed in the Abbey archives, was a long handwritten one (dated January 2, 1942) addressed to the Abbot at the instigation of Father Robert McGann, the Novice Master. The document (a canonical requirement) sums up Merton's early life in the world, his various schools in France and England, his travels and his dramatic conversion experience in New York while doing graduate work at Columbia University. It is a remarkable letter, in retrospect: it turns out to be a synopsis of what would one day be *The Seven Storey Mountain*, which the Abbot later urged him to write.

The majority of the letters of Part I, "The Early Monastic Years," extending from May 1941 through December 1959, are addressed to Frater Louis's monastic superiors—Abbot Frederic Dunne, until his death in 1948, and to Abbot James Fox from 1948 onward. With the election of Dom Gabriel Sortais as Abbot General in 1951, there follows a series of letters dealing not only with the spiritual problems of a young monk but increasingly with the problems connected with the publication of his books. At the same time he was seeking counsel from Dom Jean Leclercq, a Benedictine monk from Clervaux, in Luxembourg, which continued to his death in 1968. A number of Benedictine monks from St. John's Abbey in Minnesota became friends, including Fathers Colman Barry, Godfrey Diekmann, and Kilian McDonnell. As this monastic trio edited several magazines and journals at their abbey, Merton frequently contributed articles to *Worship, Sisters Today,* and *The American Benedictine Review.*

Part II, "The Middle Formative Years," embraces the period from 1960 through 1964, during which Merton was Novice Master, still writing and beginning to get more involved in ecumenical conversations with Baptists, Disciples of Christ, Presbyterians, and Episcopalians of the area. These letters are less parochial, and reveal Merton's growing interest in matters of social concern as well as the religious traditions of the Far East. More women were now admitted to his world, such as the Carmelite Prioress Mother Angela Collins, of the Louisville Carmel, where Merton would stop and offer Mass when he was in town for a doctor's appointment. Then there was Sister Mary Luke Tobin, another neighbor from nearby Loretto, who was president of this pioneering group of American religious women and who was to be the only U.S. woman observer at Vatican II.

The only "Cold War Letter" included in this volume was the one Merton wrote to Sister Elaine M. Bane, a Franciscan experimenting with the solitary life at Allegany, New York. (It was dated July 4, 1962, and is numbered 91 in the "Cold War Letters.") Mother Myriam Dardenne, another regular correspondent, was the leader of a group of Belgian Cistercian nuns who founded the Monastery of the Redwoods in California. This group passed through Gethsemani and became acquainted with Father Louis; it was the beginning of a lifelong friendship. During this period Merton wrote frequently to two Benedictine nuns of Stanbrook Abbey in England: Dame Hildelith Cumming and Marcella Van Bruyn. The correspondence began in 1962 in reference to the publication of a little book on Guigo the Carthusian, which was actually a letter of Guigo that Merton translated and introduced with a short essay. The correspondence dealt with everything from monastic renewal to social concern to liturgy and, of course, fine printing, one of Merton's lifelong passions.

Since the question of censorship comes up in many letters, it might be well to explain the procedures followed during these years. It was of course necessary for publications to gain the approval of the diocesan censors, and in most cases this was arranged between the publisher and the Chancery Office of the diocese; since Merton's books were published for the most part in New York, permission was sought from Cardinal Spellman and his successor, Cardinal Cooke. Prior to this, the censorship of the Cistercian Order had to be obtained, and generally this turned out to be the more problematic of the two. Besides examining the author's orthodoxy in matters of faith and morals, the Cistercian censors were concerned about the "appropriateness" of a given publication. Would the book tarnish the image of the Order? Would it scandalize the young? Should a contemplative Cistercian, for example, be interested in publishing his journals?

Many of Merton's difficulties with censors involved the publication of his journals, like *The Sign of Jonas* and later *The Secular Journal* and *Conjectures of a Guilty Bystander*. The publication of *The Sign of Jonas* was temporarily stopped after the book was already in galley proofs; it was only through the impassioned plea of Jacques Maritain in his native tongue to the Abbot General, Dom Gabriel Sortais, that the book was allowed to be published. The "French connection" saved the day!

Latin terms were used to designate the approval of the Cistercian Order as well as the diocese, such as the *Nihil Obstat, Imprimi Potest,* and *Imprimatur*, formulas equivalent to saying: let it be published, no objections to its being printed. This was followed by the name of the cardinal, along with those of two diocesan censors and two Cistercian censors. It was not an easy thing for heterodox teaching to pass through this kind of censorship. Today the demands are less stringent; the local abbot simply appoints a "reader," who can be a member of the community. Thus the work of censorship has been greatly eased and has become more efficient and probably more effective.

I discuss the question of censorship in some detail since it greatly affected Merton's writing almost from the start, and caused him (and others) no little amount of anguish. Such was not the case, however, with personal letters to people within or outside the monastic life. Here Merton, as in his private journals, was free to express his ideas about renewal as well as his unique insights as a spiritual director. It allowed him utter frankness in dealing with problems of renewal, no less than in counseling his many correspondents.

The third part, "The Later Solitary Years," covers 1965 to 1968, after Father Louis had been granted permission to resign his office of Novice

Master and retire to a hermitage on the property of the monastery. These letters reflect the great joy he experienced in living alone, establishing his own schedule of rising, times for prayer and manual work, times for meditation and long hikes in the surrounding forests, preparing meals and listening to the rain on the roof of his cinder-block hermitage. With the election of a new Abbot, Father Flavian Burns, in January 1968, there is increased exchange with other monasteries, and even a couple of visits to places like the Redwoods Abbey in California and Christ of the Desert Monastery in New Mexico.

Then a momentous invitation came for Merton to participate in the meeting of Asian monastic superiors in Bangkok, Thailand, in December 1968. There were many letters on this subject before the final approval came. Merton wrote to his Benedictine friends, Dom Aelred Graham and Dom Jean Leclercq, about making contacts with the Tibetan monks in India and the possibility of meeting the Dalai Lama. Both monks were very helpful in making this pilgrimage to the East one of Merton's greatest delights. His letters to Gethsemani from Alaska make clear how much he looked forward to Asia, and with what great enthusiasm he entered upon the venture. As paradoxical as it may seem, he was at the same time very much concerned about finding a more solitary place for a hermitage after his return from Asia. His social side and his desire for solitude remained in fruitful tension right up to the end.

The last letters, from Calcutta, New Delhi, Dharamsala, Darjeeling, Madras, Colombo, Singapore, and finally Bangkok, all manifest Merton's dedication to his monastic vocation and his willingness to submit his ideas to his Abbot and to work things out gradually for a future hermitage. The rumors which circulated following his death—that he had abandoned his monastic commitment and would have left the monastery or that he had given up his Christian faith to embrace Buddhism—were untrue. The truth of the matter is established beyond doubt in these last letters from Asia.

The old adage "Absence makes the heart grow fonder" characterizes many of Merton's letters to Gethsemani from the Far East. In his last letter from Bangkok, undoubtedly his final one, written to his secretary just two days before his tragic death, he ends by saying: "I think of you all on this Feast Day [December 8, the Feast of the Immaculate Conception]. Also with Christmas approaching, I feel homesick for Gethsemani . . . Best love to all, Louie." These nostalgic lines bring the present volume to a close. The letters Thomas Merton wrote in this "school of charity" confirm the enduring values he proclaimed tirelessly throughout his life.

BROTHER PATRICK HART
Abbey of Gethsemani

I.

The Early Monastic Years
1941-1959

Our studies and writing should by their very nature contribute to our contemplation at least remotely and contemplation in turn should be able to find expression in channels laid open for it and deepened by familiarity with the Fathers of the Church. This is an age that calls for St. Augustines and Leos, Gregorys and Cyrils!

THOMAS MERTON
IN A LETTER TO JEAN LECLERCQ,
APRIL 22, 1950

To Abbot Frederic Dunne, O.C.S.O.

Frederic Dunne (1874–1948) was Abbot of Gethsemani when Thomas Merton first made a retreat at the monastery in Holy Week, 1941. Returning to St. Bonaventure College in upstate New York, where he was teaching, Merton wrote Abbot Frederic his first letter, expressing gratitude for the retreat. Frederic Dunne had come from a family of printers and bookbinders in Zanesville, Ohio, near the birthplace coincidentally of Merton's mother, Ruth Jenkins. It was natural enough for Abbot Frederic, who valued the printed word, to encourage the young poet to write and it was also fortunate for Merton, as subsequent events proved.

St. Bonaventure College, New York
May 1, 1941

You must undoubtedly have received hundreds of letters like the one which I am about to try to write, from people who have had the privilege of spending a few days in retreat at the Abbey of Gethsemani, and returned to the world again deeply moved with gratitude to Almighty God for having been able to see what is there to see. For it can be more truly said of this community than of the most active imaginable, that it is that city which is set upon a hill, and cannot be hid.

I don't think it would be possible for any human being, certainly for any Christian, to set foot inside the Abbey without at once realizing that he is in the palace of the Queen of Heaven, and since I have been there, I cannot deny that I believe that the prayers of your community are among the only things that are keeping the world together in this horrible and dangerous time, when even those of us in the world who try to be sincere Catholics and followers of Christ, are really shot through with the most insidious indifference and complacency and false, facile piety. We outside are yielding, without knowing it, to the proud and self-indulgent standards of the world that is all around us, and never find it out, unless we chance upon the rare places, like Gethsemani, where the monks never forget how, in a garden, the apostles slept and the Lord was betrayed.

The work of the monks is not merely that they remain prostrate before the tabernacle while the whole pagan world wanders in the terrible unhappiness of a desert of sin. But it is also that they remain watchful while we, who call ourselves Catholics but are only weak and unprofitable servants, thinking that we watch and pray, are sleeping almost as deeply as everyone else. Truly, if we were good Catholics, the whole world would be different: many would see us and be converted. How much of the punishment that is falling on the world are we responsible for, who are nothing but proud and complacent and lazy and pleasure-loving Catholics, and a scandal to people who are being hunted up and down by their sins, and looking for a place of refuge!

We are asleep, and our prayers are little more than trances. We are inarticulate, we are deaf-mutes: and only you, who have been silenced by a vow, really have your tongues loosed, and can speak, because you are not concerned with arguments and justifications before men, but only with speaking to God and His angels and His saints.

We, with our prayers cluttered with cares for ourselves, for our comfort, and for our safety, and for our success in some project that will get us money and reputation, we think we pray, and we are only talking to ourselves, because we only love ourselves! Where would we be if we did not have you to pray for us!

Then may Almighty God hear your prayers for the rest of us, and awaken us from our selfish sleep, and arm us in this battleground where we have let ourselves at last be surrounded, because we were thinking only of peace in terms of fleshly rest, and had forgotten we were given, on earth, not peace but a sword.

It is not necessary for us to ask that you pray for us, because if you hadn't already prayed for us, we would be lost: and when we have said, in our hearts, that we believe in the Communion of Saints, that is as much as if we had written a hundred letters, asking for your prayers. However, I am enclosing a very small check, and beg you in your charity to have said two masses for my particular intention.

The twenty-six-year-old Tom Merton arrived at Gethsemani on December 10, 1941, and was given a room in the guest house. After three days he was received into the novitiate, and on February 22, 1942, was given the habit of a novice and began his novitiate life. At the suggestion of his Novice Master, the future Abbot Robert McGann (of Holy Spirit Monastery in Georgia, which Gethsemani founded in 1944), Frater Louis penned a letter to Abbot Frederic Dunne explaining his conversion experience, detailing the various places where he had lived and studied until the time of his entry at Gethsemani. It was probably an effort to fulfill the canonical requirement stating the various dioceses in which he had lived for over a year before entering Gethsemani.

[Gethsemani Novitiate]
January 2, 1942

At the suggestion of my Father Master, I am writing out for you this outline of the main facts of my life and education, including, in particular, the circumstances of my conversion and vocation.

I was born Jan. 31, 1915, in Prades, France, in the diocese of Perpignan, of Protestant parents. My father was a native of New Zealand, my mother an American. Both are now dead; my mother died when I was six, my father in 1931. I have no knowledge of having received even a Protestant baptism. It is barely possible that I did: but no record exists of it, and no one is left to tell me.

In 1916 my parents brought me to America. I lived here until 1925 when I returned to France with my father. Then I went to the Lycée of Montauban—a public institution of secondary education, for two years. In 1928 I was sent to England, where from 1929 to 1932 I attended Oakham School at Oakham, Rutland, in the Diocese of Nottingham. This was my address from the age of 14 to 16½. After that I came to America and lived most of 1933 with my grandparents at Douglaston, Long Island, in the Diocese of Brooklyn. During the scholastic year 1933–4 I attended Cambridge University, in England, on a scholarship in modern languages. My home address, however, was my grandparents' residence—50 Rushmore Ave., Douglaston, Long Island, N.Y. In fact this was really my *home address*, although most of the time I was away at school, from 1931 to 1934. But I actually lived there from 1934 to 1939. During that time I attended Columbia University, where I got a B.A. degree, and later I pursued my studies and took an M.A. in English, and even did some work towards the degree of Ph.D. I taught English at Columbia one term.

My next address, 1939–40, was 35 Perry Street, New York City, in the Archdiocese of New York.

After that, from June 1940 to December 1941 my address was St. Bonaventure College, St. Bonaventure, N.Y., in the Diocese of Buffalo. There I was employed as an assistant professor of English.

As to my conversion: I had been brought up without much religious training of any kind. My grandparents gave money to the Episcopal Church, but never attended it. My father was a just, devout and prayerful man, but he did not like the Protestant cenacles in France, and never went to the length of becoming a Catholic. He died a good Anglican. The school I went to in England was Anglican, but I protested against the liberal teaching in religion we received there, and because it seemed to me to have no substance to it, I proudly assumed that this was the case with all religions, and obstinately set my face against all churches. Thus from the time of my leaving Oakham School until 1938, I gradually passed from being anti-clerical and became a complete unbeliever. The consequences of this in my life were disastrous. My only concern was with earthly things; thinking myself passionately devoted to "justice" and "liberty" I began to take an interest in atheistic communism, and, for a while, I held the "doctrines" of radicalism, concerning religious institutions: namely that they were purely the result of social and historical forces and, however well-meaning their adherents, they were nothing more than *social* groups, which the rich made use of to oppress the poor!!!

Suffice it to say that I could not be happy holding such beliefs; and the earthly life, which promised happiness on a purely natural level, had instead brought me great disappointments and shocks and miseries: and I was making bigger and bigger mistakes and becoming more and more confused. I began to realize that my interpretation of the natural order was very mistaken.

As a result of studies and reading which familiarized me with the works of Etienne Gilson and Jacques Maritain, but particularly as the result of the work of God's grace which now began to move me with the most urgent promptings of desire, I began going to Mass at Corpus Christi Church, West 121st Street, New York. And there, I soon began to take instruction and was happily baptized on November 16, 1938.

After that, with many graces from God and many instances of stupidity and ingratitude on my own part, I began, too slowly, the long-needed amendment of my life. In September 1939, considering that my life was still far short of what I desired, I began to pray for a vocation to the priesthood. At that time I was considering the Order of Friars Minor. I even sent an application for admission to that order, and was accepted: however, before beginning the novitiate, I recalled an incident of my past life, and believing this made me unworthy to be a priest, and supported in this belief by a friend who was a priest, I withdrew my application and did not enter the novitiate. Instead, I went to work at St. Bonaventure College, in order to live as nearly as possible the life I would have led if my hopes had not been disappointed. I then discovered that this life also was too easy-going and worldly and relaxed for me; it was well that I had not gone on and entered the Franciscan novitiate! However, I became a Franciscan Tertiary, and by means of daily Communion and other sources of Divine Grace, attempted to advance in the paths of Christian life.

With the passage of time, I was still much unsatisfied, and having heard of the Trappists from a friend [Dan Walsh], I decided to make a retreat here at Gethsemani, which I did during Holy Week, 1941. From the very first moment of entering the monastery I was overwhelmed with the holiness and sanctified atmosphere that filled it, and by the end of that week I was filled with an intense desire to enter this community. However, I still believed that I had no choice in the matter and that, being "unworthy" of the priesthood, it would be useless for me to ever think of applying to be admitted here. Nevertheless I was praying for a Trappist vocation against all hope. The whole situation made me intensely miserable. I returned to my work, and all the impressions I had brought from Gethsemani remained with me all summer—and grew in strength, with my desire to consecrate myself entirely to God as a monk—or if not as a monk, by some other perfect sacrifice of the world: just what, I did not know: but I thought of going as a permanent worker with Baroness de Hueck, in Harlem, where I did actually spend two weeks.

During this time, I was so much at a loss for an answer to my question, for out of shame at the situation in my past which had created this problem, I dared consult no one about it—I finally resolved on saying some prayers and opening the Bible and seeing what answer I would get in this way. With great amazement and fear I read the first words that my eyes fell upon, and they were *"Ecce eris tacens!"* [Behold, you will be silent!]— the words of the angel to Zacharias. Even at this surprisingly clear indication of what I was to do, I remained uncertain for some time, and made a retreat early in September at Our Lady of the Valley [Cistercian abbey in Rhode Island].

Finally, this fall I decided to consult another friend, a priest, and one more learned and experienced than my former adviser. This time I was told that the problem I had in mind was no obstacle to my becoming a priest—which turned out to be the case when I submitted it to your consideration through Father Master, on my arrival here.

I came to Gethsemani December 10, and was admitted to the community on the Feast of St. Lucy, December 13; and now with many prayers and thanks to Almighty God I beg Him to make me, the least of all His servants, totally His so that my past life of rebellious sins and ingratitude may be burned clean away in the fire of His infinite love—for which I know I humbly share in the merit of your prayers, my Reverend Father!

Before making temporary profession, Frater Louis made out a will for the period of three years preceding solemn vows. This document throws interesting light on a provision he made in a letter to his godfather, Dr. Tom Bennett. Obviously, there was uncertainty in Merton's mind as to the whereabouts of "the person [he met while at Cambridge University] mentioned to [Dr. Bennett] . . . in my letters, if that person can be found." But it does manifest a responsibility for past actions on the part of the young monk.

February 17, 1944

I, Thomas James Merton, in religion frater M. Louis, formerly of St. Bonaventure, State of New York, now of Gethsemani (Trappist Post Office) in the County of Nelson, State of Kentucky, being about to make my simple vows in the religious community known as the Abbey of Gethsemani (a corporation under and by virtue of the laws of said State of Kentucky) of Cistercians of the Strict Observance, make the following dispositions concerning my property.

1. I hereby designate Robert Lax, of the Olean House, Olean, New York, as recipient of the yearly dividends from the stock held by me in the firm of Grosset and Dunlap, Inc., 1170 Broadway, New York,

N.Y. until such time as I shall make a further settlement of my property.

2. I reserve to myself all right, title and interest and all other real and personal property that I may now possess or may acquire during my time of simple profession.

3. I hereby appoint the Right Reverend Frederic M. Dunne, Abbot of the said Abbey of Gethsemani, or his successor in office, executor, administrator and trustee of the entire income of my property, both real and personal, until such time as I make my solemn profession in said religious Order.

4. Should I die during the term of my said simple profession I give and bequeath my property as follows:

a) The shares in my Optional Savings Shares Account No. 101533, held in the Railroad Federal Building and Loan Society, 441 Lexington Ave, New York, N.Y. to be divided equally between my sister-in-law, Mrs. Margaret M. Merton, of 61 Camden Street, Birkenhead, Cheshire, England, and my guardian, T. Izod Bennett Esq., M.D., of 29 Hill Street, Berkeley Square, London, W.1.—this second half to be paid by him to the person mentioned to him by me in my letters, if that person can be found.

b) All the remainder of my property, both real and personal, to which I may have any right, title or interest at the time of my death, I give and bequeath to the before mentioned Abbey of Gethsemani.

Given under my hand and seal this 17th day of February 1944.

[Signed]   Thomas James Merton   fr. M. Louis, O.C.S.O.

Signed, sealed, published and delivered by the above named frater M. Louis in the presence of us, who at his request and in the presence of each other and in his presence have hereto subscribed our names as witnesses this 17th day of February 1944.

[Signed]   M. Robert McGann
M. Walter Helmstetter

To Abbot Frederic Dunne

March 6, 1944

As our profession is drawing close, I suppose I ought to have something to say for myself, although really I can't find anything that is not simply trivial. If it is a question of telling you what great progress in virtue I have made—I simply don't know whether I have made any progress or not, and seem to have no way of telling. But over and above that, there is nothing that disgusts me more than trying to analyze myself, and paying attention to my "progress." *Regnum Dei non venit cum observatione* [The Kingdom of God comes not with observation].

And yet, Our Lord said *"Vigilate!"* [Watch!]. But that is another thing again: for the vigilance of desire is my whole life. It is all I have to offer Jesus. I have no virtues (nothing striking), and I am full of all the trivial and embarrassing weaknesses that only a fool would be surprised to find in himself. But I do want Jesus to come. And to come quickly, to me and the whole world. *"Deus meus, ne tardaveris!"* Si moram fecerit, expecta eum ["My God, do not tarry!" If he delays, wait for him].

And thus with my loins girt up and with the lighted lamp of faith in my hand, I sit in the absolute darkness where He has placed me, and hope against hope for the cry *"Ecce Sponsus venit, exite obviam ei"* [Behold the Spouse is coming, go forth to meet him].

All I am interested in is, not myself, but Him.

And yet my "self" is always clamoring for attention. What of it? If I keep waiting for Jesus in patience, and look only for Him, the clamors will eventually die down.

As for profession: when (and if) I lie prostrate before you on the Feast of St. Joseph, I shall be begging God to deliver me from the bitter burden of all my *self-will and own judgment*.

That is the only cross that is *too* hard—the cross that makes every other cross crush us to the ground. If I can only get rid of these, all other crosses will be light and easy.

Therefore I hereby present you with all my will, all my judgment, all my powers of body and soul to do with as you please, according to the Rule and Constitutions and the counsel of our Savior.

And I desire and beg Jesus to accept this holocaust, through you, for three intentions:

1) For His peace on earth—that is, that He may dwell in the hearts of men and end this war.

2) For my brethren in the monastery—for whom I promise that my desire and confidence shall be without limit, that they may become great saints. And I offer up my every act down to my last breath for these, but especially my superiors.

3) For all that I ever knew or had any connection with in the world, that all those with whom I was associated in my sinful life may be saved.

There will be many other intentions, and I know you will help me with your prayers always to please Jesus with the vigilance of loving faith, so that at last I may be able to say *"Quae placita sunt ei facio semper"* [I do always the things that please him].

To Dom Vital Klinski, O.C.S.O.

Dom Vital Klinski (1886–1966) was born in Poland and entered the Cistercian abbey of Achel in Belgium in 1904; he was elected Abbot of Achel on August 29, 1920, but resigned his office in 1927 and entered Gethsemani on November 19, 1927. Merton's "silver jubilee" greeting and joyful sketch with an abbot's mitre can be dated on the feast of the beheading of St. John the Baptist, August 29, 1945. Dom Vital, Merton's confessor during these years (which explains the text in part), died at Gethsemani on June 3, 1966.

[August 29, 1945]

I only attempted to draw the mitre, not the jubilarian underneath and in it. On such an occasion as this, that would require a Michelangelo. But anyway all best wishes on this happy day of your silver Jubilee as a Father and Abbot of souls—our "Pastor Bonus" in whom we see only Jesus. All our prayers are for you—especially of course our Holy Communion, Holy Mass and Rosary on this day. And in honor of the decollation of St. John Baptist I present you with my own head—that is, judgement and will, on a silver platter. *Ad multos annos!* [Many more years!]

Vivat! Vivat! Feliciter! [Long may he live! Happily!]

Your devoted son,
fr. M. Louis

To Abbot Frederic Dunne

[undated—probably 1946 or 1947]

Dear Rev. Father,

As you will probably have many notes to read tomorrow, I am sending *St. Lutgarde* [drawing done around the time he was writing *What Are These Wounds?*] to wish you a happy feast, instead of writing a note. She will tell you all my good wishes and prayers for you on this day. Your devoted child in Jesus,

fr. M. Louis

Abbot Frederic died while traveling to Gethsemani's foundation of Holy Spirit Monastery in Georgia in August 1948. Shortly before leaving, he had placed the first copy of The Seven Storey Mountain *in the young monk's hands, and he seemed more pleased than Merton. Abbot James Fox (1896–1987), who was the*

superior of the group of founders in Georgia, replaced Frederic Dunne as Abbot
of Gethsemani. The first of Merton's letters to the new abbot, undated, was
doubtless written in the spring of 1949 and apparently refers (as do later letters
in the series) to the fame and notoriety which resulted from the publication of
The Seven Storey Mountain *in October 1948. Abbot James remained Merton's*
superior for the next twenty years; he resigned his office in January 1968, the
year of Merton's death, and lived a semi-eremitical life until his own death on
Good Friday, April 17, 1987.

To Abbot James Fox, O.C.S.O.

[Spring, 1949]

Another protocol from Chop Suey Louie the mad Chinese poet.

It is just to say that I am picturing that immediate goal that Dr. de Quevedo [visiting psychiatrist] wants us all to aim at. What is it? It is this: a very obscure, quiet, unknown, unnoticed monk: a little guy who goes quietly around without attracting any attention for anything whatever, not complaining about anything and not expressing opinions, doing what he is told and being completely docile and blank as far as the exterior goes—except of course for a happy sort of an expression. I want to be as near as possible to nothing and nobody in the community—and everywhere else too—as a monk can possibly be. The reason for my wanting this is that I am altogether sick of myself and I want to do everything I can to cease existing as an ego outside of God.

I do not aim at the heights, I aim at the depths. Not at what is exalted and spectacular but what is humble and unenviable and unattractive and blank. I aspire to become a nonentity and to be forgotten. In the present situation it will take a little deliberate work to get to be that way and I don't see quite how to go about it, but anyway I'll make an honest effort, and ask Jesus to show me the rest of the way. I have got more to get rid of than anybody else in the community.

May God bless you, Rev. Father, and give you grace to guide and lead this great big community. No man can do it. God has got to do the job. But He will. And I will keep seeing Him there, doing the job. And I'll cooperate by disappearing into His will and being whatever He wants me to become which, I hope, is nothing.

May Day of Recollection, 1949

I am glad to be having this day of recollection before ordination, instead of after. My personal ideal in the priesthood is one of complete obscurity and simplicity. I ask Jesus to make me a purely contemplative priest. He has plenty of active workers, missionaries, preachers, spiritual directors, masters of novices, etc. But He has so few who are concerned with Him alone, in simplicity, silence, recollection and constant prayer.

I beg Him daily that I may always be one of those few, and that I may live the life of pure union with Him that was led by the forgotten saints.

I want to be a forgotten and unknown saint, hidden in God alone. I feel entirely out of sympathy with all the activity and noise of our day and age. Publicity may be necessary for the Church, but I beg God to spare me from it, and from all the constant movement and action and preaching and talking and business and display which seem to have become part of Christian as well as worldly life. All that is not for me. May God preserve us from it and keep us for Himself alone in silence and prayer—a life of obscure suffering and devotion to Him in the humblest things. I know you are praying for me and be sure I am always praying for you. Please give me a big blessing . . .

[Summer 1949]
. . . You can guess that the two hours between 2 and 4 p.m. Sunday afternoon, when you let me go out into the woods, were two of the happiest hours I have ever spent in my life. When I am alone, Jesus is with me at once. I am "never less alone than when I am alone." When people are around, I find it a little difficult to find Jesus. As soon as I am away from others, Jesus is there and all is at peace.

I think that in those two hours I understood things I had never known before about Gethsemani and about my own vocation. It helps a great deal to see Gethsemani from the outside. Inside we are so close to one another and to our own little interests that things get out of perspective. And we are so much on top of one another that we forget the marvelous solitude that Gethsemani really is, I mean even physically! Few monasteries in the world can beat our situation, as far as isolation is concerned. It only remains for us to take advantage of it. I am not talking about others. God has His plans for each one of us. For me, it remains to take advantage of all the wonderful opportunities the Sacred Heart is putting in my way. It may seem a little funny, it may look funny to others: I mean, I am a little outside the common life. But it is *for* the common life, Rev. Father, that Jesus draws me apart. He knows that solitude is something that I need in order to make me *appreciate* the common life and enter into it more *fruitfully.* If you only knew what it meant to me to be able to go into choir and sing the praises of the Sacred Heart after having been with Him out in the hills!

And out in the woods, too, I was conscious that every step and every movement of my heart which leapt up to the Holy Trinity in perfect unison with the heartbeats of Jesus's Sacred Heart, all this was the continuation and expression of my Mass that morning. Gee, it was perfect. I felt more myself than I have been for years—but the Mass is making me more myself day after day and so is the vault [the rare-book room which was given to Merton for writing].

This is only to say, then, Rev. Father, how much I appreciate your broad-mindedness and your help in letting Our Lord form me in His own way. And above all, dear Rev. Father, I want to promise and assure you that I won't be ungrateful. I mean with my whole heart to make use of these dispositions of His will, through obedience, in order to strengthen my vocation and to be a useful member of the Gethsemani community and a true Cistercian monk. I know that if I do these things I will be travelling the right path. Not only you, but Dom Dominique [Abbot General] was so explicit and firm in telling me to take the opportunities offered by this writing job and use them in the interests of contemplation. Everyone says that my true vocation has been marked out by the peculiar circumstances of Gethsemani plus this job. At the same time, it will be my joy to get out to the common work when I can, and I shall do so regularly once a week, or more often if you so desire. I am glad to have the certainty that God wills me to travel to Him not only in community but also with the solitude He has provided for me. How ungrateful I would be to complain when He has gone out of His way to smooth out my path to Him. May Jesus bless you in everything and show you more and more how to lead us all by the ways of contemplation and peace and teach us to rely more and more on Him to guide us through you.

So I renew my vows and promises of obedience and everything else I can renew and a few other things besides, and give myself to the work of paying attention to what goes on in the sanctuary so as to become a worthy priest when the time comes, a humble and obedient and peaceful priest, one who will vanish into Jesus and no longer be seen. Then my whole life can be one of love and contemplation and union with Him. He has been very good to me in keeping me out of all the noise and fanfare that surrounded the centenary, and I hope He will continue to do so.

To Dom Humphrey Pawsey, O. Cart.

Dom Humphrey Pawsey, a Carthusian monk of St. Hugh's Charterhouse in England, which was planning an American foundation, learns from this letter of Merton's how publicity works in America.

June 21, 1949

It is a long time since I have written to you and I cannot remember whether I have acknowledged the two volumes of Denis that finally completed our set, as well as the charming little volume of Meditations on the Sacred Heart.

We have celebrated our centenary here with unavoidable fuss. If you Carthusians ever come to America you will have to be more heroic than you ever were in preserving your purity against the incursions of this incorrigibly curious and enthusiastic "race," if you can call it such.

One reason why I have not written to you is that I have been too ashamed of myself. Perhaps you have heard some rumor of the awful notoriety that has descended upon me as the result of having suddenly become a "best seller" as an author. My Superiors—meaning especially the late dear Dom Frederic, God rest his soul—had me write a book which happened to be my own story. I wrote it, for better or for worse, and it has already sold two hundred thousand copies. An English edition, somewhat chastened by the critical talent of Evelyn Waugh, has now appeared and if you have not seen *Elected Silence*, I shall have the publisher send you a copy. Over here it was called *The Seven Storey Mountain*. What is stranger still, a book on contemplation which is strictly ascetic and mystical and in no sense popular [*Seeds of Contemplation*] is now being devoured by the public of this land, selling especially in Hollywood, of all places. I utterly give up trying to understand what is going on.

Perhaps you can guess, dear Father, that, all joking aside, this situation is extremely painful for me and is the occasion of a deep interior struggle which makes me ask myself if I can possibly continue in an atmosphere of such activity in which, for instance, one is liable to be called up on the telephone by newspaper reporters and in which a house full of retreatants is thirsting for autographs. Please remember me in your prayers, and perhaps your Venerable Father Prior would also pray for me. I cannot be more explicit but he will understand, I am sure. My vocation is contemplative and I simply *must* fulfill it . . .

Our dear Lord has strengthened me against this business by bringing me to the conclusion of my theological studies and so to the priesthood. And without doubt there is nothing that can happen to a man on earth, even American publicity, that cannot find superabundant compensation in the Holy Mass. Be sure that I remember you and all your Order when I am at the altar. Jacques Maritain told me to send a copy of the book to Dom Porion [Carthusian Procurator General], and I did so, receiving a charming letter from him, in return. On the other hand, my Superiors do not want me to have anything more to do, in an active way, with the Carthusian foundation, so here the matter rests, as far as my own poor part in it may be concerned. I did get in a recommendation to one Bishop, however. For the rest, it is in my prayers.

We sent you a big, flamboyant book of pictures of Gethsemani which we put out as a centenary souvenir. It makes Gethsemani look so gorgeous that when I read it I forget my troubles. Don't let it upset *you*. Remember that paper is patient, and takes anything.

We can still absorb some more volumes of Denis, paying for them or bartering for them as you please, starting with his commentary on the Psalms for our Utah monastery.

To Abbot James Fox

September 10, 1949

Hoping this will not be too late to catch you at Cîteaux [in France], I am enclosing some notes which I wrote out for Fr. Timothy [Vander Vennet] with suggestions for building up our theological course next year. You may have time to meditate on them on a train or somewhere—and perhaps you might see fit to submit them to someone in the know over there and get their reaction. The idea is of course to make Gethsemani, as you said, a sort of West Point or Annapolis for Cistercians. We should really organize our little seminary and make the house a center of really first-class studies in spiritual theology, especially Cistercian Fathers and mystical theology, with stress also on the canon law and other points so necessary for future superiors. This really involves a sort of long-term plan. It should be something settled and definite and in my opinion it would almost merit a small, separate seminary building where there would be plenty of space for classes and study, quiet atmosphere and so on. It is so hard to get away from organ practicing, power lawn-mowers, tractors, etc., and although I am pretty impervious to noise I still feel the strain of working with the traxcavator going. It would be easier on students' nerves, etc. One extremely important element about this plan would be to expand the range of studies *without putting an inhuman burden* on the students. In many cases the classes would have to be discussion groups in which texts would be read and commented on then and there, with each one offering his own little contribution. This would minimize the danger of boys going off and cramming their heads with facts and cracking their brains with memory work and just generating a whole lot of nervous tension, without any outlet or expression for what is going on inside their heads. I believe that is one of the big sources of nervous trouble in our life.

In any case, I know you agree that the Holy Ghost really seems to want a center of spiritual studies somewhere in the Order in USA and Gethsemani seems the logical place because we have such a good library, although Utah would have the right atmosphere and climate. It would take care of part of the winter problem in Utah.

Another point that might be worthwhile asking our Reverendissimus [Abbot General] about. Suppose we put up a little chapel in the woods behind the lake, about twenty or 25 minutes' walk from the monastery. This would enable a monk to get away once in a while and be a center where one might have little retreats in solitude and silence, especially valuable for those with heavy jobs, guestmasters, cellarers, brother cooks for seculars, priors, abbots even! There they could get away. This plan would allow of several interpretations.

1) A small chapel: one could let a single monk go and spend the

whole day there perhaps. Key to the place in possession of first superior, permission only given by him, of course.

2) Small chapel to which a group of five or six might be allowed to go and spend the day, leaving abbey after Chapter, reciting offices in common out there, but separating at other times to read and pray by themselves in the woods. They could take some food along for a frugal "dinner" and return home for supper. This plan seems to me to be the best; it retains a certain cenobitic element. One might do this two or three days in succession, with a "retreat master" preaching two short conferences, in the case of retreats prescribed for ordinations, solemn professions, etc. Novices would generally not go out there, at least at first. It should be reserved for the mature members of the community.

3) A regular little *grange* in the woods with a chapel, dormitory, refectory, kitchen and scriptorium, all very small and simple, with a monk permanently in residence (guess who??) and a brother also. These two could take care of the place, and retreatants could come out almost any time, singly or in groups as big as five, not more. I think this would be ideal, myself. The "master of the grange" could be a sort of retreat master as well, but nothing elaborate about the retreats! Leave everything to the Holy Ghost and let individuals find themselves and get back on their feet alone with God in the woods. This grange could be farther away from the abbey and deeper in solitude.

Naturally the strictest silence would always be observed out there and whatever meals would be served, if it were a regular grange, would be very frugal and simple. The grange idea would be something like a Carmelite Desert. I am really deadly in earnest about this. It seems to me we have a wonderful solitude here, as good as can be found anywhere in the Order, but our big crowded, cramped abbey in the middle of it robs most of us of the fruits of the solitude. I am convinced that this project would do an immense amount to help us advance in contemplation and divine union, above all it would break down the *rigidity* and cramped spirituality that some get into, and I know the younger generation would blossom out and expand mightily with such an opportunity. What do you think, Reverend Father? It will bear thinking and praying over, anyway. I hope the Holy Ghost will work something out for us. I know for my own part that in the last year I have drawn more fruit from my little opportunities to be alone with God, which you have so kindly given me, than I could have got from almost anything else I can think of. Everything is very well under control at Gethsemani. If you were away in spiritual retreat in the woods, instead of on business, it would go just as well, wouldn't it? May our dearest Lady lead us ever into deeper and deeper solitude and silence and into the peace of divine union.

The following letter was written to Dom James Fox while he was making a Visitation at Our Lady of the Valley, a Cistercian monastery in Rhode Island, which later transferred to St. Joseph's Abbey, Spencer, Massachusetts.

October 1, 1949

This is intended to find you safely landed and established at the Valley. First, will you please give the enclosed article, "The White Pebble," to Fr. Gabriel to censor? It is the story for that collection of conversion articles they are getting up at Notre Dame.

Second, here is a revised schedule for that theology plan. I talked it over with Father Timothy. Both he and and Father Prior say they are very anxious to see these changes made and Fr. Timothy told me to draw up this plan after our discussion. He does not feel that two three-quarter-hour classes every day would be possible, and I agree with him. This plan seems to embody all the features of the old one. I am sending it to you so that you may have time to think it over some more, and perhaps consult with the authorities on the subject at the Valley. You will notice that there is an orientation course for newcomers. Fr. Timothy is very strong on this and kept suggesting that it should be adopted. It would require arrangements with Fr. Gerard. There are also intrusions into the schedule of Fr. Lambert and Fr. Andrew. Perhaps if you see fit to go on with this plan we ought to have a meeting of the faculty and Fr. Gerard and talk the whole thing over and reach a final settlement. Meanwhile I have a clean copy of this in case it would be worthwhile showing it to the Archbishop.

In a way I am tempted to envy you having seen various of our houses in Europe but everything has been very beautiful at Gethsemani. By some miracle of grace the Holy Spirit has begun to soften my hard heart and I have broken down so far as to feel a wonderful exultation at being united to such a community of saints as we have here. Rev. Father, I wish I could explain to you what gets into my heart and simply carries me away. The Mass has done it more than anything else. But all of a sudden I have seen what it *means* to be a member of Christ, and have developed a sense of what we are all made for and heading for, that wonderful union in Him, "that they may be one as Thou Father and I are one, that they may be one in us . . . Thou in me and I in them." I have begun to long for the perfection of that union with an anguish that is sometimes almost physical. I feel very small and very cheap when I see the beautiful sanctity and purity of the souls in this house and it would be a pleasure and a great honor for me to kiss the feet of such people. However that does not prevent me from going off to the woods when I can. I need to get away to catch my breath and get my equilibrium and cool off before I burn up altogether.

I have not yet written to our new Father Immediate but I'll send him a copy of *The Waters of Siloe* anyway. People seem to have approved of it in general, around here, as far as I can see.

I have discovered a poet in the house. Father or rather Frater Thomas, in the novitiate, sent me through the regular channels one or two very nice, tender, sensitive little verses which show a great love for Jesus and a great fraternal charity. He is one of the souls that have made me suddenly feel so small and so anxious to love my brethren. I guess he prayed for me and that softened me up. Incidentally the Carmel in San Francisco has adopted me as their brother and they say a prayer to St. John of the Cross for me every night after Compline, and maybe that has something to do with the change in me too. Anyway the Holy Ghost has been trying to get in under my hard old shell and purify me a little.

We are all anxious to have you back with us, so don't linger too long with the monks of the Valley. However please give them my love and ask them to pray for me, and above all give my most affectionate regards to dear Dom Edmund [Futterer, Abbot of "The Valley"]. I hope he is well. And please ask him to bless me. I am burning up with curiosity to hear what the Holy Father had to say and all about everything in Europe. Did you hear anything about a meeting that is supposed to be planned, for all those who are working on St. Bernard for 1953? The history Commission is getting it up . . . The meeting is to be next year.

The house is now completely bursting. You better get back or there won't be any room for you. I think we have two hundred and three . . .

To Dom Damasus Winzen, O.S.B.

Dom Damasus Winzen (1901–1971), a monk of Marialaach in Germany, came to the United States during the Hitler years and founded the monastery of Mount Saviour near Elmira, New York. Merton was especially attracted to this simplified Benedictine monastery.

Holy Week, 1950
Thank you very much indeed for the two sets of "Pathways" and above all for your kindness in sending one as a gift. I look forward to the one on the Psalms, especially as I have just finished a longish study on the Psalter as a means to contemplative prayer. I wish someone would do a good readable translation of St. Augustine's *Enarrationes*—or of some of the best of them. It would be invaluable. I should be delighted to get Fr. Rembert [Sorg] on "The Theology of Manual Labor." I had not heard of it. Dom Odo Casel we have in French—is there anything of his in English? I can read German but am generally loath to take up a book in that language if it can be found in French or English as I have to plow along slowly with a dictionary. But if Dom Herwegen's commentary cannot be had in any other language I shall tackle it in the original, since it is so extremely important. I have been looking for it for some time.

Things have been rather upset here. We have had a 'flu epidemic, our sanctuary is being torn up and rebuilt and we have had a Master of Chant from Paris trying to improve our singing. When we get back to normal, I am going to try to get some of my best students to dig into the

Fathers and perhaps in time they may produce something. Is there anything I can send you from here? At any rate I'm mailing a couple of pamphlets . . .

To Abbot James Fox

Retreat Notes, 1950

I went through the retreat with the impression of being very much talked at without having proportionate time to think. Most of the retreat was actually condensed, for me, into the time following the last conference, and this morning when, thanks to your kindness and to the mercy of God, we got out of chapter by 6:15!

I had been hoping to meditate a little on the Cautions of St. John of the Cross. I have at least glanced through them. I took them as the standard of my religious life at solemn profession and have never really lived up to them. I know they contain the secret of success. Using them I know that I can really make good use of the opportunities God has given me here. I *can* lead a contemplative life here. It takes some doing, but if I do not insist on having everything exactly my own way, Our Lord will do most of the work. My biggest obstacle is my own tendency to decide beforehand just how I want to serve Our Lord, instead of letting Him tell me what He wants. However I do think that in the last year I have gone far in getting over this—I am much more indifferent about plans and means. Please pray for me to become more and more simple and detached and ask Our Lord to bring me to that deep interior solitude which He desires of me, thus giving me a real defense against all the apparent movement and activity around about, which I sometimes allow to upset me. I certainly can't complain when I see what you have to suffer.

To Dom Jean Leclercq, O.S.B.

Dom Jean Leclercq, (1911–), a Benedictine monk and scholar of Clervaux, Luxembourg, became one of Merton's regular correspondents. The exchange began with the discovery of an unpublished text of St. Bernard of Clairvaux among the manuscripts at Gethsemani.

April 22, 1950

Another film of the St. Bernard Sermons is now on the way to you. This time I looked it over to see if it was all right and it was legible on our machine. I am sorry the first attempt was not too good: you must forgive our young students who are just trying their hand at this kind of work for the first time. Pray that they may learn, because in the future many demands will be made on their talents—if any.

I might wish that your travels would bring you to this side of the Atlantic and that we might have the pleasure of receiving you at Gethsemani. We have just remodelled the vault where our rare books are kept and have extended its capacities to include a good little library on Scripture and the Fathers and the Liturgy—or at least the nucleus of one. Here I hope to form a group of competent students not merely of history or of texts but rather—in line with the tradition which you so admirably represent—men competent in all-round spiritual theology, as well as scholarship, using their time and talents to develop the seed of the word of God in their souls, not to choke it under an overgrowth of useless research as is the tradition in the universities of this country at the moment. I fervently hope that somehow we shall see in America men who are able to produce something like *Dieu Vivant*. Cistercians will never be able to do quite that, I suppose, but we can at least give a good example along those lines. Our studies and writing should by their very nature contribute to our contemplation at least remotely and contemplation in turn should be able to find expression in channels laid open for it and deepened by familiarity with the Fathers of the Church. This is an age that calls for St. Augustines and Leos, Gregorys and Cyrils!

That is why I feel that your works are so tremendously helpful, dear Father. Your *St. Bernard Mystique* is altogether admirable because, while being simple and fluent, it communicates to the reader a real appreciation of St. Bernard's spirituality. You are wrong to consider your treatment of St. Bernard superficial. It is indeed addressed to the general reader but for all that it is profound and all-embracing, and far more valuable than the rather technical study which I undertook for the *Collectanea* and which, as you will see on reading it, was beyond my capacities as a theologian. The earlier sections especially, in my study, contain many glaring and silly errors—or at least things are often very badly expressed there. If I write a book on the saint I shall try to redeem myself, without entering into the technical discussions that occupy M. Gilson in his rather brilliant study [*The Mystical Theology of St. Bernard*]. But there again, a book of your type is far more helpful.

Be sure that we are praying for the work you now have in hand, which is so important and which implies such a great responsibility for you. Any other material help we can give will also be a pleasure. Do not bother about any questions of cost for the films. But if you do have a *tirage à part* [offprint] of one or another article by you, we would greatly appreciate it.

I had heard that you were helping to prepare for the press Dom Wilmart's edition of Aelred's *De Institutione Inclusarum* [*Instruction for Recluses*], but perhaps you have put this on the shelf for the time being. Are the Cistercians of the Common Observance editing the works of Ailred? Where are they doing so and when is the work expected to be finished? By the way, about the spelling of Aelred/Ailred: the most prominent English scholars seem to be spelling him with an "i" . . .

Rest assured, dear Father, that I am praying for you and that our students are doing the same. Please pray for us too. I have too much activity on my shoulders, teaching and writing. Please pray our Lord to live and work in me in such a way that all I do will nourish His life in my soul. I ask the same favor for you, in your travels and labors for His glory.

To Abbot James Fox

September 27, 1950

May Jesus love you and bless you and bring you home soon. Here is a problem to bother you when you are riding on the train. For the last year, the Orientation course has been a recurrent source of friction between Father Master and myself. I thought at first that this was just the usual, accidental trouble that one might expect in all institutional enterprises (whew! ten-dollar language). But I am beginning to think that it may have something to do with the very essence of the course itself.

In our last engagement, Fr. M. wrote me a note in which he stated that the course, as it is now conducted, is a violation of Canon 561 which entrusts the education of the novices exclusively to the Novice Master. And he closed in a sentence which had a "perhaps" that indicated that he thought the course as such was a violation of the Canon.

I have been praying and studying the matter. Here are some thoughts. Obviously, Fr. M. does not want to shoulder the whole burden of educating the novices. He needs assistants even in the matter of spiritual direction. He needs perhaps someone who can give conferences of the same type I am giving—with reservations. But is the concrete orientation course that I am giving what he needs? That is a big question. It involves the nature of the course and the accident of my own personality and place in the scheme of things.

An orientation course that would be completely subject to the direction of Fr. M. and would, in a sense, purely echo his own teaching, would not violate Canon Law.

An orientation course that had nothing to say about the spiritual life would be useless.

I am giving a course that has much to say about the spiritual life and is on the other hand completely independent from Fr. M. It has absolutely nothing to do with him or he with it. I try with the best will in the world to fit in with what I imagine he must be teaching them and he has done his best to favor me as far as he could. But the fact remains that the orientation course is a completely independent affair. Furthermore, the one who is giving the course happens to be a well-known author—for better or for worse. Some of the novices came here because of his books— strange as it may seem. The orientation course may have helped some of them a lot. Many of them like it. Many of them get excited about it. But every one of these things is a point *against* the orientation course. They all add up to one thing: the orientation class tends to assume the danger that some of the less balanced novices may draw comparisons one way or another—in my favor or his. Their conclusion does not make any difference: the mere fact that they are tempted to *compare* is in itself noxious. "I am with Paul—I am with Apollo—I am with Cephas. . . . Is Christ divided?" And that is behind Canon 561.

Up until now I have thought that these difficulties could be met simply by charity and good supernatural intentions. I thought they could be adjusted by sacrificing pet ideas of my own, by efforts at conformity with Fr. M.'s problems, etc. But I am beginning to wonder if the very existence of the course is not somehow a drawback. Whether or not that is true, I am beginning to see that it is Fr. M.'s opinion. He seems to be quite willing to get rid of the orientation class which only furnishes him with a lot of problems and questions to be solved and answered. Perhaps he has already expressed his views to you.

In any case, it is evident that if the Orientation course is to continue at all, for the novices, I must leave the spiritual life almost out of the picture. But if that is the case, I cannot continue the course, as the spiritual life is the only thing I seem to be able to get interested in and I think you will agree that a purely academic course in monastic history, without any reference to monastic ideals, would be for us a waste of time. Yet as soon as I begin to talk about monastic ideals I am liable to come in conflict with Fr. Master and with Canon 561 . . .

On the other hand, I still believe that it is extremely important that the Orientation course on monastic life, liturgy, etc., be given in some form in our community. It is desperately needed. It should be given in the novitiate. What is the solution? I don't know.

Possible solutions:

1) Continue to give orientation talks to the young professed, informally.

2) Drop orientation altogether for the time being and devote the time to extra classes in mystical theology which covers somewhat the same territory.

3) Make one last effort to go on with the orientation as it is: but I believe Fr. M. will oppose this. I also believe that no amount of good will on my part or on his will overcome the difficulties I have described, if they are really present.

I got back from the hospital a week ago yesterday. The doctors gave me a good going over and found no ulcers, which was a blessing. However I have various little things wrong with me—colitis, low blood pressure, badly need an operation on the nose for deviated septum, and at the moment they are trying to clear up the colitis by a diet. In fact, I am in the infirm refectory, but for the last few days I haven't been able to do much about it as the smell of food nauseates me. But I am getting better: this was the result of some medicine.

One of the things the doctors said was that I needed more fresh air. I am trying to get out to work three or four times a week. That leaves less time for class preparation et al. But I can fit in enough writing to get along, I think. It certainly is good to get out more and to keep closer to the rule. In fact I came back from the hospital with a much greater love of the rule and the monastic life. It was a grace Jesus gave me there, among others.

Got to close now and get this in the mail. The more I think of it the more I realize I need an obscure and humble life, of toil and poverty and self-denial and silence.

To Dom Jean Leclercq

October 9, 1950

It is a long time since I received your July letter which I read and pondered with deep satisfaction. It is a privilege for which I am deeply grateful, to be able to seek nourishment and inspiration directly from those who keep themselves so close to the sources of monastic spirituality.

Your remarks on St. Bernard's ideas of Scripture are extremely important to me. I have been meditating on your appendix to *St. Bernard Mystique*, and also I have been talking on this very subject to the students here. I agree with your conclusions about St. Bernard and yet I wonder if it would not be possible to say that he did consider himself in a very definite sense an exegete. My own subjective feeling is that the full seriousness of St. Bernard's attitude to Scripture is not brought out entirely unless we can in some sense treat him as an exegete and as theologian, in his exposition of the *Canticle*. Naturally he is not either of these things in a purely modern sense. But I think he is acting as a theologian according to the Greek Fathers' conception at least to some extent (see end of Lossky's first chapter: *Theol. Myst. de l'Eglise orientale*). I think that is essentially what you were saying when you brought out the fact that he was seeking less to nourish his interior life than to exercise it. As if new meanings in his own life and in Scripture spontaneously grew up to confirm each other as soon as Bernard immersed himself in the Sacred Text. Still, there is the evident desire of the saint to *penetrate* the text with a certain mystical experience of God and His revelation. This positive hunger for "theology" in its very highest sense would be expressed in such a text as Cant. lxxiii, 1: "Ego . . . in profundo sacri eloquii gremio *spiritum mihi* scrutabor et vitam" [Deep in the bosom of the sacred word I shall search my spirit and my life]. He is seeking "intellectum" and "Spiritus est qui vivificat: dat quippe intellectum. An non vita intellectus" [The Spirit gives life: indeed he gives understanding. And is not understanding life?]. As you have so rightly said (p. 488) "Sa lecture de l'E. Ste prépare et occasionne son expérience du divin" [His reading of Scripture prepares and occasions his experience of the divine]. But I wonder if he did not think of Scripture as a kind of *cause* of that experience, and in the same sense, "servata proportione" [keeping due proportion], as a Sacrament is a cause of grace? Scripture puts him in direct contact with the Holy Spirit who infuses mystical grace, rather than awakening in his soul the awareness that the Holy Spirit has already infused a grace to that spoken of in Scripture. Or am I wrong? In any case, words like "scrutabor" [I shall search] and "intellectus" [understanding] tempt me to say (while agreeing in substance with all your conclusions) that there must have been a sense in which St. Bernard looked upon himself both as an exegete and as a theologian in his exposition of the *Canticle*. Although I readily admit there can be no question of his attempting as a modern author might to "make the text clear" or to "explain its meaning." That hardly concerned him, as you have shown. But do you not think that in giving the fruit of his own contacts with the Word through Scripture he was in a sense introducing his monks to a certain mystical "attitude" towards the Scriptures—not a method, but an "atmosphere" in which Scripture could become the meeting place of the Soul and the Word, through the action of the Holy Spirit?

Perhaps these are useless subtleties: but you guess that I am simply exercising my own thought in order to confront it with the reactions of an expert and this will be of the greatest service to me in the work that has been planned for me by Providence. I am also very much interested in the question of St. Bernard's attitude toward "learning," and feel that a distinction has not yet been sufficiently clearly made between his explicit reproofs of "scientia" in the sense of philosophia, and his implicit support of scientia in the sense of theologia, in his tracts on Grace, Baptism, and his attacks on Abelard, not to mention (with all due respect to your conclusions) his attitude to the *Canticle* which makes that commentary also "scientia" [knowledge] as well as "sapientia" [wisdom]. Have you any particular lights on this distinction between science and wisdom in the Cistercians, or do you know of anything published in their regard? It seems to me to be an interesting point, especially to those of us who, like yourself and me, are monks engaged in a sort of "scientia" along with their contemplation! (It is very interesting in William of St. Thierry.)

I wish I could give you some information on St. Bernard in his relation to the Greek Fathers. I have none of my own; the topic interests me but I have barely begun to do anything about it, since I know the Greek Fathers so poorly. However, I can tell you this much: in Danielou's *Platonisme et T.M.* on pages 7 and 211 there are references to St. Bernard's dependence (?) on St. Gregory of Nyssa. The opening of St. Bernard's series of *Sermons* obviously reflects the idea of Origen and Gregory of Nyssa that the *Canticle of Canticles* was for the formation of mystics while *Proverbs* and *Ecclesiastes* applied to the beginners and progressives. I find Bernard's echo of this point an interesting piece of evidence that he considered the monastic vocation a remote call to mystical union—if not a proximate one. Then, too, Gregory's homilies on the *Canticle of Canticles* are full of a tripartite division of souls into slaves, mercenaries and spouses. Gregory's apophatism is not found in St. Bernard, but in his positive treatment of theology Bernard follows Origen. I think Fr. Danielou also told me that Bernard's attitude toward the Incarnate Word is founded on Origen—I mean his thoughts on *amor carnalis Christi* [carnal love of Christ] in relation to mystical experience. I may be wrong.

A copy of *The Spirit of Simplicity* was mailed to you but my own contribution to that work is confused and weak, I believe. I refer to the second part.

I agree with what you say about Abbé de Rancé and feel that my own treatment of him in *Waters of Siloe* had something in it of caricature. It is certainly true that Abbé de l'Estrange was much more austere than Rancé. To my mind the most regrettable thing about both of them was their exaggeration of externals, their ponderous emphasis on "exercises" and things to be done. Nevertheless perhaps that is a sign of my own tepidity. It is true that the monastic life does demand faithful observance of many little exterior points of Rule. These can certainly not be neglected *en masse* [as a whole] without spiritual harm. But one sometimes feels that for the old Trappists they were absolutely everything.

The Desert Fathers interest me much. They seem to have summed up almost everything that is good and bad in subsequent monastic history (except for the abuses of decadent monasticism)—I mean everything that is good and bad in various monastic *ideals*.

Your news of the *De Institutione Inclusarum* which you tell me with such detachment, is sad indeed. Do not think that manuscripts are only lost in Italy. A volume of our poems was printed by a man whose shop was in the country. Goats used to wander in to the press and eat the authors' copy. This fortunately did not happen to our poems. Perhaps the goats were wise. They sensed the possibility of poisoning.

I am extremely eager to get Fr. Bouyer's new book on monasticism, but have not yet been able to do so. I feel that our book dealer sometimes takes orders and then forgets about them—I mean for books to come out later. I liked his *Saint Antoine*. Still, I wonder if he does not overdo his interest in the fact that in the early ages of the Church people were so clearly aware that the fall had put the devil in charge of material things. Fr. Danielou's *Signe du Temple*, in its first chapter, gives a good counterpoise to that view—for heaven still shone through creation and God was very familiar with men in Genesis!

The other day we mailed Burch's *Steps of Humility* to you and it should be in your hands shortly. If you wish to send us something in return we would like to get Wilmart's *Pensées du B. Guigue*, if this is Guigo the Carthusian. I have never yet gone into him. His lapidary style fascinates me. He is better than Pascal. Yet I love Pascal.

Your page on the eremitical vocation was very welcome. Someone told me the Carthusians were at last coming to America. I know the Trappist who has gone to Camaldoli. He was with me in the novitiate here. I wonder if he is happy there. His departure surprised me and I think his arrival surprised some of the Camaldolese.

Cistercian monasticism in America is of a genus all its own. Imagine that we now have one hundred and fifty novices at Gethsemani. This is fantastic. Many of them are sleeping in a tent in the *préau*. The nucleus of seniors is a small, bewildered group of men who remember the iron rule of Dom Edmond Obrecht and have given up trying to comprehend what has happened to Gethsemani. The house has a very vital and enthusiastic (in the good sense) and youthful air, like the camp of an army preparing for an easy and victorious war. Those of us who have been sobered by a few years of the life find ourselves in turns comforted and depressed by the multitude of our young companions of two and three months' standing: comforted by their fervor and joy and simplicity, and depressed by the sheer weight of numbers. The cloister is as crowded as a Paris street.

On the whole, when the house is completely full of men who are happy because they have not yet had a chance to suffer anything (although they believe themselves willing) the effect is a little disquieting. One feels more solidly rooted in God in a community of veterans, even though many of them may be morose. However, I do not waste my time seeking consolation in the community or avoiding its opposite. There is too little time for these accidentals.

I close this long letter thanking you again for yours, which are always so full of interest and profit. I cannot place the reference to a contribution of mine to *Rhythmes du Monde*, maybe there is some mistake—or my publisher went directly to them. I would be interested in seeing your *Soli Deo Vivere!* I sent something to *Dieu Vivant*. I like them. Is the magazine *Opus Dei* worth the trouble of getting a subscription? I wish we could feel here that *Irenikon* was essential for us. Can you persuade us that it is? Or that it is important? The thought of reunion with the Greeks is one that haunts me.

Once again, dear Father, thank you for your advice and inspiration. May Jesus bless your great work for His glory and for the vitality of monasticism everywhere. Pray for me in my turn to be more and more a child of St. Benedict—and if it be God's will, that I may some day find a way to be something of an eremitical son of St. Benedict! What of these Benedictines in the mountains of France? Have you more information about them? I am not inquiring in a spirit of restlessness! Their project is something I admire on its own merits.

To Abbot James Fox

Quinquagesima, 1951
Day of Recollection

It seems to me that what Jesus wants of me this Lent is less external activity, more recollection, greater simplicity, humility and quiet. For this end, with your approval, I hope to reduce our writing work to a minimum during Lent as there is already much material on hand for publication. I hope to simply finish off one job promised to Harcourt, Brace for March [*The Ascent to Truth*]. For the rest I would think Jesus would want me to go more often to the common work—and to take more time for reading and prayerful reflection in view of other work—or just for His sake alone, because there is no greater or more important work than love. Since I cannot observe the full Lenten fast I hope to put myself beneath all my brethren by humble love, and always try to place their interests and convenience in all things before my own. Please bless me, Reverend Father, in Jesus' name.

October 7, 1951
Feast of the Holy Rosary

This is a report on our private retreat from September 29 to October 6. As an act of gratitude for your permission to let me make it, and also because it was something of an experiment, I will try to give you a good picture of how it went off, and also to tell you of the fruits. It has been exceptionally fruitful, I think. I spent every afternoon (except Wednesday—all-out work) outside in the woods. The morning was devoted to quiet work, trying to organize things in the vault, typing up some notes, etc. I would go out each day right after dinner and return in time for Vespers. This usually gave me three and a half hours of solid prayer in solitude. I took a book along but scarcely ever read more than a page of it. Most of the time I just entered into the presence of God and stayed quiet and let the silence sink in. Most of the time it was pretty quiet, but sometimes the traxcavator was making a lot of noise. In any case I got a lot of silent prayer. Saturday you gave me permission to try a day in the woods. I was out from Sext until Vespers (that made about seven hours in complete silence and solitude). The effect of this silence and solitary prayer, especially the last day, has been very great.

First of all, it seems that this solitary prayer has a special power to detach me from things that hold me otherwise. Things that cling to me in community life and in choral prayer, vanish quite easily when I am outside alone. I can spend hours at a time outside without an appreciable distraction. I am not forcibly concentrated on anything; I seem unable to do anything special. When I try to make my faculties act in order to intensify my union with God a sense of anxiety, frustration and discomfort overpowers me and if I keep on trying I feel spiritually—and even physically—nauseated. But then I simply rest and let Him act.

When I was out there praying alone it came to me that surely in this solitary prayer above all else I was *giving myself* to God. I have never come so close to the conviction that for once I really belonged completely to Him. This was especially strong at the beginning of the week.

As the week went on, and especially on the last long day in the woods, something else, something deep, began to get a grip on me inside. Whereas in the beginning everything had been simple, restful, peaceful prayer (not sensibly consoled, but quiet and nice) now something began to get hold of me deep down in the roots of my being. I will not call it fear, but it produced a kind of fear—nothing tangible: but I began to feel terrifically *empty* as if I was all burnt out inside and a chasm was opening out in my soul. I lost all taste for the natural pleasure which accompanied my solitude. On Saturday the woods were most beautiful, and yet I could hardly look at anything. The attitude in my mind can be summed up something like this. I was feeling (and still do a little, the day after) the way someone must feel on his deathbed, when he has to leave everything. What do I care for the beauty of the autumn woods, if my spirit is on the threshold of eternity in which autumn and spring have come to an end and seasons no more mean anything? I sat in the woods for seven hours and felt hollow. For a little while I was terribly lonely, and the more so because I knew that it was a loneliness that nothing visible or tangible could ever satisfy. I can sum up the last day in the woods by saying that I just got smaller and smaller and dwindled down to nothing in the presence of God, and since it was something remotely like dying it was not altogether pleasant and yet it was not unpleasant either. It was a sort of grim neutrality of the spirit in which everything goes dead on you and leaves you feeling more like a husk than a person.

But all this had very great fruits. Established in this solitude I just wasn't able to work up any interest in things that usually draw my mind away from prayer. At the same time, when I returned to choir, the *office seemed to become just what it ought to be,* my mind was clear and although I drew no special light from the psalms it was a great comfort to be able to sing them to God and to give Him something thereby—something that faith tells me pleases Him. Also the Mass has been better for me than it has ever been before, especially in the last three days. As soon as I go to the altar that feeling of littleness and nothingness, fear of God mixed with confidence and trust, and deep emptiness in my heart, comes over me again just the way it did in the woods. But now with Jesus on the altar, and in my heart as priest, and myself united to Him as priest and victim, there is a great sense of secret strength and of pure love in my heart, and communion comes to soothe everything that was painful about the emptiness within me, without for all that giving me any sensible consolation.

Concrete conclusions:

1) This sense of interior emptiness seems to require, as an exterior expression, the constant efficacious desire to be put in the background, the joyful acceptance of anything that causes others to be preferred to myself, and myself to be passed over and put on one side.

2) It seems that at least for me "the community life" is not the absolute and infallible solution for all problems since seven days of relative solitude have apparently done a great deal to dispose of attachments and problems that the community had in large part created and fostered. On the other hand, I emerge from this retreat with a greater appreciation and respect for community exercises, choir, common work, etc., than I can remember ever having had since my novitiate. ·

3) It seems that this solitude is the root of my gift of myself to God— but once I have this essence, then I feel ready to serve Him in active ways as much as He wills. I cannot feel that for me, *working for* God is absolutely the same as *giving myself to* God, but once I have the recollection and detachment and interior freedom required to attend to Him alone, I feel ready to do what He may ask of me, realizing that whatever it is it will be very little. But when I give in to the illusion that "work" and "generosity" are synonymous, I lose much of my interior union with Him and my work itself becomes sterile, even though I may have the intention of pleasing Him—I seem to remain far from Him. I am ashamed of the excessive writing I did between 1944 and 1949: but perhaps I wasn't fit for anything else. I know that is not what is expected of me now. I will peacefully do the little I can and if I can do nothing now I shall be glad of it, because it is better to serve God in a way that does not attract attention or win the recognition of men.

Please forgive this document—I am ashamed to write it and do not usually do such a thing: but the retreat was exceptional, thanks to you, Reverend Father, so perhaps this report ought to be an exception, too . . .

To Dom Gabriel Sortais, O.C.S.O.

Dom Gabriel Sortais (1902–1963), Abbot of Bellefontaine in France, was elected Abbot General of the Cistercian Order in 1951 following the resignation of Dom Dominique Nogues. Thus begins a long correspondence which dealt with Merton's writing, censorship, and his vocational difficulties. They were written for the most part in French, and I am grateful to Fathers Germain Marc'hadour and Henri Gibaud of the Catholic University at Angers, France, for preparing the English translations. Several other letters were discovered later and these were translated by Father Augustine Wulff of Gethsemani and Monsignor William Shannon, General Editor of the Merton Letters.

October 15, 1951

This is a rather embarrassed Cistercian author who writes to you about the "imprimi potest" [the official approval of the Order] that you were good enough to send us recently, dated October 7. I think I let Dom Dominique know that the book *The Ascent to Truth* was already in press and as a matter of fact this book came out on September 20. The publisher rushed a little, I admit, and he even had the book out before inserting a few minor corrections (not all that important, fortunately) as suggested by the censor. It was his fault and he finally admitted it (I mean the publisher). He has promised to behave properly next time for I have let him know about this, and so has the censor. So while I am responsible as the author, I beg you to believe that the publisher went ahead without consulting me all that much and that he will not do so again.

Now there remains the fact that the book bears Dom Dominique's "imprimi potest"—which was not given. Not knowing in the least that he was going to resign, and expecting as usual to receive the permission automatically, since the censors had fully approved the book, I had left his name with the publishers. And so now the book bears the name of Dom Dominique. I turn to you now in order to know what is to be done. Do you want me to change the names and put yours, which would be according to the rules, or would it be better to let the thing go, so nothing is noticed?

I would very much like to write a short note to Dom Dominique— is he still addressed as Most Reverend?

Thank you for your short note about me to Father Abbot. I tell you in return that if you are the new Abbot General I will be delighted. Not that I wish you to bear a burden, but all the same I am persuaded you would be most capable of bearing it, and encourage us to advance towards divine union. Anyway, God's holy will be done! I think it will not be altogether fun to be Abbot General at this critical moment.

Remember me a little when you speak to God, Reverend Father. I am currently the "Student[s'] Master" here. I have about thirty of them— including some beautiful souls. In return I promise I'll pray for you often at Holy Mass. Please accept my most devoted sentiments in the Lord.

To Etienne Gilson

Etienne Gilson [1884–1978] was born in France and did his doctoral studies at the Sorbonne. He taught at the universities of Lille, Strasbourg, Paris, Harvard, and finally Toronto. He was the moving spirit behind the foundation of the Pontifical Institute of Medieval Studies in Toronto. Toward the end of his life he was elected to the French Academy. Merton acknowledged his indebtedness to Gilson, especially his Spirit of Medieval Philosophy, *which he first read while a student at Columbia.*

November 12, 1951

Deeply moved by your beautiful letter, I want to do what I should have done long ago—write you a line to assure you of my recognition of a spiritual debt to you which I too sketchily indicated in the pages of *The Seven Storey Mountain*, and in a rather badly constructed section of the book at that. To you and to Jacques Maritain, among others, I owe the Catholic faith. That is to say I owe my life. This is no small debt. Can you feel as abandoned as you do when you are handing out to other people as great a gift as is the Kingdom of Heaven? But indeed, it is the privilege of those who bear such spiritual fruit to feel abandoned and miserable and alone, for poverty of spirit is the patrimony of the children of God in this world, and their pledge of glory in the world to come: "for theirs is the Kingdom of Heaven."

What greater thing can we have than to be empty, to be despoiled, to be orphans and exiles in this world? Your exile is not merely metaphorical. It is something you suffer and offer to God for the France He loves and which nevertheless tends to reject Him and those whom He sends.

Thank you for the kind words you say about *The Ascent to Truth*. In none of the books that I have written do I feel that I have said what I wanted. I do not know whether or not in this one I have said what needs to be said to any except a few. I have the consciousness of having disappointed many who wanted me to say something to *them*. Also I have an even greater consciousness that I have nothing to say to anyone except the oaks of our forest. Like St. Bernard, I feel that I can go to them and learn everything. I dare not say that like him I feel like the chimaera of the age, lest it suggest a sort of comparison between an unworthy son and so great a Father—and this is a comparison which I cannot afford to make.

Please pray for me to Our Lord that instead of merely writing something I may *be* something, and indeed that I may so fully be what I ought to be that there may be no further necessity for me to write, since the mere fact of being what I ought to be would be more eloquent than many books. Do you ever come down this way? Please do not fail to come and see us if you are ever around Chicago or any of the Middle Western cities which are "near" Gethsemani! This Cistercian house—where as Father Master of Scholastics I am eternally grateful to be able to give my spiritual children nourishment from your wonderful book on St. Bernard—will always welcome you. Consider it your home in this part of the world and come whenever you like. Meanwhile, we will meet before the holy altar of God, and I promise to remember you frequently in my Mass.

To Dom Gabriel Sortais

December 11, 1951

This is a short note to tell you of my filial joy over your election. I am very pleased for the Order, although I know that the new burden is rather heavy! But God who has chosen you to carry it will not leave you without all the necessary graces and gifts. At any rate, I know that you will know how to do everything to encourage truly contemplative life in our houses. Here, with us, it seems to me that it is in this direction that the Holy Spirit's *auster divinus* [divine south wind] is breathing. Our business is to turn Gethsemani into a real *hortus aromatum* [garden of spices] where the delicate souls sent us by God may bloom. There are many of us—too many, in my opinion!—hence a lot of problems. A formidable din due to the endless constructions! But I hope this will not last.

I have just written to Desclée de Brouwer to send you the proofs of the French translation of *The Waters of Siloe* (our work on the history and the spirit of the Order). I was bold enough to believe, Most Reverend Father, that you would not deny me the favor of a little introductory letter to this work. But I would like it all to be according to the regulations, so perhaps you, or one of the Definitors, would like to peruse it. I will make the necessary corrections. Dom Vincent [Hermans, Procurator General] has justly, no doubt, remarked about my exaggerations in regard to Abbé de Rancé. But anyway, the general meaning of the work is that we must be just as contemplative as any other monastic order, and even more so, since our Fathers of Cîteaux had, as a distinctive note of our vocation, a great love for contemplation and they used to write more willingly on the subject of divine union than on any other. Anyway, I hope you will have a moment to see to this for yourself, and to tell us what should be done with it. I would like the French edition to agree perfectly with the spirit of the Order, so that it can be used, so to speak, with some confidence . . .

To Dom Jean-Baptiste Porion, O. Cart.

Dom Jean-Baptiste Porion, a Carthusian monk of La Grande Chartreuse in southern France, and a writer of considerable distinction, later became Procurator General of the Carthusian Order with headquarters in Rome.

February 9, 1952

For my own part, as you know, the betrayal of our deep self that sometimes takes place in our effort to communicate with others exteriorly, has long been a problem. It is not easy for a writer to learn to live, interiorly, without a witness, without a potential reader. But once this intruder is expelled, we truly find ourselves, and find God—and find other men in God. We betray ourselves and one another in the No Man's Land which exists between human beings, and into which they go out to meet one another disguised in words. And yet without words we cannot find ourselves, without communication with men we do not know God:

fides ex auditu [faith comes from hearing]. You have justly assessed the balance that must be preserved between the two—so that the word of faith that is passed from one soul to the secrecy of another soul matures in both and grows into understanding: and flowers in God alone.

One of the other things that comforts me about your book is the fact that your "spirituality" is not so much a spirituality as *yourself*, your identity in God: although of course that identity is not fully expressed, as you say, in what you write. It cannot be. Nevertheless what you speak has something to do with what you are, and the point that I am getting at is: your "spirituality" is "Carthusian" without for all that acquiring a label, or fixing you in some specific category. You are Carthusian precisely because you are yourself: you are a man who loves God, in sympathy with Ruysbroeck and Hadjewich, etc., in a Charterhouse.

For me too this matter of spirituality tries, superficially, to be a problem. Yet I know it can never really be a problem because after all what I love is not spirituality but God. Therefore, when considering my "obligation" to form my scholastics along specifically Cistercian lines, and according to something called "Cistercian spirituality," I can do it with abandonment and objectivity (I hope), and still remain myself. It may sound like heresy, but personally I feel that if I become too meticulously Cistercian (according to some ideal category in the spiritual books), I will only be for my pains less of a Cistercian. Because my solution is yours: for me to be a Cistercian is to be a man who loves God in a Cistercian monastery—in sympathy with St. John of the Cross and Ruysbroeck and a few other people who are *not* Cistercians, and also with a few others who are. It does not seem to me to be a reserved or even a mortal sin to live in a Cistercian monastery with more actual sympathy for St. John of the Cross than St. Bernard of Clairvaux. Though I by no means refuse to read St. Bernard. I just cannot assert that he nourishes me as much as others do. I cannot assert this and retain my simplicity. For when I read St. Bernard, I am more drawn to study than to contemplation. He does not draw me to rest in silence and darkness: he evokes spontaneous admiration for a rather brilliant theological manner of meditating on the Scriptures which is, for me, something short of prayer. This is what the other Cistercians find in him. I therefore can find what they find. But since it is not what I seek, I cannot pretend to rest there. I have no quarrel with them: they can have their gay garden. I am happy with St. John of the Cross among the rocks. When I find God then I am a Cistercian, because then I reach the end for which He brought me to the monastery. The rest is a waste of time.

The only writing I do now is in the form of maxims—sometimes they seem to be a little like Guigo. I think he is very fine. I like his lapidary quality. I find myself beginning to use these maxims for direction (with the scholastics). I write one out—for instance a word or two of Latin—and slip it to them a day or two before they come to see me. They can think about the words, enter into them, and give me something of their own in return, so that I hope in time that direction of my best scholastics will become nothing more than a few cries—as of angels hailing one another briefly from cliff to cliff on the walls of the mountain leading to heaven. Here are several of the Latin maxims—for you on *your* cliff:

Solitudo pauperis quievit in potestate Altissimi!
[The solitude of the poor man rests on the power of God!]
Silentium coelorum sit mihi lex: et vita mea imago luminis.
[Let the silence of heaven be my law: and my life an image of light.]
Nomen meum eructavit caritas ex profundis.
[Charity uttered my name from the depths.]
Fons vitae silentium in corde noctis.
[A fountain of life is silence in the heart of night.]

It would make a nice monastic book—the first monastic one I shall have done—to produce these, with brief meditations on them in English. Perhaps twenty or thirty maxims, with meditations: not more than a hundred pages in all.

All this is just to say that this afternoon, reading your book under the young cedars, in the silence of our woods, I remembered you in God Who cannot be remembered but can only be discovered.

To Dom Gabriel Sortais

March 13, 1952

Thank you for your good letter from Mariaveen. Forgive me for the cares I have made you feel in regard to our translation. A few weeks after writing you, I learned that the manuscript of the translation was in the hands of our good Father Anselme Dimier at Chimay [in Belgium]. The latter, who was examining it for Desclée, in order to "correct the names of the monasteries," had found much more than that to correct. He is still at it; I have just written him answering his questions. So we shall not have any proofs before the month of June. Perhaps I will be able to put them in your hands when you come over to America.

I also want to thank you for your Circular Letter which has done a lot of good to all hearts. All the young men here have been attracted by the thirst for God. The very intense activity in our large community is becoming, to several, a source of anguish and temptations, and it is good to be reassured by the Most Reverend Father and to know that we do not only have the privilege but above all the obligation to be contemplatives!

Awaiting the joy of welcoming you in our house, I ask your paternal blessing, and assure you once more of my filial devotion in Our Lord and Our Lady.

July 23, 1952

Our publisher, Harcourt, Brace and Company, has just sent you the manuscript of our journal, *The Sign of Jonas*. At the same time they have set to work to prepare the edition, while awaiting all the changes that your censor will want to suggest to us. Another manuscript is in the hands of one of our American censors. We do believe you will leave intact the essence of this work. To me the essential is this: one must be able to trace the thread of a history, of an interior development unfolding itself in it: the development of a young religious who is moving towards the priesthood, asking himself rather frank questions about his contemplative vocation, about Gethsemani: who sees his questions being solved under the invisible hand of Divine Providence *disponens omnia suaviter et fortiter* [arranging all things sweetly and mightily], and lastly a series of meditations, of "elevations" if you like, or even sort of hymns in prose . . . For the minor details, the censors will be free to judge. Perhaps you will allow us to discuss this gently in case something seems to us very important. But anyway we shall leave it quite willingly, and with all our filial confidence, to your judgment. I do not say I submitted to it—as though it were a thing I did not want to do; on the contrary: *vide quoniam mandata tua dilexi!* [see that I have loved your commands].

You had told me, in the form of advice, without seeming to attach much importance to it, that perhaps I should not go on writing this journal. If this *is* your will, I shall not write it anymore. But if you see no objection, perhaps I could pursue this very easy work. It is almost the only way to produce something with all my other offices which look like obstacles. The publishers urge me strongly.

And there you are, Most Reverend Father: I am asking a favor from you which is perhaps very indiscreet, since you cannot read for yourself the book in English. And besides, it seems to me that Desclée de Brouwer has disappointed me, and has not sent you the French translation of *The Waters of Siloe*, to get a letter from your hand. I have been told nothing about it . . . and I am very confused over it all. Forgive me. Is it too rash of me to ask you, after this, to give us a brief word for the English edition of the journal? Could the censor inform you sufficiently? Do you think it would be the proper thing, or would it raise a problem for you?

Of course, since the matter at hand is an altogether personal document, it is quite different from *The Waters of Siloe*. You would like to know why I am asking you for this letter? Beside the honor that it would be to me personally, and the satisfaction of my filial devotion towards you, there is also this: the theme of the book is precisely the thirst for God which should be the very heart of Cistercian life, and at the same time I present it all not in ideal terms but in the concrete ambient of an actual monastery, just as it is, with its faults (though I do not dwell on them) and with all the charm of our Cistercian life into the bargain. A word from you would reassure the readers that the Order itself always tries to look at things from a concrete and integrated point of view, that we have never deceived ourselves by pretending to be angels on earth, but that we know that Christian perfection and union with God must be realized in the treadmill of this daily life which is not always the ideal, and that God, in short, allows himself to be found *in normal life*, provided this life is truly the life of grace and that we endeavor to live it thoroughly, and with no pretense, seeking God and nothing else! I do not say I am more honest than the others. On the contrary, I think this journal is indeed the witness of a perfectly ordinary religious, i.e. ordinarily not perfect! And I think, my Brothers in the Order—at least those who, like me, are not saints—will be able to find themselves in it.

But still I know the question is very delicate for you, and I do not insist at all. I understand very well if you cannot do it.

I'm leaving tomorrow to meet our Reverend Father in the State of Ohio to see an estate offered to us to make a foundation. Of course, there can be no question of a real foundation before two or three years. But it seems we are going to initiate formidable works of renovation at Gethsemani. Perhaps they are going (it has not been decided yet) to gut all of the old building in order to reconstruct it from the inside. The idea seems to me, at least, necessary and reasonable. But fancy the din of the machines! If we could accept an estate, and if, for example, a few went there to *prepare* a foundation, it would be a sort of refuge for them. If I were the founder, I have a very simple plan to take there half of our students in theology. We could fairly well study and work in peace there as I foresee that the benefactors would assure us the funds to hire seculars to help us in the very simple building of a house which would be ready to welcome the founders in 1954. Do not say a word to Reverend Father. I mention it because I had very strongly opposed both the rebuildings and the foundations during the regular visit, but I have changed my mind for the moment, and anyway it is not certain what is going to be done. He will probably speak about it at the General Chapter.

August 12, 1952

I thank you wholeheartedly for your letter, as kindly as it was long, which speaks to me in such a fatherly way of our poor works. Such a letter could not fall into my hands without exciting, in my heart, the feelings of a deep emotion, supernatural in origin, since faith made me hear in each sentence the love of Jesus himself for my wretchedness. I have accordingly tried to gather all that could help me to serve Him and to abandon myself more and more to Him. I thank you above all for your promise of a little prefatory letter for the *Journal* in case the latter were not totally unworthy of such a favor from you. The good monk who has taken upon himself to read it will remain the judge on this last point.

I have seen the lovely estate in Ohio. It was really well adapted for a Cistercian foundation. But as I think of other offers from our benefactors, and as I pray, I begin to modify a bit the little plan I was suggesting to you. It is a quite simple plan, which could no doubt work well, given the occasion. But since a millionaire is offering us a magnificent estate in Colorado in the Rocky Mountains, with a ready-made house, I begin to wonder whether Divine Providence does not wish thereby to tell us something a bit out of the ordinary. So I am sending you the sketch of a plan to that effect. I am *convinced* of the necessity and the timeliness of something of the kind, but I confess I am not seeing clearly all the concrete details.

Most Reverend Father, I have prayed a lot, and I have even tried repeatedly to send flying this idea, which at times seemed a little fantastic. But the more I think of the concrete situation of our students at Gethsemani, the more I see that they need, *temporarily*, a very special formation that they will never get in the present state of things at Gethsemani. Why not take advantage of this estate in Colorado to send there a whole scholasticate, while bringing very good teachers from our houses in Europe. We have all the rest: library, equipment, etc. We only lack the Superior, apart from perhaps the Father Master—if I am not presumptuous in thinking I could go on filling this job. But we don't have a *true superior* for such a house. This is what we need most.

Anyway, here are the two questions I am asking you. I do not know whether you would think it expedient to put them before the General Chapter and Definitors:

1) Would it be possible to make such a foundation, *ad experimentum*, by borrowing teachers and a Superior from Europe?

2) If that is not possible, would we be allowed to do it by ourselves with our own resources? That is to say, would the General Chapter allow in principle *the temporary formation of a separate scholasticate* that several houses would use in America?

I think that if this foundation were considered as a kind of *grange*, there would be no difficulty and even no formality—we could just go there and do our thing. But I think this would not be desirable. Such a foundation should proceed from the General Chapter itself. I think Dom James would not want to take the responsibility alone. But if you spoke to him, supposing you yourself approve of the project, he might perhaps see the opportuneness of it. He is not *against* the project, but neither is he *for* it.

September 3, 1952

I had forgotten to tell you that Dom James is perfectly informed of my ideas about the scholasticate. We talked it over at length. Since our last letter, Dom James has even seemed to want to give up the plan of the great reconstruction work. But he has said nothing about it to Brother Cellarer, who goes on making plans at full speed to overthrow the whole abbey from one end to the other. At the same time, I have been thinking a little about all the complications and dangers entailed by my plan. Finally, during Monsignor Larraona's visit, I spoke to him of our problems. He for his part told me that the Congregation [of Religious] was preparing an instruction which would perfectly agree with what I was telling him. He assured me that the monastic orders were being especially thought of in this instruction. He said to Dom James that everything possible should be done in order to secure a *quiet* milieu for the students, to free them as soon as possible from various services so that the students in the foundations should pursue their studies in a scholasticate where there would be good teachers in a favorable milieu for their studies—for example, in the motherhouse.

With all this in mind, I reduce the whole content of our two other letters to the following questions:

1) If the great constructions are undertaken at Gethsemani, disturbing the whole house, could not the students be sent elsewhere—either to a quiet house, or to a temporary foundation, non-autonomous, which would merely be a grange-scholasticate, with a few laybrothers?

2) Even apart from the question of extraordinary works, should we not think of establishing somewhere a scholasticate, quiet and well provided with teachers and directors, where the students from Gethsemani and its (at least non-autonomous) daughterhouses could receive a good intellectual and spiritual formation in a contemplative milieu?

3) If this special house should not be a foundation proper, by itself, would it be permissible to constitute it some distance away from Gethsemani, like a sort of "grange" or annex—that is to say, a small community complete in itself from the viewpoint of the regular places, with a somewhat special timetable, exclusively for the students and a few brothers?

This much for the students. If we were allowed such a project, I would still like to bring teachers from France . . . Dom James receives my ideas in principle, but he does not want in effect to let the students go, first because they work a lot in the community and render us a good many services. And then all fear a radical change in the spirit of the Order. But on the contrary, I find there is more danger for the spirit of the Order if the students are left in a very busy and noisy atmosphere, where they will be formed almost exclusively by teachers from other orders or from the secular clergy.

Dom James is going to speak to you of another, more personal problem. It is whispered in Georgia that if Dom Robert [McGann] happens to die, it is I whom they are going to postulate as abbot. The same idea may occur elsewhere. They do not know me there; they only know the books! . . . It would be a complete disaster. I am totally incapable of being an abbot, first because I have no judgment in administration or in temporal affairs and I don't have the gifts of a true leader. Quite the contrary! . . . Although I sometimes feel a temptation to want to be an abbot, yet my conscience tells me it is sheer folly. Dom James agrees, and he tells me that God wants something quite different from me. So I am always prepared to refuse any abbatial election, in the conviction that God *does not want* me to accept such an office. He *wants* me, not to abandon myself in indifference, but by the signification of His positive will, implicit in my rather special vocation, determined by the effect of our books, etc., He wants me to *refuse* all superiorship and to stay in the ranks doing the work He has to be mine—or simply to avoid the trap such election would be. I think I could not save my soul in the situation in which Dom James is . . . [see the Appendix].

Forgive me, dear Most Reverend Father, for this third letter as long as the others. I pray for you a lot, and am looking forward to your remarks on the *Journal.* I am still bold enough to hope you will give us a little prefatory letter, and I thank you for your solicitude toward the poorest of your sons in America! Please bless me, and ask Jesus to make me a saint . . .

To Dom Humphrey Pawsey

Dom Humphrey Pawsey was Superior of the Carthusian foundation at Sky Farm in Vermont by this time.

September 11, 1952

You may have been expecting some sort of letter from me. I have long meant to write you at least a friendly note, if at least I could get the time. This is something more.

Father, I will come straight to the point. I am writing to you as to a friend whose advice I trust as well as to the Superior of the Carthusian foundation. You can give me much help in both capacities.

Our Father Abbot is away at the General Chapter. When he returns, I am going to present him with a formal request to be allowed to embrace the eremitical life in some form or other. That decision is made. The question remains: what form?

I may say first of all that I have been years in making this decision— even in fighting it. I have made every possible effort to believe and obey those who told me I was supposed to be a Cistercian. I have made every possible effort to get enthusiastic about the things that make a Cistercian what he is. My efforts in this regard, sincere as they have been, have not really produced the effect which they produce in those whom I see around me, called to this life in every way. Without being exactly unhappy here, I have in fact been relying on concessions to lead a more solitary life than is the usual lot of the Cistercian. Because I have received many such concessions, my interior life has been fairly fruitful. But I stress the fact that its fruitfulness depends on the *exceptions*, not on the Rule, although I would be unjust if I tried to deny that I owe much to Gethsemani in every way. In a word, whatever good has been worked in me here has been largely due to the unusual concessions for a *solitary* life which have been granted me.

Now, here is the problem. I am beginning to wonder whether I can continue in this way. Everybody here agrees that I am called to more solitude than the average Cistercian. No director denies that this call is supernatural. Most, however, favor continuing the compromise—especially my Superiors, who will certainly raise a terrific opposition to my leaving here. I doubt if I will be able to get their permission. But, Father, I have also consulted a Father we have here who is in some way an expert in questions of vocation and adaptation. He is a former Jesuit, a man of years and wide experience, and we have worked together on some of the difficulties of the scholastics whose Father Master I am. (For instance, Fr. L. who wrote to you last summer who is definitely *not* a Carthusian prospect.) I have discussed the whole question with this experienced Father, and his judgment is flatly that I *do not* belong here and that I *do* belong in a Charterhouse—assuming I can get into one. (The question whether a Charterhouse might want *me* is something altogether different.) This Father says that I need the solitary life, and that this life is not doing me any good. His judgment confirms what my own conscience is telling me very clearly. I *cannot evade* the fact that the intense activity which fills this whole house and in which I myself am engaged is actually creating obstacles to my deeper union with God. I feel exactly in the same predicament as a person working in the active ministry in a town or city. The job I have here is just as gruelling as that, in some respects, and the consequent publicity, correspondence, etc., etc., is absolutely obnoxious. I feel that I must leave all that at all costs. As I said above, I mean to make every possible effort to get permission for a truly solitary life, and I mean to take whatever permission I can get. I believe this to be a serious moment of choice in my life, one upon which depends my deliverance from a future of even more heavy and useless activity and perhaps of responsibilities which I am not in any way equipped to shoulder and which my conscience clamors against. I am not referring to the ordinary duties of Cistercian life, but to the fantastic responsibilities which arise in a monastery which has grown out of all proportion to the requirements of a truly contemplative life, which is invaded with tourists and visitors, and so on.

My whole feeling in the presence of this situation is like that of someone who desires to live a life of virginity, but who is left in the world surrounded by people whose horizons are bounded by marriage and family life. To these others no doubt it may seem like "laziness" to evade the responsibilities of the married state. But Our Lord had different ideas. I live surrounded by men who work hard and sacrifice themselves generously, but who are wedded to their jobs and consequently are nourished and built up by the work which only tears me down and gets between me and God and empties my soul.

I am therefore writing to ask you if there is any chance of my being accepted as a Carthusian. My desires go out to the Charterhouse before everything else, first because if I had been able to become a Carthusian instead of a Trappist in 1941, I would certainly have done so. Secondly because I believe the Carthusian life is the safest and best way to find God in solitude—certainly safer than the business of being a hermit on my own, which nevertheless I will try if nothing else is possible. If you do not take me, the Camaldolese will. But frankly I am a little dubious of Camaldoli—because they would probably want to exploit my name and make me write more books. The third reason why I want to be a Carthusian is that I am fairly sure you would discourage me from writing any more, and that is what I want. Finally, the Camaldolese would undoubtedly use me to make an American foundation. With you I would never be a superior. I assure you, Father, that I want to get away from activity and take on the one job that really means something: that of being silent and of serving God in peace and humility, out from under the eyes of men, alone in His presence. I am essentially quite a simple person and to me complications are only a snare. The Charterhouse seems to me to offer the best guarantee of simplicity and humility and solitude and peace. I beg God to guide you in your answer. If it is affirmative, then the real job begins: that of convincing my Abbot that I should go. If it is negative, then please tell me what you would do in my position—give me some good alternatives. Besides Camaldoli I have thought of the following: joining Père Henrion in Tunisia; looking up some Franciscan hermits in the Balearic Islands; starting out on my own in the Rocky Mountains or somewhere (I'm not tough enough for that).

Incidentally, I know all about your life—or think I do. The only thing that might bother me is the breaking of sleep, but since I lose a lot of sleep here it could scarcely be any worse than the common dormitory, and it is easier to go without sleep in your life than in ours. I have a slight stomach ailment which my advisor believes is simply a functional disorder caused by lack of adjustment and overwork in this community. He says it would clear up in a Charterhouse and I think he is right.

Well, Father: there it is. May God give you light . . .

To Dom Gabriel Sortais

September 27, 1952

I no longer know exactly where you are located now, but I send this letter to Rome! The General Chapter ended about ten days ago, I suppose. Dom James has written nothing to me in regard to the *imprimi potest* [for *The Sign of Jonas*], but the publisher indicates to me a vague message—it won't be long. I know you are very busy, and I beg your pardon for disturbing you. It is not to demand anything whatsoever. Perhaps the account from your censor has indicated to you—which is true indeed—

that this "Journal" is the product of a rather special spirit. That is, that the author is always speaking of solitude, and there is in it really a spirit more eremitic than cenobitic. In this case, maybe you find yourself embarrassed to write a prefatory letter. I foresaw it, and I wanted to inform you about it, but maybe I lacked precision, maybe even frankness. But I assure you this lack was more unconscious than anything else, for it is only these last days that I have realized the question from all its angles. In truth, I have an ideal which is more personal, perhaps, more particularly "mine" than I thought. Unconsciously it happens that by asking you for a prefatory letter, maybe I wanted to show that "my" spirit was truly quite Cistercian. I don't say it was the spirit of the Order, but a spirit that could in a pinch be accepted in the Order. But I begin to wonder if it is really true after all.

If it is not true, I have no right to a letter from you except only from a purely personal point of view. But I should not in conscience ask you to subscribe to my ideal, as head of the whole Order, if you did not really intend to say that this spirit was quite acceptable with us. Now, at the same time, if this spirit is not acceptable, there arises for me another problem of conscience which I spare you for the time being. I only ask you to pray for me and bless me, for I suffer a little in the midst of this problem. I think I must inform you that my "project" for a scholasticate was also, without my knowing it, an unconscious expedient to create a more solitary and more "contemplative" milieu for myself. Now to present this type of project under pretext of doing some good for the Order is to risk changing and even warping the true spirit of Cîteaux. I have neither the right nor the desire to do so. In short, it seems to me I must absolutely in conscience determine if *my* ideal (which I am morally certain is willed by God for me) can be reconciled with the spirit of Cîteaux. If not, I must absolutely avoid any step that would turn to its detriment. But at the same time, I must go on following the vocation God has given me without hindering the progress of others or leading them away from their own path.

I beg your pardon, dear Most Reverend Father, for exposing you to endless embarrassments by my lack of foresight. But I assure you in all sincerity that I have not done it intentionally. I was not yet seeing clearly enough to avoid all the pitfalls. I do not know if your letter is already on its way or not. At any rate, I am expecting an answer to this one, as a confirmation to this letter—just tell me by a simple word, either granting or refusing the publication of the letter. The publisher is getting a little impatient, and I would not like to inconvenience him too much. As for Fr. Maurice's objections, which I do not understand very well since his letter went straight to Dom James, but judging from his remarks on the proof sheets and his notes, I see they are questions of style and composition—questions of *literary* craft and not of censorship proper. I have sent him a mild protest, and am still awaiting his answer. I will make all the corrections he is asking for, without appeal. I hope he will all the same be good enough to leave me my own style, and to allow the publishers to judge if the public is going to accept my nonsense or not . . .

September 30, 1952

Do me the favor of reading this letter before the other, longer one. I have just received your letter from Igny, for which I thank you sincerely and express my deepest respect for your sincerity towards me. I realize for the first time that I have been unjust, when I only tried to be sincere and objective. I have not distrusted enough my own opinions. You are right in saying that this is to be attributed to a spirit more natural than I knew. Above all—I did not think of it while writing—there is in this a great lack of virtue. Maybe when I was writing "Aux Sources du Silence" [*The Waters of Siloe*], I thought I was a good religious. But now . . . maybe I am not religious at all.

Forgive me if I don't rewrite the letter about *The Sign of Jonas*. I think you ought to know the facts I mention in it to you. But after what you say about "Aux Sources du Silence," I distrust my feelings as regards the journal. Only the situation remains very delicate though—it is partly my fault and partly the publisher's fault.

The wound you give me, dear Most Reverend Father, is salutary and merciful. But it remains a wound. I express my gratitude for it, and I assure you of my contrition. I can see that unwittingly I have hurt Jesus by speaking badly of His saints. I will accuse myself of it at confession tomorrow, and I will try to do penance. I won't multiply words, I already have too many of them on paper.

After reading our second letter, you will judge about *The Sign of Jonas* as you like. Maybe the title is rather well chosen: I am only good to be thrown to the whale! I am not a saint but I *want* to be one, in spite of my wretchedness . . .

September 30, 1952

Second Letter
(Written before the other. But I ask you to read this one after the other.)

Dom James' letter has informed me—surprising me a little—of your decision about the journal, *The Sign of Jonas*, after the assessment of the manuscript by Dom Albert [Derzelle] and another Cistercian Abbot. I received the news with much joy, and I wish I could have quite simply answered with my peaceful and gracious *"fiat"* [let it be done]. I am doing so in advance, anyway, if you do not accept the remarks I feel I should make in this letter.

Indeed, Most Reverend Father, if the question was of a manuscript that had never been through the hands of a publisher—and what is more of an American publisher—the affair would be very simple. But now the publisher, as he accepted the manuscript, and knowing that the idea of a journal would not be, of itself, repugnant to the spirit of our Order, immediately started to make known the forthcoming publication of this work. So that *The Sign of Jonas* has already been ordered in several hundreds at least by bookshops. Everywhere one sees it announced, by advertisements, etc., and certain book clubs have already guaranteed a considerable sale by making this book their selection for the month of December, I think. I have asked Mr. Robert Giroux, the publisher, to send you the details of the business aspect of the affair.

So there you are, dear Most Reverend Father: if *the entire book*, as it is, is withdrawn now from the market, there will be universal consternation and scandal. First, it will be said that if the book has been rejected by the censors of the Order, it is because there must be awkward stories about the life of the Trappists, and even something shocking. People will jump on this chance to denigrate us. Even though these suppositions are not made, then the non-Catholic will sneer, seeing one more proof of what they say about censorship in the Church. In short, if *The Sign of Jonas* does not appear in the form of a journal, there will be very serious embarrassments for the Order and Gethsemani—and for the publisher, naturally.

Now Dom Albert does not reject *the substance* of the book. It appears that he accepts willingly all that is spiritual in it. He only rejects the trifles, the banal details of the life, etc. Do you not think, Most Reverend Father, Dom Albert's objections could be met by the following steps:

1) Retain the "genre" and the form of the journal. Publish the spiritual substance, with enough "vignettes" and local color and movement to give this book the true character of a journal, lived and lively, though somewhat impressionistic. But then suppress all that would seem over-banal. Dom Albert would only have to send us a) the list of the passages to be totally suppressed, b) the list of the passages to be modified according to his views. The book, thus purged, would substantially remain all that the readers expect from us, and there will be no scandal.

2) In any event, to protect our (i.e. my) miserable "reputation" (!) in Europe, one could, if you demand it, refuse all the translation rights in Europe, and even the rights for a London edition, only retaining the possibility of selling the rights in South America—a thing that would make no impression in Europe.

But still, after saying all this, I must accuse myself of negligence. Had I known that the publisher was already preparing his publicity, and had I guessed you were going to refuse permission to publish all the book, as it is, I could have prevented this embarrassment. Besides, I must accuse myself of disobedience. For while knowing that the publisher wanted to start the printing I only gave him a *conditional* [O.K.], telling him he could carry on as long as he was ready to make notable changes after the censor's decision. I had thought I could do so because you had told me the idea of a journal was not, in itself, to be rejected. I had not looked close enough, and I should have absolutely forbidden the printing. The book is not completely printed, but—I don't know the French phrase—it is "set up in type," ready to be printed. Now, this does not change the face of the question, which depends not on the work but on the advertising and the sale of the book, done independently by the publisher before even consulting me and starting the printing.

I assure you, dear Most Reverend Father, that I am infinitely sorry for my negligence and I ask your pardon for having disobeyed you. I beg you to give me a good penance for it, and I promise I will never, after this, let anything whatsoever be done by a publisher before the acceptance of the whole manuscript by all the censors. In fine, I simply expect from you the expression of God's will, and I promise to accept it with joy, remaining more devoted to you than ever. The publisher, who is a former college friend of mine at the University, a good Catholic and a friend of Gethsemani, will do the same. Believe me, my dear Most Reverend Father, that I accept your will with the joy and affection of a true son while expressing my grief and promising to do better henceforth . . .

To Dom Albert Derzelle, O.C.S.O.

Dom Albert Derzelle was Prior of Caldey Abbey in Wales at this time, and an English-language censor of the Order.

October 16, 1952

I had delayed for some time in writing to you, since I thought perhaps a letter from you might be on its way about *The Sign of Jonas.* I am sorry, Reverend Father, that you have had so much trouble with this book which our Reverendissime [Abbot General] gave you to censor for him. It is not difficult for me to see why you objected to the book. Yet I hope you will forgive me if I once more bring up the subject; I have already written to our Reverendissime Père about it, but the letter is no doubt wandering all over China looking for him. He may in time receive it with a favorable reply. I now write to you at the suggestion of my own Father Abbot, Dom James.

Plainly, the situation is this. Through the over-eagerness of the publisher, which I was not sufficiently zealous and prudent to control, *The Sign of Jonas* had already been set up in type and widely advertised before you had finished censoring the manuscript. This was a lamentable error for which I have accused myself to our Reverendissime. Nevertheless the fact remains that the book has been accepted by several book clubs and is already ordered in advance by many bookstores, so that the readers in this country are eagerly awaiting its appearance. I thought I ought to point out to the Reverendissime that if, at this juncture, the book does not appear it might cause such suspicion and calumny of the

Order and Gethsemani—they will think it was suppressed because of scandalous facts or something of the sort. In view of this, and in view of the fact that Dom James assures me that you do not object to the spiritual content of the book which, he says, you suggest publishing in some other form, we would like to ask you the following favor.

Since you approve the publication of the spiritual content of the book *in some form* and since it is very expedient that the book should appear explicitly as a Journal so as not to arouse too much adverse comment and suspicion, we would like to ask if you would not permit as much of the book as you approve to appear as a Journal and to preserve the Journal form and the thread of the story. I have asked the Reverendissime if he would not permit this also. In the case that this is permissible we would then like you, if it is not too much trouble, to indicate to us what passages *must* be deleted, and what may be kept with slight modification. Naturally we would like to keep as much as possible, but we bow to your superior judgment as censor and leave the final editing in this matter to you.

We have also suggested to the Reverendissime that we would refrain from granting any rights for publication in Europe, if he or you so desired. This would take care of one of your great objections to the book, namely that it would be received with disfavor by European readers. And yet I would like to point out that one of the passages to which I am sure you objected on these precise grounds—and to which one of the American censors also objected—was accepted and printed in *Dieu Vivant*. This is the incident about the hunters walking on the enclosure wall which has all the triviality and apparent uselessness which, as I understand, forms the basis of your objection to the book.

Dear Reverend Father, I perfectly understand your attitude towards the book, and that of our Reverendissime. I agree with it myself. The book does not have the seriousness and sobriety one would expect of a Benedictine monk. But I feel that this failing can be largely corrected, while still leaving the book some of its character. You see, I was expressly *avoiding* anything that sounded like a "spiritual journal," since I felt that it would be indecent for a person with as little spirituality as I have to pretend to publish a volume all about his interior (?) life so early in his days, or indeed during his lifetime at all. It was precisely in order to avoid this *faux pas* that I went to the other extreme and endeavored to make the book light and simple and matter of fact, describing things and events exactly as they are, so that a person outside the cloister might have something of the experience of knowing what life is like—for better or for worse—inside the walls of Gethsemani. Certainly, if you feel that this book is too frank an avowal of my own religious limitations and of those of Gethsemani, we cannot let that impression be communicated to the public. However, I am sure it can be avoided without sacrificing anything that gives the book a living appeal for the average American reader. I think the instinct to which it might appeal is a legitimate curiosity and might, in spite of everything, lead to good spiritual fruits. At least that is the opinion of our editor, a good Catholic, who is also very much in touch with the taste of the cultivated readers in this country.

In the end, however, I confess that the whole idea of a Journal has always appeared to me as an indecency—although I enjoyed writing it. It remains to be seen what Jesus wills in this matter, and I pray Him to guide you and the Reverendissime if any change is to be made in your decision. I hope you will be able to save the substance of the book; otherwise the editor, my friend, will be in serious difficulties and so will the monastery.

In closing, my Reverend Father, I beg your blessing and your prayers. Please ask Jesus, through the intercession of Our Lady, to begin at last to make a good monk of me, for I am aware of nothing but shame for what I am at present. I say this in deep sincerity, trusting that it will win me your prayers and those of your community. It is a terrible thing when a religious as poor in virtue as I am, and as full of misery as I, is nevertheless regarded as a person worthy of consideration by some people. May God forgive me for this scandalous illusion which, however, it was never my intention to create. Surely *The Sign of Jonas* will lead people to at least suspect the truth. Is not that a merit?

To Dom Gabriel Sortais

November 4, 1952

The other day, as I came back home from work, I found your good letter, so kindly and paternal. Your kindness renews my feelings of regret for causing you some pain by my imprudence, and I assure you once more that I will not do it again! I have notified the publisher of your decision, telling him to make, as soon as possible, the corrections Dom Albert will indicate to him. Of course, we have already made the corrections asked for by the American censors.

You tell me that both publishers—the one in London [Tom Burns of Burns, Oates] as well as the one in New York [Robert Giroux of Harcourt, Brace]—have raised a campaign of blackmail [Maritain's letter of protest, etc.]. I have not been aware of what has happened, and I did not even know that the English publisher had meddled in this affair. I had only asked our publisher here [Giroux] to communicate to you the details of the publicity which had been done around the book. This publicity had already been begun, without my knowing anything about it, before your visit to Gethsemani. At that time, the manuscript had already been delivered for the most part to the publisher, but they had not yet begun the printing work. [Since it had been passed by Gethsemani censors, it had been set up in galley proofs by the publisher.] I sincerely regret the embarrassment the publishers have caused you by their indiscretion. Really, it is my fault. I understand quite well that, having the book in press, they behave as "money men" since they run the risk of losing quite a lot of money if the book were suppressed. As I read over these sentences, I think I must have made grammatical mistakes. I will content myself with saying once more, from the bottom of my heart, my sincere regret, as much for this affair of *The Sign of Jonas* as for the errors in "Aux Sources du Silence."

During the month of October, I examined myself many times, and noticed I really lack religious spirit. At the same time, Jesus was kind enough, in the adorable plans of His divine providence, to lead me along a way full of trials and I very often feel myself in a state of blindness and impotence. I have never had such a feeling of my own wretchedness. No doubt this is salutary for me: but I assure you, my dear Most Reverend Father, that I am scared by the nothingness that opens like an abyss in my soul. Pray to the Blessed Virgin to hold me very near to her, in this darkness. It is certainly not the moment to discuss with Reverend Father the question of a solitary life. However I have unfolded to him what was going on in my soul: but I don't need to take a long journey in order to find the desert: the desert is myself . . .

To Dom Humphrey Pawsey

November 18, 1952

It is some time since you kindly wrote and asked me to come up to Vermont to talk things over. This will not be possible, I fear.

As you say, it would be better if things could be arranged in my present circumstances, and I think that all the indications of God's will seem, at present, to point in that direction. I cannot hope to understand or see clearly, but as long as I know what His will is, I am glad to accept it. The chief ambiguity that confronts me is that all who tell me to stay here tell me to do so for the sake of the contemplative life, while staying here seems in fact to involve the sacrifice of the contemplative life. An interesting dilemma which is enough of a source of anguish for me to need many prayers. I hope I can count on yours . . .

To Dom Aelred Graham, O.S.B.

Dom Aelred Graham (1907–1984), an English Benedictine monk from Ampleforth Abbey, was at this time headmaster of Portsmouth Priory School in Rhode Island. He had written a rather negative article on Thomas Merton in The Atlantic Monthly *[January 1953], one of the first really critical reviews of Merton and his writings. The following letter was the first of a series exchanged between them.*

January 15, 1953

This is just a note to thank you for the article you wrote about me in the *Atlantic*. It reached me in a roundabout way the other day and I feel that I have profited much by reading it. On the whole I think you have treated me with true Christian charity. If there be any misunderstanding of my position, it is probably my fault. I think, at bottom, your objection is basically due to a clash of temperaments more than anything else. For my own part I have always felt that the things I write do not at all represent what I would really like to say.

Above all, I realize that the Spirit of Christ and of His Gospels has not been given the prominence He should have in my writings, if they are to be the writings of a true son of St. Benedict. I beg your prayers that I may grow in true charity and humility and that I may really breathe forth the "good odor of Christ" in every place. From now on I probably will not be writing very much. I have a rather heavy responsibility, however, as spiritual director of our scholastics here. I will value your prayers—and any other points of advice you may see fit to give me. I assure you that I have no desire to be a reformer, that I do not really mean to enlist the whole world in the pursuit of a contemplation that can only be the gift of God, and that I am by no means a second Rancé. Finally, I am as worried as anyone else about the inordinate publicity which is being received by the Trappists and Gethsemani . . .

To Abbot James Fox

January 20, 1953

I thought we ought to have a name for the new "refuge" and I chose the name *St. Anne's* [an old toolshed moved to a wooded hill overlooking the hills to the east], if you approve.

Having been out here almost all day for two days, I find time goes by much too fast, and it is always time to go home much too soon. It is the first time in my life—37 years—that I have had a real conviction of doing what I am really called by God to do. It is the first time I have ever felt that I have "arrived"—like a river that has been running through a deep canyon and now has come out into the plains—and is within sight of the ocean.

Funnily enough, it is out here that I have for the first time discovered the real Benedictine values as they are meant to be. *Silence, simplicity, poverty, peace,* and above all I seem to be much more able to keep my eye on the *will of God.* Out here there is no complexity and no confusion—there is no contradiction between work and prayer, everything is in unity and all is truly centered in God.

I am glad Our Lord did not let me die before I could taste something of this: it is the real thing, at least for me, and with a little of this life, I feel that I can really prepare for death and for heaven. Thank you again for allowing me this privilege of being so close to Jesus, even if only for a little while.

To Father Barnabas M. Ahern, C.P.

Father Ahern, a Passionist Scripture scholar, was teaching at the Passionist seminary in Louisville at this time, and occasionally gave Scripture lectures to the Gethsemani community, and thus Merton would sometimes call upon Father Ahern for counseling and advice.

January 22, 1953

Many thanks for your kind and solicitous letter. If a cryptic sentence of mine led you to believe that I was contemplating a "radical change," I owe you some clarification. No, I am not changing to another order. I agree with the reasons you give for not doing so, although I think that in some respects you are too absolute: for after all, *all* transfers are surely not a matter of emotion. My limited experience with the scholastics shows me that a lot of them really do not belong here and that God's will surely seems to be that they try something else. Of course, simple professed are still "under probation" so that is not at all strange. I have seen misfits beyond that stage, and I agree that perhaps they got as far as they did on emotion rather than faith . . . On the other hand, there are men here from other Orders who did well to come, and whose presence here is no indication that the time spent elsewhere was wasted. I can also see the possibility of someone quite legitimately leaving here for the Carthusians but I think it would have to be a very rare case, with very strong indications of a special reason willed by God. And I have been told by one director that such indications were found in my own case, but since he also agrees that these indications may lead to a solution nearer home, and since Father Abbot takes that view, and since I feel myself that this is what the Holy Ghost wants: that is the step that is being taken. It will upset no one, because I hope very few people will ever know much about it.

However, I will really value your reactions. In some sense it is a more radical step than the other—that is, if it goes as far as I hope it will, one day.

As you know, the monastic tradition has always allowed for the quite normal development that would take some cenobites into solitude as hermits. St. Benedict recognized this in his Rule. The Camaldolese have adapted St. Benedict for hermits. The Cistercians, while being more intransigently cenobitic even than other Benedictines, commemorate three Cistercian hermits in the Breviary—a good proportion, of our fifteen or so saints! One of them received permission to live as a hermit in the Holy Land from St. Bernard himself. You have probably also seen the recent issue of *La Vie Spirituelle*, "Bienheureuse Solitude" which takes up the question. Some of the articles are quite interesting. There remains no real question of the rightness and fitness of hermits existing in dependence on established monastic communities.

The question has always been one of practical application to individual cases. Our abbots retain the power to grant these special permissions. If they have not used that power lately, to any great extent, there is no reason why they cannot use it whenever they see fit. We are not planning permissions here that would cover more than one case, at the moment. And so far, Father Abbot, who understands and sympathizes with what appear to be rather special needs, has granted me a permission which allows for a good chunk of the day in solitude, on some days, without any interference with the regular schedule and without creating any scandal in the community.

I have been fretting over this question for some nine years, Father. No matter how hard I have tried to convince myself, I have never really succeeded in quite believing that the ordinary routine of Trappist life is exactly what I am called to. It is just "not *it*." With me it does not *work*. That is to say that it produces effects in me which are more or less opposite to what it produces in those who are really called to it. Quite simply: the perpetual motion of exterior exercises, the constant presence of a lot of people and also often of a lot of machines, instead of helping me to pray and liberating me from myself, tends to get me tied up in myself to a point that is really harmful. To be alone, with real silence, real solitude without material responsibilities, and able to really sink into God, straightens everything out. Father Abbot's conclusion: "Solitude, for you, is medicine," and he gladly gives me a good amount of it. In effect, I am a part-time hermit. This began recently and it has cleared up almost everything. It has put the liturgy back on its feet for me, and has helped me to face the job of directing students a little more serenely. Last fall I just about cracked up, under the business of leading what was effectively an "active life" and trying to convince myself that this was what it meant to be a contemplative.

One point remains, and it is important. It is an interior matter, close to the heart of the question. Such a step may possibly be regarded by many as a kind of "defection," a retreat from duty, a concession to self-will and human weakness, an eccentricity. Since I am still putting in a good day's work as director, I feel no special qualms about the "duty" angle. But one of the things that I think I must face and work out, and which requires the integrity I asked you to pray for, is this: it may well be a temptation, but the refusal to face it, the fear of it, has been making a mess of my interior life. It seems to me that what I find in solitude is so much worthwhile, so truly the thing I am *really called to* and so much the real reason for my existence on earth, that it is worth facing the accusation of defection, of being a bad or eccentric religious, in order to get it. Such accusations are not forthcoming, but they might occur. Let them, then. If my really finding God is to be bought at that price—it is still too cheap! Frankly I don't think there will be any but pharisaic scandal at what I hope to do in the future. Those who know about what I have hoped, already understand it perfectly. I hope, in the future, to be able to live completely as a hermit. How I am going to get there is in the hands of God. But that is what I was asking you to pray for.

In résumé: I really believe that Our Lord wants me to follow this course now. It is a course which, in itself, accords with the monastic tradition and can be fitted into the Cistercian life. It is something which some theologians (Dom Anselme Stolz, Dom Jean Leclercq—both Benedictines—and others) feel *ought* to be brought back into its rightful place in the monastic setting. It is fully approved by my Superiors and not only approved but advised by directors. I am going forward leaving the future development of it all in the hands of God, working through my own Superiors. But there remains the personal anguish of travelling a road on which there is a great danger of illusion and on which I will undoubtedly meet many critics and many obstacles . . .

It seems to me that if I give myself to Him in the most complete possible solitude—I mean whatever solitude may be permitted to me in my present circumstances—I will be doing a work more pleasing to Our Lord and more fruitful for the Church than if I wrote more books. In order to do this, my Superiors have gladly taken me off the job of teaching Scripture and have let me cut down on writing. As far as the writing goes, I do not feel that I will ever write anything worthwhile, if I cannot have access to the depths which solitude alone seems able to lay open to me. In other words there is simply no point in my rehashing other people's books, as I am not a true theologian and cannot do so effectively.

To Dom Gabriel Sortais

February 12, 1953

Today we are reading in the refectory your beautiful letter on *lectio divina*, and it seems to me that you touch here a definitely capital point. Yes, it is true that our love for God easily falls into tepidity and aridity when we do not come unceasingly back to the knowledge of His love for us. In truth, it is His love which is at the same time the cause and the term of our loving knowledge of Him. It is His love that invites us to find Him everywhere, in the Scripture, in nature, in our own hearts, in our duties—and I add my own voice: in solitude!

But I was not intending to compliment you on this fine paternal letter. On the contrary, it reminds me of the painful fact of your illness. I remember how eagerly you left everything aside to write me, from Japan, as soon as you knew I was in a difficult plight. And what have I done? Already a fortnight or more has passed before I address you a little filial note, in order to assure you of my pain and my prayers for you. But now, it is your circular letter itself that accounts for my apparent lack of virtue. I endeavor all the same to spare a little room for prayer and reading in the somewhat active life I am leading with our forty students. But after all, this work is not really much in itself . . .

The day before yesterday a copy of *The Sign of Jonas* was sent to you. I am ashamed of it, and I would have liked to spare you the sight of this poor work which caused you such pain. It is still not the end of the miseries with this book. The publisher had pictures which had been delivered to him, in which "the monk" was not recognizable—for he is always seen from behind. Unfortunately, without even asking our permission, the publisher has allowed these photos to appear in some newspapers, letting it be known that the monk in question was me. After which, no pictures at all, even those in which the monk's face cannot be seen. I am very sorry, my Most Reverend Father.

Apart from all this, the impression is however that the book will do a little good, to recompense us for all this trouble. 60,000 copies have been sold before publication, and with the second printing we reach 75,000. Very serious persons, writers, critics, etc., seem to think it is the "best" (i.e. the least bad) of our books: this not only from the literary point of view, but also from the point of view of its spiritual influence, given the peculiar circumstances of the U.S.A. . . .

March 13, 1953

I was just going to write you a word to tell you how glad I was to hear of you, via our Reverend Father, who visited you during your convalescence in Canada. But here comes your good letter. I hasten to answer you with filial love, as I accept the dispositions you are suggesting to me as a writer.

The question of the journal is very simple. You ask me if this task is not bound to hinder my intimate relations with God. Well, if it were God's will that I do this task, He would Himself see to it how to protect me. As I wrote *The Sign of Jonas*, I felt clearly I was doing His holy will and, though I had a few distractions, I think my interior life did not suffer too much. But now you are showing your wish to see the journal cease. Since this does not please you, I willingly discard the work, which kept me busy only very little as a matter of fact. It is no longer God's will that I write this journal. Of course my relations with Him would be hindered. There we are. I find the answer is very simple.

How kind of you to take care of this question of solitude which preoccupies me. I find that what embarrasses me most is the duty to direct the students' souls. Since my thoughts are directed to persons concrete and known, and not to the rather hypothetical reader, I find in it more distraction and contention, and I unwittingly lack fidelity to my particular grace, by endeavoring to adapt myself too much to the tastes of others. There is here, as everywhere, a danger of artificiality, of falseness. But here again God takes care of our inevitable errors. He takes upon Himself even the distractions we undergo out of love for Him, in the duty of guiding the souls towards divine union. I don't lose too much by it as long as this charge does not reach proportions quite unreasonable for a Trappist, and besides, Dom James, who understands the situation very well, gives me the occasion to make good for the intervals and to pray a little and seek for recollection and solitude when possible. I think you too will favor such a step, which is quite necessary.

But there remains something I want to ask you. I don't see very clearly, in your letter, and I wonder whether it forbids me to do *any* work as a writer.

1) Is it your will that I don't write *any more* a *single* book?

2) Or do you want me not to write a book while I am Student Master?

3) Do you allow the eventual publication of the conferences given to the students, and of the main ideas of their formation? All the same I must write them [for the students], and I get them photocopied. So it is a more or less unavoidable *work*.

4) Or, apart from the journal and every autobiographical and formally "personal" narrative, would you allow a book provided it does not hinder the interior life and does not disagree with our monastic ideal—e.g., meditations, studies on the interior life, lives of saints, studies in Holy Scripture, etc.?

In principle, my Most Reverend Father, any work as a writer should be for us *rare and exceptional*. If you want to know what I frankly think, before God, in my own case, I will tell you this: what I find most embarrassing is to try to do a scholar's job, to speak as an historian, a dogmatic theologian, etc. I also have more or less given up writing as a *poet*, but sometimes an idea may come, it gets written, so to speak, of its own accord, and it helps to *deepen some insight* about God, about the spiritual life, etc. Also fragments of meditations, *impersonal and objective*, upon the truths of faith, our relations with God. It is these fragments (in the line of *Seeds of Contemplation*) that seem to me to be our affair, if we write anything at all. But if I must go on working along this line it will remain, for me, as for the others, *rare and exceptional!*

I ask you these questions with simplicity, precisely to know where I must direct our efforts. A few years ago, with Dom James' approval, I signed a contract with our editor [Robert Giroux] aiming at the publication of four books of which one has been delivered [*The Ascent to Truth*, 1953]. The others were to be a life of Saint Aelred [not completed], a book on Saint Bernard [*The Last of the Fathers*, 1954], a book on the Holy Mass [unwritten]. I assure you I have very little taste for these works, all of which seem to demand a little erudition. There remains the fact that I am under an obligation of providing him (the publisher) with three more books.

Besides, I *am* convinced of the truthfulness of what you say about the dangers of a writer's life. One may think one has very pure intentions, but publicity is an altogether nefarious thing which seduces us in spite of ourselves. Also the preoccupations of success, of the diffusion of the book, etc. I have resisted them with all my strength, but I am sure I have not avoided being wounded many times . . .

To Dom Hubert Van Zeller, O.S.B.

Dom Hubert Van Zeller (1905–1984) was a monk of Downside Abbey in England and well known for his many books and articles on the monastic and contemplative life. He wrote to Merton saying not all the English Benedictines agreed with Dom Aelred Graham's rather negative appraisal of Merton and his writings.

[Summer, 1953]

Thank you for your letter which covered me with confusion. I did not mean to enlist you as a reviewer, but I will be a most happy and honored author if you do write about the book. And I feel that the works of Merton occupy too great a proportion in the books assigned to you *ad usum.* I have three Van Zellers in the somewhat large collection which I call the scholasticate library, in order to save my face and salve my conscience. They are *Daniel, Isaias* and *Moments of Light.* The latter is particularly good and has helped one of my students very notably. Your lively approach to Daniel completely entranced another (who needs to be entranced, as he is seriously ill and is having rather a rough time of it). I am wondering if you have some other books on the Scriptures. In fact I know you have, but I have not yet been able to get at them and this letter is to be interpreted as an act of shameless and mercenary begging for one or another of them. In return, if they would be useful, I could send you some mimeographed notes of conferences and such, that form part of the *dura et aspera* which our scholastics have to suffer in this valley of tears.

The reason why Dom Aelred wrote his article about me [for *The Atlantic Monthly*] is probably that he feels the Trappists ought to be taken down a peg. We do not mean to give the impression of blowing our own trumpet in this country, but unfortunately that is the impression the "Black" Benedictines seem to be receiving. There is nothing new in this, since St. Bernard had to face the same problem, and the foundation of Cîteaux seems to have been surrounded by a certain amount of name-calling which would have been better left alone. However, the best thing we Cistercians can do about it is to pull in our horns and not make too much noise about ourselves. I sympathize with the aspirations you speak of: I think they exist in many monasteries. They exist here too; and one of the chief reasons why I think the Cistercians ought to be a little quieter about themselves is that they (we) do not have as much of the primitive

St. Benedict as they (we) suppose. If there is a real need for the simple, unadorned Benedictine life, the life provided for in the Rule as it stands, the Holy Spirit will certainly provide for those who seek that life . . .

To Abbot Augustine Moore, O.C.S.O.

Fr. Augustine Moore (1911–) entered Gethsemani about the same time as Thomas Merton, but was sent to the foundation of the Holy Spirit in Georgia, and was the American Definitor in Rome at the time of this letter. He was elected Abbot of Holy Spirit Abbey in 1957, following the death of Abbot Robert McGann.

May 10, 1953

I am appending to this letter the notes of a tirade I delivered to the scholastics after the visitation, explaining various points Dom Louis [Abbot of Gethsemani's Motherhouse of Melleray in France] had brought up. Could I have them back, please, when you are finished? You will find in them a reference to the use of the term scholasticate, which Dom Louis does not absolutely reprove. He simply discourages the use of the word in the sense of a separate group within the community. He has in mind Mount Melleray, where the scholastics have their own private scriptorium and where they go out to work separately from the rest of the monks. As long as the word does not lead to or imply such a state of affairs, it is okay. We are avoiding it here.

Functions of the Master of Students: Dom Louis simply ironed out a few details, after repeating that the fundamental duty of the Master is to *continue* and *deepen* the monastic formation given in the novitiate, to make sure that no *deviations* creep in as a result of studies, independent reading, etc., which should continue to be controlled. He does not seem to place much stress on the priestly formation of the scholastics which I think very important, but we do not disagree.

The Master of Students carries out his functions chiefly in conferences and direction. Dom Louis approved the setup we have here, for these things. They might be done differently elsewhere. With thirty-five to forty scholastics, I do not have time to take the solemn professed on a regular direction schedule. I take the first year professed twice a month, the second and third year professed once a month. I also have seven or eight regular penitents who come once a week. The solemn professed can come when they wish, Saturdays are kept open for them. Others too can come in between times if they want to.

As for conferences—I give one a week, Sunday after Benediction. Then when they make retreats I give retreat conferences—one for each minor order, three for each major order or for profession, but these conferences are optional. Usually we make retreats as follows: Go out for the morning work, then take the whole afternoon off for prayer, reading.

Conference usually comes half an hour before vespers. It is a lot nicer that way—in the old days we spent most of the time of retreat changing and going to Fr. Amedeus's conferences!!

The main thing Dom Louis did was to make clear the fact that the Prior takes care of all the material needs of the scholastics—looks after their needs when sick, etc. The M.S. does this only indirectly—drawing to the attention of the Prior or infirmarian that such and such a student needs care. Prior receives accusations for breach of rule, gives public penances, etc. M.S. has no disciplinary function. Here the Fr. Prior also takes care of the investigation of candidates before ordination, as directed by the instruction of the S.C.R., "Quantum religiones omnes" (see appendix to Creusen, "Religious Men and Women in the Code," pp. 287 ff.). Note that Cistercians are not obliged to follow this instruction in points that conflict with our private law: these differences flow principally from our "unique" privilege of being able to receive candidates to solemn profession without necessarily intending to advance them to major orders. Hence in n. 14 of QRO (Creusen, p. 294) it is not necessary to require all candidates to make application for advancement to orders before simple profession. In fact, however, Dom James and probably Dom Robert will ordinarily not receive anyone to simple vows in the choir, unless they are fit for ordination and desire to go on to orders. Hence in practice all will make application anyway. In n. 17, which by the way applies before the subdiaconate, we make them take the oath in these terms. Dom Louis thinks the first lines can be changed to suit our privilege: I don't see why they should be. This oath is taken after solemn vows, usually. I wrote up a new form which they sign here *before* solemn vows, and I'll try to get one from Fr. Prior. This is an "extra."

Before the first minor order and before subdiaconate, we send out a written form requesting all who have known the candidate closely in his formation (novice masters, professors—NOT regular confessor of candidate) to write out their frank opinion of his qualifications. This is kept in the archives. The investigation is repeated before subdiaconate and there follows a vote in the private council. Two candidates for major orders have been rejected this year, in this way. The investigation before minor orders is more of a formality since it comes so soon after simple profession. Nevertheless we have to be very strict about simple profession, especially in regard to their mental balance. In my opinion any tendency to strain is sufficient for rejection, unless it can be corrected entirely in the novitiate.

The Definitors are very anxious to get us to send men to Rome and I hope to be able to do so within a year or two. That will mean brushing up their Latin in a big way, in order that they may not reach the Eternal City as *complete* rubes. One of the big Trappist sins is accepting candidates for the choir who know little or no Latin. Dom Louis says we *must* wait until they have completed six years (unless we take them in as oblates and give them their humanities here). In my opinion Dom Louis does not mean a six-year-in-six-weeks fresh-air course. The professor sneezes and you miss a whole semester.

One of our problems here is nervous trouble which comes from various sources in my opinion.

1) They come in with the jitters in the first place.

2) They come in with a false notion of the monastic life, and do not lose that false notion in the novitiate: cling to the idea that they have to be something exalted and brilliant. They are exceptional people. They get this from some of our propaganda (mea culpa) which tends to give the idea that we are the light of the world. In fact, we are *ordinary* people.

3) Many run into a conflict between ideals and facts.

4) Many try to force their way to sanctity by sheer strain. No matter how much they may claim to be "above" consolations, their interior life tends to be nourished by emotion. They are constantly turning inward to examine their emotional "tone," and think that union with Jesus can be measured by a "feeling" of peace, relaxation, happiness, etc. If they don't hear the right "tone" inside, they try to produce it by strained recollection, forcing things "out" of the mind. Hence they conceive every sense impression, every memory, every idea, to be an obstacle to prayer. The community, the liturgy, everything becomes a potential distraction. Choir becomes a distraction—often they do another bad thing: become obsessed with the "quality" of the chant, as if the chant had to be materially perfect before you could begin to pray. Chant never perfect, ergo you can never get around to beginning to pray . . . etc.

5) All in all, we suffer from the disease of perfectionism, which is the biggest obstacle to true perfection because it dries up the interior spirit, kills real faith, makes us concentrate on ourselves instead of Jesus, puts a "false Jesus" in our hearts instead of the real Jesus Who is a Savior. He is not waiting for us to become angels before He starts to love us. He loves us because we are imperfect, not because we are good but *because He is good* . . . Most of them believe this only in theory. They are obsessed with their own miserable little "perfection" and "imperfection."

This is turning into an Encyclical, and I haven't even time to write a postcard. Please give my love to all the scholastics and ask them to pray for me and my own little gang (some of them are really the best I have ever seen at Gethsemani, which is saying a great deal). Jesus has been very good to us and to them. Some of them actually have a little common sense, which makes their fervor and their spiritual idealism really something staggering, at times.

To Dom Jean Leclercq

May 18, 1953

Forgive me for my delay in answering your good letter. *Jonas* is already being translated [into French] for Albin Michel, so I regretfully decline your kind offer. It would have been an honor to appear in "Tradition Monastique," in which series I already know your volume and that of Père Bouyer. By the way, has the promised Casel volume appeared in this series yet? I am anxious to see it. Now for your questions:

1. The XIV Century manuscript of St. Bernard is marked as n. 4 in the list of manuscripts and incunabula contributed by Dom Edmond Obrecht to the studies in *St. Bernard et son Temps*, Dijon, 1929, vol. ii, p. 133. I send you a photograph of the page with the "I" which, in fact, is of no interest.

2. I am not doing any work on a book on St. Bernard and there has been no announcement of any such book; hence I don't think it is in competition with your *St. Bernard Mystique*. If it gets finished—or started—before 1955, I will be surprised. The plan still exists, but I have no time to work on it.

3. The remark about the monks of the Common Observance understanding the truth of a statement of Sertillanges on the intellectual life which Trappists are incapable of understanding does not seem to me to be an injustice. The statement of Sertillanges is true, and there is no injustice in saying that someone agrees with the truth. Nor was it intended to be disparaging. However, if it appears so to you, perhaps they will themselves be even more sensitive about it, so I will delete it from the French edition, along with a lot of other things which will be of no interest in France. One of the censors of *Jonas* (in English) was a European. Then, too, I think the book shows clearly that I do not consider the Trappist life the highest form of contemplative life, because I believe such a theory to be plainly false. The Trappist life is a solidly austere form of the monastic life, which has its limitations, which offers opportunities for a man to become a contemplative, provided the opportunities are not ruined by excessive activity within the monastery. We have something of the spirit of St. Bernard but we have no monopoly on it. From the little I know of Hauterive [Cistercian monastery in Switzerland], I am certain that they are just as good a monastery and just as proper for the contemplative life as Gethsemani—with perhaps certain advantages over Gethsemani. I do not despise the Common Observance at all, nor do I despise the Benedictines (as Dom Aelred Graham seems to think).

The more I reflect on it, the more I realize that all the monastic ways to God are most worthy of praise, and that, in the end, there is no point in asking who has the most perfect interpretation of the Rule of St. Benedict. In the end, however, what I most personally and intimately feel about at least my own place in the framework of things is echoed by the remarkable articles of a certain "S" in *La Vie Spirituelle* of last October and again more recently. Do you happen to know who this "S" may be [Sainsaulieu], and would there be some chance of finding him and writing him a letter? (See "L'Erémitisme dans la vie spirituelle," *V.S.*, Oct. 1952.) I also by the way enjoyed your article in *Rhythmes du Monde*, now reproduced in *Témoignages*. I hope more and more to withdraw from the field of professional writing—or at least to appear in it only as an occasional author of disjointed meditations. But I do earnestly beg your prayers that I may seek God with greater love, and that He may deign to open to us here in America the ways of solitude, within the framework of our monasticism. This, I think, is much more important than any books. I thank you again for your letter which, as you see, was stimulating . . .

To Sister A.

Sister A., a young Carmelite, had met Father Louis several times at Gethsemani when she came to visit her brother, a member of the community and one of Merton's students. The friendship continued after her entrance into Carmel.

May 21, 1953

The invitation was not steamed open and there was no evidence of ink eradicator, so I presume you wrote it all over again. On the 8th I included you in a Mass I was able to offer for Sister C. who wrote that she was making her profession on that day. Meanwhile I will try to do the same for you on the 25th. Clare Luce gave me some Masses and stipulated that they were for *me* but insofar as a theologian can juggle with the intention I will make use of all the probable opinions that permit me to apply the impetratory fruit primarily to you. The propitiatory fruit is much more needed by me than by you anyway.

A., I think your soul is just as it should be. Do not try too hard to see anything special in yourself or in your actions. You must be very simple and value all the little ordinary things of Carmelite life for no other reason than that they are pleasing to Jesus. Soon the life will seem just as ordinary as every other life. Probably does so already. And that will strike you as strange. You will feel as if there were something lacking. Nothing is lacking, if you have the faith to see that there is one big difference—the only difference; you are leading an ordinary life that is *entirely consecrated* to God. It is not yours, but His. It is unbelievably hard for many religious to convince themselves in practice of this great truth. Everybody knows it in theory, but few ever live by it. They go through life looking for "something else" that isn't there. They are always uneasy, always extending themselves outside and beyond the actual into strange and non-existent possibilities. What is valuable is what is real, here and now. The present reality is the reflection of an eternal reality, and through the present we enter into eternity. That does not mean that everything becomes shadowy. The saints more than anyone else appreciate the reality and value of everyday life and of created things around them. They appreciate them not for themselves but for Jesus—in Whom they all exist.

You have the sense to see that it makes little difference whether you are doing a dull task or going through a consoling ceremony. They are all in a sense "indifferent." But I would suggest, while seeing that indifferent character, that you also see the individual value and reality of each one. In itself it is nothing. Done for Jesus, it is immensely valuable. We have to see not only the nothingness of things and not only their value but their nothingness and their value both at the same time. In that way we avoid a temptation of contemplatives who despise ordinary things not so much because they are nothing in the sight of God but because they are boring to ourselves. Boredom and detachment are two different things. This may seem strange: but sometimes, when prayer is dry, it is good and praiseworthy to look at some real created thing and *feel* and *appreciate* its reality—a flower, a tree, the woods (for you, the garden!) or even a person. (But there you had better be careful.) Just let the reality of what is real sink into you, and you find your soul spontaneously begins to pray again, for through real things we can reach Him Who is infinitely real. At the same time, we never forget that their reality is also relatively unreal and that we must not become attached to it.

It is too late to give you advice about general confessions. In such cases if you have little or nothing to say be glad of it! That also applies to direction. Do not feel that you have to pull teeth to manifest your state of soul. That is the way you are . . . There are some people who manifest themselves better by keeping quiet. In trying to put themselves into words they falsify themselves—or rather they get away from the real picture without meaning to. I think the reason why you have trouble in talking about your soul is that you are too straight to want to say things about yourself that would not really be you—and that you really have nothing to say. You know that within the silence of your own soul Jesus is present in a way that is too perplexing to be talked about and it would embarrass you extremely to try to analyze it all. That is the other thing you must not do: do not poke around too much down there in your heart, let Him be! Let Him rest. He finds so few hearts in which He can enjoy a little silence. Those Who say they love Him are always pushing and nagging, with their complaints, demanding His attention like spoiled children. How He desires to find a soul that has grown up enough to just *be* with Him. May He give you a deep and mature soul that can resound to the depth and simplicity of His own presence. That is true spiritual childhood.

I still mean to write about books, but not now. Next time you write, perhaps you could tell me a little about what you have so far found interesting, what has helped you. I'd say by all means read St. John of the Cross but not *only* him. Mix him up with plenty of variety, and above all get to know the New Testament.

You are at the beginning of a long and beautiful road—beautiful because it is so plain. The only thing you need to remember is not to seek your own pleasure along its way. If you seek pleasure you will never find it. If you seek to please Him, you will please yourself much more. For Jesus takes the greatest pleasure in the soul that has no greater pleasure than to please Him.

To Dom Gabriel Sortais

June 3, 1953

. . . A very great composer, Paul Hindemith, has written me asking if I could write a poem that he could turn into a cantata for orchestra and choir. I sent him the preliminary notes of a work. He was very pleased with it. He came to see me here. After our conversation I did more work on this project and I have finished a first complete version of it. I am awaiting Mr. Hindemith's reaction. Meanwhile [for censoring] I have sent the text to Fr. Paul [Bourne], in Georgia. He is quite pleased with it, and he tells me he has sent you his thoughts about it. Now I was not asking him for the final *nihil obstat*: only his reactions. There will be some more work to do. I wanted to be *sure* that this work would be approved [of], in principle, before I committed myself definitely with Mr. Hindemith. Fr. Paul says he finds *nothing* to disapprove in this project. The subject is theological: *The Tower of Babel*—the theme is the "word" in man's life—the word perverted by sinful pride. God's Word that comes into the world to restore the order destroyed by sin, themes of division and unity, etc.

I frankly confess to you that I intend to wait for a change of censors before letting this work fall into the hands of Father M. . . . He knows nothing about modern poetry. He has inadmissible prejudices against every work of this kind, to such an extent that he has always said that my efforts in this genre were sheer folly. Maybe he is right, I don't know. But anyway, the critics do not think as he does. For all that, he has never refused a *nihil obstat* to our poems. If you insist, I'll send the text immediately to Fr. M. Otherwise, I ask your tentative permission to let the project go ahead, in view of the favorable decision of Fr. Paul. After the text has been definitely established, according to the demands of Mr. Hindemith, I will submit it to censorship in the ordinary way, to get the *imprimi potest* after the two *nihil obstats* of our censors. I intend to do this after the General Chapter. Meanwhile, Mr. Hindemith will probably have written a good deal of music around the poem. I do not want to let him go ahead, if *the whole project* is inadmissible. But it seems to me that Fr. Paul's opinion will serve you as a guarantee of its relative value.

So I ask you, dear Most Reverend Father, to tell me:

1) If I can let Mr. Hindemith go on, and wait for the normal censorship, foreseeing some detail changes, about which they will certainly raise no difficulty.

2) If I must get Fr. M.'s *nihil obstat* immediately.

3) If the opinion of some other censor would be enough to assure you of the value of the work, while waiting for the normal censure after the completion of the work.

It seems to me that the third possibility is the best. So, if you like, I will send you the text of the poem, and you can give it to whomever you please to see what it is about.

But in short you see that the regulations, however detailed they are, do not take into account the case when the initiative for this or that work comes from outside, and when there might exist relationships between the author and the publisher, or someone else, even before the first censorship. Of course, Father Abbot's permission is always presupposed.

I thank you wholeheartedly for your good letter, which tells me very clearly how to understand the author's task in a Cistercian monastery. I promise to conform to it faithfully. At the same time, I write next to nothing. As you point out to me, I give pride of place to the charge of Father Master of the Scholastics, which is the only thing to do anyway, since we have so many of them.

Dom Louis [Abbot of Melleray] made a good regular visit. His secretary [Merton] had a lot of work! In the course of the visit he saw the poor little woods which is practically the only refuge of those who want a little silence here. He also saw in it a little hut, where one can take refuge when it rains [St. Anne's Hermitage], for we have torrential downpours which last half an hour during all the summer. He did not look very pleased with the hut, but he said nothing. Besides, it is you yourself who fully approved of our woods. This is what gives me room for a bit of interior life. Meanwhile, since last year I have suffered from nervous trouble, more and more acute; I sleep very little, etc. I am very pleased to accept the cross—in the form of continuous noise and din (of the machines) during the office, the work, etc., but in short it gets on one's nerves, even when it is accepted.

I assure you that the vocation problem is to me just as agonizing as ever. But I seek only God's will, and I don't want to cheat in trying to impose my ideas on the Superiors. I am more convinced than ever of the necessity of a truly solitary, truly contemplative life, and I am just as fully convinced I will never achieve it by making complicated projects. I thirst for God even unto death, and I am aware of being at the same time a great sinner and a totally useless chap—and also a fool. So much the better . . . I am not seeking any solitude with abjection. In the eyes of the world, one might say that my life was hardly "abject." But I am not in the least "the writer Father Merton"—within me, things are different. I do not pretend I have reached the seventh degree of humility: for what I find in myself angers me and discourages me . . .

To Dom Hubert Van Zeller

August 3, 1953

You have already forgiven me, I am sure, for my delay in thanking you for the books. I wanted to read them myself before writing, but Father Abbot's secretary had purloined *Jeremias* and one of my most slow-reading and meditative scholastics took, and still has, *Ezechiel*. But I have enjoyed *Jeremias*, the prophet I am reading this summer in any case. I am beginning to find him almost my favorite among the major prophets, and perhaps the reason is that he was involved in that mysterious discovery of the Law in the Temple which always excited me. I am glad you think Helcias was his father.

The scholastics are reading and loving both *Moments of Light* and *Famine*. Both help them to like the interior poverty and dryness inseparable from a life which is not one of exaltation.

Our cow barn burned down the other evening, in the middle of the meditation. I became involved in the most active meditation I ever made in my life and came out with the skin burned off a section of one hand. We were very happy that the fire did not spread to everything else in sight, as it might well have done. If you see Fr. Bruno James, please thank him for his last letter. We are harvesting vegetables and I have no time to write at the moment . . .

To Dom Gabriel Sortais

August 13, 1953

Our Reverend Father Dom James wants to publish and disseminate in the United States the official translation of the Encyclical [of Pius XII] *Doctor Mellifluus*. We were planning to edit a little volume including the translation, an introduction that I have written, the dates of our Father Saint Bernard's life and the list of his works. Besides, we have already received a prefatory letter from Cardinal Fumasoni Biondi and, if you agree, we would very much like to ask you for another letter from yourself, to put at the beginning of this volume.

Our New York publisher [Robert Giroux] shows some interest in the project [*The Last of the Fathers*], which is extraordinary. If the book gets published eventually by this house, it will be disseminated everywhere in America and will reach readers of all classes. The two American censors have already granted the *nihil obstat* for our introduction. I think it is not necessary to have the official translation go through their hands.

Now it is about this translation I am writing you, Most Reverend Father. Dom Jean [Leclercq] in Rome informs me about this, that Westmalle has exclusive reproduction rights for translations emanating from the Vatican. Would you kindly intercede on our behalf with the Reverend Father Abbot of Westmalle so that he may, as soon as possible, have the English text of the encyclical sent to us and let us know at the same time the terms under which he would dispose of his rights for the publication in America of this document.

I need not tell you that the Westmalle translation will never succeed in getting disseminated in the United States, above all on a large scale. But if you think it good to allow us to do this edition, the encyclical will be in everyone's hands in this country. I think Rome would be very pleased.

As for the financial side, the affairs with Westmalle can be arranged by our agent. What is most important for us at present is to have in our hands the English text of *Doctor Mellifluus*.

If our New York publisher eventually did this volume, Westmalle would gain something from it. If we are reduced to do the publication by ourselves, I hope the Abbot of Westmalle will not charge us too much for the rights.

I hope your health is gradually getting better, my dear Most Reverend Father. Do not work too hard—the Order needs you and your example. Do *not* leave us too soon! Bless me and our students. I now manage to accept God's holy will with a little more generosity, and I ask you to forgive me last year's complaints and moanings. I do see that it is not a question of living according to my own lights or the leanings of the heart, but only according to divine good pleasure. The reading of the encyclical has done me a lot of good, and I want with all my heart to become a son worthy of our Father Saint Bernard. There are moments when I seem to be very near despair, as I see my faults and take note of how far all of us are from this ideal here where one seems to be plunging more and more into materialism. But I see that the question is not to understand but to obey and love. God sees everything, and He can bring everything to a good end. He wants it!

To Dom Jean Leclercq

August 21, 1953

You must think me a very churlish and ungrateful person to leave your letter so long unanswered. We have had a busy summer, with much harvesting and other farm work. In addition to that our cow barn burned down and we have also bought a new farm, so that everyone has been exceptionally busy and I am two months behind with practically all correspondence.

Our monastery would like very much to order four copies of Cardinal Shuster's *Vie Monastique*, and we will also be looking forward to Père Dimier's book on monastic observances. I am presently dipping into a manuscript of his about his war experiences but I do not have time to read it continuously although I find it very interesting.

Above all I want to thank you for your *Dottrina del B. P. Giustiniani*. I find it most useful and am glad to have it, particularly because it would otherwise be quite impossible for me to make the acquaintance of his personality and ideas. You have given us a valuable source. I hope books will appear on all the great Camaldolese figures. Dom Giabbani sent me some pictures of Camaldoli and it is both beautiful and inspiring to me. I can well believe what you say about their having the true contemplative life at Frascati. I know nothing of that particular *eremo*. I would be interested in having some pictures of it as I may perhaps do an article on the Camaldolese—by way of exception, since I do not write for magazines anymore. This would be in the hope of helping them make a foundation in this country. They are needed.

I find that in some monastic orders there is a kind of selfish and dog-in-the-manger attitude towards other orders and other forms of the contemplative life. One illusion that is very strong in this country still is the idea that the eremitical life is essentially "dangerous" and "impossible," etc. Some monks who claim to have a high contemplative ideal will actually run down the solitary life, and show a preference for the rather intense activity which is inevitable in a big, busy monastery of cenobites. It is all very well to have a big, busy monastery, but why claim that this is the highest possible ideal of contemplation? The French have a good word for that: *fumisterie* [practical joke].

I was amused to think that I am supposed to be speaking on the radio. It is a great ordeal simply to speak to the monks in chapter. What would I do if I had to speak on the radio? I have not been out of the monastery for over a year, and then it was only for one day's journey. The only talk I have given outside the monastery was through the grille of the Louisville Carmel. I do not imagine that perfection consists merely in staying inside the enclosure, but the fact remains that I hate to go out and am very glad that I never have to do so. The last thing I would ever desire would be to speak on the radio. . . .

To Father Charles Dumont, O.C.S.O.

Father Charles Dumont, a monk of Scourmont in Belgium, and editor of Collectanea Cisterciensia, *was instrumental in establishing an English-language counterpart called* Cistercian Studies. *Merton collaborated in providing articles and reviews for both journals.*

September 2, 1953

I am about two months late in answering letters, so please excuse me. I shall be sending you the microfilms of Father Sage as soon as possible. I have never had time to work on them and do not know how much help they will be.

Thank you for your kind words about *Jonas*. It is a problematical book in the Order. Many have not liked it. I did not expect them to. Dom Leclercq thinks it will not be too well liked in Europe either. The Dutch publishers are afraid to bring out a translation. The book, they say, is not phlegmatic enough for Holland. In that case I shall have to resign myself to the loss of Holland, as I am not at all phlegmatic.

Where did the legend arise, that I would be going to Dijon? My journeys are all into the woods here. I have not been to Louisville since I was naturalized. It is true I made a day's journey into Ohio last year when there was some talk about a new foundation, but this came to nothing. But Dijon! . . . I would like very much to have any material available on the conference there. And I am glad I did not have to go.

Please tell Father Anselme Dimier that I have his manuscript and find it very interesting and that I am looking forward to his book on monastic observances which Dom Leclercq has announced. Pray for me, Father, and for my scholastics. They are such wonderful monks. They gave some very good conferences on St. Bernard, conferences that belied the hasty note of mine that was published in *Témoignages*. They *do* love and understand his spirit.

God be with you, Father. May your work on Aelred bear much fruit . . .

To Dom Gabriel Sortais

October 19, 1953

When he came back from the General Chapter, our Reverend Father Dom James spoke to me about the affair of that book published in England with an advertisement that shocked the Reverend Mother Abbess of Stapehill [Merton's endorsement of Lucile Hasley's *Reproachfully Yours*]. I understand her attitude well. I had never known that this indiscretion on my part had gotten to be known as far away as England. This rather un-monastic remark, which I had made in a private letter to the lady who had written the book, had scandalized nobody in the States. But I do think that in England they find it unpardonable. I am very sorry for it. I do not want to defend myself, but to reassure you a little, Most Reverend Father, I will say that this remark was made by me four years ago. I did not understand then all the repercussion of each of my words, but now I am beginning to become, I hope, a little more prudent. Anyway this affair makes me take again the resolution never to say anything in the way of advertising, not even to write prefaces or magazine articles: nothing, only a few discreet books. I am very sorry to cause you grief again. I will not do it again. Forgive me and pray to the Blessed Virgin that she may obtain for me much more prudence and savoir-faire.

The affair of our foundation is working out very well. I had written our last letter quite unaware of what Dom James intended to do, but also fearing some imprudence. Now I do not oppose his project at all. I would not have protested if our Father Prior had not seemed very uneasy about the foundation, of which he knew nothing either . . .

To Dom Gregorio Lemercier, O.S.B.

Dom Gregorio Lemercier was Superior of an experimental Benedictine monastery at Cuernavaca in Mexico at this time.

October 23, 1953

It was a pleasure to get your letter because it was a letter from a monk, for a change. I make no scruple about answering it at once. The problem you mention is close to my heart, and I hope I can help you by my prayers, even if my advice is not much use.

Machinery in the monastic life: this is getting to be one of the most important problems of monasticism. The Cistercian houses in America are deeply involved in it, and in my own opinion what we are doing is less a solution than a capitulation. We say there is nothing to do but involve ourselves in complete mechanization, because this will solve so many other problems that the price is worth paying. It solves, for instance, the problem of making a living, the problem of time, the problem of independence. It makes it possible for us to survive as monks.

I would be inclined, myself, to make a distinction in that last sentence. It makes it possible to survive: *concedo*. As monks? That is another question. I am not positive as to the answer. Here are a few observations, for what they are worth.

First of all, monks ought to avoid two extremes. On the one hand, we cannot let ourselves simply become a communist collective farm in which the material interests of the community overwhelm all other considerations and in which technology and machinery absorb everything. But on the other hand we cannot isolate ourselves so completely from society that we become a museum or an antique shop, playing with ancient implements as a kind of eccentric protest against the machine as such. The monk is not of this world but he nevertheless is in the world, not as a museum piece but as a living and organic and functional member of the human race in which he makes present the Mystery of Christ.

Therefore it is inevitable that there be some machinery in our monastery, and ordinary farm machinery presents no special problem. However, as soon as one has machines one enters into the technological attitude of mind that is eating the heart out of modern life. The more work you do, the more you have to add to it. Machines save labor only in order to make more labor. They bring with them a constant expansion of activity. New works are planned, requiring new machines. When the works are finished, more works have to be devised in order to make further use of the machines that would otherwise lie idle. A monastery that relies heavily on machines will be constantly promising itself a time, supposedly about to come soon, in which the pressure of work will be reduced. "We must push this one big job, and after it is finished everything will be all right. We can rest." This is pure illusion. One big job leads to another bigger job.

The monks become restless and avid for change and new projects: work has to be created to keep them quiet, or rather they create it to keep themselves quiet. And they make a lot of noise doing it. One soon arrives at a pure illusion of the contemplative life, an imaginary desire for contemplation which deludes itself that it is real because it is always "hoping" for a contemplative situation in the near future. Actually such monks, without realizing it, unconsciously create work for themselves in order that they may *not* be forced to remain in the "idleness" of contemplation. They are tired of God, without realizing it . . . It is the story of the builders of Babel, whose tongues are confounded by God Who does not wish to see their city. It is the misery of the children of Israel asking to go and sacrifice in the desert and being told that they must build bricks without straw. We all have in ourselves the tendency to look back to Egypt when the taste of manna becomes insipid.

I have had a chance to verify the effects of machine work on the spiritual life of individuals. They can maintain a rather artificial and strained spirituality—a prayer of ejaculations forced through the clenched teeth of activism. It may seem good, because the work demands a sacrifice, and machinery is noisy, it grates on the nerves, it irritates. But the sacrifice is also deadening. It dulls the sense of spiritual things. A monk who spends his work time constantly with a machine has no taste for silence outside his time of work. He is careless about the way he walks, how he handles things, slams doors, throws books down roughly and so forth. There may be a genuine spirit of sacrifice, but the spirit of prayer becomes coarse and thick-skinned. The delicate sensitivity to the inner motions of the Holy Spirit loses all its keenness, and is replaced by another spirit— tense, hard, complicated, cold.

I am now speaking of the effects of extremism. Whether the machine you mention would produce these effects is not for me to say. The monks could perhaps have enough variety in their work to save them from being completely warped by it—they could take different shifts with the machine. A slightly noisy machine is not bad. We have machinery in our cannery here which makes noise but does not disturb prayer much, and it is not too hard to work with it. Perhaps your project would involve nothing more complicated than our cannery, and therefore I would say it offered little or no danger from the point of view of machinery and noise. (However our brothers work late at night sometimes in the cannery and this is not good.)

I must close, dear Father. Other duties call me. I will only say that I have been glad to speak to you on this subject, and shall be interested to hear of your future developments . . .

To Dom Jean Leclercq

November 5, 1953

It was a satisfaction to me when Father Abbot gave me permission to write the preface for your volume on Paul Giustiniani [*Alone With God*]. The preface is completed and is on the way to you by surface mail. I was happy to write it, and happy to go over your book again. I feel that it is especially important that the true place of the solitary in the Church should be brought out at this time when there are so many who despise contemplation and when even in the monastic orders there is a tendency to go off the right road precisely because the values for which the solitary exists are not appreciated. If my preface does not suit you, please feel free to alter or cut as you see fit, but let me know. Perhaps I could go over the proofs of this preface.

Regarding the material side of the question: may I depend on you to get this preface censored by the two censors of our Order for the French language? I do not know who they are, but Chimay could tell you. All other material questions in regard to what I write are dealt with by an agent and he will be in touch with Plon in due course.

It would indeed be a great pleasure to receive you at Gethsemani and have you preach our retreat. I sincerely hope that Divine Providence will bring you to America and that we will have this satisfaction. I was glad to hear of the theological conferences at Dijon and look forward to seeing them in print.

Returning to Giustiniani—could the Camaldolese at Frascati perhaps send me a picture or a relic of him? Even some pictures of their *eremo*. I am still hoping to write a little something on the Camaldolese, to make them known in America. Any information or books they send will be useful to me and to their own cause.

I certainly agree wholeheartedly that the monastic orders have much to learn from one another, and we in America have much to learn from you in Europe. We are very isolated and provincial, I am afraid, and our undue sense of our own importance may perhaps delude us that we are the only monks in the world. It may not be possible for me to satisfy the desires of my own heart, but at least I can continue to have zeal for God's truth and for the monastic ideal.

To Dom Gabriel Sortais

December 9, 1953

I thank you for your kind letter of the 4th. It was very nice of you to communicate to me the observations of the censors about the French translation of *The Ascent to Truth*. I had already seen this translation, and without reading it in great depth, I made a few corrections in it and crossed out a few pages (so as) to make it shorter. For the theological side and the French style I asked Fr. Benoît Lavaud, O.P., from Toulouse, to revise it. He has done so, and I thought his corrections would suffice. The censors do not agree with him, so you send the translation back to me.

My dear Most Reverend Father, I thank you for your kindness and your paternal thoughtfulness. But I do not know French well enough to recast this work for publication in France. To redo this work in English would be a waste of time. So, given that this book would not be "truly useful" (I quite agree about this), don't you think that the best would be to cut it off at once and refuse the publication of the book?

True, we have signed a contract with Editions Albin Michel, but if you refuse your *imprimi potest* they may complain a little, but we don't have to pay attention to it. So there we are, Most Reverend Father: I admit that this work is a useless book, a failure. For my "reputation as a writer" it does not interest me at all. For the honor of the Order—that is different.

Since I cannot redo this work in French myself, and since the translator is incapable of bringing into it the necessary lights and since I do not want to disturb the solitude of one of my Cistercian Brothers in France, let us forget this poor book altogether. I am waiting only for a definitive word from you so as to write the publisher that the *imprimi potest* is refused to this work.

The arrangements made by the General Chapter in the timetable seem to me very wise. Far from diminishing the fervor of our devotion towards the Blessed Virgin, I find that the suppression of the Little Office [of the Blessed Virgin] on feasts of Mary helps a lot to sing the canonical office with more devotion towards her. I think that the longer intervals will help us to lead a more interior life, provided they are taken advantage of. I promise you to do so myself. I think the Blessed Virgin invites me, during this Marian Year, to a more silent life, more humble, more hidden and more solitary. I will try wholeheartedly to correspond to this loving invitation. I have no greater happiness than that of being alone with Her, and having nothing to say to men . . .

To Dom Hubert Van Zeller

January 30, 1954

I was very pleased with your letter about *Bread in the Wilderness*. It was, I am sure, just the right reaction. It is pretty much my own. I look at the big red book, and think how handsome and expertly printed it is, and I look at the statements on its pages and wish they had been written by somebody else—indeed it seems as if they were. By now I am so used to feeling this way about some of the things I write that it is becoming a habit. But I don't feel quite that way about *The Sign of Jonas*. Your generosity in the review of that book utterly confused me and put me to shame. However, the Abbot General will not have any more Journals! I have no particular desire to write any more Jonas. His wish does not stand in the way of the sober affirmation that that is the kind of thing I write most naturally. It doesn't really matter what I write. But on the whole, I am glad that I do not have to write another *Bread in the Wilderness*.

My latest effort is a purely journalistic job on St. Bernard and the encyclical. Meanwhile, Hollis and Carter [in England] will produce *Bread*, I think, more modestly and with less expense. For my own part, I am busy with St. Paul. The course is very beneficial to the professor. I do not know about the students. I am teaching it in a room which was painted (through my own misjudgment) in a wild flamingo pink, and I think that is the only reason why they are almost always awake. It has been asserted that *no* one could sleep in such an atmosphere.

Above all I am grateful for *Watch and Pray*. We are doing a series of conferences on the prophets. I started the thing off with Isaias, and by autumn it will have reached the last minor prophets, some of whom are to be accounted for by our scholastics. So they will have something on Nahum, Aggaeus, Zacharias, and so forth. I like Zacharias very much. The man who is at work on Nahum seized the volume before I had read a few words: but I had time to see that you have plenty of material and I rejoice.

I hope Fr. Bruno James was not offended at my delay in sending him a copy of *Bread*. The first edition was sold out rapidly and books are hard to come by. Why the first edition was sold out rapidly is something I cannot explain, except that a book club was disposing of it for little over half the price, and large crowds ordered it for the sake of the pictures.

I hope, too, that by this time you have not had any more operations and that things have settled down peacefully. My medical exploits are much more modest than yours. I went to Louisville the other day for an allergy test and found out that I am very sensitive to a lot of things which abound in monasteries—like dust and bacteria, milk and cheese, and so forth. I did not need any tests to tell me this. However I now take some kind of serum. The test was fun, and after it was over I rushed to the library where they have a lot of good records, and played Erik Satie's "Three Pieces in the Form of a Pear." I do not say Satie is the greatest of all musicians, but it seems to me he is the one to whom I respond most simply and most completely. He plays the melodies that I have a tendency to invent when I am wandering about the fields with a shovel. Then, to crown everything, I procured an ancient copy of Leacock's *Nonsense Novels* to feed the scholastics who are getting too strained. So far I have kept it hidden from them, and have secretly been indulging my taste for sheer insanity. Now all I need is *Literary Lapses* and they can put *me* in the straitjacket . . .

To Dom Gabriel Sortais

February 17, 1954

I thank you belatedly for your good letter and your decision in regard to the translation of *La Montée vers la Vérité* [*The Ascent to Truth*]. I am in contact with good Fr. Bernard of Cîteaux. We shall work well together, and things will work out for the best, I am sure.

M. Biemel, of Desclée, informs me that the manuscript of *Exile Ends in Glory* was sent to Rome a few weeks ago. It is about the latter book I am writing you now, dear Most Reverend Father. You probably know that this book is the biography of our Mother Berchmans, deceased Abbess of Our Lady of the Angels [in Japan] in 1915. I am sure that the "holiness" of this worthy Cistercian has a lot to do with the expansion of the Order in Japan, as far as the religious women are concerned. I also know your concern for the progress and prosperity, both spiritual and material, of our houses in the Far East. I dare, then, to ask you once more for a little prefatory letter for this book, translated from the English, and which appears now in France. It is not only for myself, but for the Trappistines in Japan and for those who love Mother Berchmans that I dare to make this request. I assure you it will be a very great pleasure to think that this poor book will perhaps be worth something more in the eyes of the French readers, due to the presence of a letter from our Father General. I suppose the book will succeed in getting through the censorship. Besides, I think the translation could have been done better, and I will be very glad to allow all the changes to be made, even the greatest which the censors will have suggested.

At the same time, I have been waiting a long time for the reaction of the American censors to our manuscript *Viewpoints* [later entitled *No Man Is an Island*]. I had sent the two uncorrected manuscripts so they will have found quite a lot of things that I have already corrected myself. But I will change all they want.

For myself: a lot more peace and interior solitude. Life is becoming more and more simple, although I am working a lot and meeting a great many obstacles. I am accused of harming the scholastics by my somewhat solitary spirituality. I try the best I can to be very objective in the conferences and not to insist on my own personal ideal, for which, so they say, there would be no room with us. I do everything with the utmost peace and interior liberty. I do not wish to be Master of the Scholastics, but I accept to be so. I would want with all my heart to pass to another Order, an eremitic one, but I agree to stay here if Dom James insists. It is not to please myself that I try to guide the souls entrusted to me, and it is not to please myself that I am at Gethsemani. For the rest, I am sure God wants from me the spirit of interior solitude which gives me peace. But if I am mistaken, and it will not be the first time, I will try to correct myself as far as possible. For if I have peace, it is above all by admitting frankly that I am not a saint at all, not even a good religious. Both I would very much like to be, so as to please God. I will never achieve this by deluding myself. I am what I am and God is God. He loves me, and I try my best—to love Him in return with all my miseries. But in all and above all I try to remain *in the truth*.

If I speak to you about myself, it is because I know you mainly as a "Father," more than as "General," and I know that my Most Reverend Father is more interested in his sons' souls than in their labors.

April 14, 1954

Thank you very much for your good letter of the 6th, which has done me a lot of good, for I was a little discouraged. It is probably because of my great self-love that I must struggle inwardly in an absurd manner, instead of keeping myself in peace here. But I will make it, I think. I have just spent the best Lent in my twelve years at the monastery— thanks above all to the changes in the timetable. Life is more quiet—at least relatively, for we all bustle about a lot here.

What you tell me about the Carthusians does not surprise me, and I agree altogether. It was while writing *The Sign of Jonas* that I could see for myself that I was not made to be a Carthusian. I sleep rather badly here: things would not be better with them. And I do think I am resigned to my fate as a writer.

As you say, the attractions that are really true come from God. He wants them. So, He wants for me this tendency towards solitude. But I must make an effort. I must even dare to face up to certain religious who have not enough of this respect for true contemplative solitude. I specify a little: for I see that things have not made themselves too clear.

I would obviously be in the wrong if I wanted to make Cistercians love the Carthusian life. It would be a very great injustice to orientate cenobites towards the hermitage. I assure you, Most Reverend Father, that this I have never done. On the contrary, there is one of the students who wants to change orders, but I am convinced that God wants him here, and I tell him so. It would be very easy to make him leave, if I did the things I am accused of doing. When I speak of exterior solitude, I endeavor to do it in the sense of Saint Bernard, whom I do not fail to cite. I speak very little of this solitude, as I concentrate my conferences above all on charity, obedience, and the virtues of the common life, etc. Let anyone consult the notes of the last two years.

This is what I am reproached with: 1) Fr. R.—who fancies I try to push *all* of the students towards solitude and *infused* contemplation— preaches in chapter that one must *not* desire infused contemplation, and even aiming at it makes us run the risk of becoming insane . . . 2) Others do not seem to understand that the little woods where we walk, and which you have seen and declared "necessary," and which Dom Louis approved of in an explicit manner at the last visit, is as a matter of fact quite proper. That is the "solitude" Fr. P. reproaches me with. 3) Maybe I speak somewhat too much of solitude and contemplation in our writings. This gives the impression that I am a sort of visionary maybe. I am reproached with it. But now, they can reproach me with anything they want to, so long as I am on the right path. Now as you say in your letter: "The religious who wants to (and seeks it, for this presupposes an effort, a constantly fostered tendency) finds solitude . . . What a service it is to the Church to make a monastery enter into a more silent (because more solitary) path . . ." I was very glad to read these words, for I was beginning to think that such words were never to be heard among us (and all the same it is the *true* monastic life!).

I feel well in the common life except that the intervals are often taken up by the students (we have more than 30 of them), and during working time I often have to prepare the conferences, and do a bit of reading and meditating. But I think I *am* as faithful to the common life as the other officers of the monastery, with the exception of a sleeping room (otherwise I hardly sleep at all) and a relief at the refectory due to the fact that I cannot digest milk products.

For the rest, when you return to Gethsemani, you will see everything. Somewhat *extraordinary* efforts are required in a community like ours, where the noise of the machinery never stops from morning till night.

Most Reverend Father: I have said I spent a good Lent. That is to say I have acquired a little insight into myself, and I see I have exerted myself like the nervous man that I am. It is a transparent fault wanting to blame others for my own miseries. I am a more difficult fellow than I realized, less humble than I thought. Because I lack humility, I enrage at seeing myself so imperfect, so weak, so lazy. I would want to be a saint without doing the work to achieve it. I would want to be canonized without renouncing myself. It is not new. I understand this well in others, but in myself! . . . Maybe I dreamed of a happy solitude to dispense myself from becoming a good Trappist. Too bad! *Nunc coepi* [Now I have begun].

I do not renounce solitude, the true solitude that God wants of me, the one that is paid for by relentless efforts. And I will try to do better all my duties as a Cistercian—by accepting the nervousness that has become my cross at present . . .

To Dom Jean Leclercq

April 27, 1954

I have just written to the [literary] agent [Naomi Burton Stone]. I suspect that Plon is unjustly penalizing you because the agent sought some kind of material settlement for the [Merton] preface. I had not stopped to think that this might happen. The only reason why I use an agent is quite obvious—it saves me an immense amount of correspondence, contract work and business worries. If I did otherwise, I would never have any time for anything except business. I simply leave all cares to the middleman. This of course has its hard-boiled aspects, since the agency is bent on making a living out of percentages. I do not think it is altogether fair of Plon to retaliate by threatening the future of your series, although in a way I see where that is logical—with the logic of the jungle.

However, if it will help your series at all to publish a book by me, I have a small volume on St. Bernard about to appear. It is very slight, not a formal life, simply a brief introduction to the saint and to the recent Encyclical. It has three parts—a sketch of his life and character, an outline of his works and teaching, and a commentary on the Encyclical—followed by the text of the Papal Document itself. I had not even thought of allowing this book to be published in France. When you see it, you will probably agree that it adds nothing to the number of excellent studies of St. Bernard, including your own. I do not think it will help your series except accidentally. If the appearance of the author's name is of any use to you, I will consent to let this book appear in France—without worrying about what may happen to my reputation. I will send you the book as soon as I can procure a copy. It is not yet off the press.

I can agree with what you say about the Benedictine life. The more I come into indirect contact with the Benedictine houses of Europe, like yours and La Pierre-qui-Vire, the more I appreciate the depth and solidity of the monastic spirit, and profit by contact with it. It is indeed a paradox that you do now in fact have much more real silence and peace than many a Trappist monastery. I never felt any sympathy with Rancé's ideas about erudition, and I am sure that the work done by Benedictines today in this field is perfectly monastic and truly fruitful in the line of monastic spirituality.

The last thing in the world a monk should seek or care about is material success. That which I see in my own labors is as much a surprise to me as it is to anybody else. Nor can I find in myself the power to get very interested in that success. I do not claim this to be a virtue, because I have never really understood money anyway. I do not know how much our books have acquired. The figures are not communicated to me and, if they were, I would probably not understand them anyway.

Please do not feel yourself obliged to write a review of *Bread in the Wilderness*. My only way of getting a copy to you was to have the publisher send you a review copy. If however you do write a review I shall feel very pleased and honored . . .

To Dom Gabriel Sortais

July 3, 1954

I have just received the letter from Fr. Clement [Abbot General's Secretary] from Cîteaux of June 27. I also have written Albin Michel and to our agent so as to stop the French translation of *The Sign of Jonas.*

Most Reverend Father, you had written me from N. D. des Anges [Our Lady of the Angels] on November 11, 1952, as follows: "I see no objection to your new book (*The Sign of Jonas*) being translated into any language when it has been corrected." I admit that these words had surprised me a little, but there was no mistaking their signification. Maybe you had meant to say something else or, writing hastily (as you yourself say in the same letter), you had not thought about it properly. After all, it does not matter. I only tell you this to reassure you about my spirit of obedience.

Now I am going to drop a line to Mme. Tadié, the translator. I think I did send *Bread in the Wilderness* and *The Last of the Fathers* to Rome. This last book has been accepted by Dom Winandy and Dom Leclercq for the collection "Monastic Tradition." The other has been accepted by Fr. Danielou. A Spanish translation of *The Sign of Jonas* is being done; and also of *The Ascent to Truth.* Our poems too are being translated for Editions Casterman . . .

To Dom Jean Leclercq

July 28, 1954

Yesterday I heard from our Reverendissime Père and I hasten to let you know that he raises no objection to the publication of *The Last of the Fathers.* So you may proceed with it as fast as you like. Also, about the translation, that too is settled. It seems that Albin Michel had already advertised or announced *The Sign of Jonas* and it was not possible for the work to be stopped altogether. Consequently we have no need of any other work for Marie Tadié. It is therefore to be published, but will be censored and abridged by our Abbot General himself and two censors. I

don't expect that very much will remain after they get through with it—
the two covers, the prologue and the epilogue, no doubt: with a few pages
in between.

It is true that religious in Europe are not yet used to Journals, but
the secular reader in France certainly has begun to acquire a taste for
them. Witness the success of the Journals of Gide, [Julian] Green, and
Du Bos. I am glad my own Journals will be expurgated, but in the long
run it would seem to be not a bad idea that, for once, by way of exception,
such a production should come from a monastery. I would give anything
for a Journal, even the most trivial, written in 12th century Clairvaux.
But then, indeed, they did *not* keep journals.

There is just one thing about *The Last of the Fathers*. If I get time
in the next ten days I would like to write an extra page or two on the
spirit of St. Bernard, perhaps also on his youth and early formation (which
ought not to be completely passed over in silence even in a sketch) and
perhaps on one other point. Please bear with me for a few days and leave
space for the inclusion of these pages. If I have them by the fifteenth of
August I will send them. If not, I will let you know by then and you can
go on without them.

The thought that the publication of this book in your series will aid
the appearance of the Giustiniani volume is one which gives me great
satisfaction. I feel much more gratified about being a writer now that I
see that I can help other authentic testimonies of the monastic spirit to
appear. I shall do everything I can to let you have another book, in order
to help your series. Please tell your good Father Abbot that I feel that I
am really doing the work of God in collaborating as much as I can with
your series, and will feel that my own writing is thereby inserted in a
truly monastic context. There is a special satisfaction in collaborating with
one's brothers in Christ, and I do not like the idea of an isolated and
spectacular apostolate. No doubt I must have the courage to face the
enemies that this isolation makes for me—even among priests and religious. But for my own part I prefer to be a member of a team, at least
to some extent, than to be a soloist exclusively. However, since God has
singled me out for a kind of isolation, I will certainly accept it, together
with its consequences. That is certainly nothing new in the Church.

To Dom Gabriel Sortais

August 6, 1954

If I tell you I was after all a little pleased to know that *Le Signe de
Jonas* was going to be published all the same in Paris, it is not because
your will was not done as you wished, but because I had some moments
of confusion and serious disturbance as I thought of those contracts and
of my obligations. But I hope that now everything is arranged for the

future. There only remain detailed clarifications that will be done later on.

1) As soon as a book appears in an American edition, we shall send it to the Definitory, asking to have it examined from the point of view of opportuneness of the translation. Now normally this question of opportuneness would be decided once and for all in this preliminary examination. But—

2) If there are specifics: e.g., such a book which would be opportune in Chinese but not in German: should not the one who examines it say so at once, or have it examined by another?

For I have just received the contract for the Japanese edition of *The Seven Storey Mountain*. I think Dom James signed it without consulting you, which appeared altogether in accordance with your will, since this book has already been translated into most European languages.

In short, these questions will be easily decided if the examiner simply says: such a book is approved as translatable into all languages—or such and such language and not the others.

Moreover, I promise you to be careful about all I do along this line, and I have already warned the agent who, naturally, proceeded automatically to negotiate contracts for the translations. As a rule, authors are not involved in these contracts at all, but leave everything in the hands of an agent, which is really very convenient for me. It will not be less convenient if the agent waits for the moment of the approval that we shall request each time from Rome.

I am very sorry to know that I have given you so much work on the eve of the General Chapter, Most Reverend Father. But I know that the cuttings will do this book good, which needs some pruning. I thank you in advance, and I assure you that I deeply appreciate your paternal solicitude towards me . . .

To Dom Hubert Van Zeller

November 4, 1954

For a long time I have been getting notes and letters from you and have let them go by without answering. Nor do I even have time for a decent answer now. One thing, however, cannot wait. I think in one of your letters you mentioned coming to America. If you do, of course, I hope you will come to Gethsemani and Father Abbot will give us a chance to talk together. However, the main thing is that he asked whether you would like to preach our retreat. He is thinking of course of the year 1956. We are having our next retreat in January 1955, and that has already been arranged. But if you were here in January the following year, we would very much like to have you if possible. He asked me to take this up with you, and I am eager to hear about it . . .

A few weeks ago, by some miracle, we actually started reading Dom Cuthbert Butler's *Benedictine Monachism* in the refectory. That has never been done before, and it was not done this time either. We got as far as the third chapter. It would have been interesting to go right through such a book in a Trappist refectory. There might have been riots, etc. Most interesting. Whatever may be the shortcomings of the book, I think he is still one of the best and surest interpreters of the mind of St. Benedict— yet in the end there is a tremendous difference between his interpretation and St. Benedict. As for me, I have got to the point where I stop interpreting. It is all I can do to wedge in a little solitude here and there, and that is what occupies me more fruitfully, I think, than haggling about the "ideal." For the rest, the students and St. Paul keep me busy, with my various projects . . .

To Abbot James Fox

November 29, 1954

This is a report on our four days' retreat. They were four pretty busy days, and in fact I only had four half-days of retreat after all. Yet there were many graces and I think it was one of the best retreats I ever made, in spite of the numerous obstacles and apparent difficulties.

First—the realization that there are problems that one doesn't have to solve. One only has to live in the midst of them, to stay with them, and find God Himself in the mystery which they engender. That has plenty of consequences—a fuller acceptance of Gethsemani and of God's will, without any lessening of desire for solitude—for the second effect has been a great intensification of the need for prayer and solitude, but for real, immediate, accessible prayer and solitude—the need to reach out and grasp every fragment that can be had right here at hand, and not to lose any of them.

I hope you agree—I think you agree—that once again my business is above all to make as much solitude and prayer for myself as the Cistercian *cadre* permits and presupposes, and to reach for the silence and aloneness that a monk must have above all.

In any case, the more I see others leaving here, the more I am strengthened in the conviction that I should stay and do what God wants me to do *here*, even though it may seem like being a square peg in a round hole, and may win me the disfavor of some, plus contradiction and criticism. Provided only that I really do God's will and not my own. I hope you will always tell me frankly when I am not doing what you want, because that is my one big safeguard, on which everything depends.

So—to conclude, I want first to thank you for all the chances you have let me have—to beg your pardon for my failure to use them as well as I might have—and for perhaps not being always humble about things here, speaking my mind too brutally and without sufficient restraint . . .

To Dom Gabriel Sortais

December 13, 1954

Marie Tadié has written me to tell me you had been kind enough to go to her house and patient enough to listen to her. Thank you . . . She also tells me that your review of *The Sign of Jonas* was very merciful. Thank you again.

It is precisely about this poor work that I am writing you today. The question now is about a Dutch translation. Two years ago, Het Spectrum publishers refused this book, telling me that the translation would not be appreciated in the Netherlands. Now another Dutch house is asking us for the translation rights. I think Dom Vincent, or someone else, could well tell us definitively what should be done. Or else, since you yourself know the book, perhaps you could advise us—or give us an indication of your will in the present case.

As you already know, I am in contact with the monks of La Pierre-qui-Vire [French Benedictines]. I send them from time to time some piece for their journal *Témoignages*. I find them very congenial and I am glad I can help Benedictine monks. As you also know, the unpublished manuscripts that I send them in English go through the French censorship only *after* being accepted and translated. Dom Claude Jean Nesmy seems to understand well the risk of this procedure, and is willing to take it. So it is understood by all that their acceptance of a piece from me means no limitation of the powers of the Order's censorship. And it would really be too inconvenient to do otherwise. Please tell me if you agree. I have just finished a text of some thirty pages for them—a text which is due to appear in a book of photographs evocative of monastic life and spirit—a truly remarkable book from the photographic point of view. I will soon be sending the text, which they will translate and send to you later on.

Finally, Most Reverend Father, I filially tell you a word about my own affairs. I begin to see that I have struggled too much with the Holy Spirit without knowing it. I resist too much. I do not want to submit, alas. I *want*, yes . . . but what submission! For my "problem" is rather artificial, abstract. Indeed, I cannot doubt in the least that He wants me, so to speak, "solitary": but it is for Him to say to what extent solitary, fool that I am. No. This is definitely not the question. It is not *my* solitude I seek, but *His* solitude. And that solitude, I begin to see, is quite incomprehensible. I just have to be myself, to be faithful to His grace, not worry about useless questions, and not want to have a "label" which places me, in the eyes of the world, in any spiritual category whatsoever.

God knows well what He wants of me, and I know too that I must remain a little quiet, and let *Him* go about it Himself. And if I am tempted to think that I am not in my place, well, it is precisely what He wants. For if one is solitary, one is an "exile" with no place that is really his own. I am sure I would not be happier in the Charterhouse than here. I am certain that anywhere I would write books that would not be books of Cistercian spirituality, nor Carthusian spirituality, nor of the spirituality of any school but simply books by Thomas Merton: which means, no doubt, very unspiritual books.

To finish, Most Reverend Father: you no doubt remember my idea of taking a vow never to accept an election as an abbot. I have made this vow already, but I have always wanted to make it between the hands of the Most Reverend Father General. Would you allow me to make it now?

Because I am not a good monk, and because I am not a true Cistercian, and moreover because I would certainly be a very bad abbot and would do a lot of harm in such a position, I made the vow never to accept any election as an abbot, either at Gethsemani or in any other Cistercian monastery. I make this vow because I sincerely believe it is God's will, and because I have been indiscreetly spoken of as a future abbot in one of our foundations—where they do not know me.

Finally, Most Reverend Father, I wish you all the graces of the Christmas festivities. We are all, really, poor and solitary men and the most miserable are those who believe they are somebody and have something. As for us, we are all the same in the company of the shepherds in the cave of Bethlehem. God be praised for it . . .

To Dom Hubert Van Zeller

February 8, 1955

It has been ages since I received your letter and the pages describing your project for a foundation. By now, for all I know, you may have made the foundation—although, as I am aware, monastic foundations move even slower than monastic correspondence.

Your project looks very interesting and I think you ought to keep working on it *in this country*. I do not know what the reaction of St. Meinrad's has been, but there are plenty of other Benedictine abbots here. Certainly America needs a contemplative Benedictine foundation. Of course, there have been a few, but what are they in such a big country?

In my opinion a contemplative life that is slightly easier than that of the Cistercians is a very urgent need in America. And also a contemplative life that is a little less agitated and noisy than ours at Gethsemani.

It seems to me that if you have a retreat house you will fill another great need, and make bishops very happy. A priest of Gethsemani left here to try to found such a house in Ohio but I do not know what kind of success he has had.

In any case if you come to this country I look forward to seeing you at Gethsemani. And I hope you will give us our next retreat!

In your foundation perhaps you might make provision for a hermit or two also. There is nowhere in America where one can find true solitude.

To Dom Gabriel Sortais

March 6, 1955

I am deeply touched by the solicitude you always show about our writings and in particular your last step to help me understand well the situation of *La Montée vers la Lumière* [*The Ascent to Truth*], for which I thank you. I have read attentively the evaluation of the reader to whom you handed this translation, and I am very grateful.

For my own part, it would seem to me at first that this work does not deserve being considered, and that we should simply put aside this badly written book.

But on the other hand, there are the interests of Marie Tadié and the publisher—perhaps also those of the apostolate.

I am very glad I can put this work of adaptation in the hands of a religious who is able to do it, and who would accept to do it—but I leave the final decision to your discretion. If you think you can find someone who can do the job, and if you think it is worthwhile, I am willing to let him do it. In the case of the eventual publication of the book thus adapted, my collaborator would get half of the income that the author would normally get for the French edition—this is agreed by Dom James.

I repeat, that for me personally I would really prefer to put this book aside. But I hesitate to make a final decision for some reason of this kind. You see the question more clearly than I do, and I beg you to make the decision yourself as to whether this book should be put on the loom once more. If you say *no*—I shall be very pleased . . .

To Dom Jean Leclercq

April 27, 1955

Our Regular Visitation was finished just a few days ago, during which the Visiting Abbot concentrated his attention on what he called "a hermit mentality" in our monastery. He strongly disapproved of it although recognizing in a private conversation that on my side, I had a particular spirit, that I did not enter into "the pattern," and that he did not really expect to see much change in me. But altogether, we have reached a point at which I think that I cannot, or even should, remain at Gethsemani, or in the Cistercian Order. There is truly no place for me here, and altogether, I am very glad that the Regular Visitation has swept away the little ineffectual compromises which my Father Abbot had thought up in order to "arrange matters."

They are willing to receive me at Camaldoli d'Arezzo. I have a friend who is willing to pay my steamer fare. I have even made a vow myself to pass to a "solitary and contemplative" life (something about which I have thought for a long time). Well, there remains an enormous obstacle: my own Superiors. I believe that my Father Abbot will try to hold me back at all costs. I am going to ask him not only permission to go to Camaldoli (which he will refuse peremptorily). I will tell him again of my intention to write to the Congregation [of Religious] to ask for a transitus [permission from the Holy See to transfer to another order], provided that he does not oppose this in advance so as to block everything. But it really seems to me that because they more or less recognize in the Order that I have an eremitical spirit, it would be unreasonable to insist that I stay here after this spirit has been officially disapproved. I do not know what is going to happen. Only I ask you this: Could you answer the following questions for me:

1. Is it true that they do not truly live a contemplative life at Camaldoli, that "silence is poorly observed," that the Prior entirely disposes of the hermits' vocations, that he can send them back to the cenobium against their will, at his own pleasure? (These are the things they tell me to make me give up my idea of going there.)

2. Can the vow to pass to a more solitary and contemplative life be made by a Benedictine monk, or is this incompatible with our vow of stability?

3. Do you think it would be better to go to Camaldoli or to Frascati? I am thinking of Camaldoli because Dom Giabbani wants soon to make a foundation in America, and I am in touch with him.

4. If I cannot go to Camaldoli or Frascati, could you tell me where I could find an analogous eremitical life, apart from the Charterhouse?

5. If I go to Camaldoli I am a little afraid of being exploited as a celebrity. Do you think that there is a real danger of that? If so, how can I escape it?

6. Is there a way of submitting an application for transfer in such a way that it would be accepted even if the Superior of the house is against it?

In fine, I do all this believing that God wants it of me. I really believe that the time has come for me to *have* to do something for myself, for nobody here is going to do it for me. It is evident that my Superiors are themselves not going to do anything to smooth the way for me to become a hermit. I am doing everything with a good deal of peace, with the same feelings that accompanied my entry into the Church—with the sensation of having my hand in the hands of God. I do not know where this is going to end, but I ask you above all to pray for me.

I have written this in French so that your dear Rev. Father Abbot [Dom Jacques Winandy] also may read it. He may have a word of advice to give me because he is in favor of eremitical vocations. He doubtless knows how much must be suffered in order to open the way to the desert. I ask him and you also to bless me. Above all, pray. I shall be very happy to receive your advice. If you want to talk this over with Dom Maurizio, I would be pleased. Let them at Frascati also pray for me. I would like to join our ex-brother Brendan there. If one could believe that they will make an American foundation, I would rather go there than to Camaldoli. But having spoken of this to Dom Maurizio, I ask you not to tell any others.

So there, my dear Father. I am glad at having friends who can help me. Here I have a director who is favorable to this change but he is leaving soon to make a foundation . . .

June 3, 1955

Many thanks for your letter of May 26. I wish I had received it sooner. Early in May, having consulted the Carthusian Father Dom Verner Moore at Sky Farm, I received from him a very positive encouragement to transfer to Camaldoli and my director here thought I should follow this suggestion, so I applied for a transitus. So far nothing has been heard from Italy however, and Father Abbot is very much opposed to my going to Camaldoli, and I suppose his objections may lead to the refusal of the transitus, although the Abbot General says he feels that if it is the will of God he sees no reason for my not going. Things are still in a fluid state however, and with Father Abbot I am earnestly trying to reach the final solution. One thing is certain, everyone more and more seems to agree that I should not stay in the precise situation in which I find myself at the moment. I honestly believe, and so do my directors, that being a cenobite is no longer the thing I need. However, I have no desire to become a preacher of retreats at Camaldoli either, still less an exploited celebrity, although I do feel that even then I would have far more solitude and silence there than I have here. I may be wrong.

However, Dom James is very interested in the question and he has even proposed to place before higher Superiors the possibility of my becoming a hermit in the forest here. If this permission were ever granted it would solve all my problems, I think. The forest here is very lonely and quiet and covers about a thousand acres, and there is much woodland adjoining it. It is as wild as any country that would be found in the Ardennes or the Vosges, perhaps wilder. I could be a hermit without leaving the land of the monastery. One could begin the project gradually and imperceptibly, for the government is putting up a fire-observation tower on one of our hills and the future hermitage could be in connection with this. One could begin simply by being the watchman on the tower and gradually take up permanent residence there. Unfortunately the higher Superiors, as far as I can see, are absolutely closed to any such suggestion and even refuse to permit a monk to work alone on the observation tower. Dom James is placing the matter before the Abbot General.

Apart from this the best suggestion seems to be that I should secretly enter a hermitage of Monte Corona, and live there unknown without writing or publication, as a true solitary. Dom James is not fully in favor of this but he has given me permission to write and inquire about it. I have written to Dom Maurizio. Dom James does not want me to leave the Order, mainly because of the comment that would be excited among souls. I think however that I could leave secretly enough to keep that comment at a minimum. It would never be more than a rumor, and there have been so many rumors before that people would not pay much attention, until it was all forgotten.

I am waiting still to hear from your Father Abbot. I will value his suggestions. Meanwhile, the main purpose of this letter is to ask about the hermit who lives 50 miles from Clairvaux. How does he live? Does he entirely support himself? Does he receive any aid from the monastery? Does he have any contact with seculars? How does he say Mass, if he is a priest? Tentatively we are planning here a life in which food could be brought to me from the monastery in the seasons in which I could not grow enough for myself—bread, rice and so forth. It would not be necessary to go to the bishop, would it, since I would be living on the monastery's land.

I was interested to hear there was a hermit at La Trappe under Rancé.

I value your prayers in this time of mystery and searching. It is more and more evident to me that someone must go through this kind of thing. By the mercy of God, I am one of those who must pass through the cloud and the sea. May I be one of those who also reach the Promised Land. Whatever happens, I shall certainly write much less and I have no desire to become a "literary hermit." I feel that God wills this solitude in American monachism, even if someone has to leave America temporarily to find it . . .

To Dom Maurizio Levy-Duplatt, E.C.

Dom Maurizio (Jacques Levy-Duplatt) was born in Antwerp, Belgium, in 1903. He was a member of the Benedictine community of Clervaux in Luxembourg until 1946, when he passed over to the Sacro Eremo Tuscolano at Frascati, Italy. For forty years he held the office of Prior in several of their hermitages. He was Prior at the time of this exchange of letters, when Merton was considering the possibility of a transitus to the Camaldolese hermits.

June 3, 1955

I have just reread two letters I received from you a couple of years ago and am encouraged by your sympathetic understanding to write to you this important and confidential letter now. It is the result of a recent reply I received from Dom Leclercq.

It is no secret to you that I have had, for more than ten years, the most ardent desire to lead a truly solitary and contemplative life, and that I have found myself increasingly out of place in the framework of a narrow cenobitism in which there is necessarily a great amount of activity and not the desired amount of silence or solitude. In the past months, since the beginning of the year, I have seen this desire warmly encouraged and blessed by several objective and prudent directors, three of them not Trappists and two of them here in the monastery. At the same time, in our latest regular visitation, our Father Visitor took strong action against an incipient "eremitical mentality" in the community. Needless to say, that mentality is thought to emanate from one person, and I readily admit that I have the mentality of a hermit rather than that of a cenobite. I felt that this visitation was the indication that God willed me to take steps to seek a truly solitary life and to break with the cenobium. I consulted a Carthusian director, and he urged me very strongly to seek a transitus. I had been assured by Camaldoli that I would be received there, and I felt that doubtless I ought to make a trial of the solitary life— at Camaldoli.

Meanwhile, my Superiors have mixed feelings about this step. The Abbot General says that while he does not like passages from one Order to another, he will not prevent my leaving to become a Camaldolese hermit if it is the will of God. Dom James is of course very much opposed to my leaving the Order. Since, however, he sees that the case is serious, he has indicated that he would be very willing to try to get a fully official permission for me to live as a hermit in the woods here, which would be the ideal solution. However, knowing the higher Superiors, I feel that this would never be blessed by their approval. I may be wrong.

Meanwhile, of course, the wisdom of going to Camaldoli itself has been called into question, especially by Dom Leclercq. It seems that I would not be able to lead a purely contemplative life there, and that I would only be exploited as a "celebrity" which would make the transitus a farce. There remains another possibility.

Acting on certain indications in the letter of Dom Leclercq, I am turning to you as to a source of hope. Will you tell me first of all if I would be accepted in your Congregation, and secondly, if I could be accepted in such a way that the hidden and contemplative life would be perfectly guaranteed: I mean in the following way. I would leave Gethsemani secretly (of course with the proper permissions) and travel to Italy and enter one of your *eremi* (probably not Frascati, since it is so close to Rome and since two other Americans are there)—I would enter under an *assumed name* as an unknown American priest and no one but my Superiors would know my identity. I would not engage in any publication or any contacts with the world, but would simply live as a true hermit. In this way I would certainly be able to give the solitary life a serious trial, which is what all seem to agree to be necessary for me to do at the moment. Above all, it would not create the noise and comment that a publicly known admission to Camaldoli would cause.

Father Abbot has permitted that I ask this of you although he is not himself firmly convinced that it is the right course as yet. But it will help us to make a decision.

Could you please tell me something of your various hermitages, and if there is one more suited to this plan than the others, let me know. Should I write to the Superior of that hermitage, or could you ask him the answer to the above questions for me? I have never seen a copy of your constitutions. Is it possible to obtain one?

I can speak Spanish better than Italian. My health is in general good except that I have a stomach disorder which makes it impossible for me to eat dairy products (milk and cheese) and at Gethsemani my diet has been supplemented with eggs all the year round. I might have trouble with the divided sleep, but I think Our Lord will take care of these minor difficulties. They do not seem to me to be important. I may add that I am now forty years old, and after over thirteen years at Gethsemani I feel that perhaps I have begun to acquire some of the maturity necessary for the solitary life. One thing is certain, that my directors and I agree that I no longer perfectly fit into the situation in which I find myself and the change is very desirable.

As I said above, the ideal solution would be the permission to lead a hermit life here in the woods, and before further steps are taken we will do what we can to obtain such permission. But my feeling is that if the permission is not granted, then I should perhaps follow the plan I have just outlined for you. I hope you will agree and I will value your suggestions.

I took steps to obtain a transitus to Camaldoli before I received the letter of Dom Leclercq, as the Carthusian Father I consulted was so positive on the point and my director here agreed with him completely. However it is very possible that Dom James' objections will cause the transitus to be refused. If the transitus is granted, would you consider it advisable for me to accept it and go to Camaldoli? It would destroy the efficacy of my plan to keep everything unknown. I will meanwhile ask Camaldoli if they would be prepared to accept me incognito.

For my own part I feel that the Holy Spirit is indeed at work in all this and that He will eventually lead me to the solitude He has prepared for me. The solution of being a hermit here is the most satisfactory but by no means the easiest. Perhaps the surest and most likely to succeed would be the plan to become a hermit of Monte Corona in secret and unknown.

I recommend all my spiritual needs and especially this great problem—or mystery of my vocation. Ask Our Lord to give me the grace to become a true solitary and to be forgotten by men and really live for Him alone. If it is His will that I continue to exercise some kind of apostolate, He will show it. But I feel I should go in the direction that leads to the heart of the desert, if it be possible for me to do so. May God bless you and your novices, and your *Eremo* of Frascati. I eagerly await your reply and all the advice the Holy Spirit may inspire you to give.

To Dom Jean Leclercq

August 11, 1955

Thank you for your last letter. I am sending this together with a note to your good Reverend Father Abbot to thank him for writing to me about his hermit. He certainly seems to have a very good situation, and I envy him. If I ever manage to become a hermit here the difficulties will be much greater, but that is nothing special. The very idea of the solitary life is to live in direct dependence on God, and in constant awareness of our own poverty and weakness.

I have also received a letter from Frascati in which they say they will be quite willing to receive me to make a trial of their life, incognito. I could remain with them without being a writer, in true obscurity and solitude. My Superiors do not wish to give me permission to make this trial, as far as I can see at the moment, but I should very much like to visit Frascati and other places where the eremitical life is led. Here again I must rest in my poverty and let God provide.

At the moment, it does seem that there is a real chance of my being allowed to live in solitude here. Higher Superiors have softened their rigid opposition to some extent, at least admitting the eremitical solution in theory. But Dom James, my Father Abbot, is showing himself more and more favorable to the idea, and I believe that insofar as it may depend on him, I can hope for this permission. Meanwhile on the material side, the way seems to be preparing itself. The State Forestry Department is erecting a fire-lookout tower on one of our big hills, a steep wooded eminence in our forest, dominating the valley by about 400 feet. I have been put in charge of this work with them, and they are going to erect a small cabin there, in which one might conceivably live. It will be an austere and primitive kind of hermitage, if I ever get to live in it. In any case, I depend on your prayers and those of all who are interested in helping me, that Our Lord may be good to me, and if it be His will that I may live alone in our forest. In the meantime I think I can count on a semi-solitary life for part of the year as the watchman on this fire tower. That will be beautiful—unless it is disapproved by higher Superiors. But they have seemingly permitted it as an experiment. Again, I beg your prayers.

I have stopped writing, and that is a big relief. I intend to renounce it for good, if I can live in solitude. I realize that I have perhaps suffered more than I knew from this "writing career." Writing is deep in my nature, and I cannot deceive myself that it will be very easy for me to do without it. At least I can get along without the public and without my reputation! Those are not essentially connected with the writing instinct. But the whole business tends to corrupt the purity of one's spirit of faith. It obscures the clarity of one's view of God and of divine things. It vitiates one's sense of spiritual reality, for as long as one imagines himself to be accomplishing something he tends to become rich in his own eyes. But we must be poor, and live by God alone—whether we write or whatever else we may do. The time has come for me to enter more deeply into that poverty.

The main purpose of this letter is this: I am cleaning out my files. There is one manuscript which I think ought to interest you for your "Tradition Monastique." It is a short, simple collection of meditations on solitude which I wrote two years ago when I had a kind of hermitage near the monastery. I still have it, but it is no longer quiet. Machines are always working near it, and there is a perpetual noise. Nobody uses it very much, except on feast days. But at any rate these pages on solitude are perhaps worth sending to you. They will make a small volume, better I think than *Seeds of Contemplation* and more unified. Tentatively I am calling it simply *Solitude* [published as *Thoughts in Solitude*].

The manuscript is being typed. Let me know if you are interested, and when it is finished I shall be sending it to you.

I look forward with great interest to your study on the eremitical life. I recently reread your pages on the hermits of Cluny, and wonder if you ever published the article on Peter the Venerable and hermits, which you spoke of some time ago. I should like an offprint, if you did.

Finally, I am still hoping to hear some news of the Giustiniani book.

I am glad that Our Lord is slowly and mysteriously opening out a new way before me. I am glad too that you have been in the mystery, and have contributed something to its working out. I trust you will stay with me by your prayers, and on occasion by your good advice.

To Dom Damasus Winzen

August 22, 1955

It is a long time since your last letter. Forgive me for not answering sooner. If you sent anything on Marialaach, it has not reached me. Let me know if you did, and I will try to see that it is not lost, and that it is sent back to you if you need it.

It did not altogether surprise me that Fr. B. found the labor rather hard at Mount Saviour. I foresaw that this would be his main difficulty in a young community, but it does not seem to me that this alone is an indication that he should throw over the whole idea of a monastic vocation. In my opinion—speaking in terms of your letter of a month ago—he should make every effort to test his monastic vocation and give it a good try, especially if he likes the Mount Saviour idea as such. After all, you will not always be in the foundation stage, and things will settle down later on. I entirely agree that he should follow your advice and regard this as a necessary training in the *bios praktikos* [the ascetic life]. However, since that time you probably all have new light on the subject.

I am distressed that Dom James does not allow me to receive mail from Fr. B. or write to him. It would have made things a little easier for him, I feel, and I would have liked to help out. However, if my Superior does not wish it there is nothing I can do. He gave me permission to send you these thoughts, at any rate, and I trust the permission includes my best wishes to Fr. B.

What you say about studies and the monastic life would probably not only be not understood but even opposed by many here, but they do not understand the monastic spirit. It certainly seems to me of crucial importance that monks should be first of all *monks* and that they should get their roots firmly sunk into the monastic life and that the studies for the priesthood and thoughts of the priesthood do, in fact, distract them from this when they are assumed at the wrong time. I have also known students who have had to leave, who might have made good choir monks if they had been left alone after their profession. About this and many other important things, little can be done in the established order of things in a place like Gethsemani. The work is reserved for you. Yes, I know Dom Lemercier too, and admire his little monastery at Cuernavaca. I have heard of the Ashram, in South India, but know nothing much about it.

About the word "contemplative"—it has been much abused in this country—everywhere. I am perhaps partly to blame for its misuse in America. I am gradually beginning to learn a few things about it. The thing that annoys me most is the purely negative sense the word is given by most of the "contemplative orders." It means "not active"—in the sense of not in the apostolate—it means being behind a wall instead of outside one. Result—such contemplatives lead neither the contemplative life they claim to nor the active life (in the ancient sense) on which a truly contemplative life would have to be founded. I can only conclude that it is essential for us to understand what the *monastic* life really is and to remember that the "contemplative" life is a special gift which all monks should desire and some may receive—in the sense that all should "seek God" truly and desire to know Him not conceptually but as He is.

To Dom Maurizio Levy-Duplatt

September 5, 1955

Thank you for your very kind and complete letter about my problem. Thank you especially for your invitation to come to Frascati and try out your life incognito. In my opinion this would be a very valuable measure and I wish I could avail myself of your invitation. Perhaps later.

Meanwhile, however, the question of whether or not I may be allowed to live a hermit life here in the woods of Gethsemani will be fully discussed at Cîteaux by Dom James with our Father Immediate and our Father General. Will you please pray that a right solution may be reached?

It still seems to me that there is an inordinate hesitation and timidity about the solitary life in the Cistercian Order, due to the fact that so many of the Superiors have an *a priori* and absolutist insistence on the common life as the universal solution for all problems. That this solution is not always quite realistic, and that it results sometimes in the warping and harming of souls, is sometimes quite evident. I can only pray that what seems to me and to my directors to be a genuine call to solitude in my own life, is not simply steam-rollered in this manner.

However, of one thing I am sure. God has all things in His hands, and we will never comprehend the depth of His inscrutable wisdom. *O altitudo sapientiae et scientiae Dei* [O the depth of the wisdom and knowledge of God] . . .

To Dom Gabriel Sortais

October 18, 1955

I thank you for your good letter from Cîteaux. I had to wait for Dom James' return and the result of the election at Genesee before answering you, for everything holds together, and before arriving at the final solution of the problem I had to know everything.

First of all, I am now quite convinced that God does not want me to be a Camaldolese. Your advice, along with the advice of the Most Reverend Father Larraona [of the Sacred Congregation of Religious] and even of Monsignor Montini [later Pope Paul VI], give me the most complete assurance that it would be most imprudent for me to leave Gethsemani, or at least the Order, and that there would not be much to gain. So I am quite sure I know God's will on this point, and I accept it willingly with the most complete peace and without regrets. This gives me the opportunity to sacrifice an appeal, a dream, an ideal, to embrace God's will in faith. Forgive me for worrying you, perhaps out of a lack of faith: but I could not tell in conscience before the solution of the question, that it had received its answer—at least the answer that would have had the power of convincing me from the subjective point of view. Now, it is over, and I promise you I will not worry you any more with this business.

Does God want me to be a Cistercian hermit? You advise me not to seek a life of total solitude. But you have told Dom James that I could be allowed to make the trial of the solitary life here. I thought at first that God wanted this trial of me, and I was going to ask to do it, knowing that Dom James would probably give me permission. Now, at the same time, one of our officers has been elected Abbot of the Genesee [Walter Helmstetter], which is very inconvenient for Dom James, since if I were to leave for the woods, he will have to replace two of his Father Masters at one time. So I thought I must, before God, leave myself entirely in the hands of Dom James, and *he* has decided to give me the office of Father Master of the Choir Novices to replace Father Walter (the new Abbot of the foundation). You see how poor we are in personnel when it is I, the *only one* that Dom James can entrust with the novices without having to seek a dispensation.

Perhaps you will say that Dom James is quite imprudent to make this choice. To protect him, and to protect the house and the novices, I have made a vow (it is only the third private vow I have made!) not to say anything to the novices that would diminish their respect for the Cistercian cenobitic life and orientate them towards something else. If I happen to violate this promise, I will have to notify the Father Abbot. I will try to do all that is possible to give them a truly Cistercian life, cenobitical and liturgical. Pray for me. Above all pray that I don't set them a bad example.

So I will have the opportunity to make a second novitiate myself, and to reimmerse myself completely in the true spirit of my vocation. If, after that, the appeal to solitude persists, and if Dom James will allow it, maybe I will ask, after three years, permission to live in the woods. Dom James wants me to be Novice Master for three years to allow a young priest to be trained for this job.

There only remains for me to assure you of my regrets for having afflicted you with my problems, to ask you for your paternal blessing and your advice for my new job. I assure you of all my filial devotion and my entire loyalty in the Lord. Maybe I am not the best of your sons, but I love you all the same as well as those who are holier than I.

To Dom Jean Leclercq

December 3, 1955

You had heard from Dom Gabriel Sortais the issue of the discussions about my vocation. But you had evidently not heard all that eventually came about. It happens that I am now master of novices! In fact I am somewhat more of a cenobite than I expected to be. Strange things can happen in the mystery of one's vocation.

As I am master of novices, Father Abbot desires me to devote my full time to the souls of my charges. He will not allow me to consider your kind invitation to join you in your project on the psalms, although I want to express my gratitude to you for asking me. In any event, I feel that I would not be erudite enough to join you, but my job in the novitiate makes it entirely out of the question. I shall cease to be a writer at least as long as I am in charge of the novices. The prospect does not trouble me. I care very little what I do now, so long as it is the will of God.

Will He some day bring me after all to perfect solitude? I do not know. One thing is sure, I have made as much effort in that direction as one can make without going beyond the limits of obedience. My only task now is to remain quiet, abandoned, and in the hands of God. I have found a surprising amount of interior solitude among my novices, and even a certain exterior solitude which I had not expected. This is, after all, the quietest and most secluded corner of the monastery. So I am grateful to God for fulfilling many of my desires when seeming to deny them. I know that I am closer to Him, and that all my struggles this year formed part of His plan. I am at peace in His will. Thank you for your part in the affair. If you see Dom Maurizio, will you also thank him for all his kindness and for the invitation which, alas, I was unable to accept?

I am delighted to hear that Giustiniani has finally appeared. I have not yet received a copy, but I am hoping that some will come soon. Did I ask you for a dozen of them? That would be a favor I would appreciate. I would like to be able to give some copies to friends who would be very interested and help to make the book known; please let me have at least this many in "service de presse."

I am very glad that you like the meditations [*Thoughts in Solitude*]. I do not feel the book is adequate or complete. But since I can do little or nothing to remedy matters now, I will have to leave it as a fragment. I look forward to hearing news of it. I entrust you with the care of getting it approved by Dom Gabriel Sortais.

In conclusion, then, will you please thank Dom Gribomont in my behalf and express my deep regret at not being able to accept the general invitation which he has extended.

Please pray for me and for my novices. Your course on "Grammar and Eschatology" sounds interesting, the only thing in the title that I find difficult is the word "grammar." That, precisely, is the hook. If you publish these lectures in a volume, I hope you will not forget to send me one.

Meanwhile for my part I am happily lecturing on Cassian. What could be better material in my situation? Although I cannot live like Abbot Isaac, Nesteros, or Piamon, I feel that they are my fathers and my friends.

Let us remain united in the Holy Spirit, and wait the coming of the Lord with our lamps burning in the night of this world.

February 6, 1956

It is already a long time since I had the pleasure of receiving your finished and published work on Giustiniani—after all this wait. It is a splendid book, and reading it again in French I do not hesitate to say that it is the one of your books which I most enjoy. I think it is really a landmark in spiritual books of our time, even though Giustiniani is not himself a figure of towering importance. Nevertheless this statement of the perennial value of the eremitical life is an important one, one which needs to be made, and one which will have a significant effect. I predict that it will be in fact one of the most influential of your books—perhaps not by the number of the souls it influences, but by their quality and by the depth of their reaction. I am very happy to have been able to write the preface and thus appear in the pages of this significant volume.

My new life as master of novices progresses from day to day. It is an unfamiliar existence to which I often have difficulty in adapting myself. I sometimes feel overcome with sheer horror at having to talk so much and appear before others as an example. I believe that God is testing the quality of my desire for solitude, in which perhaps there was an element of escape from responsibility. But nevertheless the desire remains the same, the conflict is there, but there is nothing I can do but ignore it and press forward to accomplish what is evidently the will of God.

Returning to the question of the Giustiniani book—I believe an English translation would be very desirable and you might be able to interest an American publisher in the idea—for instance, the Newman Press, Westminster, Maryland. Or the Mercier Press at Cork in Ireland. In any case I am convinced that the book ought to appear in English. However, I doubt whether I can help you in any way beyond making these suggestions. I have abandoned all writing now and my Superiors wish me to keep free of all contacts with publishers, except of course for those made necessary by the books still waiting to be published . . .

To Abbot James Fox

Day of Recollection, February, 1956

Welcome home! Don't work too hard now that you are back.

On this day of recollection—going over the past weeks—I am beginning to realize that I am something of a problem and that I need plenty of grace now. I am coming to a crucial point in my life in which I may make a complete mess of everything—or let Jesus make a complete success of everything. On the whole, my nerves are not too good and I can't rely on my faculties as I used to—they play tricks on me, and I get into nervous depression and weakness. However, I have to react by faith, by love of the Cross, and work especially to give an example of monastic regularity and simplicity. Anyway, I put myself entirely in God's hands. I renounce my desire for anything but His will. I have plenty of peace and trust though everything is *really* dark. But I hope it is the darkness before dawn.

To Father Charles Dumont

August 19, 1956

Thanks for your kind note written at Caldey. I am pleased and grateful to have you as my translator, in the article on Adam. If you wish to have it multigraphed I would be delighted to have about twenty copies—or is that asking too much? I am afraid we cannot do it here as my novices are busy with many other jobs. I myself give them multigraphing as we are trying to get out a series of lectures on Cassian—just elementary things. I can always send copies over there if they are desired.

As for an American Cistercian magazine, I think the hopes are very poor; it would probably turn into a rather cheap sheet full of news bulletins to seduce rich benefactors. I regret that I can offer no better hope for the time being. England, I should think, would be a better prospect . . .

To Father Thomas Aquinas Porter, O.C.S.O.

One of the Cistercian censors from Holy Trinity Abbey, Huntsville, Utah, Father Thomas Aquinas had been rather negative in his criticism of Merton's small brochure Basic Principles of Monastic Spirituality.

August 27, 1956

When I was at Collegeville recently, Dr. [Gregory] Zilboorg, who is a good judge of character, assured me that I was much more aggressive than I realized. This accounts for the fact that my letter to you was probably much more violent than I intended it to be and I deeply regret if I have wounded you. It was certainly not my intention to do so.

Since that time I have heard from our Most Reverend General that you have considered giving up the charge of censor and he lays this at my door. Again, it was certainly not my intention to provoke anything so drastic. Indeed, I do not feel anything you have taken up with our Reverendissime is really my business and I shall refrain from commenting on it. I would only like to point out what I meant by the letter which caused all the trouble.

Father, it seems to me that the difficulty is not so great. Most censors, when there is question of corrections, make a distinction between the corrections upon which they insist and those which they only suggest. An author, certainly a Trappist author, is always eager to comply with the censor, but at the same time, when the correction affects some very minute point and involves perhaps a mere matter of opinion, the author would like a little freedom so as to spare his text from the sort of mutilation involved by the forcible injection of a technical phrase. I certainly felt that by your *demanding* some of the changes in *Basic Principles of Mon-*

astic Spirituality, I was being unnecessarily cramped and the effect on the work, if this principle were pushed to its conclusion, would be a bad one.

On the other hand I am certainly grateful for all the care with which you have checked my theological statements in the things censored by you, and I have always done my best to put your desires in effect. In the case of *Basic Principles*, I felt I was entitled to make representation since the Dominican in Rome supported me on those three points.

But anyway, dear Father, you know there are no hard feelings on my part and I am sure there are none on yours. Authors and censors inevitably tangle once in a while, and if you are thinking of not being a censor I am also thinking of not being an author either. Not because of conflicts, but because of other work.

I regret to inflict some more of my stuff on you. You were, I believe, one of the censors of *Tower of Babel*. It is appearing with a collection of poems, many of which have been censored by others and have appeared in print over the last eight years. I enclose a few poems for the volume which have not yet been censored [*The Strange Islands*].

By the way, when I said *Basic Principles* was with the printer, I did not mean there was a contract one could not get out of. The printer had given us an estimate which, I believe, is perfectly legal and he was waiting to get to work. But of course I was wrong in trying to use that as a motive for hurrying you, because the censor has no need to pay any attention to such things, as we have no business getting the thing printed until he gives the green light. Sorry, Father. Pray for me, and God bless you . . .

To Dom Gabriel Sortais

September 1, 1956

When I received the *imprimi potest* for *Basic Principles of Monastic Spirituality*, etc., I perused the criticism of the three censors, recognizing at once the scrupulous style of good Fr. Thomas Aquinas in Utah. I also noted that the third censor, the Dominican in Rome, had sided with me on three counts. So I wrote to Father Thomas to ask his *permission* to omit those three "corrections" that he imposed with all the others. I also told him, without malice, that if a correction was really not necessary, it would be a pity to *demand* it. In effect, the other censors always make a distinction between the necessary, which is imperative, and the accidental, which is only suggested.

In effect, the censors of [*Thoughts in Solitude*] seem to me reasonable enough. I can see without difficulty that they have done me a good service, and I will make their corrections as I see quite well that they are imperative. I have no grudge against them; on the contrary, I am very grateful to them.

As for Fr. Thomas Aquinas from Utah, I deeply regret I have hurt him. But I do not think at all I have told him anything whatever unjust. The author certainly has the right to make remarks on these three points, since the third censor had sided with me . . .

If Fr. Thomas Aquinas wants to resign, it is not my business. I accept him willingly as censor. But I think all the same I do a service to the Order and to the writers of the Order by saying, gently, that this censor might well take into account the context, which sheds light on the meaning of the author. Many a time he interpreted me in an unfavorable sense and he demanded clarification the context provided in abundance. I am always quite willing to render my text clearer, but when a censor asks me to qualify the phrase "without Christ there is no salvation"—then I insist all the same on saying that this seems to me slightly idiotic. I will *make* the corrections, as much as he wants, but don't I have the right to tell him what I think of it, provided it is charitable?

But, Most Reverend Father, if you want me henceforth to make no remark, I'll make none. I don't mind. I did not get angry, I simply wanted to express my thought to him. I repeat, I have no complaint about the censorship of [*Thoughts in Solitude*]. Of course it is annoying to have to redo several pages of the book but in sum it is not bad . . . You don't realize, no doubt, the difference between this censorship and the other. It is not the length that matters, but the reasons—or the unreasonableness—of the censor . . .

Forgive me this fuss, Most Reverend Father. You think no doubt that I have a lot to do with the censors. But it is about very small texts, or else about things written before. I write next to nothing; I am very pleased and fairly busy with our novices who are all good little novices. I have received many graces since last year, and I can assure you that I would never again begin the attempts for a change of Order. I like very much the new timetable. I find time for prayer and for my own interior life, and besides, I have received the great grace to know a little the causes of my faults. On top of that I also see the means of bringing some correction to them, and I do hope that I am going to make some progress with God's grace. But that will not be easy—nor always pleasant.

I know that God loves me much, and that He has been very patient with me. My life becomes more and more a question of graces and a confession of my wretchedness. I know that I am not a saint, but I am happy because God loves me and draws me towards Him always—He who is the Father of the poor . . .

To Abbot James Fox

January 25, 1957

This has been, I believe, a very good retreat for me, one of the best since I entered. In the last year I really think I have grown a little, not in any spectacular exterior way but in depth and in simplicity and, I hope, in honesty with myself. For the first time in fifteen years I can begin to hope that my vocation is getting to be really solid, although I have no illusions yet on that score. But one thing, now I know that I am not just looking for some spiritual kind of self-satisfaction but honestly want to do the will of God, not that I expect it to be always easy. But I really want to give myself simply to His will and seek Him in His good pleasure, and not worry about what becomes of my precious aspirations. I beg Him to give me grace to carry this through in spite of darkness, depression and disgust. I know I yet have to grow very much in the spirit of faith—and need much more hope.

January 26, 1957

This note supersedes yesterday's because I wrote our retreat resolution too soon—the best graces came at the very end, crystallizing everything out. What God wants of me is to abandon myself completely into the hands of Our Lady as a child and stop worrying about anything, but leave everything to her. In that way I don't have to wonder where I am going to get the strength, hope, etc., in fact I won't have to bother my head about the "how" of anything. And that is the answer as far as I am concerned. Alleluia. *Ora pro me* [Pray for me].

To Dom Gabriel Sortais

February 7, 1957

Since Christmas, I have wanted to take a little time to write to you. The letter I wanted to send you would have been the first for a long time which would have had nothing to say about business, books, worries, but would simply have shown you how happy and content I am to be at peace, in the novitiate, with nothing to write and out of contact with outside affairs. Alas, here I am once again obliged to give you explanations to assure you that I have neither intended nor caused the unfortunate incident that has arisen.

My Most Reverend Father: since I have not been writing, Dom James has completely severed my connections both with my agent and with my publishers. I have not written to the one or the other. I do not know what is going on. I do not understand what is happening most of the time. I did not know that an Italian edition had been published, or by whom, or in what condition. I did not know that this edition had not been passed by the censors. I did not know that it contained photos of Gethsemani (I certainly did not send any) and, finally, I did not know that the text lacked the important chapters about the Benedictines, the Carthusians and the Cistercians.

I know only this:

1) In 1954 the monks of Pierre-qui-Vire asked me for a text for "Silence dans le Ciel." I sent them a text—one already too long, "Silence in Heaven," destined at the same time for Camaldoli—Dom Giabbani had asked me for this. Pierre-qui-Vire sent the original text to Camaldoli. Now this was the one that the American censor decided needed to be changed.

2) In summer of 1955, as you know, I had come to the decision to go to Camaldoli myself. Having heard that I wanted to leave Gethsemani, Dom James forbade me all correspondence not only with Camaldoli but even with any director outside the monastery. In short, a complete iron curtain. If, on the other hand, Dom James had dealt with the situation in a less arbitrary fashion, I think that everything would have been much simpler and much less bothersome for all of us. At any rate, it has been totally impossible for me to communicate with Dom Giabbani about the subject-matter of this book since 1955. I did not write him. I was unable to know what point the publication had reached.

3) In 1955, with the approval of both the censor and the monks of Pierre-qui-Vire, I rewrote the book, now called *The Silent Life*, with the alternate title: "Living in Silence." I wrote three new chapters about the three Orders mentioned above. Later on I wrote yet another chapter, but it has no bearing on this matter. The whole thing had been censored and accepted. At this point I told my agent to send Dom Giabbani the three chapters on the Benedictines, the Cistercians and the Carthusians. She told me she was going to do so. But at this very moment things became so mixed up that about thirty beautiful photographs were lost either by the agent or by the American publisher. Therefore it is possible that all this confusion caused the mix-up with the Italian translation also. I simply do not know.

4) Pierre-qui-Vire first of all published chapter one of "Silence in Heaven" as the whole text of "Silence dans le Ciel." And later on the second text, a longer one, appeared under the title *The Silent Life* and the French translation, "La Vie Silencieuse" is under way. The book is unknown in Gethsemani. No one here is allowed to read it, but they do not even suspect that it exists. You can see, therefore, the answer to your question: "Is there another circumstance I can think of that might account for this unfortunate omission?" If these difficulties continue to multiply, it may be because Dom James is trying to settle things himself without understanding them very well. But on the other hand I am glad not to be involved in it myself. When Dom James asked me some questions following your letter of January, I explained everything to him, but very likely he did not understand it clearly. I also told him to explain to you that I had had nothing to do with Camaldoli and that I could not control the Italian edition in any way. Very likely he forgot to tell you that.

As for the error concerning the censors, I was *never* told who was the censor of the book. I believe that Dom James communicated the censor's name directly to the publisher. I learned who it was only after the publication of the book.

Having said all this, Most Reverend Father, I believe that is all I can explain to you. How did these three chapters come to be omitted from the Italian translation? I simply do not know the reason at all. I did my very best to guarantee their inclusion, but what I was able to do was very little indeed.

So as not to make this letter a litany of troubles, I want to tell you, Most Reverend Father, that I am doing fine and that I am truly happy and at peace. There is a serenity in the novitiate. Everything goes well. Silence and solitude exist, at least to a degree. I am trying to be a monk. I am not writing and I do not think of writing anything whatsoever. True, I still have two or three manuscripts that are going to be published, but after that the name of Thomas Merton can be forgotten. So much the better. I continue to seek God through the somewhat strange and solitary path that is mine. More and more I try to pay no attention to myself. I know that I am in God's hands and that I cannot see what He is in the process of doing. Please bless me. I am sorry for all these problems, Most Reverend Father; fortunately it will be all over soon. I remain devotedly and loyally one with you in our Lord.

April 16, 1957

I make quite willingly the corrections you demand in *The Silent Life* as well as most of those that the censor has suggested. I send you the copy of the page I have just written for Marie Tadié. And I leave it to you to change what does not please you, for I do not think I have succeeded altogether in making these corrections well myself in French.

When I was writing this work, at the moment of a crisis in my religious life, I was not looking at things in an altogether normal way, no doubt, and certain expressions which slipped into it allow a glimpse into this state of mind to someone who looks closely. But at the same time, I do not reproach myself as if it were an infidelity towards the Order, with the fact that I have expressed opinions which most of the Abbots in the Order would not accept. I did not think I was compelled to conform on all points, in this book, to the official doctrine of the Trappists, given that I am not an official spokesman of the Order but a simple individual, and besides everybody knows that I speak according to my own thought, and I don't make it a virtue to repeat mechanically what the others think. I don't think I harmed the Order by acting thus, for the well-informed reader while deploring my errors of judgment (which I deplore myself) could appreciate this somewhat unusual frankness. Know that after all the Protestants are still accusing us of servility and lack of frankness.

I am not saying this to justify myself. After two years in the novitiate I realize the necessity not to muddle up the souls in our monasteries with opinions that may disturb them. So I content myself with conforming exactly to the ideal of the Order not only in the formation of novices but in my own spiritual life. You know that I thought I should renounce the personal ideal which inspired some pages of this book.

Besides, I am quite sensitive to the acuity of your own problems, and I do not want to bring an addition to them. I simply promise you not to say again things which might inspire sinister interpretations in the minds of certain readers . . .

April 16, 1957

I wrote you this morning to tell you with how much good will I wanted to obey your demand to make certain alterations in our work, *The Silent Life.* But thinking of the second paragraph of that letter (which is gone already), I think you might misunderstand me. In effect, when I was saying, in the American way, that I did not regret having spoken my opinion frankly, it is quite possible that you, who are European, may think I am intransigent, not to say stubborn. No, Most Reverend Father, this is not the case. I do not make any claim, I do not ask for the "right" to express myself in my way. I don't have this right the moment my Superiors think I am in error. I accept their decision with my whole heart, and I prefer to obey, I prefer to renounce the expression of my own thought in order to submit to theirs because faith tells me that true liberty is found in obedience through love of Christ.

All that was understood in this morning's letter, but I wanted it all to be completely clear. I love obedience, and out of love of obedience I have also renounced writing. I would not want for anything in the world to give you the impression that I obey you grudgingly, or with bad will, while thinking that I am "right all the same," for I know that even he who would be truly right from the speculative point of view, would no longer be right if he left his opinion to make a dent in his obedience. And moreover, I don't think myself infallible. Anyway, I would never want, even "being right," to express an opinion which would disturb the souls in our Order. I think now that you understand me better, and I repeat to you the assurance of my entire devotion, for Christ's love.

July 5, 1957

Your very kind letter, written from Koningsoord in May, reached me here in July, having re-crossed the Atlantic twice—for it was sent from here to Melleray. Why, I hardly know. There was a transmission error, no doubt.

But anyway I feel an urge to express to you my deep gratitude, given that I have the feeling of being a somewhat difficult monk, for I fear I might push to the limit the good will and benevolence of my Superiors, who are very patient with me for that matter. But you reassure me completely, and I see that we understand each other perfectly, and that you trust my intentions: they at least are good. Anyway I try to make them good as far as possible.

Dom James surprised me a little by asking me to write a pamphlet on the monastic life this summer, but it amounts to very little indeed, and I finished it quickly. I tell you this because for my part I really thought I would never write anything as long as I was Father Master.

And now, leaving aside these writer's affairs, I will speak to you a little of our novitiate. For me, it is a quite comforting office, the one of Father Master. I like this work very much, and the novices—and all the same I had always feared such an "activity," thinking that it would eventually ruin my famous "contemplative life." But no such thing has happened. I still have both the taste and the opportunities for prayer and solitude (in the Cistercian sense!) and quite a lot of silence. We can manage, above all, with two sub-masters.

What is most interesting is the number of Ibero-American postulants. Especially priests who want to come from South America. We try to sort out these vocations by making them consult priests who are in contact with us in the different large cities there, and we prolong their postulancy, especially when they scarcely know English. Fortunately, I speak Spanish, for we have already had two of them who had hardly any English at all. In parenthesis, there is going to come in September a Hungarian seminarian, who escaped from the Reds last November, and who seems to be all right. We have at present three priests from South America in the novitiate, and a postulant who as a poet is fairly well-known in Nicaragua [Ernesto Cardenal]. We expect the arrival of an Italian priest who is at present in Chile, and of three more who are priests or seminarians in South America. Lastly, there are two more cases which are being examined, a seminarian from Puerto Rico, and a Canadian missionary who was in Santo Domingo and who speaks Spanish. All those that we have accepted (and we have refused many others), seem to adjust fairly well here, but they are mainly Spaniards, or people of European race who come through South America. We shall see later on what the true South Americans are like when two of them will come to us from Colombia. It appears that this country is one of the best.

Dom James also told me that we had been offered several times estates down there to make a foundation. Of course, he refused, for it is not yet the moment. But it seems that this moment is drawing near quite soon, and that in two or three years we shall be able to go ahead all right. Thus, after praying a lot, and thinking about the situation, I thought it my duty to tell Dom James that I was ready to go on the foundation if he wished me to, especially if he needed a Father Master who knew Spanish.

Of course, I don't know what will come out of all this and I leave it all in God's hands, and for my part I am pleased to live from day to day in the present moment, without worrying about the future. But all the same, I think it would be a great grace for me if I could offer myself to help make a foundation in South America, if it is God's will. I tell myself from time to time that maybe I don't have the health, etc., and above all that I don't have enough virtue, and that maybe I am deluding myself, but the Holy Spirit may see to it, and He will settle everything if it is God's will. Dom James does not say yes or no, which is quite wise. My confessor approves of my desires. Anyway, it may be that by this sacrifice I can "make up for" all that I may have lost by the sins and the miseries of my monastic life, provided that I am not going to add to it yet more of them.

This is what is perhaps an illusion above all: but I think of the thousands of Indians down there, and of their poverty, and of the good that could be done by a quite poor, quite simple, quite Benedictine monastery, in their midst . . . for example in the Andes in Ecuador. The climate of the mountains even on the equator is wholesome and quite propitious to our life. Or again, in Peru, among the descendants of the Incas: but the land is poor down there. One could better make a living in the direction of Bogotá, Colombia. That is perhaps the best in South America. It appears that the Cardinal down there has invited Dom James to make a foundation and offered him lands, but it was at the moment of the foundation in California.

I let my heart speak, for I know that this also interests you very much. If it is a dream, too bad! I leave myself in God's hands, and if others make the foundation, well so much the better. But I think the moment for such a foundation is going to come soon, and I cannot think of it without a very deep emotion. Maybe this is an indication of a grace from God for me. If you have a moment to tell me your thought, I would be delighted to know it. And I think that you will tell me I am not yet a good enough monk to go on a foundation: it is true. Or else that it is an illusion, and maybe this is true, too.

We have at present thirty in the novitiate; that is a dozen more than in the beginning of June. It is enough. A larger novitiate would be too large for the formation of each one. All the same we receive two or three more next month. The others who come from Latin America will be here by the end of the year. In the meantime, some will leave, no doubt . . .

To Abbot James Fox

Abbot James Fox was away making Visitations; hence the following letter assessing the possibilities of a foundation in South America.

July 15, 1957

Well, we are really sweating at last. I think the summer has arrived in honor of St. Stephen, so that we may do a little penance. I hope it is cooler where you are—by the time you get this you will probably be at the Genesee [Trappist monastery in upstate New York] . . .

I have been reading up a little about South America—I didn't manage to get anything from the library in Louisville when we came to see you off, I forgot it was the 4th of July. But I got some from the U. of Ky. instead. It is an eye-opener. Ignorance is bliss. When you get to know more how things are it sobers you up a bit. Any foundation we may make there in the future will probably be harder than anything so far, but it may also be more fruitful. Here are some considerations.

1) Any tropical country, even though one may be at a high altitude, will provide the community with lots of special sicknesses. In Colombia a big proportion of people die each year from dysentery (!)—there are lots of intestinal parasites.

2) Another drawback of high altitudes is that the ability to work is cut down very considerably. No pep and strength. The natives are not usually very zealous either.

3) A particular drawback of Colombia is the political situation. All S.A. countries are politically unstable, but in Colombia, things are set up for a very bad revolution: and if this comes, the Church, having been totally identified with the conservative political party, will get it in the neck very seriously. There was a prelude in 1948 when convents were burned, priests killed and mutilated, etc. The people are largely illiterate and are subject to intense political propaganda beyond their intellectual level so that they can go berserk very easily. From the point of view of relative safety, it would be better to found in a country that has *already gone through* its main anti-clerical upheavals and where the Church is to a great extent *out* of politics. Mexico would be a case in point, but South America is preferable to Central America.

4) Another difficulty in the Andean countries is the lack of communications—one can get around easily enough by air, but there are practically no railroads and roads are very poor. Freight gets through with great difficulty and hazards and one would be cut off from supplies. To found in the Andean countries would mean largely getting along on nothing—without machines, etc., to a great extent. It would be very hard to get parts, supplies, etc., when needed.

5) Colombia is a half-Indian country. Ecuador is mostly Indian, like Bolivia. Venezuela is mixed up Indian and Negro and very tropical, with all attendant drawbacks.

6) Nevertheless, Colombia remains a very attractive prospect with all its drawbacks. The people in general are very good—when they are calmed down. The land is rich, lots of things will grow, there is a good climate. However, at the moment, as far as I can judge, it would seem that everything tends to tip the balance in favor of Argentina and Chile, and maybe Uruguay. Argentina and Uruguay are the only really white countries in S.A. and it might be wiser to start there. Chile is also very

good, in the fertile valley near Santiago—and very accessible. You can get things there.

Well, I just thought I would register a few thoughts. Maybe on this trip you may get a chance to consult someone who really knows a great deal about it all. I hope you do . . .

To Dom Gabriel Sortais

December 30, 1957

On December 28 I wrote the letter you wished to Mme. de Hueck Doherty. I also wrote at the same time to the publisher. Today I have just written to the agent. So everyone is informed. I asked Mme. de Hueck Doherty to be kind enough to take into account the wishes of the Order and my Superiors, to which I submitted myself entirely. I am morally certain that she will comply with your will, and that you have nothing to fear about the publication of this early [pre-monastic] work which so much worries the Reverend Father [*The Cuban Journal*, which was eventually published under the title *The Secular Journal*].

I do hope that your operation went well and that you are beginning to recover. It is not for me tell you that maybe you work too hard. The burden of the whole Order is certainly heavy, but still you share it with others, fortunately for you. Anyway, I wish you a good rest, and even a somewhat prolonged convalescence so you may recover completely . . .

January 27, 1958

I am pleased to know that you have been operated on with success and that you are at present convalescing. May God restore you to complete health, and to the joy of living for Him.

I have just received a letter from my friend Catherine de Hueck, the one who holds the rights of my *Secular Journal (Cuban Journal)*. She tells me, I foretold you, that she accepts your decision, and that she abandons herself to God's will. I see that it is costing her a lot, but that she does so with entire and altogether admirable generosity. She also tells me, in parenthesis, why this costs her. They could have bought a new car to transport the nurses in the abandoned country where there are poor farmers that she helps; they might also have made a little building for those who come and join their institute; they might even have helped a family in distress. In addition to her, some priests are also grieved by our decision.

When I think that Christians who are destitute must remain so when one could easily help them, I wonder if God does not want me to tell you discreetly: Would it not be possible to suppress in the book those passages which the censor cites? In truth, there are many of them. One might perhaps change the expressions here and there, suppress the overly shocking sentences, without damaging the substance of the book which, all the same, does not consist altogether of reprehensible things. I even think that the censors have not really reached the true heart of the book with their criticisms. In sum, would it not be possible to publish the book corrected and pruned, for these extrinsic reasons as one of the censors said?

Mme. de Hueck has not suggested this, but in the situation she describes it seems to me that it is an act of Christian zeal to try to do what is possible for these people who are suffering. Do not think, dear Most Reverend Father, that I suggest this out of stubbornness. I only indicate what she told me, and what seems to me to be correct. You have a better judgment than I; you see things from a higher perspective than I do.

If you think one could adapt the manuscript for publication so as not to put off these good people, nor offend pious ears, you just have to send back the observations of the censors, and I will make *all* the suggested changes. You will tell me that the book remains an indifferent, worthless book. On this point my agent, who is in no way a credulous or easily deluded person, thinks rather the contrary. The moment it is certain that it will not offend anybody, don't you think that the book could be published? I leave this entirely to your judgment . . .

We have just completed a very good retreat preached by Reverend Father Dom Eugene Boylan [Irish Cistercian Abbot], whom I find very friendly. This is really the best retreat we have been given in the time I have been in the monastery . . .

To Jaime Andrade

Jaime Andrade is an artist from Quito, Ecuador, to whom Merton was writing in regard to a statue of the Blessed Virgin and Child for the novitiate library.

March 3, 1958

I thank you very much for your letter, and I am going to explain to you my ideas about the work proposed, a statue of the Blessed Virgin for the novitiate library in this abbey.

It is a question of a statue in tropical wood, dark wood, of 1 m. 50 more or less. We already have a base of stone of about 60 to 70 cm. in one end of a room not too large, which has two windows on the south side. The statue will be on the east side, a little in the shade (unless one turns on artificial lighting). Behind the statue there would be a simple white wall, without any decoration.

I ask you to make a drawing for us and tell us how much you generally charge for a work of this type. Later I will try to gather enough money to pay you, and in case I am successful, will have the joy of telling you positively and definitively to begin the work. I have available about $400, no more, because I am not rich. We are still among friends in a rich country, only Father Abbot does not yet understand how one could spend a thousand dollars on a statue. Well, let me know, and I will try to persuade him. I can also tell you that I have some friends, artists and writers, who would be very interested in this project and certainly some journals here would publish photos of your statue, etc.

I said I was going to explain my ideas . . . For me, this work seems to be of great importance, and that is precisely why I want to give it to you. You are a sculptor; I am a monk and a priest: this means we are both consecrated men, men with a vocation that is more or less *prophetic*; this means that we should be witnesses to the truth, not only to intellectual truth, but to mystic truth, the integral truth of life, of history, of man— of God. We should be witnesses to the *Incarnation*, but that does not mean that we should be occupied with the contemplation of a nice, sentimental [Christmas] "Nativity." The Nativity of God in the world develops in the history of man. The Christ lives in the history of the people, not of rich and powerful people, not of powerful peoples, no, but in that of the poor. The advent of God in the world and the judgment of the world takes place in each moment of history.

So, for me, the "Nativity" of God, of the poor and unknown God, of the powerful and majestic God, Savior and Judge, can be contemplated in the Indian of the Andes, and in all the peoples of South America (as in all the peoples of the world). Here we are "contemplatives"—or we should be. So then, the novice who enters this monastery should see, not the sweet and false image of the Holy Virgin, but the reality—the Virgin Mother of the Indians of the Andes, holding in her arms the Christ incarnated in the flesh and blood of the true America, and of the Indians who received us and fed us centuries ago so that we would be Americans like themselves. Here we are, North Americans, and by and large do not think much of the Indians there. This is why it is not a question of producing a shock they would not understand. But at the same time we should learn to see God not only in the old forms, almost dead, of a Europe whose historic mission is coming to an end, but incarnated in the forms of the country whose mission is in the future.

I am persuaded that in this I have the truly Christian and prophetic point of view, and I rely on the fact that all true religious art, be it Christian or pagan, of America is concentrated in the countries of Ibero-America. Alejandinaho of Brazil, I think, had that same vision, in spite of his more European forms: I say the same thing of the great artists of the past, as well as of the present, in Ecuador.

You can see that this work has a highly spiritual meaning, in the true sense of the word "spiritual"—spirit is *life*, reality, reflection of the transcendent reality of God in its image, man. If I have the mission to form contemplative monks—above all some Ibero-American vocations—I have the duty to form them not according to a dead formalism, but according to the inspiration of the Spirit of Truth, who speaks not only in words and abstract ideas but above all in the concrete, in the "incarnation" of the Divine Logos in humanity.

I think that none would understand me better than you, dear Jaime Andrade, artist of Ecuador!

To Father Kilian McDonnell, O.S.B.

Father Kilian, a monk of St. John's Abbey, Collegeville, Minnesota, was much involved in the ecumenical apostolate. He was also editor of Sponsa Regis *(later renamed* Sisters Today*), to which Merton frequently contributed.*

March 14, 1958

I wonder if you can do me a favor. The novices here have their breviaries full of very sad holy cards, and I am secretly planning to descend on them, take away all their favorite trash, and impose on them something good. It is a quixotic scheme, no doubt, for a Father Master to hope to clean his house of all the trash that accumulates in corners and crannies. However, I am inspired to make the attempt.

There are some that I definitely know I want: of these I send you the numbers. Then I beg you to look for some more from the Liturgical Press—of the same character as the Marialaach card which I enclose. I like very much this artist whoever he is. I think he is very fine . . .

I want to compliment you all on the sacred art issue of *Worship*, especially your own article . . . I was delighted with the last number of their (clerics) *Scriptorium* and warmly applaud the translation of Mabillon, also the article on Tillich . . .

To Dom Gabriel Sortais

March 27, 1958

Here I am among the censors! I am truly embarrassed in this new and unaccustomed position, in which I predict I shall not be struggling nearly as much as those who were involved with my own manuscripts. I can say, quite calmly, therefore, that I see no problem about the publication of this poem (a single poem) that was sent to me . . . I foresee, however, that there is going to be a whole procession of poems, since the Reverend Mother . . . seems to believe that I am going to send the *nihil obstat* by return mail and that the poem will be published the following week. Maybe she also thinks that I am going to supervise the poetic education of this little sister. I am sure she does not understand.

You ask me for my opinion about this poem. To tell the truth, it is a sincere little poem, on the "cute" side and totally feminine—it is like hundreds of poems of the same sort. I see nothing new in it, but I suppose that nobody is now trying to do anything new. It is a poem for a popular review and that is all: nothing more, nothing less. I shall refrain from criticizing it severely. Why should I? It seems to me that Reverend Mother and the sisters . . . may be encouraging the poetess, but I must beg you not to let me fall *in os leonis* [into the mouth of the lion] and become her poetical mentor. Perhaps if she writes more, a group of poems could be sent all together . . .

I wish you a very happy feast day, Most Reverend Father, and I promise you my prayers and those of my novices. We are still very happy here in the novitiate and things are going well with our 18 young men and two young professed. We still have quite a number of postulants from Latin America. Some are fine, but others lack the aptitude for the life of silence and contemplation. We shall see . . .

I have made all the desired changes in *The Secular Journal* and in order to bring a little more spiritual interest to the book, I have added a few pages, taken from the original manuscript, that deal with my religious vocation. I shall gladly delete them if the censor does not like them. I say "the," because I am sure that the other censor, who has already seen the manuscript, is happy with the book as it is.

To Father Kilian McDonnell

June 8, 1958

Another SOS. I am putting out a little book on Sacred Art. We are doing the job here, at least in Louisville. I am in need of illustrations.

What I need is first a batch of some very good traditional stuff— icons, Byzantine mosaics, Romanesque sculpture, good architecture. Then some good examples of medieval art, ms. illuminations, sculpture, Angelico, and so on. I would like a small selection of *really bad* "sacred art"—pseudo-modern, or kitsch, or whatever one can get, including if possible the Cathedral of Barcelona . . .

July 21, 1958

This has been my first chance to thank you for your wonderful help in getting such a fine selection of pictures that I could use in the book. I have picked out quite a few to work with, and sent the others back quickly, as I did not want anything to happen to them. I noticed that the boards on which they were mounted warped easily in this clammy Kentucky heat, and so I thought the best thing to do was to get them back as fast as I could. I envy you your Minnesota weather—though this also may be an illusion; often when it is very hot here it turns out to be very hot everywhere. But I am happy anyway to have received such help from you and I think the book is going to turn out well. Please pray that it may do so. I am just publishing it here and that makes for difficulties— and special satisfactions as I shall have the fun of planning it all myself, which I like to do . . .

To Jaime Andrade

July, 1958

. . . If I were free to do what I thought best myself, or if I could get permission to do it somehow (and perhaps some day it might be possible), this is what I think I would do:

I would like to embark on a new form of monastic life, a very simple kind of life, a small monastery of six or seven very carefully chosen monks with the same aspirations: living for instance in the country near Quito a life fully integrated in the life of the region, and in the soil, yet also fully in contact with the intellectual life of the Capital.

I would *not* carry on any special "work" or "apostolate" (this is where the mistake is generally made by so many). I would not have any arguments to sell to anybody; I would not try to "catch" people and make them go to confession, etc. Preferably I would not even dress as a priest or as a monk, but as an ordinary person. I would live a life of prayer, of thought, of study, with manual labor, and writing, a life not only in contact with God in contemplation but also fully in contact with all the intellectual, artistic, political movements of the time and place. But I would not intrude into the life of the place as one with a "mission" or a "message"; I would not try to sell anybody anything. My function would be (as it must be in any case) to be a man of God, a man belonging to Christ, in simplicity, to be the friend of all those who are interested in spiritual things, whether of art, or prayer, or *anything valid*, simply to be their friend, to be someone who could speak to them and to whom they could speak, to encourage one another, etc.

As I conceive it, the usual error of the priest is to barricade himself behind an "apostolate" that separates him from everybody else. The basic assumption of this equivocal position is "You need me, but I do not need you. You need my help to be saved, but I do not need yours," etc. Actually of course it is true that the priest has the sacraments, but otherwise he is a man like every other and it is good that he realize it. Also we are all alike struggling for truth in the world, and the possession of spiritual formulas still does not enable one to see especially clearly in the darkness of the political and intellectual chaos.

So I ask you in all simplicity: what do you think of the idea of a small monastery near Quito, a monastery that would be a retreat of silence as it should be, a place of simplicity and work and study, and also a place where ideas and problems could be discussed, or where one could come just for a rest. I would try to make money for it by writing, and there might be a kind of educational project of some kind. But mainly I think just of *being* there with those who are there, and to be in contact with everybody who would want that kind of contact, and without any *arrière pensée* [ulterior motive]. (It seems to me that what is traditionally thought to be the "Jesuit" technique—of using a cultural and intellectual approach as "bait"—implies a certain sort of cynicism and a basic disrespect for the values of the spirit. My approach is quite different. I believe that *all true spiritual values are bound up together*, they all rise and fall together, and that consequently there is no sense whatever in considering one as a decoy for the other. And I am the enemy of all kinds of manipulation in the apostolate, because manipulation ruins all truth and sincerity and is an insult to God.)

The question you might reasonably ask is: why do I not want to try this in North America? I don't know; I believe, on a kind of instinctive basis, that this is not yet needed here. The country is perhaps not yet ripe for it. South America is.

Basically, also, I am a revolutionist—in a broad, non-violent sense of the word. I believe that those who have used violence have betrayed all true revolution, they have changed nothing, they have simply enforced with greater brutality the anti-spiritual and anti-human drives that are destructive of truth and love in man. I believe that the true revolution must come slowly and painfully, not merely from the peasant, etc., but from the true artist and intellectual . . . from the thinker and the man of prayer.

To Dom Gabriel Sortais

October 29, 1958

I beg your pardon: this is a *very urgent affair*.

My friend Boris Pasternak, winner of the Nobel Prize for Literature, is, as you know, under terrible pressure from the Soviet leaders. He is in very serious danger.

I wrote the enclosed letter to the Union of the Soviet Writers, as a protest. But of course this is not going to achieve a lot. What can help is the open publication of this letter in free countries. I instantly ask your permission to publish this letter in any language, as soon as possible. If, for example, one wanted to put this in some newspaper, like the *Osservatore Romano*, could somebody take it upon himself?

Be patient with me, dear Most Reverend Father, but it really seems to me that this is an exceptional cause. I know Pasternak from his books, from letters, in which he manifests to me a very great comprehension, a very friendly understanding, and a lot of kindliness towards some of my writings. I admire him a lot, and we agree with each other very well. I wish I could help him. I would reproach myself bitterly for not having done so. Forgive me, dear Most Reverend Father, and give me permission to let this letter be published at least in English, as soon as possible . . . [See letter of January 26, 1959.]

To Jaime Andrade

November 20, 1958

I am grateful to you for your long and interesting letter, and for your thoughtful, sincere answer to my question about the idea of a monastery . . .

What you say about the difficulties of a monastic mission in Ecuador seems to me to be very reasonable and just. I had thought much the same things myself. To make the kind of a foundation I had imagined might well bring me in conflict with the more conventional-minded of the clergy, and I know for a fact that I would not be long in the same region as Falangist priests from Spain without a radical separation and deep-seated conflict. This would not help matters, and would tend to defeat the purpose of the foundation. On the other hand, of course, nothing good and nothing new is ever done without opposition, including opposition from other priests.

Ideally speaking, the kind of monastery I imagine would have not only a cultural mission but also a social one. Our aim would be to strive, to some extent, to lift up the Indians physically, morally, spiritually by providing a clinic, encouraging education, cooperatives, art-projects. The monastery would be perhaps the nucleus of a farming community of Indians. What I am saying now, of course, is more a project than a definite plan. The elements I have just enumerated would not fit in with any idea my Superiors might have, and would be outside the scope of a conventional foundation of our Order. Therefore I probably could not get permission to make it. I am just telling you what I would *like* to do.

Another difficulty to be expected would be opposition from orthodox Communist groups. Lenin said that the worst kind of socialist is a Christian socialist—and he was right in the sense that we are the kind who can do most (ideally speaking) to give people real happiness and therefore to make them more impervious to the appeals of materialism.

The greatest difficulty of such a foundation would, in short, be the greatest difficulty that someone like myself must face everywhere in any case. It is the inevitable difficulty of one who refuses to accept passively a solution proposed by a reactionary group on the one hand or a totalitarian group on the other. It is the great spiritual and physical hardship of going forward without the support of a powerful or influential group, of isolating oneself from those whose thinking is done for them by party lines or authoritarian decrees, and honestly striving to think in depth and clarity for oneself, under the eyes of God—a life of obedience to the truth which is hard to see and which is not seen by one who does not seek it himself with all the strength of his spiritual and physical being.

Actually, there is no immediate likelihood of my attempting such a project as the one I have described. My Superiors are cold to it, if not actively opposed. As we stand now, they would not permit me to do it or offer me any help. If they made a foundation in South America it would be the kind of thing I would not like to be associated with—a big, mechanized, efficient North American hacienda, very productive, in contact with the established wealthy classes and the higher clergy and out of contact with the Indians. Under such conditions it would be utterly impossible to have the kind of contact which I desire with the people like yourself to whom I believe I must address myself. I could not face you without shame. Hence in practice my own idea is still little more than a dream, and it is not likely that I will be able to do anything about it. Yet one never knows. Things can suddenly change. And because my idea is, I believe, a really good one, I feel I ought to keep thinking of it and examining its possibilities.

I certainly do not think I yet have the strength to face the struggle that would be necessary to carry out my idea under the conditions that exist in Ecuador. In actual fact, to do what I intend to do, I would probably have to live practically on the level of the Indians myself. To try that in a strange country with a climate and conditions which I have never known would be to invite failure, even apart from all the other difficulties.

At present I have my hands full simply thinking my way into the clarity of an unconventional position and standing by it, resisting the powerful appeals of the massive groups and their authoritarian philosophies, and their sinister claims to be right because they are powerful and massive. Yet I know in the depths of my being that this is what we have to resist with every fiber and every nerve and every breath that is in us. The massive, powerful groups are *not* right. Even the Church is right only insofar as she preserves, behind the façade of power and authority, the humility and poverty of Christ: and this humility and poverty often have very little to do with the façade. Nothing at all. And those who cling to the Church because of her façade sometimes have nothing of her true inner reality.

It follows as a most bitter consequence of this that one must ever run the risk of being thought wrong, of being thought evil and misguided, not only by the powerful community "church" but even of being thought a bad Christian and a rebel by other Christians. I do not say by the Church, because I have no intention of getting myself officially condemned. But I must certainly expect to be attacked and vilified by theologians and by certain of the clergy—as Maritain, for example, has been attacked by the Falangists in unanimous chorus.

This being the case, if I were to arrive in Ecuador with an ill-considered project, I might as you suggest only add to the unhappiness of a country torn by too many conflicts already. This I would certainly not want to do. And I do not intend to do it. But spiritually, yes, I already live among you, and your conflicts are in my own heart. Meanwhile, I have very much to learn and I am only beginning to realize how much.

May your statue of the Virgin and Child be to me a reminder always to seek that truth which is hidden among the poor of this earth and is inaccessible to the mighty. And may it be a reminder to hope in the future of man, when Christ shall rise from among these poor and build a new world.

To Father Kilian McDonnell

January 26, 1959

At long last the permission to use these articles has come through. All our routine censorship is routed through Rome, or rather through the Abbot General, who is always on the move; one never knows where to find him. In addition he has lately been ill. Hence the inordinate delay.

So here are two widow's mites, one of them longish. I mean the one on the "Way of Perfection" which I have divided into two parts, provisionally, as I am sure you will want to run it serially rather than in one issue. Fr. Godfrey [Diekmann, editor of *Worship*] says he likes to break things up into paragraphs with subtitles. The "Way of Perfection" is more or less like that now. You can do more to it if you like.

Please tell Fr. Godfrey that everything is all right for the Easter articles too, they have been censored and passed.

When these are printed may I please have a dozen copies? And would *Worship* send me a dozen also? I can always use them to send to friends in foreign parts and what not—it is a help to be able to give something to people who send us books or other things. I would appreciate it.

Perhaps later on in the year I might be able to write two more articles for *Sponsa Regis* but I do not promise anything as I can never tell what may be coming over the horizon. In this I am no different from anyone else, except that what comes over the horizon is usually enough to keep me quite busy.

I tried to persuade Father Abbot to get Fr. Paschal or someone from Collegeville down to give our retreat in 1960. I hope something comes of it. This year we are awaiting the usual Redemptorist or Jesuit (it is always a secret), and will be on retreat the second week of February, so please pray for us . . .

To Dom Gabriel Sortais

January 26, 1959

I have received your permission to publish various articles and also your letter on the subject of the seventh article about Pasternak. I am quite willing to accede to your desires on this matter and I am giving up the project of publishing this article which does not meet with your approval. As a matter of fact, I have several times asked myself if I should publish this article. I was hesitant about doing so. Your letter has solved the problem. It no longer exists. I am grateful to you.

At the same time it seems that I must address myself to a misunderstanding that I find in your kind letter—a misunderstanding that seems to call for some explanations. These I want to make with simplicity, without any desire to excuse myself or to put myself in a more favorable light in your eyes, but simply to do (and I may be wrong in this) what I believe is my duty to the truth.

You have judged my article on Pasternak not after your own personal reading of it nor after a reading done by someone who was acquainted with the subject; instead you follow the opinion of someone who does not know what it is about. No doubt, if the article is judged from a superficial point of view, it may seem amusingly odd for a "monk" to be writing about a "novel." But in judging a moral action, we must not forget the circumstances.

Why did I get interested in Pasternak? Out of sheer curiosity? This is what you seem to believe. On the contrary, it seems to me that there is in Pasternak an element that is deeply spiritual and deeply religious. This is no illusion, everyone acknowledges it. Besides, he has written some religious poems which are among the greatest, the most profound, and the most Christian of the century. Good enough.

While nearly everyone believed that Pasternak's revolt was political or literary, the stance that I chose to take in my article was that his revolt was a-political, anti-political and in truth spiritual. Not only spiritual but Christian. In taking such a position I never for an instant had the feeling that I was betraying my Christian or my contemplative vocation. On the contrary, I believe that my vocation as a contemplative writer *demands* this kind of testimony of me. (Elsewhere I have told you about my uncertainties in this regard.)

It seemed to me, in effect, that to understand Pasternak's witness as only a political or literary reaction was totally to distort the work of this great man. At the same time one has to prove this. And this is something that I have not done adequately, since this would require a more in-depth study of his work, of his symbolism. This, as I say, I have not done, though I wanted to do it. But clearly it is a task that is beyond the capabilities of a Cistercian. I do not think any more about it.

It does seem to me, I must add, that the voice of a monk might well be the one necessary to point out the religious significance of Pasternak's works. It may be that I am wrong. I am quite willing to accept that. But at any rate I assure you that, in writing about the Christ of Pasternak, I found myself face to face with the Christ whom you accuse me of not loving. Of course love is not the same with everyone. *Alius sic, alius vero sic* [Some in one way, others in another]. And it is very true that Pasternak's novel is not a treatise on ascetical, dogmatic or moral theology.

But it may be that you think that I do not read anything else? Is this possible? It has been a long time since I read this book and a long time since I wrote this article. As a matter of fact, I put this on paper just after the letter to Surkov—at the time when you seemed to be more or less willing to deal with this matter.

The article was sent to the censors in November. It took them three months to read it; hence it is hardly fair to say that, while the whole world had forgotten Pasternak, a Cistercian monk was still thinking about him. Moreover, if it were true that I was in such a situation, I would be very proud of it. This man needs someone to think of him, especially in prayer. I would never want to be one of those who easily forgot him.

Most Reverend Father, I know that you are not well and I do not want to keep boring you with the same things. But I would at least like to give proof of my good will and honesty. I make no pretense, alas, of being a holy monk or a great contemplative. But I assure you that I try to be faithful to the vocation which seems to be mine and will continue to do so with God's help. If mine is not in every way a traditional type of vocation, there is nothing I can do about it.

Yet it is impossible for me not to feel, interiorly, the importance of a great manifestation of the Christian spirit in the climate of Soviet Russia; and it is impossible for me to believe that my contemplative vocation demands of me a complete indifference toward the soul and work of a Pasternak who appears to me to be just as great as a Claudel, but of course not quite so Christian and *Catholic*.

If you disagree, then I am quite willing to keep my inner convictions to myself and not express them to others. In any case I do not plan to write any other articles about Pasternak or other similar subjects, unless I receive from you a different expression of your point of view. In short, I do not plan to write very much. Just a few little liturgical and spiritual essays growing out of my lectures in the novitiate.

In conclusion, Most Reverend Father, I hope that I did not give you the wrong impression when I said I was in the process of losing my vocation. On the contrary, it was back in 1955, when I was thinking only about my own spiritual life and especially about my personal aspirations toward prayer, that I was in danger of leaving the Cistercian Order . . .

March 2, 1959

May I be allowed to ask you to reconsider, for the good of souls, for the good of the Church and for the glory of God, an earlier decision that you made? It concerns something very important, very serious, of grave import for justice, freedom, truth and the Kingdom of God.

Boris Pasternak, who has written as a Christian and who has given a witness that is both Christian and spiritual in his writings, has just disappeared. I am certain that his end is not far off. He might even be dead at this very moment. If he has died, he is truly, at least in the broad sense of the term, a martyr. But not everyone would be able to interpret the spiritual and Christian meaning of his witness, especially given the fact that political interpretations would obscure the truth that he stood for.

Since last fall, though I was not able to follow this case in magazines and newspapers (to which obviously I do not have access), I have nonetheless received information of the highest authority through Pasternak's publisher (who is a friend of mine as well as of Pasternak, and who has close ties with a great many people who have seen Pasternak and spoken with him in Russia since he was given the Nobel Prize, and up to the time of his disappearance "on vacation" where he could have had contact with strangers). Hence I have had access to everything that is known, without having to deal with newspapers, etc.

I leave the judgment to you, but it seems to me that I have a very serious duty to complete my article on Pasternak and to put the whole truth on paper. And to publish it. It is a question of giving a Christian explanation of Pasternak's witness which is both heroic and Christian. This affair has moved the hearts of everyone, but most profoundly it has touched those who are writers and intellectuals. It is about an event that has happened in the very midst of the spiritual life of our time. To dissociate myself from involvement with this action which is so extraordinary would be for me a betrayal: a betrayal of my particular vocation, a betrayal of Jesus Christ. At least this is the way I feel.

So as not to involve the Order in this event, I would be quite content to be allowed to publish an article under a pen name. Of course this would deprive the article of a good deal of its power as a Christian witness on Pasternak's behalf. But if you are unwilling to let me publish this article under my own name (and I beg you to let me do so), then at least permit me to publish it *incognito*. The secret could be very easily kept, since no one would expect such a document from a Trappist. But at the same time, if I published it under my own name, people would hardly be shocked, because it is more or less known that I am a friend of Pasternak.

You know that I submit myself entirely to holy Obedience. I implore you to listen to me, Most Reverend Father; but if you believe that this project is out of the question, I submit myself to your judgment and God will not regard me as a traitor to my conscience. But I beg you on my knees at least to let me publish this report under a pen name . . .

To Father Mark Weidner, O.C.S.O.

Father Mark at this time was Novice Master at Our Lady of Guadalupe, the Cistercian abbey in Oregon.

April 15, 1959

Please forgive me for taking so long to reply to your letter. It got buried under the pile, and I have only just got to it.

First I am sending you a reading list which we follow loosely (very loosely) in the novitiate. We revise it every year and I haven't got around to the 1959 edition yet. When I do I will include some books by Conrad Pepler.

For the Novice Master—well, it goes without saying that Bouyer's *Meaning of the Monastic Life* is fundamental. One doesn't have to agree perfectly with absolutely everything he says. Dom Jean Leclercq on St. Bernard (in French) is also good, and Gilson's *Mystical Theology of St. Bernard* is a must. Also I would say Dom Cuthbert Butler's *Western Mysticism* is not bad but controversial. You should know it. I assume you are familiar with the mimeographed material that comes from the Maison Généralice and from Chimay and places like that. The notes put out by Fr. Francis Mayhieu when Novice Master at Chimay are very good.

Here are authors I recommend in a general way: Guardini always fine. Bouyer, Danielou, De Lubac (some books), Josef Pieper (Thomist), Von Balthasar (controversial but generally very good).

I especially recommend the series of conferences on Obedience, Poverty, Chastity, Common Life and other "problems of the religious life" originally put out by the French Dominicans and published here at Newman. They are essential, and you probably know all about them. Then, too, the Etudes Carmélitaines are very good. Some have been done in English (Love and Violence, Conflict and Light); Sheed and Ward does these.

If you have not read Cassian thoroughly you should. Also the *Verba Seniorum* (Desert Fathers). I am bringing out a translation of this latter (in part) and there is a new book of selections from the Desert Fathers being read in our refectory (by whom?). It is very good.

I suggest that for background you be somewhat acquainted with such odd and disparate subjects as Gandhi (very important, I think), Dorothy Day, psychoanalysis (Karen Horney is a useful author for us), liturgical art, and the spirituality of the Oriental Church (Fedotov's *Treasury of Russian Spirituality* is fine).

I pass over as obvious the great theological writers who are right up our alley, like Scheeben and Vonier. And of course top priority belongs to our own [Cistercian] Fathers. Guerric is one of the easiest to break into in Latin. And perhaps the most representative. You know of course that a publisher called Mobray in England is bringing out brochures of translations of our Fathers and other medieval texts.

Now I have to spring over to see our Father Immediate—so I close in haste better late than never . . .

To Dom Gabriel Sortais

May 22, 1959

I talked yesterday with Dom James who advised me to write you this letter about a project which interests him a lot and in which I have a little share, too. There is question of an admirable collection of photographs of the monastery by Mr. Shirley Burden, a very distinguished artist (in this photographic genre), a great friend of the monastery, and a highly respected personality here in the U.S.A. You are going to see the collection; I need not insist on its very obvious qualities.

Mr. Burden wants to publish these photographs in New York by a publishing house, and wants to start negotiations, but he cannot go ahead without knowing if this project can be approved by the Order. Of course, not being a member of the Order, he need not submit to censorship like a religious. But since his topic is photographs of a monastery and some monks, it is obvious that he must think of possible objections on the part of our Most Reverend Father General! Dom James is altogether pleased with the book, and so am I. But one finds in it several pictures which clearly show *the faces* of certain monks and laybrothers. The difficulty is this: without these faces, the book of photos will completely lack sense for a publisher. With the faces, it is a highly impressive document. The faces one finds in it are truly moving—and there are not many, at the same time.

This is my personal opinion: one might publish this book without mention of the name of the monastery. It is quite simply a Cistercian monastery (rather Trappist, since Dom James always insists that Gethsemani is Trappist first of all—and the word Cistercian has not caught on in America). Of course those who know Gethsemani will have no difficulty in recognizing it. There is really no question of publicity for the house or for those who will appear in the book. It seems to me that to allow these images will be a great good for the believers and for the Order. The book is very true, very sincere, and in very good taste.

Without the faces—the book cannot be published. It would be a great pity: it would really be regrettable. So I join Dom James, pleading for this good Mr. Burden and for his work. I hope you will be kind enough to allow us this exception.

For my part I have written a preface of three pages, which will naturally have to go through the censorship. I suppose Dom James has taken the necessary steps—or else we can send this preface to the two censors who examine in the usual way the "short articles."

To Dom Jean Leclercq

May 22, 1959

Some time ago questions were asked about the French translation of *Thoughts in Solitude,* [entitled] *Les Chemins de la Joie.* You remember that you had this translated by a Benedictine nun and it was to have been published by Les Editions d'histoire et d'art. I remember that I myself complicated matters somewhat when I hesitated about the publication of this book in English or in French. The French ms. was sent to me and I returned it eventually with the consent to its publication.

Nothing more has ever been heard of it. Recently there was a question of offering to some other publisher the French rights for this book. I heard this from my agent, and told them to hold off until we could find out something definite about your translation. Will you please let me know where matters stand? If your publisher does not want this translation you have, perhaps it could go to some other publisher. Let me know please.

Most of the trouble comes from the fact that I have been out of contact with you for so long. It is a pleasure to greet you again, and to ask your prayers. I heard Dom Jacques Winandy is in Martinique. I hope he will pray for me too. I naturally keep a certain desire for solitude in my heart and cannot help but hope that some day it may be realized. But I no longer have any thought or desire of transferring to another Order. I believe that to move from one institution to another is simply futile. I do not believe that there is any institutional solution for me. I can hope however that perhaps I might gain permission to live alone, in the shadow of this monastery, if my Superiors will ever permit it. I do not think that there is any other fully satisfactory way for me to face this, but to seek to live my own life with God. I am not pushing this however, simply praying, hoping and waiting. I hope you will pray for me also . . .

To Father Kilian McDonnell

August 22, 1959

After a little delay I am sending you the new version of the "Spiritual Direction" material. It has been considerably lengthened and I think it ought to make a good pamphlet. Perhaps that is something more ambitious than you at first intended—it will not just be a reprint pure and simple.

At the same time, however, I felt that additions and clarifications were needed.

You have full permission to use anything you like or can from the "Art and Worship" material for *Sponsa Regis*. No one else is using any, and *Jubilee* is the only one who has printed any of it before. *Sun* never rose, so everything is clear. I agree with you that Sisters hold a key position in this whole battle for sacred art, and I take very seriously any idea that will help them to appreciate and promote good taste and religious quality in art. Often they are a bit passive, though, and think that once they are supposed to be interested in sacred art, they have to promote everything that looks modern, with no regard to its intrinsic merit. Would you want me to write a few paragraphs of earnest exhortation to Sisters, to precede any material of mine on art you may be using? Suggestions as to how to proceed would be appreciated. I do know that what I try to do in the novitiate to make people understand sacred art usually runs up a stone wall in the minds of those who were considered very good boys by the Sisters and were therefore given special attention. I am much happier with the ones the Sisters thought were naughty; they are usually my best subjects. They have open minds and are willing to take in something unconventional.

I do think the whole issue of sacred art has been terribly confused by the stupid fashion for radiator-cap-modern-pious art in which all that one asks is that the Blessed Virgin look like a Bermuda-rigged sailboat taking into the bay. Which reminds me that I still envy you your vacation in the Bahamas, and hope you are feeling better. Everything you say about your new Church sounds exciting. I look forward to the day when I might possibly be able to admire it, finished, and face to face . . .

October 3, 1959

Here we are with the note for nuns on sacred art. It turned into a little article on its own. I have inserted a few sentences in my own impossible handwriting but I hope that will not drive the printer out of his mind. You will check and see how the copy looks. I hope it will be sufficiently clear. I also added the last paragraph in single space rather than go over the page for just one line or two. So I hope it will be adequate.

Naturally, any material that you can use from the expanded "Spiritual Direction" article can go into *Sponsa Regis*. If I remember correctly there was something at the beginning that would make a short article in itself.

I have a few poems of Robert Lax here, and I think you would like some of them. I am presuming his permission to send you one or two, and there are more. He can be reached at *Jubilee*. I think it would be a good idea to have something of the sort in *Sponsa* and liven up the magazine. Really it seems to me there is no reason why *Sponsa Regis* could not be a very rich and vital little magazine, with a few things like this. I'll try to think up some other ideas, too.

One thing that would certainly be easy, and I think there is a crying need for it, would be just to print a page or two, in each issue, of really good spiritual texts, from the Fathers, from the saints, etc. I will try to suggest some as I go along, if I get time. Also unusual liturgical texts from other rites. Your scholastics would be able to dig up things like that all over the place . . .

By the way I hope this sacred art piece isn't too rabid for your readers. I don't know how conventional they are, but most of them must be pretty much that way. I hope they aren't shocked. Of course in the printed word the approach is indirect. It will take a few minutes for them to realize what I am defending and what I am attacking. They won't have it jump right out at them like a Kacmarcik Madonna . . .

Wasn't it sad to hear that [Dr.] Gregory Zilboorg was dead? I just learned it yesterday. A great and good man, and may God grant him rest and eternal life . . .

To Dom Jean Leclercq

November 19, 1959

Here I am again and it is the same subject of *Les Chemins de la Joie*. My New York agent in Paris is negotiating *another* translation. I have not written to Wittman, but he has evidently set aside the one made by your nun in Landes, not wanting to publish it. But I like this translation very well and I will help your Sister. I think that the simplest thing will be for you to request the translation from Wittman, and have it published where you like. Besides, it is now the job of you people. But if Hoffman succeeds in getting his business done, all the work will have been useless. On my part, I shall go back to Father Abbot so that he shall not sign any contract with any other publisher chosen by Hoffman. He is a very opinionated fellow. It is understood, is it not, that you (the Abbey of Clervaux) have the *rights* of the French language for this translation at present. I will take the normal author's rights (10%) for us, and it is up to you to fix things up with the lady translator. But it is quite certain that if Hoffman succeeds with his ploy, then there is nothing left.

There you are. I do not know if it is as simple as all that. I am not a "business man," fortunately.

Now I shall tell you, in confidence, something more interesting and more monastic. I have asked the Congregation of Religious for an exclaustration so as to go to Mexico, and become a hermit near the Benedictine monastery of Cuernavaca. Dom Gregorio will take me on and encourages me very much. This is really what I have been looking for for a long time. I have good hopes of succeeding with the Congregation, but the Superiors are dead set against this move. Dom James is at present in Rome where the Abbot General has summoned him. But though knowing that this must have something to do with my case, I do not know exactly what may happen. There must be some other matter there, because I do not believe that they have made Father Abbot come to Rome merely in order to block my indult. At present there are some questions which have arisen respecting another monk from here, who has the same problem as I, but with certain canonical complications which are perhaps the fault of the Superiors . . . But in spite of that, I still have hope that at the same time they will let me go to make the experiment. I am very happy and I think I shall succeed well with the grace of God. Truly, I am who I am and I always have the writer's temperament, but I am not going down there to write, nor to make myself known, but on the contrary to disappear, to find solitude, obscurity, poverty. To withdraw *above all* from the collective falsity and injustice of the U.S. which implicate so much the church of this country and our monastery.

I tell you this (and I beg of you not to talk about it) in order to ask your prayers, and also, if you should happen to be in Rome these days, to take my side somewhat with Dom Gabriel, who respects you very much. (To him, yes, you may speak of this.) I even reckon a little on the Procurator of the Benedictines—but this is up to Dom Gabriel, I think. In a word, if you can do anything for me, I beg of you in your charity to do so.

In any case, if the matter fails this time, I will continue. I do not think this is the time to let go whatever it may be. My Benedictine vocation is, I am sure, a solitary vocation, at least relatively, and primitive. It may be that my health cannot withstand the intestinal illnesses in the tropics; in that case I shall recommence the attempt elsewhere, perhaps in Europe or in the regions of the U.S. where there are Indians. If you write a word to me on these matters, I beg of you to address it to me *sub secreto*—conscience matter . . .

II.

The Middle Formative Years
1960-1964

*The world has changed much since my entry into the
monastery. It is no longer the society which I lately knew,
the world of my youth, of my parents. I think of myself
as an exile two times, three times over. The way toward
the Homeland becomes more and more obscure. As I
look back over the stages which were once more clear,
I see that we are all on the right road, and though it be
night, it is a saving one.*

THOMAS MERTON
IN A LETTER TO
PIERRE VAN DER MEER,
JULY 28, 1961

To Father Kilian McDonnell

January 13, 1960

The latest *Sponsa Regis* has arrived and I have just read it from cover to cover. I think it is really fine, and I like every word of it, not excluding the article on p. 133. I especially liked the Arts in the Juniorate and hope you will tell Sister so; I think it is excellent. Bishop Dwyer was most encouraging and stimulating; I hope I can get it read here in refectory. Fingers crossed on that one. I enjoyed yours very much too, and Fr. Cloud, in fact everything. I hope the magazine will reach a lot of people that need to be reached and will do a lot of good, will liberate, open up souls, open eyes. *Illuminare Jerusalem!* [Be enlightened, Jerusalem!] Let this be part of our contribution to the Epiphany of 1960.

I hope you haven't lost courage in regard to Lax's poetry—it is really good, simple stuff and worth a try; I think it is deeply spiritual, in all its transparent simplicity. Too simple at first sight. I hope you will use it.

The proofs have come. I have still to receive any remarks from the censors of the Order and hope to heaven that they won't suppress huge chunks of it. Pray for me and for the book. Your placing of the insert from Baker is ideal. Do you mind waiting a little before I return the proofs?

Thank you for Dom Cyprian Vagaggini's book which I am slowly reading with very great satisfaction. It is solid and deep and, again, liberating. *Veritas liberabit vos* [The Truth will make you free].

About *The Merton Reader*, all things are in complete confusion. I suspect that my new agent is lost in the woods completely and I helped matters by believing him too readily when he blandly announced that *you* had been selected by Harcourt, Brace as editor of the project . . . But what I have done is this: I have written and told them that I think there is no hope whatever of the book coming out if it is done by Harcourt,

Brace . . . Have you heard anything about it? Probably not. You would certainly be a very good and acceptable editor and I would welcome such a project on those terms . . . Let's hope that this tangle gets straightened out . . . [Thomas McDonnell of Boston was the editor of *The Merton Reader*, which was eventually published by Harcourt, Brace.]

January 29, 1960

The censor has finally come through. As I rather anticipated, there were a lot of picayune corrections, where "almost" has to be substituted for "not quite." So I have made almost, or not quite, all the corrections he wanted. Some of them were just too trivial to involve breaking up the type and resetting it. I am very sorry. Of course these censors give no thought at all to the labor and expense that may be involved by the corrections they suggest in their ivory towers three months after they ought to have sent in the *nihil obstat*.

I suppose each one of us thinks he is the only religious who has trouble with censors. Alas, we *all* do. Lately I have had a few good experiences in this matter. I had done a book on the Desert Fathers, some translations from the *Verba Seniorum*, and D. T. Suzuki the Zen man had come in on it with an essay comparing the Desert Fathers to the Zen masters, in a way that showed a rather good grasp of some basic patristic ideas. But this has been thrown out of the book by the censors, on the ground that all my readers would instantly become Buddhists. This shows what wonderful confidence we have in our faith, doesn't it? That is how much we trust the power of the Gospel message. I hope you will remember this problem in your prayers; I want to be able to use this little bit of East-West dialogue somewhere and somehow, if I can. It is interesting and seems to me to be a step in a new and right direction . . .

Father Barnabas Mary Ahern will be giving us some Scripture conferences here this year, since he is stationed at Louisville. I hope they will be good ones, and think they will.

I am glad Frank [Kacmarcik] is keeping his head above water and defending the cause of sacred art step by step. The other day Bob Rambusch sent us a small ikon, a Hodigitria, he had acquired in Salonika, I believe. Or perhaps even on Athos, though I am not sure. Today we re-blessed it and put it up over the altar of the Blessed Mother in the novitiate chapel. It is very simple and charming, chipped a bit here and there. Bob had it well cleaned in New York. I am very happy with it . . .

To Sister L.

A nun with an active religious congregation working in the Orient wrote Merton about the possibility of her transferring to the Trappistines.

March 31, 1960

It seems to me that probably some of my letters have not reached you. I sent the only available copy of the book about Mother Berchmans, and this also perhaps did not reach you . . . I believe you will never get into a Trappistine convent in Europe or America, due to the fact that the distance is so great and the risks are so considerable that no one will take the chance of accepting you merely through letters. If you still want to be a contemplative nun and can find admission to some convent of another Order there in the Orient, I suggest you try to do so. But I seriously doubt whether it is practical to go on hoping to become a Trappistine. Such great obstacles seem to show, in actual fact, that this is not God's will for you . . . You must also be practical and not let your hopes become a vain escape from the actual responsibilities of the life where you find yourself at the moment. I would therefore accept the difficulties of your present situation as God's will, make a heroic gift of yourself, and accept all that He wants. If then He wants something else for you, He will certainly know how to bring it about. Do not be discouraged. He loves you very much. If you were the only person in the world, and needed Him to do so, He would descend to earth again and die for you. How then can you fear that He will abandon you? Trust in Him and repay His love with your whole heart . . .

To Dom Gabriel Sortais

April 21, 1960

Enclosed is the letter I have just received from Jacques Maritain. It is a reply to the one I sent you a copy of a few weeks ago. In principle he favors the dialogue in the form of a book; you can read his reasons. As for me, I dread the work involved and all the bother one will have to put up with from the censors, but I must confess that I think that the best solution would be to publish a book that would include some short essays by me, Suzuki, Erich Fromm (well-known psychoanalyst and writer), Paul Tillich (a Protestant theologian) and perhaps Mircea Eliade. But to be on the safe side and fully in accord with the Rule, I think it would be necessary to have not only my preface, as [Maritain] suggests, but also a final chapter by Father Danielou who is a specialist in these matters.

This, therefore, is the solution I propose, Most Reverend Father. If this is agreeable to you, I shall set to work on it. Otherwise they would have my essay published along with the one by Suzuki in a review or an anthology. My response to that is quite adequate, I think.

After you have read Jacques Maritain's letter, I would appreciate your returning it, as I have no other copy.

As I have told you, I have no great desire to do this work, difficult and delicate as it is, but if you give me permission, I think it is the best thing to do in the situation. But in that case I beg you to let me know your desires about the censorship. I would suggest, in addition, an unofficial censor, either Father Danielou or some other French theologian equally competent, whose point of view might represent a better perspective than our American censors—whom I do not desire to replace. Please don't get me wrong! Forgive me if this suggestion is not to your liking. I make it in all simplicity.

We now have in the offing two books which include various articles which have been approved by various censors. I think that the names of all the censors should be listed at the beginning of the book, with your *imprimi potest* last. By the way, in order to publish the book [*The Behavior of Titans*], we are waiting for the approval of two pieces, "Prometheus" and "Confessions of Crimes against the State" (a short satire on communism). To publish the other book we await approval of "Notes for a Philosophy of Solitude," "The Primitive Carmelite Ideal," and "A Renaissance Hermit." This second book is called *Disputed Questions* and I can assure you that after my experience with these articles, the title is indeed the right one. When I receive these approvals, I shall use their dates in the publication of the book. Is that correct?

I know that you are very busy, Most Reverend Father, and I regret bothering you with these matters, but I am in a rather difficult position, with all these works piling up one on top of the other because of the delays. You are the only one who can help me out with these matters. I thank you in anticipation with deep filial affection, in our Lord.

April 29, 1960

Since the beginning of the regular visit, which Dom Colomban closed last night, I have hardly had a moment to write you. But you know, of course, that I fully and unhesitatingly accept your good decision on Suzuki's article—a decision taken with the prudent advice of Father Paul Philippe. So this is the solution, and we are going to try to present the two articles in a magazine, or better in a collection of the type of an annual anthology of poems and articles, which my publisher is putting out.

The regular visit was quite peaceful; we are very fond of Dom Colomban, who is very discreet and paternal. He incites us to become more and more silent and contemplative, and urges us to a very spiritual practice of this Cistercian silence, while we listen to the Word of God in our hearts. He also narrated to us your visit to the Holy Father—a consolation for the whole Order. The Holy Father has had sent to me, too, very poor monk that I am, a paternal message to tell me that he approved of a few discreet meetings in the form of colloquia or of informal retreats with some distinguished guests who come here from time to time, and with professors of Protestant theology, writers, etc. These are discreet, rare contacts, but which seem to help these souls to understand the Church, or else if they are Catholic, to deepen their love of God and their Christian faith. I assure you that I am not launching into a new "career" but I still keep the taste and the practice of solitude. But these restricted contacts seem to do good and seem to help me a little, too. Naturally, it is only with Dom James' permission that I make these contacts, and according to his will.

I try to put into practice, for the novices, the program that the *ratio studiorum* suggests to us. I think we are fairly well established here to be able to give the full and integral course which they advise for the novitiate at least. Dom James will send all the details to Rome, so I will not waste time describing them here.

When I say above that I accept the decision about Suzuki, that is not the whole of it: I want to make myself quite clear, I *prefer* your decision which saves me a lot of work and above all a heavier exchange of letters . . .

May 21, 1960

Only today has Dom James, back from his regular visits, handed me your observations on the censorship of the "Notes for a Philosophy of Solitude." If I had known what you thought about it in all earnestness I would never have written you a letter like that of the other day, which must have appeared to you altogether carefree, ironical even, maybe even rebellious. I have too much pain in writing you now to want to make useless explanations. What I tell you is a fully serious admission, which comes from the bottom of the heart with sincerity.

I have the impression of what it must feel like for a sick person who thinks he simply has a cold to discover suddenly that he has tuberculosis. I don't have the temptation to ask myself if the physician is mistaken. The diagnosis is too serious. The case is urgent.

I am going first to make scrupulously all the corrections that the censor asks of me. I am going to change what displeases you in the article on Mount Athos, without it having been asked of me. I change this not simply because you don't like it, but because I am wrong in speaking in this way. I am wrong in speaking without prudence, and in giving such painful impressions. I spoke like a fool: I am a fool, I am an idiot.

I am going to change not only the passages pointed out in the article on solitude, but *all* that might give an impression of scurrility, levity, lack of respect for the Church and for the Superiors. I was wrong in thinking that it sufficed to obey promptly when asked to do so, and in not thinking more seriously of the effect of my interior attitudes. I do not ask you to think that I am not malicious. You are a Father, so you must know it. For my part, I must accept the responsibility for my imprudent writings. I confess that I attach too much importance to my subjective sentiment of having good will. Good will does not suffice. I thank you for pointing out to me this serious fault. I ask you to forget the other letter, and to forgive me in God's name.

I am not going to begin again to write on the subject of solitude. It is finished. I have nothing to say. I will try to be a good monk and to live as a solitary the best I can, according to the will of my Superiors. I have always tried to do what my Superiors wanted. I thought I accepted their will last year. And I accept it now. I am not saying this to please you; I am saying this before God, because it is the truth, and I know that you like the truth. I have never tried to flatter my Superiors; I speak to them straightforwardly, as I think. And I accept what is answered to me. Perhaps it is somewhat in the American way that I do that: then, pardon me. You are also a Father; you will understand.

I am going to pay attention to this error you point out to me; I am going to study with care all the aspects of the question. I am going to do all that is possible to correct myself. I beg you to help me with your prayers. I am going to write fewer articles. I will avoid seeking written dialogues with non-Catholics, except for the particular persons whom I can help, in private, to find the faith.

P.S. As I reread the censor's remarks and your good letter, I must tell you all the same that the censor interprets my words in a sense that I certainly did not intend, though I am responsible because of lack of care in my expressions. I must tell you, not to excuse myself, but to testify to my faith in the Holy Church, that I did not want at all to say and I have never thought that a Christian should prefer the interior voice to the voice of obedience!!! What is said on page 29 is not "a direct attack against the Superiors." I don't speak of Superiors in the context *at all*. It is the Father Censor who makes them enter it. But above all on page 28 he has completely *overturned the meaning* of what I meant. I precisely said that the solitary was tormented by agonizing isolation in which he could not have *the security of obedience* to a Superior!!

That is what I said, and meant to say. Of course, since the Father Censor took it in a dangerous sense, I am responsible; I should have been cautious.

I confess that I feel very wounded by this interpretation and by your doubly severe judgment. It is my fault, really, but the wound remains.

In the hands of this Father there are still other manuscripts that he might turn and interpret in this way. I shall change them. I am wrong! But above all do not think that I disobey once again!

Also in the book *The New Man*, written in 1955 and passing only today through the censorship, one will want to change certain expressions one will find somewhat risky maybe. Do not worry! I'll do whatever possible to avoid all that may shock . . .

To Father Kilian McDonnell

May 31, 1960

We are now typing out the ms. of "Liturgy and Spiritual Personalism" and I hope to get it off to you, or rather Fr. Godfrey, today or tomorrow. I hope that will be in good time. Unfortunately there are still the censors. I will try to prod them a little, and see that they get the thing cleared by the end of June. They have been more terrible than ever this year, holding things up for ages and then coming through with fabulously pic-ayune and absurd demands, some of which have got the Abbot General up in the air—for he gets in on these things too. Our censorship is explicitly designed to discourage writers and writing. I mean that literally.

What I want to write about now is the book *Spiritual Direction and Meditation*. I know it is all set up, and I wonder if you could make sure that it is not delayed any longer. The reason for this is that I have two other books coming out this year and it is to the advantage of all concerned if they can be properly spaced. The sooner the *Spiritual Direction* book appears, the better it will be for everyone. Farrar, Straus have a full-length book [*Disputed Questions*] in galleys now, and this will probably be out in the late summer, if all goes well. The more time you can put in between the appearance of the Liturgical Press book and this one, the more chance you have of selling yours . . .

Why don't you and one or two Benedictines come down here for a little visit, retreat, rest and so on? I have permission to organize some small, "special" retreats cum discussion and informal consideration of things that are important to us and to the Church. A couple of groups of Protestant theology professors, some professors from Bellarmine College, some Negro artists, maybe some beatnik writers—who knows? I think it would be very appropriate if some Benedictine editors, writers, or just Benedictines period, came down. The whole idea is to keep these things very informal, not under any circumstances to treat the affair as a move-ment, and rather to regard it just as a personal visit. Groups of five to ten people, for three or four days, and not too many in the course of the year. So far it has been going nicely. So do please consider yourself invited and bring anyone else who is interested—Benedictines first . . .

To Mother Angela Collins, O.C.D.

Mother Angela Collins had been Prioress at the Louisville Carmel until shortly before this letter was written. Mother Peter of the Holy Face replaced her as Prioress in Louisville. Later Mother Angela was to found a Carmel in Savannah, Georgia, as subsequent letters will reveal. Merton's correspondence with this dedicated Carmelite Prioress was mutually beneficial.

September 16, 1960

It is about time I wrote you a few lines to congratulate you on your new solitude and leisure. I hope you are enjoying them and that you will find yourself very close to God in everything. That is my prayer for you in any case. I came by Carmel the other day and had a few words with your new Mother Prioress [Mother Peter of the Holy Face], and I presume she said "hello" on my behalf.

The new book [*Disputed Questions*] I told you about is finally published and I am sending you a copy. It is for you primarily as I do not know to what extent it will interest the whole community. It has for example the articles on Pasternak of which I spoke to you. I do not know if this will appeal to others or even to you. But you will like the "Notes on Solitude." Perhaps that part will appeal to you most. You already know the section on Primitive Carmel. I hope the Friars of the Order won't be upset by it—some of them might. Who knows?

My desires for solitude continue. That is to be expected. Do keep me in your prayers. I don't know what may ever come of it. Work has not yet begun on the little retreat house on the hill, but at least the contractor has been to look at the site. If we get a lot of rain, the work will be held up as they will have a hard time driving through the field up the hill. However I do get what solitude I can.

I am realizing more and more that my big task is within myself. This is imperative. I am seeing what are the depths of my pride, and what an awful obstacle it is. In the old days I used to think about this problem in unrealistic terms: confusing pride with vanity. I know I still have vanity enough, but now for the first time I am beginning to see into the naked depths of pride. There is something one cannot explain in words: this tenacious attachment to self, and the virulence of it, which would make one stop at *nothing* in order to protect this inner root of self. And to see that I do in fact do all sorts of evil, properly camouflaged, in defense of this root of self. The problem is that it is all tied up with our clinging to life itself, which of course is a good thing. The desire to *be*. But the desire in us is not only to be, but to be our own idol, to be our own end. It sounds nice on paper but it is a bit sickening in reality. Do pray for me, and don't go and tell me I am humble, because that is not true except on a superficial, exterior level. Pray for me to be humble, and really humble. Not with the fake, inert sort of humility that excuses all kinds of hidden pride and prevents us from doing God's work. But with humility that is deep and afraid of nothing, of no truth, and which is completely abandoned to God's real will. How hard that actually is . . .

To Father Kilian McDonnell

September 19, 1960

Too bad you could not make it. However, it was just as well, as the other ones got sick or for some reason could not come just then. I find it is a bit complicated for us to try to get people together from different places. About the best I can manage, without a periscope, is to get a group from one place.

What I suggest now is this: I may or may not get a few people down for Thanksgiving, but whether I do or not, why don't you come? One thing I am beginning to realize is that better than planning groups is inviting individuals. I find that many prefer to come down just by themselves and have a quiet time and talk a little . . . Consider yourself invited down for Thanksgiving and bring someone else if you like. You may or may not run into a discussion of some sort . . .

I shall keep the Munster idea in my prayers, certainly. And I hope you will have a fruitful time in Ottawa. I keep you in my prayers, above all. About being a monk: have you run across the splendid biography of Staretz Silouan who died on Mt. Athos in 1938? Called *The Undistorted Image*, by Archimandrite Sophrony, Faith Press, London. I have written to Arch. Sophrony, also an Athonite. Silouan is tremendous. Who is editing *Sponsa Regis?* I might do something on Silouan for them, or perhaps again not, as it might turn the nuns' heads and I would get into a hassle with everybody. Which would not be the first time. I really had to sweat blood over the essay on solitude in my new book which, if you have not seen it, I will try to get to you . . .

To Mother Sylvia Marie, L.S.P.

Thomas Merton visited the convent of the Little Sisters of the Poor in Louisville in August, 1960, about which he wrote Mother Sylvia Marie, the Superior.

October 1, 1960

For a long time I have wanted to write this letter, thanking you for all the joy that was mine when I visited your convent last August. I have also wanted to put down on paper a few words that could be used, as the Little Sister suggested, in your publication. Father Abbot has granted permission for anything I say here to be used by you.

It is certainly a fundamental truth that all religious not only work to save their own souls and the souls of others, but in so doing they manifest something hidden in the mystery of God, some aspect of the inexhaustible truth of His mercy to men. Each time we come in contact with a religious community that is truly faithful to its mission, we are struck not only by the joy of its members and by the calm, fruitful and productive atmosphere, but over and above this we are somehow aware of a divine reality manifested in their midst, seen only by the eyes of faith.

We know that Our Heavenly Father has a very special concern for the poor and the abandoned, who are the apple of His eye. We know that He pays very special attention to the needs of those whom the world ought to care for, but whom the world tends to reject. Recently I had occasion to talk to a writer from India who said he was shocked by the way the old people in American society tended to be set aside and tacitly forgotten. I wished he could have visited your community in order to correct this impression.

And yet it is sadly true that in this country, which worships youth to the point of obsession, old age is not understood. There is a kind of foolish legend about old people, a legend in which the old are rendered acceptable because they retain some vestiges of youth, but for that reason and no other. (The foolish platitudes which praise the old for being "like kids" rather than for the dignity of their age.) It is certainly very fine for old people to be full of the vigor and verve of youth, but they should not have to cling to that *alone* as a way of being acceptable to the rest of the world. On the contrary, their age itself has a wonderful quality which makes them worthy of special respect and love. This is what the Little Sisters of the Poor are able to recognize and live for. What they see in the old people is not some vestige of natural "pep," but the light and the joy and the mystery of Christ, which gives them a far greater and more wonderful energy, in spite of the feebleness of their limbs. You have been able to see in the sick poor not just "specimens" of aging humanity but temples of God, persons of unutterable dignity who have travelled to the threshold of eternity and are waiting to be called into the joy of their Lord. These are in many respects the most interesting and exciting people on earth: for they are sitting right in front of a door that may open to them any moment. There is nothing else for them to be interested in. This is a truly marvelous condition. Would that the rest of us could live like that. But those who have the cult of youth and success and pleasure are prone to turn their eyes away from this beautiful mystery. They do not want to think of another world. The mystery which you serve is the mystery of charity and the mystery of heaven, and God loves you because you love His little ones.

It was a joy for me to meet the Sisters and to speak with all of you. I felt very much at home in your midst and I hope I will be able to drop in on you again. Would you be put out if sometime I just dropped in without warning and begged a dinner from you? I might not have much time to stay long, but I would like to do this one day. If you don't mind, perhaps I will.

I close with the assurance of my prayers, and I ask you and all the Sisters to remember me before the Lord. May Our Lady bring you all many graces and joys, and may our Merciful Lord bless all the dear old people with His love.

To Father Bruno Scott James

Bruno Scott James, an English priest and scholar, collaborated with Thomas Merton on a volume of the letters of St. Bernard of Clairvaux.

October 1, 1960

It was awfully good to get your letter, and Eugene Exman sent me your news to him about the trip through Sicily. I can imagine that at times you might feel a little depressed in the midst of all that. All what? As if the black desolation around Etna were somehow to be contrasted with some supposed idyllic peace somewhere else. All of us who are called to a serious way of life are called to face the blackness of ourselves and of our world. If we have to live the victory of the Risen Christ over death we have to pass through death. Or arise out of our own death. It means seeing death and hell in ourselves. I never imagined when I was a novice and when "His lamp shone over my head" what it would mean to suffer the darkness which He Himself suffers in me. Filthy? We are utterly abominable and vile, all of us. How we can get through a day without constant retching is to me almost incomprehensible. But on the other hand it is not His will that we make much of this either. Simply accept it as our ordinary state. I wonder if you have ever run across the re-markable Athos mystic of our century, Staretz Silouan. He died in 1938, a Russian, at the Rossiko on Mt. Athos. The Lord told him once: "Keep your soul in hell and do not despair." This is a bit far from the hearts-and-flowers mysticism of our western victim souls, but it is very true, for if we descend into hell in this life we do not have to worry about it in the next. Nor is it really a matter of much choice. We *are* in hell. But a hell we can get out of if we don't try to transform it into heaven or pretend that it is heaven.

And so, joy in the Lord. Joy in hell. A scholastic question: "Whether there be joy in hell." *Distinguo*, etc. etc. etc. Where the Lord is, there is joy. If He be in our hell with us, what are we worried about? . . . People don't pay any attention to the mystery of the descent into hell anymore.

There is great joy if we do not play the devil's role and punish ourselves and one another. The great secret is to be other than devils. That is why we must be meek and loving even toward ourselves, especially toward ourselves. The fourth degree of love is to love ourselves as, and because, God loves us. This too I have learned or begun to learn in hell. Oh, the mercy of God. We are its ministers, even for ourselves. We must minister mercy to our hateful self, and to our brother in whom we most see our own condition reflected. Thus we become Christs, in no other way can we.

I am writing this after finishing my week as hebdomadary [presiding celebrant] for the conventual Mass. If I can presume that the Lord wishes to speak through me in any way, I would say He wants us all to know not to punish ourselves and not to be Satan to ourselves. Let us accuse no one, punish no one, accuse ourselves rightly of course, but not as Satan does: rather as the woman with the issue of blood, who "accused" herself by touching the hem of His garment in secret and with many, many tears, almost despairing yet hoping tremendously. This alone is our joy. Let us not swallow it back and be afraid of it. Let it burst out of us, and not remain imprisoned within us, for if it be imprisoned in our hearts our very joy will punish us . . .

I still have the novices, and many desires. Things do change, but the change does not alter anything. However our libraries are not locked anymore, not here. Perhaps we are swinging to the *other* extreme all of a sudden. What I am up against now is a small group of fanatics who are crying for a dialogue Mass—when we already have everything else under the sun that is better. This they want right after Lauds, at four in the morning, between Lauds and Prime, when there should be a quiet interval of reading, a lot of liturgical novelty and excitement. Understand my groans. They call themselves liturgists . . . .

To Dom Jean Leclercq

December 24, 1960

I learned late in the fall that you had been in America this summer. What a pity that you did not come down to Gethsemani; I would have enjoyed seeing you and talking to you. I am sure you were able to accomplish a lot of good at St. John's. I intend to read your article "La Spiritualité Vanniste" as I think I will write a study on Dom Calmet for the *American Benedictine Review*. I wonder if you can suggest any interesting materials? I am basing myself so far on the contemporary biography of Dom C. in French, on his commentary on the Rule, and such references as are made in the ordinary histories of the OSB.

My personal problems seem to be working themselves out in a way. A very fine little hermitage has been built in a nice site; it is for the purpose of *"rencontres"* and conversations with Protestant ministers and professors, but it also serves for solitude and I have at least a limited permission to use it part time. This is to a great extent a hopeful solution and I find that if I can have at least *some* real solitude and silence it makes a tremendous difference. I can at least help to stave off the kind of crisis that arose in 1959 when I felt it was necessary to change my situation and go elsewhere . . .

To Dom Pierre Van der Meer, O.S.B.

Dom Pierre Van der Meer, a Benedictine scholar of Beuron Abbey, had been a part of the "inner circle" of friends who frequented the home of Jacques and Raïssa Maritain. His book on the Carthusians of La Valsainte, Le Paradis Blanc, *was published in 1939 with an introduction by Jacques Maritain.*

July 28, 1961

It was a joy to receive your book with the very cordial dedication which you inscribed there. I am convinced that you speak the truth, because when I read your pages, a feeling sweeps over me which takes in all of your love for "our spiritual family." I feel an extraordinary affinity with that wonderful brilliance of Léon Bloy. This has been going on for twenty years, ever since the days when I took out all his books from the Columbia University Library. I noticed that Raïssa Maritain and I were the only ones who read them, (One can tell this from the library cards which you have to sign: sometimes I preceded her, other times she arrived before me, but we went through all the volumes together without my ever running into her.)

The part on Léon Bloy is wonderful. All "my" France comes back to me, with the mystery of my own vocation which my sojourn in France had prepared. The part about Raïssa and Christine and Dom Pieterke is very moving: in the case of the latter two, it's my first acquaintance with them. There's no need to tell you that I have known you for a long time, because the *Paradis Blanc* is one of my favorite books—especially the beautiful conference (in the style of Cassian) with Dom Porion. Is he well? I have not written him in a long time—since the "debacle" of my Carthusian leanings. But looking back, I have to say that my Father Abbot permits me, all the same, a substantial amount of solitude.

Tell me, Dom Pierre: Raïssa's poem on [Marc] Chagall, is it complete? I would like to translate it. It is so beautiful, such a jewel. I am thinking of a translation with a Chagall painting, a portrait of Raïssa and a short biography. It would make a nice piece for a periodical directed by a friend of mine. What do you think? At any rate, I am going to try and get a whole book on Chagall.

But how can I tell you, after all this, what I am really feeling? Reading your beautiful book is for me much more than just reading. It is a communion at depth with all of you, with God, and with myself. To contemplate His Goodness in all of our lives. I am already 46. The world has changed much since my entry into the monastery. It is no longer the society which I lately knew, the world of my youth, of my parents. I think of myself as an exile two times, three times over. The way toward the Homeland becomes more and more obscure. As I look back over the stages which were once more clear, I see that we are all on the right road, and though it be night, it is a saving one. We are very much alone, as regards the crowd which presses in around us. But as regards that "cloud of witnesses," well, that is something altogether different . . .

To Sister Helen Jean Seidel, S.L.

Sister Helen Jean was Mistress of Novices at the Loretto motherhouse in Kentucky at this writing. Merton on occasion received permission to visit Loretto and give talks to the novices.

October 9, 1961

This morning I got a nice note from Mother Luke [Tobin], and I had been intending to write to her to thank all of you for the very happy afternoon spent at Loretto on the 4th. However, I recollect that she is going on visitations.

First I am enclosing a few copies of the notes on mental prayer I have given to the novices. There is nothing much to them, but they may serve a purpose. Then too a lot of things could be said to clarify the rather jumbled thought I was giving out the other day.

Perhaps some day I will make a more complete set of notes. But in any case, to avoid giving wrong impressions, perhaps I ought to add the following thoughts: In training them for mental prayer, they must of course receive a real *training*, they must get discipline, and learn how to exercise themselves in various important ways. The danger is that in learning how to do these things they may get the impression that they know how to meditate. And also that they may cling to the methods learned, and never know when to let go. So really, while learning how to use the mind, the imagination, the will, etc., they must also learn when to let go and when *not* to use them too much. And of course there are no clear rules for this as it differs with each individual case. If one emphasizes not only discipline but also suppleness, flexibility, freedom of spirit, and so on, it ought to preserve the right perspective.

There is a rather good book by Brillet, *Meditations on the Old Testament*. In fact it is in four volumes. As a meditation book it is not extraordinary but it does tie up meditation with the reading of the Scriptures. Since the Scriptures are the word of God they are certainly the ideal way of opening up a meditative approach to Our Lord, dialogue, response and communion with Him in faith, hope and love. And that is what meditation is. Since there is so much richness and solid meat in the Scriptures, and since reading of the Scriptures tends to be objective and simple, meditation on them can also preserve us from too much self-conscious and reflexive activity.

As I said the other day, the curse of meditation is watching ourselves meditate. Again, I think it is important for them just to become aware of the fact that there are many things they *can* do in meditation if they have to, without necessarily doing any of them very much. It is good to know how much one can fall back on, in a crisis. Yet it is good to go along without relying on methods, but on God Himself, provided one's faith is mature enough to permit this.

I wish I had had a few more minutes with the novices and postulants: they gave me much more than I was able to give them. But I certainly enjoyed it. I think you have a fine group and I hope they will all advance happily and peacefully in the ways of the Lord who has loved them and called them . . .

To Dom Gabriel Sortais

April 28, 1962

Yesterday Dom James gave me the report of the censors on "Target = City" and at the same time your letters of April 17 and January 20. So I am at last in the know. I am going to try as objectively as possible to give you the required explanation.

First of all, I am quite distressed by the accident which caused the uncensored version of "Christian Ethics and Nuclear War" to appear in the *Catholic Worker*. It was entirely against my wishes and against my expressed orders. This article was to have passed through the censorship and appeared first in *Jubilee*: the modified version appears in it in May. The editor of *Jubilee* was in consternation. Whose fault? There was a sudden change in the editorial staff at the *Catholic Worker*. The new editor found the article and put it into the publication. So the fault lies with the former editor who knew very well what he ought to have done; I had told him that several times and he had *formally promised* to wait. It is a disappointment which disconcerts me as much as it does you. I immediately wrote a letter to the *Catholic Worker* asking for an explanation as to its publication.

For the article "Peace and Christian Responsibility," on receiving the *nihil obstat* I allowed the publication of this article. Now, only after I asked Dom James if by chance there was not some correction suggested by the censor who had refused to approve the article. He said there was, and he gave me the very helpful observations of this censor. If I had been able to make the corrections before, I would have taken advantage of them. But anyway I brought in many corrections and clarifications to this article which appears a second time in a collection of testimonies. And also in the *Catholic Worker*.

You have no doubt remarked that the English censors had much less difficulty in accepting an article which protests the nuclear war than the American censors. Besides, it seems to me that the American censor who so formally condemned "Peace . . . Responsibility" and "Target = City" has really interpreted my thought wrongly. I am in no way a pacifist in the sense he condemns. On the contrary, I only say that *total* war, *massive* nuclear destruction, without distinction between the combatants and the civilians, is against Catholic moral doctrine. It is what Pius XII says very clearly, as does even the theologian whom this censor quotes textually for two pages of his report without really seeing certain nuances . . . But it is useless to discuss these things with you. I do not want to discuss. I intend to obey quite simply.

I want to accept wholeheartedly, and with joy, the decision never to write anymore on war. Besides, this does not make me sad at all. This work is enormously difficult, quite repugnant, exhausting and unrewarding. To do nothing is very convenient, and I am relieved of it from that point of view.

For my part, I would like quite simply to end my letter here, but there remains a question that I put to you only because my confessor told me to do so. I no longer write anything to be published on war. (Of course, if I say something in a letter to a friend, or in private notes, I suppose this does not go against your will.) But I have once more revised the two articles which had already gone through the censorship, i.e., "Peace . . . Responsibility" and "Christian Ethics." With additions, these articles form a short book, which is already completed, and which is being copied. A publisher has asked me for this book. My thought, and that of Dom James, was to submit this book to the reading of the two censors who had approved the articles in their original form. Now, the censor (the third, I think) who finally rejected "Target = City" insists that I send nothing more to him for censorship. I am quite ready to do what he wants, even in the case of this book which is based on already approved articles, but revised with corrections and clarifications. I must tell you that the book is much longer than the two articles, and that there is quite a lot of new material, especially on the tradition, the Fathers, etc.

I am not asking for indulgence, Most Reverend Father, I only seek God's will. I am not asking you to spoil me. And moreover I will be only too happy to make the sacrifice of a completed book, which cost me a lot. I simply tell you the case, and if you want to stop it at this point, I would be very pleased. One has to finish somewhere all the same.

Anyway, whatever happens I will no longer write anything on war and peace if it is your will. I am going to try and write and publish only things that are clearly the subjects one expects from a monk.

One word to finish with: maybe you wonder why this question of war and peace worries me? In a letter that Dom James showed me yesterday, I think I see a kind of contempt for this kind of monk who strayed into a monastery only to allow his head to be filled with secular preoccupations. Perhaps it is the truth. I do not deny it, for I don't fancy I am a good monk. But may I assure you that it seemed to me I was acting at least as a Christian? I don't claim to be a good Christian: I am altogether unworthy of the graces God has given me. I don't expect to become worthy of them one day, but I try to love Him with the heart I have, which is not very much, and no doubt for the true monks it is somewhat a ridiculous thing, this heart, especially when one knows well that one must not listen to the heart: but anyway I have this weakness. Now I very seriously think there is a real danger of a nuclear war, and a *massive* nuclear war. Do you know what that might mean? I don't have to tell you. The United States might "win" and survive. France and England would not have the same luck . . . I wanted to tell you what I thought. No doubt it was imprudent, unscientific, preposterous. Not all think so, including atomic scientists. There are quite a lot of very well-informed people who think I am not altogether wrong. The article "Peace . . . Responsibility" has appeared in *Commonweal* in early February. Shortly after, the Lenten pastoral of the Cardinal Archbishop of Chicago was on peace, and this pastoral contained some ten sentences copied exactly from my article, which shows that the Cardinal was not altogether in accord with the Father Censor.

I have told you this not by way of defense but by way of explanation. I have written quite enough on this subject, and people know what I think: so I am not totally responsible for what is perhaps going to happen. If you ask for silence on this subject, and you do ask it of me, I obey willingly and with much joy. As for the book, you can say what you think, I am not attached to this project one way or another.

I hope this is the last time we shall have such explanations between us, Most Reverend Father. I am going to do all that is possible on my part to avoid such things in the future . . .

May 26, 1962

I have just received your good letter of the 12th that Dom James forwarded to me from somewhere, Mepkin I think. You tell me very clearly what I wanted to know, your will. I thank you for it and I am glad to have it since it is what God wants of me.

From the point of view of the obligation I might have had towards my countrymen in this situation, I think I did say what was needed and my opinion is known. It is not necessary to say more than what has been said already. People should know indeed that my opinions are not those of the Order. What I said clearly was this: that in war, in any war, either nuclear or "conventional," the Popes have said that when the destruction is "massive" and "total" and "uncontrolled," and when thousands and even millions of human beings who have nothing to do directly with the war and who are perhaps neutral are annihilated, it is a crime. I thought that that needed to be said because it is not clear here. What is said by the American theologians is that one must use strength, even nuclear, to stop the advance of the Communists. For the public, it is understood that distinctions hardly exist, or do not exist at all. There are American generals who publicly declare themselves ready to launch a total, massive, nuclear war against Russia any time, and that it should be done, that we already have good reason to do it, etc.

As far as I know I am nearly the only known American Catholic writer to have said quite plainly that this situation leaves us in an occasion of very serious sin. I said so, and people know what I have said. If they believe for that reason that I am a Communist, too bad! We, too, have our boys *à la OAS* [*Organisation Armée Secrète*, opposed to De Gaulle, and to Algeria's independence], and they are the ones who have more influence perhaps in our monasteries.

There we are, Most Reverend Father. I accept your decision joyfully, and of course I agree on the motives that you suggest to me are the true ones, and the normal ones. I am quite willing, and I know that God will accept my good intentions such as I can have.

Besides, I assure you that I am very happy these May days, especially today which is the 13th anniversary of my priestly ordination. I think of Our Lady's intervention in my life, and my enormous debt towards her. I am glad to belong to her, too, and to hide in her Immaculate Heart. She will take care of the nations of the world . . . and of the things that are going to come perhaps. So, I am very thankful in my monastic vocation, my vocation at Gethsemani, my vocation to be a strange and funny creature, a sort of twentieth-century juggler. But my brothers tolerate me and they love me; I also love them very much. God will do the rest.

For the *Catholic Worker*: do you ask me to write nothing more for them? Or nothing more on war? They have the poem on the women's prison that the censors have not yet sent back to me. I want to tell you that Dorothy Day, who founded this movement and this paper, is one of the holiest persons among us, highly respected by those who really know what it is. I also want to tell you that a book is appearing which contains a preface approved by the censors and one of the articles already published long ago: it is an anthology by several authors. There is nothing new from me, and it is already in press [*Breakthrough to Peace*]. I think you already knew . . .

To Sister Elaine M. Bane, O.S.F.

Sister Elaine, a native of Cambridge, Massachusetts, entered the Franciscan Sisters of Allegany, New York, in 1947. In January 1959, a group of six sisters with Sister Elaine "in charge" inaugurated the Cloister, or "retiro," to provide a contemplative lifestyle within the Allegany community for those sisters who felt called to that life. She wrote to the Novice Master at Gethsemani, asking for suggestions he might have on orientating the sisters from an active to a contemplative life. To her great surprise, the Novice Master turned out to be Thomas Merton.

[*Cold War Letter 91*]

July 4, 1962

This is not an adequate letter, but I do want to get some kind of reply into the mail for you, as the project of the "retiro" sounds most interesting. It is something that deserves every possible encouragement and I want to do my bit. I will try to remember to fill an envelope with materials that might be of use to you and get it off in the next couple of days. You can guess however that I have not much time for handling mail, and secretarial facilities are, well, rudimentary. I don't want to overburden the novices, and that is the only "work pool" to which I have access. One or other of them do help out though and I am grateful.

Transformation in Christ is a difficult book, and I let the novices read it without however pushing them. On the other hand Von Hildebrand's *Defense of Purity* is, it seems to me, a superbly spiritual treatment of chastity. There is a lot about marriage in it, but I feel the novices ought to appreciate the married state which they are renouncing. What good to renounce it if they do not know its dignity? For a retiro however the needs might be different.

Bouyer on the *Meaning of the Monastic Life* we regard as standard. In an older context, there is Dom Marmion, always safe and solid. Bouyer's new *Introduction to Spirituality* is a bit advanced, but I should think you might be able to use it. A perfect biography of St. Therese which is very useful for all religious is the *Hidden Face* by [Ida] Goerres. We always like Guardini here. To my mind he is one of the most important and articulate Catholic authors of the moment. He has good things on prayer, faith, and so on. *Prayer in Practice* comes to mind as excellent. Fr. Danielou is liked by the novices and I like him too. Also Hubert Van Zeller.

These are just a few books that spring to mind as I write. I will try to dig up one of our novitiate reading-lists and put it in the envelope I hope to send. I remember St. Elizabeth's well, and you have a lovely place for a cloistered contemplative life—except perhaps for the trains, but who cares about a few trains once in a while? Are you right in the old convent, or are you somewhere apart?

Remember that in the enclosed and solitary life, your solitude itself will do an immense amount for you. The sisters need not strain and struggle and worry too much about "degrees" of prayer. The great thing is to be emptied out, to taste and see that the Lord is sweet, and to learn the way of abandonment and peace. Littleness is the chief characteristic of the solitary, or else he is not a genuine solitary. Silence is a rare luxury in the modern world, and not everyone can stand it: but it has inestimable value, that cannot be purchased with any amount of money or power or intelligence. The gift to be silent and simple with the Lord is a treasure beyond counting and it almost takes care of everything else, at least in some souls.

I wish you all success and send you every blessing. Do remember me in prayer please; I keep hoping eventually to get permission for a more solitary life, though I do have a fair amount of solitude now, thanks be to God.

To Father Ronald Roloff, O.S.B.

Father Ronald Roloff, who was at this time a monk of St. John's Abbey, Collegeville, became involved in a lively exchange of letters with Thomas Merton. This is the first of the letters Merton wrote him that has been discovered. Many more will follow on the subject of contemporary monasticism and renewal.

September 26, 1962

Dom Leclercq has just been here for a flying visit. Naturally we spoke a little of the rather heated controversy about Benedictine spirituality that has been going on particularly in the pages of the ABR [*American Benedictine Review*]. Though I feel that this discussion is being conducted in terms that are really none of my business (you have reduced it to a completely intramural and family affair of your own), I thought I might as well make an observation since I myself was mentioned, with a gentle sentence of excommunication from the Benedictine family, at the beginning of the series.

In the first place, speaking personally, I would like to say that I think most Benedictines judge my statements almost exclusively in the light of earlier books in which I was much more rigid and doctrinaire than I believe I have since become. There has, I think, been a slight evolution in my thought about the monastic life from *The Waters of Siloe* (which I regard now as a rough and immature essay) to *The Silent Life* and even more recent essays, such as some of those in *Disputed Questions*. What that evolution may have been exactly, I do not attempt to say myself at this point. But I do feel it is a reality, and though I have by my early and more impetuous efforts deserved to get shoved into a pigeon-hole, I still meekly protest.

About the controversy: as I say I am not competent to enter into the details of what is for you a family affair. But standing on the other side of the street, vis-à-vis your family, and yet a member of the Benedictine family at large, I would like to say this. I personally feel that more confusion than clarity is ultimately going to follow from discussions that separate Benedictine vs. Trappist vs. Cistercian, and which build up little card houses of "Cistercian spirituality," "Benedictine spirituality," etc. These classifications may certainly have a validity and usefulness of their own. But as Novice Master in a monastery of Benedictine monks of the

Cistercian reform, I feel myself obligated to instruct the novices not in a fanciful "Cistercian spirituality" but to try as best I can, in all simplicity, to give them a *monastic* formation in elements which are *common* to us all. I have never found it relevant to stress the fact that we don't have parishes and that you do. *Ut quid?* You are monks, we are monks. The big thing is, do we really seek God?

Do we really keep our vow of *conversatio morum* [conversion of life], which is the very heart of our monastic consecration? Are we really men of prayer, men living in the Spirit, men given over to the Spirit of God that He may use us as He wills, whether to dwell in us silently, to praise the Father in the liturgical assembly, to announce the message of salvation, to labor in poverty, to study divine truth?

It seems to me that we all need more and more to deepen the grasp we have of our rich monastic heritage, and the closer we get to the source, the more fruitful and splendid our lives will be, in all kinds of varied expressions and manifestations. It seems to me that the monastic life is wonderful precisely for the way it embraces so many varied approaches to God. And it would seem that what we need today are monastic communities that are more and more aware of the opportunities they possess in this regard; opportunities for special kinds of apostolate and for special kinds of contemplation, for eremitical solitude, for community projects in study and research, for special ways of poverty and labor, for peculiar forms of monastic witness, for unusual and pioneering dialogue. We have not scratched the surface of this rich land of ours that our Fathers have left us. This does not mean that we are not working at it manfully in many ways. There *is* a monastic movement of great vitality everywhere, including America, and your discussions are part of the stirring of life that this implies. Naturally, not everyone can do everything. One must limit himself to certain reasonable choices and commitments. But it seems to me that we could all be of much greater help to one another if the entire monastic movement in America were more cooperative, if we all felt we had a common task and a common ideal, in which we could help each other mightily by God's grace and fraternal encouragement. Certainly I know this spirit has been growing in the past ten years, and I know it will grow much more, especially when we Cistercians come to realize that we can offer much by opening up a little more to our Benedictine brethren.

At the same time I feel that one of the difficulties is that we all tend to become prisoners of particularities which are too limited. One of the drawbacks of the conventional, stereotyped idea of the "Trappist" (an idea which has a firm basis in reality) is that it tends to be narrow and out of contact with monastic realities, by reason of a certain voluntaristic insistence on a few select aspects of observance. I wonder if, on the Benedictine side, priests are not to some extent hampered by being too confined in the routines and machinery that have been devised by the secular clergy, especially in this country. This I say with the realization that someone can easily prove I don't know what I am talking about, and I would be hard put to it to prove that I am right. It is only an intuition which may be falsified by any number of factors; I thought however I might mention it.

One last thought: there is the perennial problem of monks who are not quite at home in one or other branch of the monastic family and who have to get dispensations to pass through the gate into the next garden where they will be more at home. This it seems to me could be obviated to some extent if our monastic families allowed more latitude for different kinds of solution within their own framework. But here too I speak as one less wise, and certainly without authority.

These thoughts were on my mind this morning so perhaps the Lord wanted me to put them down. I do hope you will not find them in any way out of place. I repeat that I am not at ease putting my foot into territory that is not really mine, and it would not be at all out of the way if the entire American Benedictine community shouted to me with one voice to mind my own business. But what I have written I have written in a spirit of fraternal solidarity and interest. If I did not feel to some extent one with all of you, there would be no reason to comment on the fact that I was declared to be not one of you.

To Etienne Gilson

October 11, 1962

Yesterday evening I was discussing a project of mine with Dan Walsh, who is teaching philosophy here, and we agreed that it would be a good idea to write to you because you are the one most qualified to help me out. So I am doing so in all simplicity.

For some time I have been very interested in the 12th-century School of Chartres. The more I come to know of these Masters, the better I like them and the more I am convinced that I ought to work on them quite seriously. I have read a great deal of John of Salisbury in Migne, of course, but I am also getting into William of Conches, through the texts in Parent's book, *La Doctrine de la Création* . . . and also in *Moralium Dogma* (Holberg). I am acquainted with the more accessible sources, like R. L. Poole, Huizinga's "Essay on John of Salisbury," and so on. I can also get Clerval from a nearby Protestant seminary.

Thus far I have no need to bother you. But when it comes to serious work, then I must turn to you for advice. And more than that, for loans of offprints and so on: for I presume you must still have offprints of some of your own studies (V.G. the one on "The Cosmogony of Bernard Silvestris," etc.). I would take great care of them and return them. I do not have access to the periodicals that contain the best studies. We do not have here the AHDLMA [*Archives d'Histoire Doctrinale et Littéraire du Moyen Age*] in which I understand there are studies on Gilbert de la Porrée. I am also told there is a Mlle. d'Alverny who has done studies on the Chartrains.

I will also obviously have to get into the manuscripts, but it is possible that at St. Michael's there may be typewritten or mimeographed transcripts of some of the important texts. For all these things, I ask your help and your intercession with the ones concerned. I am indirectly in touch with the librarian at St. Michael's but I am not sure whether he is in a position to help me.

In any case, it seems to me that the "wisdom" of the Chartrains has a character and a beauty of its own that has been too long ignored. It seems to me that chapters like the introduction (cc. 1 & 4) of Bk. ii of the *Summa contra Gentiles* reflect something of the Chartrain spirit. I would like to read them in the light of St. Thomas, with of course due attention to his developments and steps forward. I would also like to read them, naturally, in the light of the Cistercian reaction. Not only the official reaction against them, but also the inspiration which some of the Cistercians derived from Chartrains. Can you tell me where to look, among the Cistercians, for Chartrain themes? I suppose Isaac of Stella would be an obvious place to look.

What interests me most of course is their doctrine on creation, but also their ideas of man, of study, etc., and ultimately also their wisdom as a whole. I would study them as contemplative thinkers above all, and as taking a significantly different approach to God from the Cistercians of the time. And I could try to outline the similarities and differences.

In the background I would have to study Boethius, Eriugena and who else? It is strange that though I am uncomfortable with Plato, still, I am perfectly at home with the Chartrains . . .

To Father Ronald Roloff

October 21, 1962

Thanks for your very fine letter. It really threw a great deal of light on the situation, and I assure you that I feel very much involved in the problem. Don't think it is something I can look at with remote detachment from the top of an ivory tower. Basically the problem is very much the same in its essence everywhere.

But first, I have a disappointment. It was also a disappointment for me. I wanted very much to take a more active and articulate part in the discussion, and asked permission for the publication of my letter, but Fr. Abbot refused it. I am very sorry. However it does seem to me that the most elementary charity demands at least some concern and some thought on my part, in response to your letter. It is better no doubt that I just write with no view to publication. Then the jots and tittles won't matter so much, and anyway you can share the letter with anyone who is interested.

First, everywhere there is and doubtless must be a certain disharmony between ideals and realities. This is taken for granted, and to be realistic we have to accept it as a fact. To act as if it were fully possible to realize a supreme ideal consistently all the time is plain folly. So whatever we do we are caught in the machinery between the ideal and the real. We have to strive for an ideal that is not fully realizable, but we have to strive for it in a way that is healthy and realistic, not a pharisaical evasion from present obligations. And we must strive for it in such a way that even in our relatively unsatisfactory fulfillment of obligations the ideal provides a spirit and a source of grace which enables us to transcend and spiritualize everything, and thus become saints in our ordinary life.

You and Fr. W. are having a tug-of-war with both ends of this proposition. He is holding on to the ideal and you are clinging to the real. He is afraid you will be so "realistic" that you will simply give up pursuits that are traditionally essential for the monastic "contemplative" life, and you are afraid he will make such a mirage out of the contemplative life that he will undermine the energy and realism which would enable people to come to grips with their misfortunes and make the best of it. Misfortune is probably a badly chosen word, since you are not presenting the active life as a misfortune exactly, and it is not. Yet it does present a big problem, and those who have emphasized contemplation have spotlighted the problem, making it all the more painful, without doing anything to liberate the ones who have to suffer from the division. We are like the Law, in St. Paul: not very comforting. Indeed, we all of us sound like Job's comforters as soon as we open our mouths.

There is certainly no question that the troubles of the Sisters, with their heavy load of work and active duties, will not be alleviated by talking about the things they might do if they were in some other, better situation. Yet on the other hand, I think it can always be said that discussion of a question may stimulate the interest and the momentum necessary to change the situation. There *is* a monastic revival going on. One may well be dubious about its ambiguities and its numerous false pretenses, but the reality is nevertheless there. Now if ever is the time when something can really be done not only to bolster up the dispositions of the individual, but to change his whole situation. Hence there is merit in raising the questions raised by Fr. W. provided they do not just dissipate themselves in smoke and idle talk.

Take the battle cry of *"lectio divina."* Certainly we have raised this cry here long since, and in the last fifteen years or so a great deal has taken place. You are probably not aware that the Cistercian life (let's forget about Trappists), even with its claims to contemplation, is basically an active life: *bios praktikos.* Not only in the ascetic sense, but in the sense that a great deal goes on in the monastery, including a great deal of work, profitable work, highly organized and pushed hard by operators who know what they are doing and who know how to get others to work for them (within limits). There is overwork here as well as anywhere else. We lose people who go into work too deeply, solemn professed included, just as we lose people who are slack, uninterested, vague, etc. Here too, just as with you, the term "obedience" is invoked to cover a multitude of evils that are in themselves utterly obvious.

However in the last decade significant things have happened, due to a general movement throughout the Order in favor of lectio, study, a more contemplative spirit and so on. A very top-heavy schedule full of extra offices and community exercises has been considerably alleviated, trimmed down to quite intelligent proportions, and it is now possible to breathe much more freely and to take more time for reading, thought, personal prayer, etc. The liturgy is also much more stately and leisurely, much improved in every respect, better for one's inner life, better as service and worship of God.

It is true that a lot of people have taken advantage of this leeway to waste time diddling around. This is the perennial trouble in contemplative orders which really have an "active" spirit. A large number do not really *want* lectio, meditation and the rest. They are glad of time to stretch, and they spend hours shaving, shining their shoes, standing around and watching the clouds go by. I fear that the inevitable result of this will be a general cutting down on the precious time we have gained and an overall return to work as (practically) the dominant consideration in the life.

Conversatio morum, then. I think this is the term that needs to be understood, because it is the very heart of the problem. It is what makes the difference between the monk and the non-monk, provided it is taken in a broader than the technical sense. I mean it should include something more than just a pledge to live in a cenobium. (I think the spirit of *conversatio morum* covers solitaries as well as monks who are in parishes.) The great thing is the monastic metanoia, the inner transformation, the newness of monastic life. Where this is effected by the grace of God and by a deep formation in a community, then I think there is nothing the monk cannot handle. The great thing is then making real monks from the inside out, as far as possible in the atmosphere of true monastic silence and prayer in their novitiate and student years, and perhaps longer. A longer, more thorough, more gradual formation in the monastic spirit to give the person a more complete command of himself under God's grace, in all the eventualities he will meet, so that he will meet them always as a man of God, living in the Spirit, and as a true monk. I suppose here I am getting into the idealistic blather so I won't go further. I hasten to add that it seems to me St. John's fulfills these conditions anyway, and could easily go further in this direction if it were desired or needed. Perhaps it is not.

Then too I would say that there could be a greater respect everywhere for the needs and aspirations of the individual who for valid and just reasons aspires to a deeper penetration of the monastic tradition and experience. Work should not be such an end it itself that it excludes these valid demands or hopes. Obviously sacrifice will always be necessary, but it should not be the automatic answer to everyone who wants more of a life of prayer: "Just sacrifice that, Father, it is just self-will."

Finally, in all true and necessary Christian activity, for soul or in any other sphere, there tends to creep in a lot of senseless inertia and useless palavering.

I would say that the great problem for the Black Benedictines in parish work is more or less a universal problem of all priests today in America: getting themselves (and even to a greater extent than other priests) disengaged from the futile routines and paperwork and "public relations" gags and all the rest of the trivialities that have entered the life of the priest in America in proportion as he has become a business man and an operator like other business men and operators. For further details see my perhaps scandalous review of Jim [J.F.] Powers' new book, which Fr. Godfrey tells me he will print in the next *Worship*.

Here I think it is most important for the spirit of *conversatio morum* to operate, not just picking the Benedictine priest up by the hair of his head and depositing him in a desert cave, but delivering him from the waste motion and the burden of nonsense and triviality that *seems* to become, so easily, an "essential" part of priestly life. I am sure there must be a thousand tasks that are supposed to be important and which, if everybody faced it, are a pure waste of time. I am just speaking of the kind of waste motion we get into here, also, even though our life is supposed to be streamlined. It isn't . . .

In any case, I am sure there is great benefit in our exchanging a few ideas and the Lord will show us what we can do, each in his own way, to help people in the Benedictine and Cistercian life who are overburdened and discouraged, frustrated and backed into a corner of some sort, not so much [that] it is "necessary" and that the religious life "has to be that way," but on the contrary, as a result of stupidity, mediocrity in the "system itself," and general fuzziness and ineptitude in everybody's thinking.

Do pray for me, Father. We are going into a big change here shortly, merging the brothers and choir into a more homogeneous and "equal" group. The brothers will have a vote in chapter, etc. The two novitiates will become one, and so on. So we will need a lot of light and tact and submissive obedience to the Holy Spirit.

To Father Colman Barry, O.S.B.

Father Colman Barry, a monk of St. John's Abbey, Collegeville, is the president of St. John's University. At the time of this exchange he was involved with the Liturgical Press and was editor of The American Benedictine Review.

November 13, 1962

I believe I did not yet answer your letter about the publication of my letter to Fr. Ronald [Roloff]. But as he is probably keeping you informed about our correspondence, you will know what I told him: namely that my Father Abbot said he did not want this. I do think, however, that the correspondence itself is bringing up some rather fruitful points of considerable importance to all of us. Especially the question of monastic formation, the priesthood, and so on. This is the subject of much new thought here and we are putting into effect a new plan which may be very far-reaching in its effects.

About the Bolshakoff ms. [*The Russian Mystics*, later published by Cistercian Publications], only a few weeks ago I looked at it closely and saw I would have to revise it as the English is halting in places. This is quite a big job, and it took time for his letter to come back giving me permission, so I have only just begun. Consequently it will be a while before I forward the book to you. The material is really interesting and thorough; I think it will make an excellent book, if I can manage to make it more readable. I have not read the Italian version, but it seems quite good.

Finally I am reading Dom Adalbert de Vogüé's new book on the Rule of Saint Benedict and the Rule of the Master. I wonder if you would be interested in a brief review article, though the book is in French. I think he makes some important new points, and would be glad to try it if you think it might be worthwhile . . .

To Father Ronald Roloff

November 13, 1962

It is really interesting that you bring up the point about monastic priesthood in your letter of the second. As a matter of fact I think we are all coming to realize the crucial importance of this question. If it is important for us, I have no doubt it is even more so for you, for the reason which you mention.

As a matter of fact, we are right in the middle of the big change in this matter too. Let me outline the situation briefly.

1) It has always been theoretically our tradition that no choir monk needed to feel himself obligated to go on to the priesthood, and that one

could be accepted for profession in the choir without having a priestly vocation. At simple profession it has even been customary to sign the document required by the Holy See, with certain modifications peculiar to our Order, namely that ordination would not necessarily be granted just because one was a choir monk. We have always had the right not to ordain or be ordained, in the choir. But up until very recently this was more or less ignored. In practice everyone in the choir immediately went on to study for the priesthood and was ordained in due course.

2) The ordination of priests in our houses rested mostly on the kind of reasons given by Dom Leclercq: to give the choir monks a certain extra fullness in their contemplative life, a deeper participation in the mystery of Christ by the grace of the priesthood and by the holy sacrifice. But also of course accidentally there are offices in the community which should be fulfilled by priests, and there must be confessors. Also the more material consideration: the great number of Mass stipends sent in.

3) It has been rather generally recognized in the Order lately that this creates a problem. Whether the problem is usually stated as a sense of divided loyalties or not would be difficult to say. What seems to preoccupy the Superiors of the Order is the fact that after a more or less normal seminary course, with emphases that are logical for the apostolic life and have no real relevance for us, our young priests reach ordination prepared for active ministry, and without anything to do. Hence a sense of disorientation and confusion in many of them, a feeling that they are out of place, useless, badly adapted. They get frustrated and in fact quite a few have left to work in parishes. This then is the problem, essentially the same as yours in its roots, accidentally different with us. The problem of the monastic priesthood leading more or less inevitably into activity which, while reconcilable with monastic perfection per se, does in fact produce anomalies and, with us, even leads to a complete break.

4) I might remark here that one of the greatest mistakes we have made in this regard has been to assume that anyone with a priestly vocation and a desire to enter one of our monasteries had a Cistercian vocation. We have not sufficiently distinguished between the two, and have taken boys whose heart was entirely set on the priesthood and who were only interested in the monastic life in the secondary way. Add too, in parentheses, the fact that this has in the past not infrequently been an out for boys who were too slow to get the studies in ordinary seminaries and came to the Trappists, where everybody was reputed dumb and where the course was, in fact, much easier. It is amusing to note that the one man we have being processed for Beatification now is one of these, though he was very sincere and good. He would never have become a Trappist if he had been smart enough for a diocesan seminary. And in the monastery his one idea, in fact his obsession, was to become a priest. He made it, and then died. Curious that he is being beatified (perhaps) at the precise moment when the Order is coming to realize that this is the wrong way to go about being a monk.

One further note: I have known cases when a boy was being sent away as not having a monastic vocation, and he would admit frankly, on leaving, that he had planned to get his priestly education here and then leave. A fine situation.

5) What are we doing now? We are just beginning an entirely new program. Already for some time I have been insisting that the important thing in the choice of vocations for our choir was the monastic vocation, not the call to the priesthood. Also many of the novices have freely admitted that they really prefer to be simple monks and not priests. Up until a few months ago Fr. Abbot was not tolerating this, but now since the recent General Chapter he has agreed to let them try it out, and is in fact pushing the new monastic program. Hence we now have half a dozen newly professed who are going ahead with the explicit intention of remaining simple monks and not becoming priests. They are among the best in the house, actually. I do not know if they will all manage to have their desire, some may have to be ordained later, just because they do have qualities that make for superiorship, etc. But for my part I would personally support such a one all the way and would encourage him to remain a simple monk insofar as it was possible.

6) It is a matter of experience that even where the priesthood does not in any way threaten a person's basic monastic vocation and attitude, it nevertheless does have a profound effect on the interior life of the monk. It would be hard to say precisely what this effect is: certainly it complicates the interior life a little, and brings with it responsibilities even without parish work and "contacts with souls." There is something about the very fact of assuming the burden of priestly greatness and dignity which must have been one of the reasons why the Desert Fathers fled from bishops. I think this is in part more disturbing to those who have been pushed on to the priesthood directly. It might be a different matter in a monk who after years of slow maturing in the monastery received the priesthood in middle age as a crown to his spiritual life. Not that he would not be humbled by the greatness of the dignity, but he would be able to handle it better.

7) What are our new plans? First it seems that Fr. Abbot will begin to demand more than three years of simple vows. He is talking of six years. Nothing is yet certain. After the novitiate, all the choir monks, whether they will eventually go on to the priesthood or not, *continue their purely monastic formation.* This is what we all here consider to be the really important point. They will not begin clerical studies for at least three years after the novitiate. Or perhaps in the third year of "monastic formation" they may begin philosophy. I have a pet plan about a monastic pre-philosophy course which will have nothing to do with manuals but will be a sort of *lectio divina* of texts from St. Anselm, St. Augustine, Boethius, and so on. This would be a very interesting course and very important. But meanwhile, that would not be until the third year. Before that they will take nothing but Scripture, Monastic History, the Fathers

and a language. But they will not have an overloaded study schedule. They will work part of the time now allotted to studies in the clerical course. They will have a lot of time (relatively) for *lectio divina*. They will live as much as possible the plain monastic life according to the Rule, with no special adjustments such as students have. They will have a few classes, and that will take a little of the work time. But they will always have at least two hours of manual labor and maybe four every day.

8) *Lectio divina*: The plan that works here, and works well, is one of my pet schemes and I think it has caught on. After the night office, that is about 4:15 a.m., the students get breakfast and then settle down to read until Prime, which is at 6:15. They have more reading after Chapter, and receive Communion at the conventual Mass, which begins at 8 (with Tierce). Thus they get plenty of reading. For those who do not have to use this time for clerical study, this will be a great big chunk of lectio and will be of vital importance. I think this alone will make a decisive difference. Three years of that (after the novitiate) will really create a taste for the contemplative life in its simple monastic form.

I think something like this monastic formation program is definitely worth considering in your monasteries too. I am sure you will agree, and as it goes on I will keep you informed. Next year is the first year, and your special prayers will be a great gift which we will appreciate. I must close now, though there is much more I could add. Perhaps more later. I think our correspondence is going to be very fruitful for us all, I am certainly enjoying it and profiting by it.

To Father Brendan Connelly, S.J.

Brendan Connelly, a Jesuit priest at Boston College, was an inexhaustible source of books on loan for Merton, especially when he got into Celtic studies, as well as the School of Chartres.

November 26, 1962

Thanks for your good letter. I fully realize that simply to give you things without letting you give something in return is just frustrating, and I apologize for not getting down to this letter sooner. I do seriously intend to take advantage of your generosity, though it is possible that you may not have at BC [Boston College] the precise publications I am after. One reason why I have been waiting is that we are rounding up some of the learned journals that are necessary. Hence I am now jotting down a few titles, especially of articles, which we will not be able to acquire for ourselves. This in the hope that it may be possible to find them at BC.

First I had better say that I am just moving into what will probably turn out to be a long-term project on the twelfth-century School of Chartres. Hence if you know of or see anything you think will be of use in that field, think of me, please. As I say we are getting at the main sources, and such journals as the AHDLMA, and *Medieval Studies*. And I will be in touch with the men who are editing the texts in Europe. Here are some of the things I cannot get to:

A book by Cappuyns on Scotus Eriugena, in French.

A book by Paré, Brunet et Tremblay, *La Renaissance du 12ᵉ Siècle*, Ottawa. Articles:

Delhaye, something on 12 cent. Ethics in *Miscellanea Janssen*, Louvain, 1948.

Chenu, "Découverte de la Nature," *Cahiers d'Histoire Mondiale*, 1953.

Vernet, on William of Conches' *Scriptorium*, I, 1946–47, pp. 243–59.

Then I think this is a book: Liebschutz, *Medieval Humanism in the Writings of John of Salisbury*.

These may be hard. To make things easier I may send you the title of something for light reading one of these days, but I haven't got a line on anything particularly intriguing at least to me, but I will let you know if I unearth a good title.

Really it is no trouble to me to send you things; it helps clear the decks for action and it is nice to feel wanted, though not perhaps edifying. But I am grateful for your interest and kindness.

To Father Tarcisius (James) Conner, O.C.S.O.

Father Tarcisius, a monk of Gethsemani, was at this time studying theology in Rome, and wrote to Thomas Merton while passing through Paris.

November 27, 1962

Thanks for your good letter from Paris. It reached me after about five weeks, and I enjoyed it. They must have sent it over by whale. I was glad you were able to see Marie Tadié; she certainly has her troubles. As a layperson dealing with religious, she has experiences which go beyond the ordinary experiences of laypeople. We are constantly in some kind of jam, including now: so please pray for us. She and I are just two twin little doormats at the front door of the great edifice which you now inhabit. Ah me. But I offer it all up; into every life a little rain must fall, as your successor in the job of vocation director loves to say. Oceans, too.

The book of Fr. Adalbert [de Vogüé] (*La Communauté et l'Abbé*) is exceptionally good. It is one of the best treatments of the cenobitic life I have seen (seriously). It makes you realize the importance of making the cenobitic life what it really ought to be and not just some kind of a chummy picnic-cum-hairshirts. It is neither sentimental nor totalitarian, and it points up the fact that the cenobitic society is unique with a function entirely its own, and unlike any other collectivity. When the cenobium is reduced to the level of any other society, including the community of an active modern religious congregation, it loses its raison d'être and it is normal for people to feel out of place in it. That is, people with monastic vocations.

I won't waste time telling you about the waterworks, etc.

Next year we will probably amalgamate the two novitiates. It would be a logical time to fire me, and I would be delighted. However, we will see what comes. I think it is going to be a pretty delicate operation and it will have to be done slowly and carefully and without false optimism and easy clichés, or celebrations of Sunday-school euphoria.

Also the famous monastic formation—which, I understand, solves all problems for everybody forever—is to be initiated. It will be more or less a continuation of the novitiate schedule, without formal classes in anything except Scripture and monastic stuff, and not in the novitiate (God forbid). Fr. Flavian will run it. I don't know if it is going to include your professed brothers. Rev. Fr. thinks of six years simple profession for everyone. Maybe they could start philosophy before the end of that, however, if they are to be ordained. Quite a few evidently will not go on for ordination (Paul of the X, for one, Cyprian, perhaps Basil, etc.).

Big question, what to call the three new groups: choir clerics, choir non-clerics, and brothers. I suggest 1) Non-contemplative megalo-schemos, 2) Non-intellectual and non-ascetic stravrophores, and 3) Utterly disgusted rassophores.

I have now beaten my brains beyond measure to find news for you and I have reached the limit. Be sure to write again and tell me all the inside secrets of the Council, and what Cardinal Alfrink said about Cardinal Ottaviani; not however what Cardinal Ottaviani said about Cardinal Alfrink. (Enough of that. Now I have to go and write up applications for all my friends who are trying to get Guggenheim Fellowships so that they can live somewhere decent like Greece for a while.)

Be good, keep your feet dry, your eyes open, your heart at peace and your soul in the joy of Christ. May Our Lady be with you. All the best to all the brethren. If I get time I will enclose a note for Fr. Chrysogonus. If it is here, please give it to him.

To Mother Myriam Dardenne, O.C.S.O.

Mother Myriam Dardenne, previously Abbess of the monastery of Nazareth in Belgium, was the founding Superior of the Belgian Cistercian foundation at Redwoods, California, in 1962. She and her companions stopped briefly at Gethsemani en route and met Thomas Merton, whom they considered a kindred spirit. Merton later visited Redwoods Monastery in both May and early October, 1968, as he was about to leave for the Far East.

December 12, 1962

I hope you are by now well settled in your new home. I have not heard any news from you or about you, but I presume you are well and that all the Sisters are very happy and busy, and that the Redwoods have lived up fully to your expectations.

The purpose of this letter is to enclose a copy of another letter I have just written to Graham Carey, the editor of a magazine called *Good Work*, who will be interested in your projects. I hope he will write to you, and put you in touch with people who will be interested in your vestments. As time goes on I will write to other people, but I presume there is no need for a furious rush right away. Let me know if there is anything you specially need, or if there are any questions I can answer . . .

It is quite cold here and there is snow on the ground. Christmas is near. It is a real Advent, cold and silent. Next week the novices will get Christmas trees, not too many I hope, and decorate the novitiate for the feast.

Are you making vestments yet? I am interested to know. I might perhaps ask Father Abbot if we could get a set from you for the novitiate chapel. Our white set is very shabby and does not fit properly.

We have not forgotten the joy of your visit with us. It was a grace to see in you the simplicity and good sense of the Cistercian tradition, so to speak incarnate. There is a great deal of talk about monastic tradition and monastic spirituality, but actually the reality of people who live the monastic life in simplicity is much more impressive than words about it. We do not have to have too many splendid programs and doctrines if we seek and find the Lord, and this we do not in ideals only but in the realities of life. Still I am sure that one reason why you are all functioning well is that you have approached the life intelligently and with a little knowledge. Pray that we may do the same . . .

To Graham Carey

Graham Carey, editor of Good Work, *had been in correspondence with Thomas Merton previous to this encounter regarding the nuns at Redwoods. A number of Merton articles appeared in the pages of* Good Work *over the years, including sections of the unpublished manuscript* Art and Worship.

December 12, 1962

I think you will be interested in a foundation of Cistercian nuns that has been made out in California. They are from Belgium, and very superior types, with good sense and good taste in plenty. They intend to make vestments and do other things like that for a living, and the principles on which they intend to work are very sound. They are not going to strive for facile effects or for publicity, because they want to maintain a high level. They do not want to have to condescend to sham and compromise which would be inevitable in the event they got mixed up in commercialism.

Hence they will need the support of discerning people and so I refer them to you. I do not know how well established they are as yet, but they will soon want to be in contact with people who will be interested in their work, and perhaps if you yourself go out that way, or if you know of anyone significant there who might drop in on them and get acquainted with them, that would be the obvious start. When they have something to show you, I think no more explanations will be needed.

Unfortunately I have not been able to get permission to come to the meeting in New Mexico. I anticipated this, of course, but thought I ought to ask, as you seemed serious about wanting me to come. I wish I could, but unfortunately my Abbot does not give these permissions, except to laybrothers or people on business which is less esoteric than art (art is thought to be esoteric). But in any case the fact that it is a kind of convention makes it practically impossible for me, because the more public an event is, the less chance there is one might get permission to attend it . . .

To Dame Marcella Van Bruyn, O.S.B.

Dame Marcella Van Bruyn entered Stanbrook Abbey in England when she was forty-five, and after twenty-three years of monastic life left to lead a solitary life. While at Stanbrook she wrote the hymns that were included in the breviary when the change from Latin to the vernacular occurred. It was Jacques Maritain who first put Dame Marcella in contact with Thomas Merton. Stanbrook Abbey Press published an English translation of Raïssa Maritain's poetry, as well as several books by Merton, including his translation of a letter of Guigo the Carthusian and a prayer of Cassiodorus.

February 23, 1963

Since Jacques Maritain told me of your project, I have been expecting your letter. Actually I think there is even less chance of conflict than he thinks. I am not actually translating all of Raïssa's poems, or even an entire book. In fact, I have only translated the enclosed, with one more, an *inédit* of four lines which Jacques found in her notes.

These translations which I am enclosing will probably appear in a magazine called *Jubilee* in April. They will also be in a book of my own verse which includes a section of translations, mostly from Spanish. I do not even know if all of these poems I have translated will appear in the book.

Thus you see that it is not a question of two books getting in each other's way. In fact, I will try to insert a note in my own book, about your limited edition. It might help. Will you please give me the relevant details?

According to present plans, my own book of verse (including translations) is supposed to appear early in 1964. You may doubtless have published your translation before that time. But even if the two books appear simultaneously, I do not think there is the slightest chance of interference. On the contrary: between us we may prepare the way for a complete English edition of her poems "for the trade," as they say. In fact I will sound out my publisher on this, though he is perhaps not quite the right one.

You are perfectly right about the Journal and the poems. I have been so deeply moved by Raïssa's poetic and spiritual experience, and of course Jacques's too, for they are inseparable. There is a light that shines through them into our darkness and it has an unmistakable origin. Her purity of heart and her fidelity are most inspiring. I very much like the *Notes sur le Pater*. I hope they will be translated soon.

About limited editions: one of the best hand-printers in this country is a good friend of mine, Victor Hammer. He lives in a town some seventy miles from here, which is not far as American distances go. He and I have worked together on several projects: "Sayings of Desert Fathers," "Prose Poems," and so on. But he is getting old now and has given up printing. I very much enjoy this kind of thing and also believe it to be quite important. So I am always eager to hear about hand-presses that might be interested in doing such things.

For example I am enclosing a translation I did of a letter of Guigo the Carthusian. I am trying to interest a very fine printer in this: but he too has other things to do and may not want to take it on. What do you think about it? I would write a note of introduction. It is of course quite short. There are other possibilities I can think of. If I can provide you with an interesting text, I would be delighted to do so. Do please let me know: doubtless this is something that your Lady Abbess would want to decide on, but I am mentioning it here since we are on the subject of your press . . .

To Dame Hildelith Cumming, O.S.B.

Dame Hildelith, a Benedictine nun of Stanbrook Abbey in England, was the Abbey Press's printer at this time.

March 23, 1963

Thank you for your kind letter. I assure you that I am brimming over with confidence in you, and delighted that you will print the Guigo Letter. Your plans sound excellent. Would you like to let me see samples of how it might look in both types? I think I prefer Spectrum, but am not sure if I remember what the other one looks like, or if I have ever seen it and known what I was looking at. You see, I greatly enjoy projects like this, and therefore I make myself rather a nuisance. But because I do it for the joy (and I think that is really not so far, after all, from doing it for the Lord Who gives the joy) there is no need to worry about the money question. Father Abbot has no objection to my doing these things just for the sake of producing a good book. All I ask would be a few copies of the book. My only idea about this is that perhaps it ought to be quite small in format, and even then with plenty of margin: a small booklet that one theoretically slips in the pocket. I do not know if that is what you were thinking of, but I leave it all to you.

There is no trouble about proofs. Airmail is usually quite efficient. And be sure that we are in no great hurry. I have learned by experience that it does no good to expect speed even from the most businesslike and energetic Americans. They put on the speed when the fancy takes them: but the rest of the time they are speeding with somebody else. I can think of no book of mine that has not appeared without interminable delays.

I am enclosing the note on Guigo. You are right; it will lend variety. By the way, there is no need to have this censored by the Order, or as far as I know by the bishop either. I leave that up to your Lady Abbess. As far as the Order goes, it will be enough to slip in a *Cum permissu superiorum* somewhere. I thought it would be nice to have a dedication, too. It will be to the Procurator General of the Carthusians, and it could read:

For Dom
J.-B. P.

I think you could do something interesting with that. As to the number, I leave that to you. Perhaps a thousand would be too many.

It is really a pleasure to be in contact with Stanbrook and thus, I hope, more closely united to you in prayer. Be sure that I will think of other projects. For example there are some short selections from Benet of Canfield that would go nicely with an introduction. Perhaps a few poems, or a meditation, or some prayers. We will see . . .

To Archbishop Paul Philippe, O.P.

Archbishop Paul Philippe was at this time Secretary of the Vatican's Sacred Congregation for Religious. He had previously visited Gethsemani and given lectures to the community.

April 5, 1963

First of all, I have delayed a long time to congratulate you on your elevation to the archiepiscopate: I did not want to bother you with a letter that was only a personal message. However, now that I have some more important matters to deal with, let me preface them with a heartfelt congratulation and the wish that God may grant you much light and help in your arduous task. Surely the graces of the episcopate are to no one more necessary than to you, in your work as Secretary to the Congregation of Religious.

I have long felt and thought it might be a matter of duty for me to send you a few observations that might contribute, ever so slightly, to the future discussion of the problems of religious in the Council. As the novice master of this not unimportant Abbey, having been in office more than seven years, and now charged with both the laybrother and choir novices, it is possible that I may have something of interest to say, though I am aware that I have not really resolved in my own mind the many difficult questions which are concerned with the mere *formulation* of problems.

The first thing that I would like to say is that I wonder if we have even identified our problems. There are in religion, and in this house, some who think they know exactly what the problems are, and therefore have no hesitation in prescribing definite solutions. But for them the problems seem to be the same as they were four hundred years ago and the remedies are consequently the same. It is for them simply a question of "laxity" and what needs to be done is to "tighten up discipline." On the other hand, those who obscurely see that this *simpliste* diagnosis is inadequate, tend to increase the confusion by simply seeking to relax rigidity and promote a merely human and provisional, if not pragmatic, spirit of well-being and recreation. Both these views are, it seems to me, wrong. They tend to generate much confusion and in the long run the greatest obstacle to progress is not one of these views or the other, but the specious dialectic that takes place between them.

Since I have been in this monastery I have seen scores of really good subjects leave after vows, even after solemn vows and the priesthood. I think it is true that in the case of priests, the studies and the inappropriate priestly formation led to a loss of the true sense of their monastic vocation, among other causes. It is possible that the new course of monastic studies and the longer delay before clerical studies, introduced here at Gethsemani, may help to mitigate this problem. In effect, the monastic formation is now prolonged six years beyond the novitiate, before clerical studies are thought of. And it is hoped that many will not even want to be priests at all, but will be happier to remain monks. There are several very good subjects who definitely prefer this already, but there is always the fear that Superiors will override their preference, and in the end we will have a bad situation, with the non-priest choir monks being regarded as somehow second-rate. It is most important that some of the best subjects be allowed and encouraged to be simple monks and not priests.

Although it is true that many professed who have departed from this community were men who did not have all the qualities required for this life, and perhaps lacked a really sound formation, yet it must be said that some apparently excellent subjects have left. Several among those whom I have had as students and whom I have known to be richly endowed, deep, serious, and evidently called to the contemplative life, have left this monastery, all declaring, with more or less good reason, that they felt it was simply not possible for them in this milieu, and in the framework of our life, to develop as they believed God wished them to develop. Constantly I am confronted with the sincere question, on the part of the novices and young monks, who wonder if they can sincerely wish to become like the senior religious they see in the community. These good seniors are, many of them, quite regular and exact, but the novices seem to feel that the regularity of such good men is nevertheless rather empty and that their lives are devoid of any depth and value which one is led to expect in contemplatives, or in any man living close to God in silence and far from the world. It does not seem to me that this criticism is altogether unfair or without foundation; on the contrary, I think it ought to be taken seriously. It seems to me that if there is a certain mistrust for discipline and austerity as practical ideals, this may be because those who are most strenuous in praising discipline, in some monastic communities, are making discipline unattractive by the rigidity, inhumanity, and apparent emptiness of their own lives. This is a serious obstacle to the genuine growth of true regularity, seen not as an end in itself but as part of a greater and more vital whole. It also encourages the delusion of those who imagine that the answer to our problems is to be found in a spirit of recreation or in pointless novelties. There is some danger of confusing *novelty* with genuine *renewal*.

I have much to do with members of other religious institutes who inquire about admission to our Order. In most cases they do not have vocations to our life, and yet their complaints that they lack a genuine spiritual life and true opportunities to fulfill their vocation in their present institute seem to be well founded. It seems to me that one of the problems of all religious in this country is the fact that *opportunities to grow and develop along the true lines of one's vocation,* especially in its contemplative aspect, are generally lacking. Beyond the essential tasks of the institute, it seems that more or less everywhere in this country religious have to devote a great part of their time to occupations that fall outside their normal rule and vocation when they do not altogether contradict it. It seems to me that in every Order there should be provision made for *much greater flexibility* and more numerous opportunities for individuals with sincere desires for a deeper interior life to live in a more favorable milieu. The formation of something analogous to the Carmelite deserts would be very desirable, and especially in the monastic Orders provision should be made for those who desire greater quiet and solitude. They should be encouraged and helped in this legitimate desire, so that it could be fulfilled in their own Order, without transitus to a stricter Order. But

I am afraid this would require a lot of originality and new perspectives. Meanwhile with things as they are, it would seem that every opportunity should be granted for the fulfillment of true vocations to greater solitude and contemplation, and that considerable elasticity in this matter should be permitted.

Without going into further details, I can briefly indicate the context of my thought when I say that I think valid and positive suggestions can be offered by men like Dom Jean Leclercq, Dom Damasus Winzen and Dom Gregorio Lemercier, among others. Obviously not all Superiors will be able to go as far as these have done, but all should be willing to look more in that direction.

At present I believe that the situation of religious in the United States is critical, and this may be true even of those who are apparently flourishing, such as the contemplatives. I do not think that this situation can be properly understood when it is looked at only as a problem of regularity. I think it is much deeper than that, a problem of *truth*, and I believe there are not a few who feel, as I do, that a shortsighted and distorted emphasis on exterior discipline alone can serve as an evasion of the real underlying problem of authenticity. Part of the acuteness of this problem comes from the fact that the older generation has a notably different idea of sincerity from that held by the new generation. It is a fact that many of the young religious who have left our Order have felt that in various ways they were not being treated with a genuine sincerity and loyalty, and that their needs and problems met with evasive and insufficient replies.

As regards the apostolic function of contemplative communities, especially in the New World, Africa, Asia, etc., it would seem that little good can be done at the present time by large, wealthy, self-sufficient monasteries which maintain themselves in complete isolation by virtue of economic independence—and with the help of rich benefactors. This would seem to be procuring solitude at the cost of poverty, and without edification. It would seem that small contemplative communities are needed which, while preserving jealously their solitude and life of prayer, might also in discreet and limited ways offer opportunities for dialogue and spiritual communication with members of the surrounding society, particularly the intellectual and religious leaders, whether Christian or otherwise. There is a spiritual work of mercy which has almost become a corporal work in our time: offering to others some small share temporarily in the silence and solitude of a monastic setting. This does not mean "closed retreats" only, but a much more informal and human sharing in the benefits of the monastic milieu, perhaps without organized conferences and exercises, indeed perhaps better without them. This would seem to be a much more valuable form of monastic apostolate than the maintaining of parishes and schools, though these may be necessary.

For the monastic Orders to carry out their true function in the Church it seems that they should be recognized as quite distinct from other and more active institutes and that they should have their essential nature and vocation emphasized. In short, I wonder if the problems of religious Orders are not really to be solved on a much deeper level than that of organization. Our problems are problems of *spirit* and not merely of *institution*. What we lack is not merely discipline but above all profound and serious *life*. To give these problems our institutional solution which once again stifles the beginnings of life is really no help at all. But to imagine that "life" is to be understood and lived on a merely physical level is another delusion. In short, our problem is not to be solved so much by *rules* as by *men* who are alive with the Spirit of the Risen Saviour and are not afraid to seek new paths guided by the light of perennial tradition and the wisdom of Mother Church.

It is a pleasure to write you again, Most Reverend and dear Father in Christ. I have not spoken of my own affairs, since there is no need to do so. I think often of you, and remember you in prayer. I often remember the pleasant days you spent with us years ago, and hope we may one day have the joy of seeing you again.

To Dom Gabriel Sortais

Easter Day, 1963

I am writing to you not only to wish you the Easter joys, although I do so with much filial respect. But I also wanted to tell you how interested I was by the encyclical *Pacem in Terris*.

Now the Holy Father clearly says that war can no longer be used as an instrument of justice in a world where nuclear arms are possessed. Fortunately he does not need to be approved by the censors of the Order in America, for they said very energetically last year that this thesis, when I proposed it myself, was wrong, scandalous, and I don't know what more.

I still have the manuscript of the book I wrote [*Peace in the Post-Christian Era*]. Many very serious persons ask me to speak to you again about it. Would it not be permissible, dear Most Reverend Father, to recast this book while commenting on *Pacem in Terris*, for it is something very important here where most Catholics will be in complete stupefaction, since they, for the most part, believed that war, or rather the threat of nuclear war, was almost necessary to "defend Christendom."

So I ask you very humbly to think once more of this poor book, which is but the recasting of the articles already approved, and which will be a necessary commentary on the encyclical. People already know what I think, generally speaking. So there will certainly not be any scandal; on the contrary, it will be the opportune moment to make clear this doctrine which may appear so strange to so many American Catholics. You will say that the professional theologians must do it themselves. Well, they will do it, no doubt. But we must allow them the time to find themselves again, and to retrace their way to begin thinking over this question again. While my book is already finished, and only demands the additions and the clarifications that the encyclical suggests.

To Dom Aelred Graham

A copy of Aelred Graham's Zen Catholicism *had been sent to Thomas Merton, which he in turn reviewed favorably in* America.

April 24, 1963

As a matter of fact I went ahead and wrote a review. I liked the book so much and found so much in it that I agreed with that I could hardly do otherwise. The thing is that although Zen has the appearances of being a sort of fad in this country, it is actually a life-saver for many people, here at the exhausted end of an era in which thinking has been dominated by Cartesianism, Kant and so on. Certainly, as you have so well seen, a correction of perspective and the discard of a lot of useless baggage will help Catholicism a great deal: not that we don't believe, but we are out of touch with life: and that affects our faith a great deal, because subjective sincerity is not enough. We have to *be* real, not just mean to be. And the paradox is of course that we *are*: and we try to make our being real by adding unreality to it, through useless mental gyrations.

So I am sure your insights will mean a great deal to monasticism in this country too. You do not need to worry about that *Atlantic* article. I see perfectly what you were driving at, and agree. I have had the salutary experience of seeing my early books through the eyes of novices and postulants who have read them and got them all wrong, through my fault. Precisely what was lacking was the "Zen" element, which I certainly had no need to "acquire," but which I had covered up with a lot of useless concepts I picked up here, and accepted as if they were articles of faith. All the fatuous divisions between action and contemplation, and so on! These are of course necessary in discourse: but in life?

I would very much enjoy meeting you. I do not remember having heard that you wanted to come here, or that you even thought of it. But I shall certainly ask, and I see no reason why Dom James should say no.

We have a number of friends in common, and everything I ever hear about Portsmouth always sounds fine. I am particularly glad about the Zen garden . . .

P.S. I spoke to Fr. Abbot since writing the above, and he gladly gave permission for me to speak with you if you come—just let us know anytime. You are always most welcome.

To Dame Hildelith Cumming

May 1, 1963

It is a very lovely May morning here, with larks singing and not a cloud in the sky. And for several days I have been resolving to get something in the post for you to look at, in case you might want to print it. So under Our Lady's gaze I send you these texts from Benet of Canfield.

I think they are very interesting indeed and the kind of people who like the *Cloud of Unknowing* will also like them very much indeed. However they will require a little correcting and editing, and that will not be hard because the editor of the full text, from the ms. of which I took this, is at Oxford. So if you like these pieces, or if your editorial staff agrees with the choice, we can proceed. I would want to add a little introduction myself, and then the editor can at the same time make corrections and additions. She has already made a few notes in the margin of this manuscript.

The editor is the wife of the Master of St. Edmund's Hall: Mrs. Etta Gullick. She can be reached at 7 Crick Rd., Oxford.

I really think this would make a very attractive little book and one that would do a great deal of good. So I hope that you will be interested in it. And of course there is absolutely no rush.

Thank you so much for the samples of printing which arrived safely some time ago. I was very delighted and impressed with them. I can see the beauty of Romanee, especially the capitals, for use in titles. For the Guigo I myself would still prefer Spectrum. Romanee would perhaps be more in the spirit of Benet. Some of your little prayer-cards are exquisite. Your book *Unless the Grain Die* is also very fine, though I think that the great variety in it, appropriate for that book, would be too much for something like the Guigo, which, it seems to me, should remain quite plain . . .

To Father Paul Bourne, O.C.S.O.

Father Paul Bourne, a Cistercian monk of Holy Spirit Monastery, Conyers, Georgia, was head censor (now called "reader") of the Order, and one of the more benign ones. The exchange with James Baldwin never materialized.

May 1, 1963

Here is a problem for you as Head Censor: I hope you can help me unravel it. The matter is quite important. It concerns the awful race situation in this country. I have long felt that this was an issue on which something needed to be said, but I have deliberately refrained in every way from taking initiatives. However it has finally come to my doorstep in a form which makes me think that I really must take some kind of action.

You may or may not know that a Negro writer, James Baldwin, has written a powerful book on this and has got people alerted, in some cases upset. But the book is true, and it points to the truth that unless there is a change of direction, there is going to be a terrible lot of trouble. It is therefore a question of conscience for the entire nation.

Now the editor of a big, well-financed and well-edited Catholic magazine, *Ramparts*, has felt that he ought to do something about it, and he wants a dialogue, in letter form, between me and James Baldwin, for one issue some time. I cannot, for my part, refuse to consider this. It seems to me that, if I can, I am bound in conscience to try to do something. The exact tenor of the ideas that will be expressed will, of course, depend on the exchange of letters. Basically I am in agreement with Baldwin on the extreme seriousness of the situation, and on the gravity of the problem of justice involved. Also I am convinced that the mere "good will" of the liberal sector of the white race is not good enough. It has to get a lot deeper and be ready for more sacrifice and more real action. I am not of course going to make precise prescriptions, but will stick to the realm of principles, and they will be on a spiritual level.

The question now arises: it is simply not conceivable that this work be done and written and ready for publication, and be turned down totally on the grounds of being "inopportune," which is Dom Gabriel's favorite maneuver. Hence, the question of *opportunité* must be settled *first*. That is to say, the articles should be admitted as acceptable *in principle*, but of course my part of the work would be subject to any change, correction, editing and cutting desired by *reasonable* censorship. Obviously once the thing is undertaken, the problem of scandal given to a non-Catholic Negro who is already pretty skeptical about us Catholics has to be considered. If you think the whole thing should just be dropped, now is the time to drop it.

What possibilities occur? You may think of others.

a) Perhaps you and Dom James (who agrees with me) might put the thing to the General in the way most acceptable to him. Pointing out that, unlike nuclear war, this is more a *national* issue, not international, and would be considered eminently acceptable in America as coming from a monk. That I could speak on this subject with edification, and that the mere fact of my taking on the job would not give scandal, *au contraire*.

b) Or perhaps since they are "letters," one could go ahead without censorship. I don't suggest this unless you think it best, because after all they would not just be tucked away in the letters to the editor; the exchange would be a real feature with a big play in the magazine. There is no question it ought to be censored, in a magazine that is widely known and circulated like this. (I have tended to look the other way when letters of mine to literary friends have turned up, in part, in small magazines read by limited groups.) (That is not the case here.)

c) I do not know if you would feel free just to tell the censors that, as far as you are concerned, the reasons why the *opportunité* clause should be taken as fulfilled beforehand are compelling. Doubtless you would rather have the General settle that. You have been very generous about the reviews, and on that point I certainly agree with you. Also the translations.

In any case, you will be able to talk this over with Dom James, but as the editor is waiting for a reply, I would appreciate any word from you that you feel you can send along, at your convenience.

Hope you have been enjoying the visit of Dom Colomban. He is a fine Father Immediate, very understanding and good, and he gave us a really good visitation. I wonder how the Chapter of the American province (!) will turn out. Hope they don't industrialize us up to the hilt or something. I wonder whether we are not going in all directions at once. I think that for the time being the business about the Brothers has calmed down here, but I think it would be a great mistake if we ended up by just abolishing them in fact. That would be a terrible loss. And certainly it would disconcert the best of the Brothers here. I think the "Brothers' choir" business is being pushed a little too hard and too far here. I think we are threatened with a little over-organization, at times. One has to leave an area of freedom and leisure for the monk, and not regiment him into all kinds of assembly line jobs followed by assembly line prayers. Not that the Brothers' choir is like that; but it can become so. And all the eager beavers start campaigning for their idea of beautiful music: it turns their prayer life into a purgatory such as ours can unfortunately sometimes be. All because of this insatiability for collective pleasure and celebration. The simplest is best, in my estimation, and goes deepest and farthest. Away with pontificalia. I had better stop, or I will be excommunicated.

But about the dialogue with James Baldwin: I hope you can help out, and am grateful in advance . . .

To Dame Hildelith Cumming

May 12, 1963

About American distribution of the Raïssa Maritain poems: first I think Princeton is a good idea, especially as the Maritains were there for so long. The only other suggestion I have is my own publisher, one of them, who does a lot of limited editions: you could write to James Laughlin, New Directions, Norfolk, Connecticut. Explain your problem to him and I am sure he would be helpful.

Victor Hammer also mentioned the Oxford Press. You could probably make contact with them in England, but of course they do a great deal of business over here.

That is about the extent of the advice I am able to give you on this question. When it comes to the money end of it, I am afraid I am as stupid as a stone.

I do think, however, that there will be no real problem getting a limited edition to people who like Raïssa Maritain. The Maritains had many friends who were well off, in fact rolling in money. If they know about the book they will surely buy it.

Our letters appear to be crossing, so I will not add more to this one. I am enclosing a little thing with some texts from Fénelon you might like to read. I am not suggesting it as something to print. But still it is worth reading, especially in the light of *Pacem in Terris*. Please overlook the mistakes which the typist made in the stencils. We have not been able to go over every copy by hand.

I am so happy that you want to do something with "a distinctive mark" for the Guigo text. I look forward to seeing proofs (perhaps on the way) and will write at once when I receive them.

Blessings to you and Dame Marcella and all your community. I have always felt very close to Stanbrook since the old days when I realized that you had a long-standing tradition of translations, for instance of St. Teresa.

June 9, 1963

Thanks for your good letter and for the two little designs for the *cum permissu*. I find the "more carefully done" (the circular) one most attractive. I think it has a great deal of beauty and spirituality. I do hope you will use it. It will be even more effective reduced. And no one has to be able to see what it is without looking.

You are probably right about Benet, though I really wonder if the whole thing hasn't become rather a dead letter since Bremond and Co. have rehabilitated the man. Eckhart is getting printed all over the place, too, and got a very good article in the *Dictionnaire de Spiritualité*. Still, I am sure it would be better in modern English, but I have no time to do this myself. Etta Gullick might be willing to. She is a very good person and an Anglican, friend of E. I. Watkin and so on. I am sure she would be willing to do anything to make it more attractive. I like the Penguin edition of *Cloud*. There was a moderately good modernized version in this country, too, recently.

I am trying to get E. I. Watkin interested in doing a good selection from Dom Augustine Baker and making a really readable little book that would introduce people to him. I myself have never ploughed through the whole *Sancta Sophia*. But I do like Baker immensely. I think everything should be done to bring his fine things back into a place where they will be accessible. I think the whole question of Baker and the Cambrai nuns is extraordinarily interesting, a very important moment in the history of monasticism. And you know, I must confess that I did not connect you people at all with Cambrai. How stupid of me. Of course this makes it clear why I have always had such a respect for Stanbrook and have always felt close to you, and indeed now am. We have Dame Laurentia's life in the novitiate library; I got it for the novices a couple of years ago, but had not yet read it myself. I am doing so now, and enjoying it. I forget whether I sent you the notes on the English Mystics, but I am sure Dame Marcella has them. There is a little on Baker there, but I would like to do more.

The account of Dame Catherine Gascoigne's prayer is very fine. She is an admirable person. I want to get at the life of Dame Gertrude, too, but this is not a hint that I want to borrow a copy from you. I will get it from a library in this country. Unless you do have a couple of extra copies (I mean of Baker's life of her), because I would hate to see anything so precious get lost.

It is now frightfully hot here. I just got through with a five-day retreat up in a hermitage in the woods (did not sleep, eat or say Mass there, but was there for all the rest). It was wonderful, even though hot. I remembered Stanbrook there, and you. I hope you got the more pleasant kind of graces. I have a Moslem friend who feels himself urged to pray for me, and I pray for him: but when he gets the urge to pray for me on the *night of destiny* (a key point in the fast of Ramadan), I usually get a whacking cross of some sort. I don't know usually when Ramadan is, or the night of destiny (it varies), but I can generally tell if I get knocked on the head some time in March that Abdul Aziz is praying for me. I send him books about St. John of the Cross and he sends me some about the Sufis. Great people.

I will make another attempt with Fénelon. I don't know how good he really is: very limited and dry, but a person for whom I feel great sympathy.

To Dom Jean Leclercq

June 10, 1963

How are you? I do not know where this letter will find you, but I suppose the best thing to do at this season is to send it to Clervaux, and it can follow you.

What I want to ask is: can I borrow an offprint of your article on the *"Reclus et recluses dans le diocèse de Metz"* from the *Rev. Hist. Eccles. du Diocèse de Metz?* I hate to trouble you about this. I hope it is possible for you to lend it to me without too much inconvenience, or to tell me where I might perhaps be able to get a photocopy of the article, or a film or something. I want to do a little study of Grimlaicus, perhaps for the *Collectanea* or perhaps for the new *Monastic Studies* of Berryville, which is very well done.

The thing that interests me about Grimlaicus is not the rather impractical setup he has devised for recluses, but the spirit that animates his rule. It is as far as I can see the closest western counterpart to the oriental idea of the megaloschemos in the common life. This has a great deal of importance just at the present moment, when I think we need to understand the need to allow *growth* and *development* in mature monks, toward a more deeply contemplative life. At present, as you know, there is an exaggerated fear that all attempts to develop present some kind of temptation or danger, and also there is fear that if one legitimate aspiration is encouraged, a lot of less legitimate ones will arise to bother the Superior.

Things are developing well here, however. I received permission to take some time in solitude up at the hermitage, and so far I have had six full days up there, with more to come. Not allowed to sleep there, or say Mass there, but what I have had so far is a great godsend. It has certainly settled any doubts I may have had about the need for real solitude in my own life. Though I realize that I am not the ideal of an absolute hermit, since my solitude is partly that of an intellectual and poet, still it is a very real inclination for solitude and when I have continuous solitude for a more or less extended period, it means a great deal and is certainly the best remedy for the tensions and pressures that I generate when I am with the community. It is indeed the only really satisfactory remedy that I have been able to find. Distractions and "recreations" with visitors and active retreat work, etc., do absolutely nothing to help. Also this little bit of solitude helps me to appreciate the real values that do exist in the common life, though they certainly manage to get hidden when I get too much of them. I hope to take more time in retreat later in the summer or in the early fall. And perhaps get a day at a time more frequently.

There has been a lot of talk about our Monastic Formation course, but actually it does not amount to much. However, please let us know if you are in this country, because I am very anxious to have you give the group a talk if possible, or two or three even. But if you can spare us even a small amount of time I would be delighted, and we would all be indebted to you. So if you are in the Midwest, I hope you can give us a little time and I would be glad to see you again.

Any suggestions you may have about Grimlaicus will be very welcome, and I do hope I can get a look at your article. I liked very much some of your pages on St. Gregory in the *Histoire de la Spiritualité Chrétienne*. I have used your material there in a long article I have done on the question of the "Humanity of Christ in Prayer" as it was seen by the monastic Fathers. For them it was no "problem" as it seems to have been in the time of St. Teresa . . .

To Father Tarcisius (James) Conner

June 23, 1963

Thanks for your letter and for your frivolous card in Italian. Even the Italians are now infected with this awful American humor. What is the world coming to? I enjoyed your letter, and your letters to the community have been very good. I think everybody appreciates your detailed accounts of what is said in conferences by this or that one. Certainly that makes more sense than the usual chatter, and it is a real contribution. Keep it up.

Are you at Mont-des-Cats now? I presume so, and that is where I will send this. I have a lot of respect for Dom André [Louf, Abbot of Mont-des-Cats]: I think he is one of the few in the Order who really has something, though maybe there are more coming up. By the way I hope he is pleased with the Berryville *Monastic Studies*. I think they have made a very good beginning and that is something we can work on. I am doing a longish study for them on Monastic Prayer (Humanity of Christ, acc. to Cassian, Gregory, Bede, Leo, Ambrose Autpert).

The Monastic Formation does not really amount to much. It is going along quietly. It seems to be something just because for the time being they are all running around discussing it, but that is dying down too. It is just that nobody ever told the brothers that the Fathers of the Church existed, and that there was such a thing as Monastic Tradition, and that it was alive. Tradition, according to the usual concept, is ipso facto dead. If you get it from somebody else, it is dead. This is a myth, and of course it does not stop people from running around slavishly imitating the world models.

You know that Father J. left. That is a rather tragic thing, but I don't think there was anything anybody could really do about it here. I was hoping that he would get organized outside, but it does not seem that he is doing that. Pray for him. He really does belong in the monastic life. So do some of the others who have left. But not too many, I suppose. It is best that most of them have gone. One is left with a feeling that the house is full of people who have no notion what it is all about, and this is because they cannot accept the dead, but zealous voluntarism of the people who make it all consist in keeping rules, period: and not accepting this, they have nothing better, indeed nothing even as good, to put in its place. That is the trouble. And so one is always landing up with the alternative: shut your eyes and do it on sheer willpower, or else quit. That reminds me: are they doing anything about Rancé this year? This is a sort of centenary, isn't it? He is the granddaddy of the willpower boys and yet there was a lot that was really genuine and admirable in his reform. But once again, people refuse to take a really sane perspective on such things: it has got to be all or nothing. Either Rancé is the greatest saint of the Order or else he is a devil. Nothing in between. We can't accept the fact that a man can be a serious, good, in some ways admirable monk, and at the same time an obsessive neurotic, defeating himself and blocking the Holy Ghost by his own best zeal. Yet that is the kind of thing we have most of in our Order.

Really, the novitiate is very peaceful. The merger with the brothers went beautifully and I am wondering now why we took so long to think of it. It is a very good move. I think the simple fact of the Junior brothers, Junior choir, and all the novices being in some conferences together is also a good thing, even though to most of them what is said is practically meaningless. It does give an impression of unity, and I suppose that is something to be grateful for.

Well, anyway, there are basic realities in the Order that cannot be denied or avoided: one of them is the unity of charity, in the Spirit, which is able to survive all the superficial oddities that are promoted in the name of togetherness. For this we have to be thankful. The monastic life is a great thing, and there is much life in it yet, many possibilities of growth.

I don't know if I will get around to writing a book on Monastic Spirituality, but I am supposed to do one on Cassian, and maybe in my old age I will sum it all up. By my old age I mean some time in the next three years.

Well, say hello to all the Cats on the Mount. Especially to Dom André. Who is editor of the *Collectanea* now? I may review a new book on St. Anselm for them; it is very good, by a History Professor at Oxford. Anselm is very interesting, though not quite the pure monastic type that we are led to look for at the present moment. Yet in actual fact one of the greatest of monks: but with a definite eleventh-century character, I guess. But he is great . . .

To Dame Hildelith Cumming

June 29, 1963

About Guigo: here are some "precisions" on that. My advisor tells me that actually the problem of printing it as a "book" is really not a problem at all in England. It can be cleared with Burns, Oates in no time, and I will do that. But the problem does exist in America where I am in a very confused tangle with one of my publishers and it would just add infinitely to introduce even a small thing like this into it. Perhaps you could follow through with your original plan for the books to be sold in England, and do "pamphlets" for America. I think your description fits the idea of "pamphlet." I was told that a book means a "hard cover." But on the other hand there are millions of paperbacks floating around. I wonder if the flat back makes any difference? I would be inclined to think that might almost constitute a book. But I don't know about sections. This is getting to be terribly Talmudic, isn't it? I am very sorry indeed. But by all means let us think of doing it as a book at least outside the United States. And then, anyway, you are not publishing it in the United States. I really don't see the problem. How many copies would you expect to sell in the U.S., in any case?

About Dom Gerard Sitwell, I read one of his books, I think on "Medieval Spirituality," in that Encyclopedia series. I thought it was very well done, and I think as you do that he would be the logical one to work on the Baker mss. at Ampleforth. I do hope something will come of it. It does not necessarily have to be a "potted" edition of the *Sancta Sophia*: why not a decent edition of something that has never been printed before?

I have not tried to do anything yet about tracking down a copy of Dame Gertrude More in this country. But I would not want to borrow a copy from Stanbrook unless you had several extra ones, and evidently you haven't. If it cannot be found, perhaps there might be a possibility of photographing your copy. But don't let's bother with that for the moment, as I have many other things to get out of the way first.

I just got a nice letter from the librarian at Pusey House (Oxford) saying he plans to be in this country and wants to spend a few days here. Actually, we have lots of Anglicans and Protestants coming here for retreats and for conversations, and I see a lot of them. Do pray for this, please, and for all the other needs and problems of the Church in America. You probably don't know about the very active fight the Negroes are now putting up to get their full rights. And the very active resistance that is being offered by bigoted whites, especially in the Deep South. This is something for your prayers, because it may turn into a really nasty and explosive situation. In fact it already has in some places.

P.S. By the way, in the course of some work I ran across a bibliographical reference which may possibly refer to you? In the *Dictionnaire de Spiritualité*, article "Ermites," find: Ild. Cummins, "Modern Hermits," Pax, 1934. Do you know anything about this? I am interested in seeing the article.

To Father Thomas Fidelis (Francis) Smith, O.C.S.O.

Father Thomas Francis Smith is a monk of the Holy Spirit Abbey at Conyers, Georgia, who expressed an interest in the Jesus Prayer of the Eastern Church.

June 29, 1963

Probably you are overdoing the Jesus Prayer a bit. I think it is all very well for a hard-headed nineteenth-century Russian moujik to do that all day and all night, but it is not going to work for Americans today. And in any case, remember that you are adding this to an already rather heavy schedule. Our life as it stands is pretty overloaded with "means."

Personally I like the *Way of the Pilgrim* and it is a good stimulating book to read. The ideas are good, but we have to apply them to ourselves with due concern for our own situation. It seems to me that it is expecting too much to try to make our whole life center itself in the Jesus Prayer. And it is not necessary. I think that this repetition of the prayer is useful at certain times. I have recourse to it when I am plagued with distractions or half dead with sleep and can't do anything better. As for the breathing, I would get some idea of some good Yoga breathing, as described in a reliable book like Dechanet's *Christian Yoga*, and use that *sometimes*. But for the rest, the light of the Lord shines in our hearts always and all we need to do is to remind ourselves of it in the simplest possible way, and surrender to Him totally. If a simple ejaculation helps, well and good. Words do not always help. Just looking is often more helpful.

As to the inner warmth around the heart, as a result of pushing the prayer, don't fool with this. This is one of the misleading and risky aspects of Oriental prayer (see Simeon the New Theologian, who is off on this in many ways).

I think that reading some of the great Protestant O.T. theologians would help your prayer. Von Rad, for instance (without getting too stuck on his special axe-grinding), or Eichrodt. Anyway, I'll send a paper I did based on some of this material and you can see what I mean, and evaluate it for yourself. I am no Scripture scholar.

It seems to me that the Bible is a much better source of light than the Jesus Prayer. But all sources fail, except God Himself. And He is after all the most accessible. We get tired of means once in a while, and that is perhaps because we are nearer to the end than we realize.

It seems to me that we create obstacles for ourselves by setting up arbitrary division, "intellectual life" and "life of prayer." Each of us has to find the unity in which everything fits and takes its right place. For some, a certain amount of intellectual life is necessary for the life of prayer. Each must work out just what the right measure may be. And it varies, at different times of our life. The best thing is to acquire that discretion by which we can tell when to do what needs to be done, even though it does not seemingly fit in to some ideal plan of monastic spirituality. There are moments when all plans are useless. So while we cannot rely on them, we learn to rely more directly on God Himself, Who cannot fail us . . .

To Dame Hildelith Cumming

July 14, 1963

. . . Thank you so much for tracing the "Ild. Cummins" article on hermits. I really did not think you would be writing learned articles from Stanbrook in 1934, but still, one never knows. I shall gratefully read the copy that is so kindly being made, and I am delighted that I shall have a chance to read Dame Gertrude. I will take very special care of it and be sure that it gets back to Stanbrook safely. Do please thank your Mother Librarian.

You are Scotch: I have a bit of MacGregor in me somewhere, but it is mostly English and Welsh that boil about in me. I think the strongest strain in my family, on the father's side, is the Welsh. We all tend to look like my grandmother's family, the Birds, from Pembrokeshire.

The Anglican who is visiting us here wrote a history of Anglican monasticism, which he sent and which I have not read yet but it looks quite interesting. I will pray for your Anglicans, too.

Your ideas on music are of course very monastic and I am sure if you wanted to you could find some thrilling things in the Augustinian tradition. All starting with A.'s *De Musica* and coming on down into the Middle Ages, getting into architecture at the same time. Do you know that in the building of St. Denis and Chartres, and other such cathedrals or abbeys, the proportions are consciously likened to musical intervals and modes, so that the monks were aware that the nave was third mode, the sanctuary fourth and so on. There is a most interesting book about this, which I can look up if you are interested. But from what you say, I think you are more like some of the Greek Fathers, though I don't know which. I think Pope John's remark is most true and suggests many fine ideas about the chant and liturgy.

At the same time, even if Dom Augustine Baker is a little eccentric on the question of liturgy, I don't think that should keep his commentary from being published. On the contrary, I think that is all the more reason why it should be published, the right qualifications being made. He must have had his reasons, at that time, and if they were good ones they will not ultimately reflect on the *real* liturgical spirit at all, but will only help to make it understood.

I will keep the Danish and French samples for future reference. I am still thinking quietly about other possibilities, and we will see. For instance, there is a charming letter (in fact two or three) of St. Anselm to a community of Anglo-Saxon nuns of the pre-conquest nobility. The nuns are called "Seit, Edit, Thydit, Lwerun, Dirgit and Godit." He has nice things to say to them, very good and practical. It is a fine, characteristic medieval spiritual letter of direction . . .

To Dom Jean Leclercq

July 23, 1963

It was very kind of you to send the material on Grimlaicus. I will keep working on the idea of an article about him and these two pieces will be of great use, even though they are by another Leclerc without a "q." I can never figure out whether there are two or three Leclerc(q)s. Usually you are working in different fields and do not get in each other's way. There is funnily enough another Thomas Merton, in England, a "Sir" Thomas, no less, at Oxford and a collector of paintings. He is rather older and more venerable than I, so he must be irritated if people think he has become a monk and written his autobiography. I have never run across him.

Ed Rice sent me your essay on the Rule and *"presenza nel mondo"* which is excellent, and I am at present translating it for *Jubilee.* I think it will, or should, have a great deal of meaning in this country. I do not think that the American monasteries, even of our Order, have got out of this national obsession with productivity. It is one of the great delusions and temptations of the age, especially here, and it is certainly the one thing that wrecks monastic vocations, much more than the love of the pleasures of the world. Are they after all such great pleasures? We are more tempted by ambition.

Father Abbot has been away visiting foundations. His letters always give a desolating impression of cattle ranches, alfalfa crops, prunes, hay, beef cattle, diesel tractors and other elaborate machinery. And really, a few slogans about the absolute superiority of the "contemplative life" added on at the end do little to relieve this sense of desolation: a spiritual desert worse than anything else.

I envy you going to Africa. I think it is a very important place now. Toumliline is a place I admire greatly. Dom Denis Martin met and spoke to me briefly here. Naturally I did not have permission to visit with him; he is one of those "dangerous" Benedictines who are experimenting with a new kind of monastic life. I have written to him but I suppose he must be on the black list for mail, too. Perhaps some day I may travel somewhere and if I do I hope to go to Toumliline. Please give him my regards if you write to him or see him. Do please send me a copy of *Images de Toumliline.* It probably comes to the monastery but nobody sees it if it does. I am not receiving the bulletins from *La Vierge des Pauvres* either, though they did begin to come. In a word, Benedictines are dangerous here, Father! Dom Aelred Graham invited me, very kindly, to spend a little time at Portsmouth for a vacation. I was tempted to reply that it would be easier for me to get permission to take a mistress than it would be to visit a Benedictine monastery, even one that was not primitive.

In any case I hope your visits to the monasteries, etc., in Africa will be very fruitful for you and for them. If the Church would really reach all the Negroes, what life there would be! I send you a little piece I have written about the Negro situation in America. Again I am perhaps a little beyond the limits of what a monk is theoretically supposed to do, and yet I am convinced that today at least one or two monks should speak of these things, especially in America. What do you think?

I have been talking to the novices about St. Pachomius and reading some of the material translated from Coptic. He has been too little known: there is much in him that is of great interest.

To Mother M. L. Schroen, R.S.C.J.

Mother M. L. Schroen, a Religious of the Sacred Heart of Manhattanville, was at this time stationed at the General Headquarters in Rome.

August 9, 1963

This is a note to tell you that I offered Mass for you this morning. I was deeply moved by your letter about your new position in Rome, and am sure you are right in sizing up the situation as a kairos in your life. Everything is connected in the mystery of the Church and it is good, as well as frightening, to find oneself part of the same movement that produced the Council and will lead to so many other things. But if you are part of the "new Pentecost" you will certainly not have to go without graces as well as trials. One cannot do anything for the Church, today or at any other time, without inexplicable sufferings, some of which come from the Church herself, not necessarily in that which is most perfect in her. This is especially true of the Religious Life, and of the needed reform in it, about which I cannot be expected to say anything intelligent because I am really quite inarticulate about the whole thing. More than that, I cannot pretend to understand the first thing about it. But I do not think that the presently accepted ways of looking at it are quite adequate.

It is almost impossible for me to handle mail intelligently these days, so I will not attempt to write more, except to say that you can be very sure of my prayers and that I need yours. I cannot begin to talk about my own problems and I don't suppose they are either unusual or interesting, but they are problems and I have no earthly reason to suppose they will ever be solved, and furthermore I have stopped caring because they do not really have to be solved. I do not know if it makes sense for me to think of myself somehow serving the Church in the midst of them. But at any rate, I think we are indeed close to one another in the mystery of Christ today and I suppose our sense of frustration and inadequacy is probably pretty much the same . . .

You will be working in the shadow of a great Pope, and will have the good fortune to see many such people as Fr. Barnabas Mary [Ahern], to whom please give my best regards. It is long since I have been able to write to him. When I think I am busy I think of him and relax. He cannot possibly get along without a flock of charism, I am sure . . .

To Abbot Anthony Chassagne, O.C.S.O.

Father Anthony Chassagne (1911–   ) entered Gethsemani in 1941 and was thus a contemporary of Thomas Merton during the early years of novitiate and studies for the priesthood. He later became Superior of the foundation at Mepkin, South Carolina, and then was elected Abbot. He was still Abbot at the time of this exchange of letters.

August 21, 1963

. . . I have written your preface, and it is being typed. It will be on its way to you sometime. I want this note to get off now while I have a minute to write it. It is really going to require some charismatic help from Fr. Joseph [Cassant], I think, to get this book across, though it is very good. I think Newman is a very good bet, and they might publish it.

At the mere mention of censors I tend to see red, so I won't go on a tirade about them. But really this question of *"opportunité"* is absurd, at least in the completely arbitrary and irrational way in which it is handled. I see no serious objection to censorship on points of dogma and morals, and obviously the Order is interested in maintaining what is known as an image, if not an idol, of itself. But when some rather rattle-brained monks with no experience of the world, and still less of publishing, air their private fantasies about what constitutes an opportune publication, and can maintain it against the opposition of the entire publishing business, plus eminent and even intelligent persons of the laity and hierarchy. . . . Oh well.

Years ago you recommended that I get to know Newman, and I did not see your point. I certainly do now, not that I can compare my griefs with his in this matter of censorship. Have you read a very interesting book, *From Bossuet to Newman* by Owen Chadwick? It is excellent and you would like it. (Cambridge Press—you ought to review it for *Monastic Studies*, Berryville, and thus save the trouble and expense of buying a copy.) Another thing you would immensely enjoy is David Knowles' biographical memoir of Dom Cuthbert Butler. It is in Knowles' new book, *The Historian and Character* (again Cambridge Press). This book by the way gives a curriculum vitae of Knowles and helps to clear away some of the misgivings people have. It also has some good essays on Cistercian topics.

Your Bro. Bonaventure seized me violently in the Prior's room and recited to me some very bad poetry which, in the heat of the moment, I managed to recognize as being by me. In such ways does the good Lord enlighten sinners and sweetly seek to draw them out of darkness . . .

To Dom Aelred Graham

September 10, 1963

. . . Your remarks on the memorandum about vows are much appreciated. As a matter of fact, it seems to me from my readings in Pachomian and other early literature that you have hit upon a point. The earliest "commitment" of monks was apparently a promise, made among cenobites, that they would not abandon their work-group. In other words, they undertook to stay with the people with whom they were engaged in a common job. So certainly something would have to be done to guarantee continuity.

To Dame Marcella Van Bruyn

October 15, 1963

The Feast of St. Teresa is as good a day as any for a letter to Stanbrook, and I must confess I enjoy writing there much more than I do to a good number of my other correspondents. With you I feel quite at home, and I don't have to pretend to be interested in things which have no earthly meaning to me.

First of all I liked your cards very much, and your own lettering is exquisite, virile, noble, and all sorts of other things could be said about it. Thank you very much. I have now too many cards in our breviary, being attached to all yours. I do occasionally run into bits of quotes that would make nice cards, and often think of getting someone to do them, but I will not ask you if you are already overworked. And really there is no serious justification for it. One just likes to see good words nicely written: but if work is to be done at it, then I think it ought to be justified by the fact that the product will be multiplied and shared with many. It is a pity you no longer do cards at Stanbrook, but I can imagine they are not terribly practical.

You evidently do not know about the events in the American South, and everywhere in this country. I think it is something you *should* know because it is terribly symptomatic of the spirit of the age. The Negroes are theoretically "equal" to the whites in this country, but in fact of course they are not allowed to share the same restaurants, hotels, public services and whatnot. They are rigidly segregated in their living quarters and even in schools (in the South). In the last few years they have given up waiting for the white people to apply the laws that exist granting them their rights, and have started to agitate for their rights themselves. The resistance has been "nonviolent" (rather like Gandhi's approach) and in most cases very spiritual and religious in its base. One of the leaders is a Protestant pastor, Martin Luther King (a Negro), who is a very courageous and I think quite edifying Christian. The "Children of Birmingham" were schoolchildren who, in one of the Southern cities, went in procession to the City Hall, as an act of protest against the condition of the Negroes. The police would not let them carry on the procession, and stopped them with high-pressure fire hoses, turned Alsatian police dogs on them, beat them and threw hundreds of them in prison for "rioting." It was a great act of injustice on the part of the police, but the wonderful good order of the children and their indomitable religious spirit of charity, and their lack of resentment, was really a wonderful thing. It moved the whole country and the whole world. Since that time however things have not got better. In September, four such children were killed when white people bombed a Church (!) where the children were at Sunday School. There has been much criminal violence on the part of the whites, and the police are hand-in-glove with them. No one is ever caught or punished for these things, only the Negroes are put in jail as soon as they dare to manifest any spirit of protest. It is a most serious injustice, and as such it is something that needs to be known by contemplatives and remembered in their prayers and penances, because reparation is urgently needed. Also it is a very serious moral problem for this country. It is so complex that it is beyond the serious efforts of the Government to handle properly, and I personally believe that it is going to take on the proportions of a revolution, it is so serious. It may have disastrous effects. So pray for us.

The phrase "pinch hitting" means "substituting for." It is taken from baseball, when one man goes to bat instead of another, in a "pinch" or an emergency.

By now you must have received the copies of the essay on Examination and Dame Gertrude [More]. It will show you how much I have been enjoying her. I like her Apology very much, and also, of course, Dom Augustine [Baker]'s life of Dame G. . . .

Have you heard the rumor that Pope Paul wants to make Jacques a cardinal? Perhaps by now it will be fact. I think that is tremendous. Maybe Jacques would refuse, though. I hope he doesn't. In any case let us keep up our prayers for him. He will not be with us much longer on earth, but I know he will always be very close to us and we will not really have cause to "miss" him any more than we do now . . .

To Dom Jean Leclercq

November 10, 1963

First of all I hope the translation of your article on Benedictine work reached you in Ireland. It was sent on to you by the editors of *Monastic Studies*, from Berryville. I am afraid *Jubilee* did not take the article after all, feeling it was "too technical." But *Monastic Studies* will publish it.

Then, thanks for your two offprints. I was very touched by many of the beautiful references in your piece on *"sedere."* Did you know that the 14th-century English mystic Rolle was known as "the sitter"? He has some nice things about sitting as the most favorable position for contemplation. Of course the Buddhists of the Far East have many texts on this too. A Zen artist, Sengai, did a picture of a turnip with this short poem: "Turnips and Zen monks / are best when they sit well."

The one on the early history of eremitism in the West is excellent, and again it has many fine examples, as well as showing that one must not take a stereotyped view of the solitary life. For some people, the solitary life is their only way of truth, and it is *their* truth precisely insofar as it is not imposed on them from the outside. Some people are congenitally incapable of understanding this. It is a perpetual scandal, especially to the standard Cistercian mentality. On the other hand, people like Dom Augustine Baker and Dame Gertrude More have a wonderful sense of all this. I hope to do a study on Gertrude More for Stanbrook. There is also a piece of mine on her and Baker in the *Collectanea*, coming up soon, I believe.

Do you know, or can you find out for me from Dom Gribomont par ex., who is the author of the *Admonitio ad Filium Spiritualem* attributed to St. Basil, in PL. 1032? The novices are translating it here, and it is a very good parallel to the Benedictine Rule. I would like to do a short introduction, and wonder if there are any studies on it. I have not seen any myself.

Then can you perhaps persuade the monks or nuns (I am not sure which) at Etiolles to send me a copy of their mimeograph of Hausherr's study of Hesychasm? I would write to them myself but I am not sure whether they are a convent or what. I look forward to your study in *Studia Anselmiana* on Otium.

I have not yet been able to do my piece on Grimlaicus but I will get to it soon, when I have other duties out of the way.

To Mother M. L. Schroen

November 25, 1963

Thanks for your good letter of August 20. Since then you are probably well under way in your course, have doubtless seen Fr. Barnabas Mary [Ahern] again, and have accomplished much with your classes. I must say I am inspired just to hear of them. In a way I envy you. Not being in Rome or anything like that, but having a class with people from so many different places. I am hoping that some African college students will be here next year, and occasionally I have a group to deal with which is "international" in composition. At the same time I don't want to let the "ecumenical conferences" here mushroom into anything beyond handling reasonably. I feel that I must do everything I can to keep everything I do in this way quite small and simple, most informal, with nothing of the air of accomplishing anything, a few simple and friendly words and some discussion. I try to do as much as I can in a hermitage in the woods, and to spend such time as I can there myself. I try to take some of my work there, and to do a fair amount of reading and meditating there. I don't want to make you envy me, now. I do not regard this as a blissful joy but as a simple necessity like breathing, because without it I think I would simply fall apart or drop dead or something. The strong ones like you and Fr. Barnabas can take the real beating. The weaker ones like myself have to be sheltered, and I certainly intend to stay sheltered if I can.

My novices are a joy, really. About twenty in the novitiate, but I also have the juniors in classes with them most of the time. They have a real taste for Scripture and the Fathers. Fr. Romanus [Ginn], who did Scripture at the Biblicum and knows Fr. [Barnabas] very well, takes care of the Scripture. I am almost exclusively busy with the Fathers and monastic tradition, as well as the normal classes on vows and so on . . .

Everyone is deeply moved and troubled by the death of the President. Such an uncannily terrible thing: I think there is something diabolical in it. Of course this is the usual cliché. But it is so fantastic and eerie a crime, so useless, so pointlessly cruel, and it robs us of the best President we have had in years, right in his own best years, when his work for the country had barely begun. On top of that, the hysterical madness and excitement that led to the murder of his murderer, right on TV with everybody in the country (except Trappists) watching. This is a deeply shocking thing and I hope it will make everybody take stock of our condition. The nation as a nation seems to be disturbed and sick, to act in such a way, on top of all the senseless crimes that have been committed this year out of race hatred. Yet perhaps too in permitting the President's death, Our Lord has willed to drive home the importance of the work he has done so far and to impress upon the nation the seriousness of what he was striving for. All this perhaps might have been lost in the confusion of political struggle in the coming years. Who can say?

To Father Chrysogonus Waddell, O.C.S.O.

Father Chrysogonus, a Cistercian monk of Gethsemani, was studying in Rome at the time of this writing.

November 26, 1963

Thanks very much indeed for going down to Herder for the books: I hope they will be coming along one of these days and will let you know when they do. But with the new regime in force, I haven't much time to do anything on Chartres. Still I think I ought to be able to get back to it shortly. Thanks for the references too. I will be able to use them to advantage, at least within my limitations as a musician. I apologize for even using the word in connection with this pronoun.

The books of mimeographed material have gone to Fr. Roger at

Spring Bank, and I dropped him a note saying he would be welcome here. An awful thought later dawned on me: maybe he might *not*. But at any rate if he writes me a note and if I receive it, I think he might be able to get through and we could have a chat about whatever he is interested in. I would be glad to help him if I can, without leading him into a delusion.

If there is such a thing as "Mertonism," I suppose I am the one that ought to beware of it. The people who believe in this term evidently do not know how unwilling I would be to have anyone repeat in his own life the miseries of mine. That would be flatly a mortal sin against charity. I thought I had never done anything to obscure my lack of anything that a monk might conceive to be a desirable quality. Surely this lack is public knowledge, and anyone who imitates me does so at his own risk. I can promise him some fine moments of naked despair.

Of course I agree that as a theologian Chenu does not come up to Von Balthasar, but I like him above all as a historian of theology. What he has done on the 12th century seems to me to be really essential for us to get a true perspective of the Cistercians, or rather, if you like, the "Bernardines." A priest in Alaska (not a professional writer) sent down a panegyric of St. Stephen and demanded to know why we weren't like that anymore. I told him that this question had been asked before and that there was unfortunately not much use in trying to get an answer to it from me.

I presume the label "hard on Ottaviani" is another one like "soft on Communism": one that can be fished out and tied to anything under the sun that makes a conservative feel insecure. And God knows there is little under the sun that doesn't. And as you say, his health is far better than that of Pope John. Without derogating from the subjective holiness of Ottaviani (in his own way), I think one can confidently say that if they both died, Pope John would be the one who would continue to be in a position to influence the course of the Council: and in that case I think he would influence it more than Ottaviani even if the latter remained alive and John were dead . . .

To Dom Denys Rackley, O. Cart.

Dom Denys Rackley, a Carthusian at La Grande Chartreuse in southern France, was formerly a Cistercian at Gethsemani, but left during the time of his temporary profession while a student under Merton.

December 9, 1963

About liturgical material: I will send you the little I have. I do not think it will be up your alley as a Carthusian. So to make amends I am also sending some mystical theology and perhaps a few other items that might be of better service to you there. What you are not interested in may perhaps be of use to someone else. So I have picked out a little here and there. Do you know the English mystics? I suppose you are acquainted with the *Cloud*. Do you know Julian of Norwich? This is Carthusian territory, as the Carthusians once helped disseminate such texts, particularly the *Cloud* and Hilton.

As to liturgy, I hope the Carthusians will be cautious with liturgical reforms and indeed I am hoping that someone will be: who if not the Carthusians? In the enthusiasm for new things I am afraid that much that is excellent will just be dumped for no other reason than that it belongs to the past. Then later, when no one can get it back, there will be lamentations.

We have done a lot of things here that are good: for instance the brothers, or some of them, have a liturgical revival of their own, with a vernacular office, a dialogue Mass with a lot of vernacular and quite a bit of singing, etc. This is ok. But there is talk of fusing the brothers and the choir into such a unified group that they practically become one, and all have an English office and Mass and whatnot and this is pure nonsense. A lot of irresponsible stuff is going around in this regard, and no one is too well informed. That makes it worse, in a sense. As usual in these matters there are little cliques of enthusiasts who are politicking to get their ideas put through before others find out exactly what is cooking. This will make you laugh a bit: I hope it will, because I hope that such things are totally unknown among you others. But in a word, it is good to have the real solid essence of liturgical worship and participation, and bad to get carried away with the brainstorms of theorists. One of the things monks ought to do is penetrate with deeper understanding the good things they actually have. Our great danger is to throw away things that are excellent, which we do not understand, and replace them with mediocre forms which seem to us to be more meaningful and which in fact are only trite. I am very much afraid that when all the dust clears we will be left with no better than we deserve, a rather silly, flashy, seemingly up-to-date series of liturgical forms that have lost the dignity and the meaning of the old ones.

I will get my dear Dame Hildelith of Stanbrook to make sure that a batch of the Guigo Letter are sent to you there . . . I have not yet seen the text of *Guigo on Contemplation* but expect it with joy . . .

To Dom Aelred Graham

December 16, 1963
. . . I agree with you perfectly about Huxley. I felt his loss very deeply, and I do think that he was on the side of the angels all right. He was a deeply spiritual man and I am myself very much indebted to him.

The new Constitution on Liturgy from the Council is most exciting and very rich, it seems to me. I am going through it with the novices. There is great work ahead. This is the first real liturgical reform in 1600 years, and if it is properly understood and implemented, it will amount to a revolution in the sense of a metanoia for the whole Church. I know that there will be some false starts and some blunders, but the Holy Spirit will take care of us. At the same time I think that we monks will have a special responsibility for keeping in mind our own dimensions in liturgy, and not treat monasteries purely and simply as on a level with parishes. There are great possibilities for us, however, and perhaps even more interesting possibilities for liturgical forms in which non-Catholics can begin to join. However I am not an avant-garde liturgist, and I do not want to give the impression that I am bubbling over with projects. Rather I want to make it my business to try to stand up for some monastic values that might get lost in all this: for instance the preservation of *some* "sacred silence" somewhere in all the singing and reading and acclaiming that we are promised.

As for the monastic life, again I think it is terribly important to preserve the contemplative dimension of silence, aloneness, and so on. I am glad that it is there at Portsmouth. There is much danger of it getting lost in some of our Cistercian monasteries where they are beginning to get very chatty and recreative on top of the constant common life. (Recreation is only admissible, I think, when you have a room to compensate for it.)

To Father Kilian McDonnell

December 20, 1963

. . . It gets harder to keep up with mail, especially as I had a few weeks in the hospital with a disk. Certainly your year with [Hans] Küng must have been great. I am disappointed that he was not able to come here when he was in this country. I think he has a lot to say and will continue to, but it is difficult for a person to get into such fame as he has, because it automatically closes the ears of some people who would benefit by listening to him. I know he is big enough to take this and there is no problem as far as he is concerned. But it creates a barrier that ought not to be there: a willed refusal to attend to someone who really has something from God to say to the Church. Nevertheless his message will get through all right.

The Second Session of the Council was a little disappointing to some, because they thought everything was going to be much more conclusive and the "bad guys" would be totally defeated. But one has to be realistic, and I am glad that so much was said and voted on. One can continue to hope for the future.

The Council has really been something great, and it has fulfilled the promises of Pope John's reign. It has really effected a deep change in the Church and even in the world. Perhaps not as deep a change as everyone would like, or as some claim it to have made. But it has been most significant, a real beginning of renewal already. There is much more to be done, but one can be thankful for such a hopeful beginning. Time will have more to say about it, because the effects of such a renewal cannot be sudden. I have great hopes for the next years, and it seems to me that the prospect is a lot brighter than it was a year ago, and before the opening of the Council.

I have read a little Barth this year and like him very much indeed. You will, I hope, see an article of mine on Anselm in the ABR [*American Benedictine Review*], which deals with Barth's study among other things. I think that Barth is almost the one among theologians alive today that I like best, not that I am a great reader of contemporary theology. I am about to begin Rahner's new book (*Christian Commitment*). One of the problems that preoccupies me in dealing with Protestant theologians is their apparent complete discounting of nature and of the fact that man is made in the image and likeness of God, and that grace is a "new nature," etc. I can see the beauty and austerity of the approach and its religious impact is profound and in many ways very Christian, but at the same time one cannot, it seems to me, be fully Christian and neglect the other approach, "Greek" though it may sound. My old friend Jean Hering wrote on this a long time ago. I have been out of touch with him; don't know if he is alive, but I want to follow up his idea (he is a little more on my side). Have you any leads or suggestions?

I am also interested in some of the French existentialists and especially Merleau-Ponty, who is exceptionally challenging I think. Perhaps I can do a study on him. There is an austere sagacity about his phenomenology that I like, and he does not hesitate to criticize Catholic thought as a "rear guard action." I think though that the Council has drawn the sting out of that one . . .

I am beginning to think that contrary to you and to Congar, etc., my vocation is *not* ecumenical. I am not called to much discussion of any kind, of this I am sure. But still, I will keep it up when it seems to make most sense. I know you will urge me to, but I plan to be independent about it anyway. Perhaps what you say about Tillich has some connection with the above. It seems to me that the theological seriousness of American Protestantism, as I see it, is not high. It is a sort of religious pragmatism, and a lot of it is pretty flighty, with smatterings of psychology and sociology and that is about all. But enough animus to argue about the rosary. Since they now know that I am not a Curial-Marian type, they just tend to sit and listen passively and to accept almost anything. There are some good men at the Baptist Seminary in Louisville and at Vanderbilt.

I am writing mostly monastic essays these days, and studying things like Aetheria's pilgrimage, letters of Anselm and stuff by Peter the Venerable and Peter of Celles, along with Desert Fathers here and there. With poetry on the side, and I would like to continue to translate some South American poets, if I get time. My "ecumenical" bent seems to be more toward the people who have *nothing*, the poets and intellectuals and the Zen set. This I think is more my line, and yet perhaps this does not rate as "ecumenism." I don't intend however to get discussing too much with them either. What I can do for them can be done by writing, I think . . .

To Dame Marcella Van Bruyn

January 2, 1964

. . . About the two cards of the 14th-century saying: I only got one, so I presume Fr. Abbot helped himself to the other, which the Rule allows him to do and which he does, so unfortunately I cannot compare the two. The one I have is excellent, my only comment being that perhaps "XIVth Century" should be smaller than the rest. But it is a most attractive card and I have it always in the Breviary, along with all your others. The little bits on vellum are posted on my private notice board by the desk, along with the lists of things I forget or need to know, and a picture of two quails (a detail from some Venetian painting) and another picture of some rocks in Catalonia. Soli Deo does nicely with the Catalonian rocks. I am most grateful . . .

I have been hearing off and on from Jacques Maritain, who has been deeply shocked and concerned about the terrible business of the President's murder. He feels as I do that there is much more to it than the story that everyone accepts, which really does not make too much sense. But in any case the whole thing is part of the general moral illness of this country . . . It is all in many ways deeply disturbing, and of course it is symptomatic of the condition of the whole world. My articles on the Negro situation are being done as a small book in French and in the preface I refer to this, at least in passing . . .

Yes, I must admit that I am a congenital Bakerite, and that is why I take to Stanbrook quite naturally. I am in no way the kind of person that easily forms lasting connections with communities of nuns, but I am quite at home with all of you, precisely because there is this sense of liberty and informality and not taking things too seriously. I know that with you if I don't write it doesn't matter, and if I do it will be properly accepted. In any case we are united in the simplest kind of prayer, the kind that is quite alert and attuned to present reality and at the same time forgetful of self. It is liberty of spirit, not abstraction, that makes our prayer. Dame Gertrude saw this so well.

We will be on retreat here, as a community, in a couple of weeks and I hope you will pray for us. I am afraid these preached retreats rather irritate me, and are not really retreats at all as far as I am concerned. They are simply brief courses in familiar spirituality without too much time to think for oneself, though lately it has been getting better with only two talks a day instead of three. I hope to make a private retreat later in the spring. Perhaps in Lent, that would be nice. On January thirty-first I begin the "jubilee year," my fiftieth . . .

I agree with you about the constant sense of one's sinfulness, because we constantly assert ourselves, the delusion of ourselves, against the simplicity and truth of God. We cannot help it, this is our condition. Hence our life is a constant struggle with unreality, and the thing that complicates it is that the unreality in us is what seems to itself quite sincerely to be struggling for the truth. I do not really understand this at all. But the Bible is what seems to fit the situation best . . .

P.S. A "zombie" is a person, or rather a human being, that has been brought back to the semblance of life from death by voodoo and goes about with an appearance of autonomy but no soul. A rather ugly concept, but one which forcefully expresses the depersonalization of mass man.

Yes, I know the whole business about Jacques and the red hat was a fancy. I am rather glad that it was; he would never have liked it, really . . .

To Father Chrysogonus Waddell

January 4, 1964

. . . When I wrote my last letter I must have been in a state of unusual sensitivity about the cenobite hermit problem. Really there is not that much of a problem, is there? In theory and in tradition the whole thing is clear as crystal, and in practice the Holy Spirit is there to help people find solutions if they really want to. I think we are going through a phase of problem aggravation by our strictly contemporary and "western" disease of lining up white against black and black against white and deciding which half of a necessary whole contains the whole truth.

I think too that we suffer (not the least I myself) from the disease of absolutes. Every answer has to be the right answer and, not only that, the final one. All problems have to be solved as of now. All uncertainties are intolerable. But what is life but uncertainties and a few plausible possibilities? Even the life of faith, in practice, is full of contingencies, and rightly so. That is why it is a life of faith. And its certainties are dark, not absolutely clear. Nor are they the kind we can use to produce immediate conviction in the interlocutor . . .

Actually I think a few pages in P. Placide's new *Directory* say the best things that have so far been said about the cenobitic life. Certainly the function of such a life is to draw out the best in everyone, not stifle it, slap it down, kick it against the wall. Perhaps our problem here is that we prefer the security that can be gained by screwing everything down tight and keeping it that way, to the risk of letting people really discover themselves. Or else we make pseudo reforms suggested by people who have long since left and not needed by the people who have stayed.

I very much appreciate what you say about the cenobitic life in some of the (Benedictine) monasteries over there. I think that is a very realistic adaptation to modern needs. I think too that we are deliberately artificial in this respect, keeping everything down to a perfection that looks good on paper, rather than seeking a perfection that implies a real development and maturing of the monks themselves, even though it may in appearance be "less perfect." I agree too on the point of mature communication. Actually our life is lived in such a way that it generates an unusually consistent state of resentment. I think this is even unconsciously fostered, because when people are eaten by resentment they run to the Superior and give him information which he appreciates, and which helps him to tighten the screws some more, perpetuate the resentment, divide the monks against each other, draw them with more information to the center of the hive . . . etc. This is not very edifying and in the long run it is very self-defeating even for those who think they profit by it, for the ultimate target of the greatest resentment is the queen bee . . . Incidentally I suppose it is useless to speculate on who will be our next General. I have suggested Dom Leclercq and Patriarch Maximos, but I have a feeling they will not be acceptable to the Order. Perhaps Dom Willibrord of Tilburg? I wouldn't know.

Whoever it is, I will wonder what to do about the question of writing about peace and so on. I know this is not regarded as an approved monastic subject, though I sometimes wonder why we think it is noble to concentrate on producing an inner feeling of peace in ourselves, while allowing the wicked world to blow itself to hell without any concern of ours. Fr. Bernard Haring was here and strongly encouraged me to go on, and even said he would speak to Dom G. [Dom Gabriel Sortais] but I heard no more about it. I think Dom G. was strongly in favor of that absolutely appalling French deterrent system, which has no purpose whatever except to threaten cities (there is not even a momentary thought of counterforce in it) even when, if a missile attack came, there would be only five minutes in which to mount a whole reply. All this is entirely at the mercy of computers in one center, and the chances of accident are fantastic. The element of human choice involved seems to be almost minimal. It is just a giant robot affair that, given the right stimulus, will start sending bombs over twenty or thirty big cities. Completely mechanized. Of course it is still a matter of planes and of men in planes, but instrument-guided throughout. And a monk should wind himself up in his cocoon? I wonder if *this* is one of the monastic problems of Dom L.'s [Dom Jean Leclercq] course. I very strongly suggest it: what should the monk do to make an adequate judgment concerning the critical moral problems of the time . . . ? Should he consider that leaving the world absolves him from all responsibility in these matters? Can he safely leave it to others, when others have been either silent or obsequiously favorable to a solution that looks like an abdication of Christian responsibility? (At least in this country.)

About the liturgy: I hear that at Conyers the monks have voted to ask for a complete vernacular liturgy in the choir, right away. I wonder about this. I think that in the long run there will have to be readings in the vernacular, but I wonder if there are not quite a few complexities to consider. There is first of all the matter of Gregorian chant. Whatever may be my evil reputation among chant people, I am really deeply in love with the chant. I think it is certainly the greatest religious music we have available to us. I also like the Latin office myself, and am so far demented as to love the Vulgate Psalter. I know that I may have to give this up for the good of others, eventually. But at the same time I think we ought to recognize that something valuable and great in itself cannot be discarded thoughtlessly. I certainly think that it will not be easy to replace it by something objectively half as good, though of course for the benefit of those concerned, there will be immense advantages. I also hope that the enthusiasm for readings (good) will not end with interminable ones, and offices that go on until 5 a.m. each day. I think that we must not add anything without proportionately subtracting something elsewhere, or else we will end up with the old business we tried to get away from a few years back. One trouble with the innate activism of so many in this Order is that they don't want intervals and lectio; they want things to be planned for them, they want entertainment and passivity (although they mightily like to plan new forms of this). So I agree with you about one substantial lesson for a nocturn, and I would add two nocturns are plenty. And I agree heartily about the useless and trivial and often incomprehensible changes that have been made one on top of another in the last few years. Some of them will go out of effect even before they go into it, I believe. Let us at last get something solid and meaningful, done by someone who knows what it is all about, and not just according to unpredictable fancies . . .

The FBI informs me that you have sprung to my defense against the wicked Calati, in the monastic problems class. I am very grateful and sorry you did not have a more worthy and defensible cause. But it's good to feel oneself a monastic problem . . .

To Dom Colomban Bissey, O.C.S.O.

Dom Colomban Bissey (1912–   ), Abbot of Melleray, Gethsemani's motherhouse in Brittany, France, was the new Father Immediate. He made visitations to Gethsemani during these years and until his resignation in 1986. The relationship between Father Louis and Dom Colomban was exceptionally cordial.

January 7, 1964

Here are a few words for you first of all to wish you a happy New Year, and then some reflections which I hope you will allow me to make. Dom Gabriel [Sortais, the Abbot General, who had just died in Rome] has left us. Who will be his successor? If it were you, I tell you beforehand that I would not be sad.

In the Constitution on the Liturgy of the Council, it is said that only bishops and those who have a certain jurisdiction retain the right to the use of the pontificalia. Does this mean that the jurisdiction must be territorial, and that consequently abbots must renounce this dignity? You know that many here would be content if this were the case. But cannot one hold that it would be in the spirit of the Council for Dom James to give up his cappa magna [pontifical vestments] after all that? He seems to be quite willing to do so, and in any case, because it is known that he has already worn it many times, it would seem that the Holy See would not be annoyed if, without anything being said, he simply did not wear it anymore. Is it not true that Dom Gabriel did not wear his?

The monks of Conyers seem to think that they could obtain immediately the Office in English *in choir.* Even so, this seems to me to be something quick. But we must also ask ourselves: do we not think that the change is either simple or easy? Nevertheless, we must bear in mind that the traditional Office in Latin which we have is something very great and that Gregorian chant is adapted to it. Consequently, if we are going to change it, we must in any case look for something which can be sung as well as being understandable. Is it not better for the whole Order to proceed together than to let hurried changes be made by individual houses?

Allow me also to say a word about the new *Directory* by Fr. Placide of Bellefontaine. It is an excellent work of the first order. It contains strong and clear doctrine which is very traditional, and it seems that this book could do a great deal of good. But if the Father Abbots do not approve of it in its entirety, it seems to me that it would be better if it were published as it is without "official" approval (though of course after having been censored) as the work of a monk. And then something a little different could be done in order to appease the Reverend Fathers, which would become the "official directory" of the Order.

Good Fr. Irénée of Bricquebec has just sent me his book on St.

Bernard and it also is a book without a second—the best on St. Bernard and in any case the best biography . . .

I know more about it [the laybrother question] now that I have more contact with them. The better and wiser ones do not want these changes which tend to abolish their state as simple working brothers and they do not want the white habit, etc. No doubt the question of the habit is quite secondary. But it seems to me that it would be disastrous for us to make a change that would strike at the essence of the laybrothers' life. Changing their life of work would be an essential modification.

I leave you now, dear Reverend Father. Shall we have the pleasure of seeing you this year? Will there be another General Chapter in September? In any case, I greet you and ask you to bless me and my novices.

To Dom Jean Leclercq

January 12, 1964

First I want to thank you for your kindness in sending me the mimeograph of P. Hausherr's study on Hesychasm. It is really excellent and I profited much by reading it. I was able to use some of the material with the novices and now I have one of the young professed translating it. We will mimeograph the English translation and I think it will do a great deal of good in our American houses.

The other day I sent you a mimeograph of some correspondence that passed between me and Fr. Ronald Roloff, the black sheep of the Benedictine controversy in America. I don't think the correspondence is interesting or satisfactory beyond a certain point, but it may perhaps contribute something restrained and ambiguous to the "Benedictine problem" in America. I have not read Fr. Wilfrid Tunink's book but it looks good.

Dom James is off to the election of the new General of our Order. There is still much speculation of course. We wonder what we will get this time. It would be too much to expect someone like Dom André Louf, so fast. I have facetiously proposed *you* as my choice?! I don't know if you would accept the job, and so I will not press the point. If you refuse, I will campaign for Patriarch Maximos. But I suppose he will refuse also. Hence I will have to accept the one elected by the General Chapter and hope for the best. We have all warned our Abbot that he might get in as a result of a deadlock between the French and Belgian Abbots in the Chapter and now he is worried about it. Actually, if Dom James were elected it would be a victory for the conservatives and integrists and I am not too anxious for that to happen. How is Dom Willibrord of Tilburg?

I hope our students in Rome are doing well. We hear good news from them quite often. You are a great help and inspiration to them all, and thank God for that . . . I am sending you my new book of poems [*Emblems of a Season of Fury*], which are angry and obscure.

To Father Illtud Evans, O.P.

Illtud Evans, a Dominican priest from Cambridge, England, was involved with the editorial work on Blackfriars *(later* New Blackfriars*) and was a popular retreat master in the United States as well as in Great Britain.*

January 13, 1964

I have no idea where this letter will find you, but I hope you are at Cambridge. So first to the main business. I am happy to say that Father Abbot wants to ask you to give our community retreat here in 1965. That would be in January, about a year from now. We usually begin it on the 18th and end on the 26th. Would you be able to do this for us? I have no doubt that you can arrange a host of other things to justify your presence in the U.S. besides this . . .

My thing on the race question (the essay from *Blackfriars*, enlarged, and another essay) is coming out as a small book in French. I hope to send you *Jubilee*, in which I have an article on the Shakers. The race material, plus the things I managed to get published on peace before the axe fell, should come out as a book in this country sometime. At least I hope it will. As to writing about peace I am hoping the new Abbot General, whoever he is, will be more understanding than the old one. The election is this Thursday, and I hope you will speed a swift ejaculation upward for this intention.

The Pope's visit to the Holy Land has been quite extraordinary, hasn't it? I have made a few efforts to view it sternly as a pseudo event, but it certainly is nothing of the sort. It is almost an eschatological sign. The first day among the Arabs was wild and gave a shattering new picture of the Pope thrust right into the middle of the "world" that is totally alien to Rome, the Vatican, etc., etc. This was a shock, but in the long run a salutary one, perhaps the most significant thing about the visit, in a way. But of course the meeting with the Patriarch was splendid. I liked very much the little talk the Pope gave at Nazareth. A sort of résumé of Charles de Foucauld's spirituality, in a way. I am discussing it with the novices today. Simple, but a lot of spirit in it. The appeal for peace was a good gesture. As for our idiot President sending [the Pope] an invitation to the U.S. at that moment, I don't know how smart *that* was. I think the new boss means well, but has the kind of head that thinks best under a Stetson, and this is not the right kind . . .

To Mother Mary Margaret

Mother Mary Margaret, an Anglican Abbess in England, wrote to Merton about her interest in ecumenical dialogue between Catholics of the Roman and Canterbury persuasions.

January 16, 1964

Your letter of December 12 took rather a long time to reach me . . . Thank you for the picture of Abbé Couturier, whose life I have read with much admiration. And please pray for me, as I hope some day to write a study on Anglican spirituality. I have lots of Anglican friends who are spurring me on. Let me meanwhile send you a mimeograph of something I did on the English Mystics.

Perhaps some day I can write a brief meditation for you, on the spirit of Ecumenism or some such thing. I am usually quite busy and can never make reasonable promises in things like this, but it might be worth considering and I would love to do it. Have you any suggestions? It seems to me that the really practical thing to do about Ecumenism is to work at small things together when we can, and pray together as best we can, in whatever ways we can. I will keep you and your community in mind in my Masses and ask you to pray for me and my novices. Especially next week, when we will be on retreat . . .

To Sister Prisca, O.S.B.

A nun of Regina Laudis Abbey, a cloistered Benedictine monastery at Bethlehem, Connecticut, Sister Prisca wrote Merton about the Shakers in New England.

February 10, 1964

Thank you very much for sending your notes on the Shaker community at Sabbathday Lake. I found them very moving indeed. Certainly your visit there was peculiarly blessed. As a matter of fact I was confused, thinking that the only community left was at Canterbury, New Hampshire, and that there were only half a dozen old ladies there. Your notes suggest that some of the Sisters are relatively young. That is hopeful. What a pity that they should die out altogether. I have always been very impressed by their eschatological spirit, their sense of themselves as a sign of the last days and the new creation.

I have been doing a book on art and want to use some of the Shaker prints in it, or at least one. I am in contact with E. D. Andrews [see the first volume of the Merton letters, *The Hidden Ground of Love*], who has access to everything and can provide what I need, I hope. He is doing a new edition of his book on Shaker furniture and it sounds fine.

Are the Anglican Sisters in Newburgh the St. Helena Order? They have a house in Versailles, Kentucky, near here and a few of the nuns have been over. I am also in contact with the novice master at the Holy Cross Fathers on the Hudson.

The bulletin from the Philadelphia Museum apparently did not come. I am sure they must have sent it but maybe I just did not get it. I will try to find out. I would like to have whatever I can on the Shakers. There is an immense amount of unpublished material. I am afraid I will never be able to get into it deep enough to do a book on them but I want to build up my article into a more meaty one on the Pleasant Hill community in particular, with some history . . . Fr. Gregory from Mount Saviour was down for a few days, a very pleasant visit. Let us be united in prayer through Lent in the light of Christ and the peace of the desert, though the peace of the desert is always a bit militant. There is no Christian peace that is not militant, but precisely it is militant, not violent. May we grow in understanding and in joy.

To Father Ronald Roloff

February 14, 1964

That was a good, hard-hitting letter and it moved me deeply. I agree with you that there is a need for this kind of clarification. When such big changes are taking place, they must certainly be discussed intelligently and freely. This is an absolute necessity, for otherwise the pastoral meaning of the changes will be greatly lessened or even neutralized. It seems to me that your Father Abbot's approach is a very reasonable and practical one. I personally dislike sitting on committees, but I think in a large community there is no other way of really doing things satisfactorily, and I think that it is important for the whole community to feel that it is taking part in the changes, and not that changes are being made mysteriously and more or less imposed.

I would say that this is our problem here now. There has been some open discussion but only a minimum of it. The rest all goes on behind closed doors, and there are some brothers, particularly (they are the ones who are in crisis at the moment), who feel that changes are being made which they don't know, and don't understand, and which might affect the essence of their life . . . The real problem is not the changes themselves (in general they seem to make sense, or to be tending in the right direction), but the after effects, the side effects, the emotional and psychological impact of the changes. Will they in the long run unite the community and awaken a deeper life in the monks, bring about a renewal, or will they end by dissolving the community, in part, and chasing some men out of it?

It seems to me that here we are so intent on the changes we want to make, and the new possibilities in observance, liturgy and so on, that we are not paying sufficient attention to the *people* involved. In a monastic community our first concern should always be concrete, for the *persons* of the monks as they are, not abstract, the nature of the observance and the physiognomy of a desired new order. *Sacramenta propter homines*, and *regulae* also [The Sacraments are for the sake of men, and rules also].

I think that we are certainly going to have a conventual Mass for the choir and brothers in common. I have no clear idea what is going to be done about this. This is not quite up to the local Abbot as far as I can see. It will probably be left to the General Chapter, and this may mean slowing it down. This may disappoint those who are most eager for changes. I do not myself know what is planned. I have my own idea which seems to me to be fitting for our kind of life here. I would like to see an *evening* conventual Mass, after Vespers. This would probably be appealing to a lot of the brothers because in the first place private Masses will probably continue here for some time yet, and the brothers will have to serve. They don't want to serve private Mass and then get into a conventual Mass right afterward. The evening Mass could mean that we would have two big blocks of prayer: Vigils (Matins) in the morning, with Lauds about dawn, and Vespers with conventual Mass in the evening. This would leave the rest of the day pretty open, and I for one would like to see us drop Prime if we were going to lengthen the lessons of the Night Office. The day *has to be open* if the brothers are coming to High Mass with the rest. However, this is just my idea and I don't suppose it will get anywhere, nor have I tried to push it anywhere.

At the stage where we are now, everybody around here is rewriting the Rule and composing new liturgies. Great fun.

One reason why there have been so many changes with the brothers is that things seem to be more open to experiment, in the present state of affairs. There have been a couple of long Vigils in the vernacular for the brothers, and from what I hear they have gone pretty well. The danger is that those involved will decide to push this for all it is worth, without remembering some of the other factors involved, such as the work load which remains unchanged for the brothers. Thus while some will be at Vigils, others will have to assume their burden of work. These are complications that will eventually have to be ironed out.

For one thing the tendency seems to be now to arrange things so that there would be less work for the brothers. This is good in a way, that is to say the motive is good in theory. But in practice I wonder if it does not involve an occult supposition that the brothers' work (especially some of the lonely quiet jobs in the great silence) is incompatible with prayer. This would be disastrous, because the brothers who are brothers in the full sense of the word and really love the brothers' vocation, love their work and can easily pray while doing it. This is of course real manual work and a lot of it is fairly quiet and solitary, so that it does not need to be terribly distracting. Because of this the brothers can be monks in a more real sense, actually, than some of the choir. It seems to me that there is danger of this value in their life getting lost . . .

One thing though is that the brothers have really been the backbone of this community ever since I have been here. We have always had a very strong contingent of brothers; they have handled a lot of big jobs, a brother has been cellarer for years, and the brothers really run the place. This has to be taken into account. This means that we have had brothers who had in practice quite a "status" of their own, apart from canon law, and they have cut more ice in the community than most of the choir. Our functions, as far as the real work of the monastery is concerned, have been ornamental. I do not say contemplative, because I don't know just how contemplative we really are.

The brothers' life here has been one in which the brothers have run their own office and their own affairs with a certain laudable kind of autonomy under the Abbot, and with a Father Master. I think that much will be lost if they are just more or less merged with the choir and have to pick up a lot of our silly little problems. Many of the older brothers feel this very much and are hurt by the prospect, though mostly silent . . .

I can understand your liturgical experiments. They fit in with the character of your Abbey, which has for so long been a great center of Pastoral Liturgy. I think we may move somewhat in the same direction, without the participation of the laity, and I think there are plans afoot for a certain amount of vernacular even in our conventual Mass. Epistle and Gospel, for instance. When our liturgist gets back from Rome next summer I think we will have no dearth of prayers for the faithful in English and yet many other things of the same kind. What will be done about Gregorian I don't know. We have hitherto been so strongly attached to it, as if nothing else were conceivable; yet the very ones attached to Gregorian here will be the first to throw it out if it gets thrown out. That is their affair. For my part I like Gregorian and would be surprised if it could be replaced by anything one-tenth as good, but obviously I know one can't expect to remain fixed in a pattern that has lasted for a thousand years with no appreciable change.

That brings us to the *Opus Dei* [Divine Office]. There is a very strong movement on foot in the Order to get the office in the vernacular for the choir, and there seem to be optimistic hopes on the part of those who are working for this. I do not know how well founded the hopes are, but there is serious discussion (again not too open) about a complete change in the Vigils, to have them in the vernacular for the choir (this may mean also for the brothers, in some plans, but the brothers don't want this at all).

Let me respond to your own reaction to your experience on the committee. Here I think you are right on target. I want to try to say this briefly because if I get off on it this will turn into a book.

The root question is the question of the authenticity of our monastic vocation. I mean this in a concrete sense again. I am not talking about the abstract value of our vocation. I am wondering if in fact we come to the monastery and *lose our monastic vocation when we have got there.* I mean, is it somehow squeezed out of us, so that we are left with a husk of outward forms and no inner vocation? Does our monastic life become so artificial and contrived that it is no longer really a life; it is just an existence which we put up with, a set of obligations which we fulfill, having as good intentions as we can muster, meanwhile looking for living interests elsewhere?

That is the trouble with the great overemphasis on monastic institutionalism. In fact, the monk comes to be for the sake of the monastery, not vice versa. The monk is a member of the organization. He cannot be fired, but he can be urged to work hard for the purposes of the organization, whatever they may be: from cheesemaking to liturgical renewal and "contemplation." In order to ensure that the monk will be more or less cooperative, he is told from morning to night that the monastic life consists purely and simply in doing what you are told. Sanctity, doing what you are told. Just do it, and keep your mouth shut, and that is all that is required. That is *everything.* It substitutes for prayer, for the spirit of prayer, for the desire of God (I use that bad word "desire"), it substitutes for meaningful activity, it substitutes for life itself.

This is not to say that obedience is not the "heart of the monastic ascesis." It is. But merely doing what you're told is not obedience. And in order to make it obedience, a "pure intention" is not sufficient either. This unfortunate oversimplification of the monastic life is what drains it of all meaning and spirit. Then, after years of going to choir because one has been told that "this is the most sublime form of prayer you could possibly imagine, just because you have been told to do it," one suddenly wakes up and finds that the official convictions themselves have vanished. Then what? Everything is drained away. There is no interest left. The whole thing is meaningless.

This is a very dangerous situation, because at the moment I get the feeling that everyone is, as you say, more or less articulately admitting that they haven't been making any sense out of the office and have only been there fulfilling a duty. But to make this admission all right, acceptable, they are running around concocting new forms of the same thing. If the old office did not mean anything to them, where is the guarantee that the new one will mean more?

Merely singing the psalms in English is not going to make the office any deeper and any better for people who are just not interested in praying.

Incidentally I sometimes shock people by saying that with twenty-five years as an Anglican (and daily chapel services in school), I had plenty of vernacular office. My own personal feeling about the vernacular office is that it had better be good, because to me it was a relief to get the substance and richness of the Latin office we have here, with Gregorian, etc. This I know is not popular talk, but I speak only for myself. I have in the past had a choice between vernacular and Latin and made it with my eyes open.

This is not normative, it is just a personal affair. I have never had any trouble with our office as such. I have certainly been bothered to death by some of the policies in choir, and some of the monastic nonsense that has taken place under the guise that nothing is to be preferred to the *Opus Dei* (therefore make it as much of an impossible project as you can). I came here with a good knowledge of Latin and a love for the Psalms, the Bible and the Fathers. I have never had any trouble understanding the office, or "getting something out of it." But I have never bothered much to indulge in a lot of mental activity in the office. I don't try to get *thoughts*, specific thoughts here and there; I just like to get lost in the Psalms and try to let them be in my heart so that before the Lord I am this psalm, and nothing else. This is really very easy and it poses no special problem. It only becomes a problem when the entire choir gets very self-conscious about something (usually the chant) and when one has to divide his attention between the main thing and a lot of helter-skelter among the brethren.

I do feel though that for a while the vernacular may be an improvement because it will have to be simpler. It will have to be fairly experimental, and non-professional, and hence we will escape perhaps for a few years from our benighted perfectionism and just pray like humans for a while. Who knows, we may even manage to be spontaneous?? This will be welcome.

I agree with your paper on the *Opus Dei*, which seems to me simple and clear. Perhaps my own view of the office is in very minute details different from yours, but this is only a question of certain modalities. I would say that I myself belonged to a monastic tradition which did not regard the *Opus Dei* as a specific work of the monk, but rather as an essential part of his life . . . like eating or breathing. One can regard breathing as a work if one likes, but when the office becomes too self-conscious and formal, when one has the feeling that it is what justifies the existence of the monastic community, something *for which* the monks exist, then I am not at home in it. But I realize that this is a perfectly legitimate view; it is the tradition of Cluny, and I admire it without wanting to live in it for myself. However, I do not always have a choice in the matter because in practice it is widely adopted in our own Order, and it governs most of our thinking on the subject.

But your basic principles on *fuga mundi* [flight from the world], eschatological witness, and asceticism seem to me to be the real framework of the monastic life—more than that, its very being insofar as it is a search for God.

It seems to me that the monastic life is a charismatic vocation to fly from the world and seek the Gift of the Spirit. We need the Holy Spirit because without Him we cannot pray, cannot resist the devil, cannot have real peace, cannot give witness to Christ and cannot live together as a community, still less as solitaries. The Holy Spirit is given to us, in choir, in the chanting of our psalms and our response to the reading of the Word, and that is the reason for the office. Naturally one needs to understand what is happening and open one's heart to the Spirit.

When I say then that the problem is really one of authentic vocations, I think it comes to be in the end a question of whether or not we are extinguishing the Spirit by overwhelming the small sound of His voice by too much human clatter. I think the great problem of our monastic life, especially when it gets big and unwieldy, is the ungodly proliferation of human laws and regulations and systems and methods and projects and ideas. I don't care what the projects may be, how good the ideas may be in themselves, as long as they are chiefly the expedients and eccentricities of mere men looking for ways to assuage their anxieties and make themselves "happy," they will never do any good to anyone and they will not make monks of anyone. And if in order to promote all this waste motion one is perpetually told to just "do what they say" and forget about the real reason why one came to the monastery, then the Spirit is extinguished.

I know this is not well explained and is dangerous talk anyway (everyone knows that the Holy Spirit is a dangerous illuminist), but bad though my expression of it may be, I think it comes somewhere near the truth.

This does not alter the fact that we must make changes, for they are precisely demanded of us by the Holy Spirit in the Church. But we must remember why we are making them and for whom.

I won't say more. I will send you a copy of an article I wrote about Rahner's new book and its relevance to us ["The Monk in the Diaspora"] . . .

To Dame Hildelith Cumming

February 22, 1964

Thanks for your note and for the pages of Guigo. It is most attractive, everything that I had hoped for and more. I like the paper very much and everything goes well with it. The capitals (initials) are fine, and I like the margins, the type shapes up very nicely and it is a real success. I am so grateful and pleased . . .

About getting copies of the mss. in the archives at Lille, probably Dom Leclercq would be able to put me on to someone who would photograph them. Would you please let me have a description of the exact things you would want? I am afraid though that it is rather complicated to do things like this from a distance, blindfolded. You are quite right that my movements are limited (and I am glad of it) so that there is not much chance of that plane bringing me to Birmingham and my then coming down the Severn Valley to you, much as I should like to. Let us think about the archives in Lille. We have a man [Father Chrysogonus Waddell] in Europe now (some do travel; this one is studying at Rome) and I might get him on to this, as a matter of fact. He is a manuscript fiend anyway. I think I had better write to him about it. Say a prayer and something might work out . . .

To Father Brendan Connelly

February 23, 1964

The first thing that strikes me is your interest; it proves that the problem is important and universal. Obviously there is a sense in which all of us who have embraced the religious life have very much in common. I suppose the present tendency for "monks" to stand back and identify themselves as apart from "Jesuits" is due to the fact that we have for several hundred years been assimilated canonically to other Orders, so that we have suffered by it ourselves in a few not unimportant ways.

At the moment there are hopes that we can get a status of our own as *monachi* once again in the eyes of canons. This will enable us to make sense out of such things as our *ratio studiorum*, and will simplify our problems about the status of brothers. To put it in another way, it will clarify a lot of problems that are perhaps no problems at all when seen in our particular context. So that when Fr. Ronald [Roloff] was saying "not Jesuit," it was just a kind of automatic reflex, and did not imply much about Jesuits one way or the other. I agree that it is neither fair nor accurate to keep describing monks as non-Jesuits.

It is certainly true that boys who enter religion usually think just of "being a priest" and discover afterwards that they are called first of all to "be a monk" or to "be a Jesuit." Really this is something that ought to be brought out in High Schools. Though I don't suppose it makes too much difference in most cases.

Still, I do think that there are really quite profound differences in the spirituality of monastic Orders and the modern Orders, especially yours, which are dedicated to the apostolate so systematically and entirely. Doubtless the differences must not be exaggerated and the picture of religious life in the Church must not be distorted. I realize too that it is easy for people to make sweeping generalizations about the Society, when in fact Jesuit life and spirituality is a very complex phenomenon and much deeper than most people take it to be. In reading documents by people like Jerome Nadal for instance, as well as Grou and that school, I find myself in a familiar kind of atmosphere. And old Rodriguez after all uses monastic sources just as much and perhaps more than any Benedictine novice master.

I would be interested if you could give me something of an idea of Jesuit spirituality and the Jesuit ideal as you see it. I know this is a nasty and burdensome question . . . I realize that neither of us is in a position to get into a very lengthy correspondence about this, but perhaps a note from time to time might be possible.

May I finally ask a favor: one book I have been hoping to read is perhaps on a reserved shelf: Gerald Clark, *The Coming Explosion in Latin America* (McKay).

To Dame Marcella Van Bruyn

February 24, 1964

This is chiefly to wish you many blessings and graces on March 12th and to say how much I liked the last italic version of "He abideth patiently . . ." which came through. It is very charming yet energetic too. And I liked your whole letter very much. I see I misled you about my birthday. Actually I am only in my fiftieth year, and am building up to the fiftieth birthday with a Jubilee of something or other, I cannot quite establish what. In any case I will remember to read [T. S. Eliot's] "Little Gidding" on that day, if I do not get back to it before then (perhaps March 19th).

I saw some of your translations of Raïssa in the *Tablet*, not that we get the *Tablet* but someone sent the page. They are excellent. I hope we will see the book, and I am sure there is no need for broad hints about it: I will simply ask, and if I have a chance I may write a review of it, though there too with atrocious freedom of spirit I do not promise, because I really cannot. I have several prefaces to write and other short bits of things.

What you say about the flood of dispensations or requests for dispensations coming in to the Congregation lately makes me aware, again, of the great problem of vocations. No matter how much one explains vows, one does not make the matter really clear to people. There is something that seems to get in the way. No one has to make them [vows], but when he has made them he should keep them. I think that in this as in so many other things it is a very complex and ambiguous affair, and there is a subjective possibility that after a certain time, from a certain point of view, the vows cease to be a "greater good" and become a rather lesser, frustrating, ambiguous good in certain cases. Then it is important to make up one's mind that even then fidelity to the lesser good remains a greater good. Or else to really go for a better good. What happens in fact is not a definite decision but just an abdication and disappointment— like Monica Baldwin (whose book nevertheless I thought quite good and honest). In reality I have not seen many situations where it would not have been better to simply hang on, even though that may sound negative. Where are all these better goods and greater goods people think they can find? I wonder particularly where they are in the world. And after all, the Cross is the one good on which all others depend and without it we can look far to find another.

Our retreat was rather awful. Psychological counseling, mostly. But I felt a lot of compassion for the Father who gave it, a member of a wretched hand-to-mouth congregation in which they all seem to be fighting for "good jobs." He must live a rather hectic and unhappy life . . .

To Father Flavian Burns, O.C.S.O.

Father Flavian Burns was Prior at Gethsemani at this time. The Prior speaks in Chapter when the Abbot is absent; hence Merton's comments on the hermit life in our Order.

March 1, 1964

I am in profound agreement with your talks on the hermit life, etc. However there is one small point where I differ from the approach taken by you and Dom André [Louf]. It is this.

It does not seem to me practical or in accord with the deepest monastic tradition in our present circumstances to say that the "solution" is to permit rather free transitus from one "monastic" community to another.

Certainly such transitus should be possible in the rare cases where it is really needed, and it is perfectly traditional.

However I think the more honest as well as more workable way would be to reduce the *need* for transitus; that is to say to create a situation where each monastic community would seek as far as possible to satisfy all the legitimate needs of all its members including those who seek the highest perfection.

This would mean that a Cistercian monastery should be able normally to provide the solitude, partial or complete, required by exceptional cases, which would certainly be very few. Reasons for saying this:

a) Importance of continuity in the monk's vocation and in his monastic life, without serious break in the crucial period of his life. His community should be strong enough and big-hearted enough to provide him with the solitude he needs if he really needs it. He on the other hand should bear with the community patiently, until his need is clear to his Abbot and if possible to the brethren.

b) Most important reason is this: a man is not ready for solitary life until he has been able to renounce his own tendency to plan his life, and has completely committed himself to his community in a spirit of total faith. He must no longer insist on working out his own future according to his own attractions and desires. Yet he should be faithful to these desires in all their depth. Only deep faith can bridge this gap, and the faith will not be deep enough if it cannot be faith that God can and does act through the monk's own community. (Obviously there will be case where this will not be possible at all.) If a monk always has at the back of his mind the proviso that he will one day take off and go somewhere better for a "higher life," he will never in practice make this surrender and this act of faith, and consequently if he does move, he is likely to lose everything, which is quite frequent.

c) To me then the ideal would be for our own community to develop enough maturity and strength to handle this *here*, starting with temporary periods in solitude for those who really need it and have proved the seriousness of their need over a long period. And so on.

Naturally this is all ideal, and in practice some may have to go elsewhere perhaps (where????). But I think if it is presented just as a problem for which the normal solution is transitus, the immature ones who remain shaky on this point will never face the fact that they must make the commitment to live in their own community . . .

I usually see Rev. Father Thursday around 4. Could I see you then? An answer to this question will be my proof that you have read this far.

To Brother Francis Taparra, O.C.S.O.

Brother Francis Taparra, a Cistercian monk at Lan Tao (Hong Kong), was formerly a novice at Gethsemani, but transferred to the monastery in Hong Kong harbor.

March 2, 1964

Those pictures you asked for are supposed to have gone off airmail to Hong Kong in a big package several days ago. I hope they arrive safely and in time. And I hope the Sierra Club exhibit will be a good one, and that the vocation week will go off well.

You certainly are in a hazardous position there in Lan Tao. In a position where you can readily reflect that the "Son of Man had nowhere on earth to rest His head." It would not be surprising if you had to move again some one of these days, I mean the whole community. We live in a time of change and trouble and we cannot plan on having things go the way they perhaps ought to go. There will be innumerable surprises and as long as the world stays in one piece I think we can be grateful, because where there is life there is hope. Meanwhile we must trust God and realize that the monastic life is a renunciation of earthly security.

We are not oriental here, but there is a certain amount of oriental resignation in the community about the change of habits. Actually the idea was well-intentioned, but people have not reflected on the different implications of certain ideas which may be good in themselves, as far as they go. There has been a great deal of solicitude about making the brothers "happy" with "changes," without people stopping to consider that the changes are not always wanted or meaningful. One of the brother novices said to me the other day: "Who do they think they are doing a favor to, anyway?" I suppose that a lot of these changes are dictated by subjective ideas in the minds of those who think they are necessary. The general idea of putting everyone on the same footing is of course good, and it could have been attained without half so much fuss and trouble.

Things are quiet here. All the novices are in one novitiate together, and they blend well, without any trouble at all. There are not as many as when you were here. Your old friends are all getting along well. Some of those who were here with you have left of course. I sometimes hear from some of them, like Fr. Sebastian who is doing graduate work at Columbia. Fr. Bede is sacristan. Dom Walter has been trying to resign his abbacy at Genesee but the grapevine says he has not succeeded. However he has been here lately.

I must stop now and get ready to give a conference. The Superior of the Japanese monastery of our Order is here, Dom Damian. He has interesting things to say about the new religions in Japan. One of them, the Seko Gakkai, is probably going to cause a lot of trouble one of these days.

Best wishes to all of you. Let us be united in prayer that we may truly grow in faith and breadth of vision, and be able to accept anything that comes. There are reasons behind all that goes on in the world, and we do not always see them. May God give us light, faith and strength to go forward in His love . . .

To Dom Ignace Gillet, O.C.S.O.

Dom Ignace Gillet was elected Abbot General of the Cistercian Order in early 1964, following the death of Dom Gabriel Sortais. He had previously been Abbot of two French Cistercian monasteries (Dombes in 1953 and Aiguebelle in 1956). The first letter begins with a problem surrounding the publication of Merton's writings on peace and nuclear war.

March 6, 1964

I very much regret that our first contact is marked by a misunderstanding, through my fault. But before speaking about it, allow me to assure you that I accept, very willingly, the decision on the three articles, which will not be published.

When I tried, twice, to obtain Dom Gabriel's permission for the publication of a book about peace based on these articles, it was a question of the articles' material in a new form, as everything was reworked and expanded to make a book. So it was no longer the same thing. That Dom

Gabriel had refused permission to publish that book, I thought, did not change the right which I believed had been obtained for the publication of the already printed articles as is. But on thinking it over, I see that Dom Gabriel's prohibition could also have aimed at this form of publication. It is through lack of judgment and of consideration that I made this error which I regret.

I find by experience that it's almost impossible for a monk to do the technical reading required by the problem of nuclear arms. Unfortunately, I think that it is also quite impossible for a bishop. It is a very difficult question. In any case, I recognize my lack of professional competence and I am dropping this type of work (which, at any rate, I have not done for a long time).

I am heartbroken to begin a relationship, which should be cordial and open, with a misunderstanding that might create a certain diffidence between the Abbot General and one of his sons, but I assure you sincerely, Most Reverend Father, of my genuine loyalty and obedience. I beg you to give me your blessing and to accept the assurance of my most respectful sentiments in Our Lord.

To Father Brendan Connelly

March 17, 1964

Concerning your inquiry about your young friend who may have a Cistercian vocation. I don't think that agricultural school would add much. Usually the farming operations in a monastery are relatively simple and well organized by the few brothers who are in charge, and many members of the community simply do pick and shovel work, as this is all that is required of them—or else they have other jobs. For the choir, a couple of years of college would be more useful than ag. school. But on the other hand if the boy is not inclined to study much perhaps he would be better in the brothers. But even then, I think that the practical training of the monastery would be more use than agricultural school.

If he wants to enter here, the best thing would be for him to come down for an interview and we ourselves would work out what he ought to do next. That is the way we would handle it here. Perhaps Spencer would have a different approach, though I believe they are even less farmers than we are.

But, in résumé, the farming is not a very big or complex operation. Here we are simplifying it all the time. It is just a large dairy farm now, and a lot of the work is done by machine. Personally I would rather see more hard manual labor in the fields, but it is not the most profitable way of doing it . . .

To Father Ronald Roloff

March 21, 1964

The Feast of St. Benedict is an appropriate day on which to try to reply to your two long letters, and thus to wish you and your brothers a happy feast. I have tried to draft a long and more detailed reply to some of the points you bring up, and I think the attempt on my part is fruitless. We seem to be moving toward a dual monologue rather than a dialogue and I am afraid that if I try to clarify everything the confusion will finally be total. So I will cease and desist.

You have certainly attributed to me some rather depressing opinions, which, fortunately, I do not hold.

As to Christian optimism: let me confess the following and clear myself of any further suspicion of heresy. I hold that by the infinite mercy of God we have been delivered completely from sin, death, the Law by the victory of Christ and that henceforth we are cleansed from dead works to serve the living God in the brotherhood of the sons of God, the Church, which manifests Him on earth. Thereafter what matters is not to fall back under the Law, and this implies a sagacious use of the knife of discretion, dividing dead works from living ones.

I do not make this division in such a way that one comes out with "action" on the side of dead works and "contemplation" on the side of living service. On the contrary, both action and contemplation, as they are meant to be, are living service. Let's forget that division which is deceptive. And I do not place the knife anywhere between Teilhard and Rahner. Nor between Benedictine and Cistercian. We are all members one of another and, in unity and variety, we complete one another, hence it is futile to demand that we all be exactly the same (I do not accuse you of demanding this).

As to Christian friendship and brotherhood: it is to this that we are called in Christ. But in this as in everything else there is the dead and there is the living, and each case must be judged on its own merits . . .

To Dom Jean-Baptiste Porion

March 26, 1964

Last year when I was translating this beautiful letter of Guigo I thought frequently of you. When the Nuns of Stanbrook started printing it, I decided that you were the one to whom the small printed booklet should be dedicated. Out of deference for your love of hiddenness I have put only your initials in the dedication, but it will be enough to express my friendship, long silent, and my gratitude for your past sharing in my own concerns for solitude. It is with this in mind that I send you the first copy of the translated letter, and will send others when I have more. It is a most beautiful letter and I hope my translation has not fallen too far short of the original to permit it to be recognized.

As I reflect over the past and over God's grace in my life there are only two things that are more or less certain to me: that I have been called to be at once a writer and a solitary *secundum quid* [in some way]. The rest is confusion and uncertainty. At present however I do have a measure of solitude, more than I would have expected in the past, and it is the only thing that helps me to keep sane. I am grateful for this gift from God, with all the paradoxes that it entails and its peculiar interior difficulties, as well as its hidden and dry joys. I think that really there is no solitude but a solitude *secundum quid*, lodged in paradox, and that one becomes a solitary in proportion as he can accept the paradox and the irony of his position. It is the irony that is the expression of God's love in the life of the "monazon" [one who lives alone], the one who practices loneliness on purpose. The joy of the solitary is then the laughter that makes him, as the Fathers said, an Isaac, *risus*, a joke and a delight of the humor of the Lord. I wish you this joy at Easter, and know that I owe my share of it in part to your prayers.

To Mother Benedict Duss, O.S.B.

Mother Benedict was the Abbess of Regina Laudis Abbey, at Bethlehem, Connecticut. She and several members of this Benedictine community corresponded with Merton during these years.

March 26, 1964

It seems that I still owe some response to notes from several members of the Regina Laudis community, and I take this opportunity to write you all an Easter Greeting, to ask your prayers, to share with you the joy of the Feast.

First of all I was most interested in Sister Prisca's account of the visit to the Shakers. Such contacts are deeply significant and there is no question that the Shakers were deeply imbued with a spirit like that of St. Benedict. It showed in the work of their hands, which was worship in spirit and in truth.

I am grateful that someone there responded to the article "The Monk in the Diaspora," which has been rather attacked by a Benedictine of one of the big monasteries. It is strange to be up against the confused ideas of Christian optimism that struggle with one another in the Church today. To be an optimist in the eyes of some people one has to believe in the ever greater and greater success of the institutional aspects of the Church, those rather secular glories and achievements, which seem precisely to be stifling her true life and progress in some ways. But one must expect conflict, confusion, and inertia even when the inertia thinks itself to be progress. And after all, how do we know and how can we judge? Anyway, please pray for me.

There is certainly life and hope in the monastic movement, but not always where the biggest buildings and the greatest activities flourish. I always think of Regina Laudis as a place where there is genuine life, and a human dimension. Here too, in spite of our confusions and difficulties, the Lord has been good to us, and there is a living spirit and a genuine progress, especially since our numbers have grown much smaller (that is a contradiction in terms: I mean since they have *become* smaller).

May the Lord bless you with His Light and His Joy, and may the whole Church exult in His true Victory, which may not always consist in what the faithful think it to be. And may we be faithful ourselves to the grace of Easter and its liberty. I will remember you especially at the altar on Easter morning.

To Father Guerric Couilleau, O.C.S.O.

Father Guerric Couilleau, a Cistercian monk of Bellefontaine, in France, had written Merton in regard to monastic renewal, especially about some of the current observances, to which he elicited the following long letter in response.

April 7, 1964

The basic question seems to be that the Chapter of Faults simply does not fulfill any really deep function in the monastic life today. I agree with you perfectly when you say that in our daily life we operate according to one conception of man and then in the Chapter of Faults we immediately adopt another just for the duration of the exercise. In actual fact, in the Chapter of Faults it seems to me that we do not look at one another as persons at all. We treat one another as objects, and though we pretend to be sanctifying one another we are in reality only oiling up the community machine. The resulting artificiality is regrettable and in some more than others it has rather unfortunate effects. I can see that the Chapter of Faults might continue if we insist on maintaining the ancient framework in all its details. However, if we seek a genuine monastic renewal, I think it would make sense to revise our conception of this exercise.

On the other hand, thanks to you I have been led to read the "Dossier" in VSS [*Vie Spirituelle Supplément*], and the letters of good Dom Emmanuel of Timadeuc. It seems to me that he is not wrong in seeking to establish in the monastic life something analogical to the *révision de vie* [examination of life] practiced by the Fraternités. I repeat the expression "analogical," because it is quite clear from his sometimes naive suggestions and from the replies of the others concerned, that he has transferred the idea of revision to our life not without a certain fundamental modification, and I think at the same time he has reduced it to a rather more trivial level, thus bringing into focus the general tendency to triviality and "playing around" which the monastic life tends to get today. The thing that struck me most about this monastic contribution to the idea of *révision de vie* was not that it was very sincere and very much "from the heart," but that it implied a notable reduction of the *seriousness* and impact of the concept. There is no question that we need to introduce a greater element of humanity and of genuine communication into our whole life, and something analogous to revision would bring this about.

On the other hand when we do this in a strict and rigid framework of rule, we empty the concept of revision of its true meaning, because revision is precisely for people who are living outside the framework of rigid rules and seeking the guidance of the Spirit in profane situations where rules do not offer much help (since they only isolate one and enclose one in a ghetto mentality, which is what the people who practice revision most seek to avoid). This only brings out quite clearly that we monks are living in a very protected and hieratic atmosphere. In many respects this may seriously diminish the validity of our contacts and of our witness in regard to the rest of the world. Nor will the assertion that we alone have chosen a contemplative part which implies contact with the "real" reality serve our turn in this case, because God is acting and revealing Himself now in the profane sphere and we, insofar as we cling to the frameworks of the remote (let us say Carolingian) past, have been somewhat *dépassés* [outdated].

On the other hand the most authentic and original monastic spirit remains completely actual and valid, insofar as it is not a question of measuring one's acts by minutely detailed rule and observance but by the concrete and existential demands of the Spirit here and now, and of the vocation.

I think that the Abbot of Timadeuc is perfectly right. I agree with him heartily when he seeks a more human and frank communication between monks in an effort toward a *mise en commun* [sharing] of all our problems and experiences in regard to our vocation. At the same time I think it must be stressed that we are called to a somewhat solitary life and that this *mise en commun* should have in view the ultimate facing of our vocation to solitude, so that we will help one another to advance into this unknown and somewhat frightening territory, which is nevertheless that which the Lord has opened out to us. The great danger I foresee in the adoption of a diluted "revision" by us is that it will only contribute to the illusion of chumminess, togetherness, and infantile collective delusion. This helps us substitute pretended seriousness for the real seriousness of wrestling with the angel of solitude in an isolation where we cannot tell our troubles or find anyone to whom we might express them. Of course here too this may be an exaggeration and a distortion. There is a possibility of serious and mature revision, *provided that the real aim is kept in view*. It is even conceivable that with a genuinely honest and mature effort at revision it would transpire that some monks had solitary vocations to which they were being unfaithful out of fear, human respect, submission to undue pressures, etc. On the other hand I think that revision among us would more likely turn into a more subtle form of Chapter of Faults, concentrating on a friendly and undisturbing conformism and on the allaying of any anxieties that might be brought into view if the thing were pushed too deep.

Let us face the fact that if we practiced revision seriously the result would be, as Dom E. suggests, the dissolution of the Order and the desire to start something else, on the basis of the experience at Molesme, which he cites. This of course would be a good thing, but it is not something that I feel the Order is at present capable of facing, and the only result would be schism, battle, ruin for many people . . .

Returning to the original sense of *révision de vie*. There is one place where I think it definitely should be practiced and to some extent is practiced in our houses: in the realm of business and work, with the ramifications implied, relations with the outside, etc. This should also be extended to the responsibility of the monk in the face of the critical problems of the profane world, such as nuclear war, the starvation of millions of people in underdeveloped countries, the tensions between political blocs and so on. One may say that all this is a distraction. But on the other hand it happens that when monks do not concern themselves with defining their relation to these things in the light of faith, their monastic witness becomes radically falsified (vg. the monasteries that were in favor of Action Française and Vichy, and those in Germany which supported Hitler, some of them nevertheless fervent contemplative or liturgical communities).

The question has seriously arisen here in this country. A Quaker friend has said to me: why is it that you monks are not on Freedom Rides and on marches for peace, for civil rights, and so on? I have no answer except . . . shall we say inertia, infidelity or what? The answer that we are supposed to stay enclosed would be all right, if our solitude had a *seriousness corresponding to* the seriousness of the demonstrations. You may not know much about this, but in the Civil Rights movement in this country, a struggle which involves beating, danger of murder (which has frequently been carried out), and perpetual threat of jail and various forms of legal pressure, there have been Christians giving a witness that puts the monks to shame and makes our petty concern with regularity look like a gross evasion. But at the same time I am not asserting that the only thing the monk can do to be "faithful" is to leave his cloister and get involved in these things. That would lead to the most tragic deceptions, without a special charism which no one has the right to expect. But the full seriousness of our monastic life *is* demanded. The full seriousness of the life is not to be realized without an authentic and complete realization of the potentialities and demands of solitude. The adjustment of community relations on an evangelical level is most desirable but it is not the whole story, and days of desert, most desirable also, are only a beginning.

At the same time, without illusions that we would be practicing real "revision," I am in favor of modified application of the idea to our life.

To Dom Jean Leclercq

Holy Saturday, 1964

Thanks for your note about Fr. Ronald Roloff. As a matter of fact I think you have guessed that what he was saying in his letters to me was not his real mind after all. In a couple of recent letters, very long and outspoken, he shows himself to be in reality an activist who has no real taste for the monastic life in its renunciation of the world and in its orientation toward solitude. He seems to be completely convinced that the only genuine monasticism today is one which is busy with education and converting souls, while at the same time he seems deeply confused and troubled about the most genuine and normal monastic works, especially prayer in its more characteristically monastic forms. He is in a word a parish priest or a "Jesuit."

Where he came out most outspokenly was in an attack on an article I had written and sent him; I don't know if you saw it: it is called "The Monk in the Diaspora." A shorter version of it was in *Commonweal*. I sent him the longer mimeographed piece and he found it quite shocking. He accused me of pessimism, defeatism, evasion, etc., etc. All the usual accusations. He ended by giving me a sincere fraternal exhortation to renounce the pernicious influence of Rahner and to turn to the saving optimism of Teilhard de Chardin. This I found curious. The division did not seem to me to be self-evident. But apparently that is the attitude some are taking now. One is evaluated in relation to Teilhard, and by this standard monasticism is asked to abandon solitude and prayer to become more open to the world. But the division is made in a very naive fashion. My contention is that there may certainly be an exceptional apostolate for the monk, but that if it exists at all it must be charismatic. And in order to preserve this charismatic quality, the monk must first of all be entirely faithful to the charism of his vocation to solitude and the desert. Otherwise the "apostolate" he attempts to carry out will be an infidelity and a mockery, and in the end he will be neither a good monk nor a good apostle. This seems to be altogether outside his range of thinking. Or at least it is now. I think what happened was that his brethren have read the letters that were mimeographed and have accused him of becoming weak and giving in to the arguments of contemplatives.

I have read with great pleasure the wonderful article of P. McNulty and her collaborator on the Orientale Lumen in the Commemorative Athos volume. It is really magnificent and it will help me a little in my work on recluses. I am keeping on patiently and quietly in this, and will I hope eventually begin to get something on paper about Grimlaicus. I also enjoyed the magnificent quote on the Athos hermits, by a 15th-century Italian traveller, quoted in the article on the Amalfitan community of Athos. As I told you, I had previously read your own two articles with great pleasure.

Here are a couple of pieces that may interest you, including "The Monk in the Diaspora." Incidentally I wrote a long answer to Fr. Ronald but then decided not to send it. If you are interested in seeing a copy of it, I can send it to you. I do not want to waste time arguing where there is no real communication . . .

To Dame Hildelith Cumming

April 15, 1964

It is some time since the first copy of *The Solitary Life* arrived and I have not yet thanked you. Today another came, together with the little fourteenth-century cards (how beautifully done) perhaps from Dame Marcella (there was no indication). But in any case I am so pleased with the finished [book]. I think it has a great deal of character, and is just right. A great sobriety. It is just substantial enough, too. A most monastic job. Thank you so much for it. I am eager to get to something else. But I know we both have more irons in the fire than we probably should.

The first copy went to Dom Porion in Rome and I got a nice letter from him. He liked it very much. Did I ever say that I received word from a friend at La Grande Chartreuse, getting an unofficial clearance for the use of the material? He said the Prior there would like to have some copies. I am sure they would like quite a few, and I leave it to your judgment to decide according to what you have. I should think a couple of dozen at least.

The little fourteenth-century card is also a jewel. It is hard to say which of the two I like best, the one with the red or the one with the gold.

Lately I have been reading a bit about English recluses in the Middle Ages. There is a lot of fascinating material on this. But I am not planning anything yet that would be of immediate interest to the press at Stanbrook, though I may come up with an article for one of the magazines. I do still want some time or other to do a couple of letters from Anselm, but this must wait.

Spring is gradually reaching us. We have had a few late frosts, but now things are opening up. The dogwoods are just barely beginning to show. I forget if this tree was in England. I know that another that blossoms in the spring was not there: the redbud. It comes out in delicate pink clouds of blossom just about the time when the first leaves on the earliest trees begin to appear (the maples). It gives the woods a water-colourish washed look and is very pleasant . . .

To Nora Chadwick

Professor Nora Chadwick, of Cambridge University, England, had written a number of books on Celtic monasticism which Merton found very attractive.

May 26, 1964

Having just read, and greatly enjoyed, your book *The Age of Saints in the Early Celtic Church*, I am emboldened by my friend [Eleanor] S. Duckett to write you a note about it. Speaking as a monk, I can hardly say how much I have responded to your ideas and theses. As I am not enough of a scholar to find reasons why they might not be perfectly correct, I am happy to agree with you throughout. So your book has come along just when I was about to start on Celtic monasticism with my novices and students at this Abbey. I also used your *Poetry and Letters in Sixth Century Gaul* with them last year and will, no doubt, use it again. One of my students reviewed it also for our little magazine which perhaps you have seen. If not, please let me know and I will have a copy sent to you. The magazine is called *Monastic Studies*.

I have begun some work on medieval recluses, and am of course very interested in finding out more about the Irish sources of this movement on the continent. I see you quote Marianus Scotus, and there are all sorts of interesting suggestions in your book that seem to lead in the direction which interests me. I have Gougaud's *Ermites et Reclus* and *Celtic Christianity*, and have run into the standard works on recluses in England. Can you give me any other good leads for Ireland? I am especially eager to get at the poetic material in Kuno Meyer, which I have never seen before, and probably will find a thing or two there. But I would greatly appreciate if you would give me some good leads for Irish hermits and recluses and their influence on the continent.

Really this letter does not say what I want to say about your book. What is so delightful is to meet someone who is completely "in" the monastic movement of our own time (though you may not realize it), for you think just like some of us and have the same longings and joys in monastic solitude of the Celtic type. Actually in the Monastic Order today there is quite a struggle afoot between the partisans of this ancient tradition and the more active and busy types of our time. Monasticism remains a very living reality, and one which is not necessarily defined by enclosure walls.

I had a year at Cambridge a long time ago, and with Mr. Telfer as my tutor I should by rights have come in contact with some of the Chadwicks, but never did. I am afraid that at that time the seeds of a monastic vocation were very, very dormant.

To Sister Felicitas, O.S.B.

Sister Felicitas, an American Benedictine nun, wrote Merton in regard to integrated monastic communities.

June 3, 1964

Today happens to be the feast of the martyrs of Uganda, and I think I had better answer your letter at once. Thank them for this push, because if I let the letter go, God alone knows when I would be able to answer it.

The first thing that I think we can do as Benedictines, I mean precisely as Benedictines and not merely as Christians engaged in good works of one sort or another: we can take Negroes into our communities and simply *be* Churches as we ought to be, families in which there is no distinction of race, color, etc., one in Christ. This seems obvious. There is of course the difficulty of attracting a lot of Negro vocations. I suppose all of us accept them, I take this for granted. We have only one here at present and no applications recently. The point is that the first and best thing we can do is worship and love God together, white and black, in one family, thus being a sign of the Risen Christ in the world torn by prejudice and hate.

Where Benedictines have a parish I think they ought to be in a special position to appreciate the need of forming an integrated parish with families visiting together, warm interrelations between the races, and holding the fort against flight of whites from a neighborhood that is threatened with "deteriorating."

For further ideas you can write to the Monastère Bénédictin, Box 16 (I think), Bouaké, Ivory Coast, Africa. They have just had a big meeting there about Benedictines in Africa, their role, etc., and they can give you all the information you need. Or maybe someone at St. John's can tell you about this.

To Father Hans Urs von Balthasar

Father von Balthasar's writings were much read at Gethsemani at this time. Eventually he arranged for a German translation of some of Merton's poetry. Pope John Paul II made him a cardinal shortly before his death in 1988.

July 3, 1964

My friend Dom Jean Leclercq writes that he recently had the pleasure of visiting you in Basel and that my name was mentioned in the conversation. I am honored and happy that it was, and it is with pleasure that I follow his suggestion in sending you some of the unpublished texts that have been emanating from the novitiate here. I also send you a recent volume of poems, as Dom Jean said you were especially interested in poetry.

It is a comfort to me to know that you, whose works we know so well here and whom we so profoundly respect, should be interested in such things. Too few theologians are, I imagine. But you are an Origenist: how can you fail to be alert to the seriousness of the poetic word, which has its own special place in the world of the sons of God since Adam was appointed to name the animals. After years I have I think learned to be a poet without guilt because I am after all not that much of a poet. But I am completely convinced that without the emergence of an occasional poetic word into consciousness, my monastic life would be fruitless. Theoria demands not just gazing but response and statement. Don't you agree? Statement of course in the sense of praise or lamentation (for in our day there is much to lament and the monk, *cujus officium est lugere* [whose function is to mourn], ought to be able to raise a cry like an Oriental mourner over the world in which we now live).

I have found too by God's grace that other poets, particularly in Latin America (where splendid poetry is being written), have come to be a part of my life and of my monastic vocation too. One of them, whose name you will find in my own book of poems and with translations and a letter, is editing a very lively and vigorous magazine in Nicaragua which is gradually becoming international, that is to say more than Latin American. This poet, Pablo Antonio Cuadra, has asked my help in suggesting people who could provide deep and interesting texts whether on poetry, or culture, or theology. He is after Gabriel Marcel, etc., in France and I believe that you would be one to send him something to translate from German.

You will also receive some monastic texts that have been mimeographed here, and a couple of offprints. I would be most interested to know what your own latest publications are. I am very fond of your neighbor Karl Barth and have written on his book on Anselm (which is wonderful I think). I mean to send him the essay when it gets printed. Have you ever done anything on Oriental religion? I have been in contact with a Master of Zen Buddhism, and in fact had an exchange with him that showed him to have a "natural" grasp of the Patristic approach to Paradise and the Fall which is most remarkable. He understands it much better than many technical theologians and indeed many monks.

I am so glad Dom Jean suggested my getting in touch with you. Do you travel to America? If so I hope you will let us know and we will invite you here to give us some talks . . .

To Brother H.

Brother H. was a member of a Bruderhof community in the United States, and had written Thomas Merton about a possible visit and sharing some of the common problems of contemporary community living.

July 4, 1964

Please forgive the long delay in replying to your very kind letter and acknowledging the two fine books you sent. Life here is not exactly geared for much correspondence and so it takes time to answer letters.

First of all let me say how much I enjoyed the little book on Eberhard Arnold's life and spirit. It was certainly a very moving and genuine religious experience to read this simple and direct account of a Christian life stripped down to the real essentials. There is no question that there is a similarity of spirit between your Brotherhood and our Monastic Order. We should indeed be in touch with one another. It is unfortunate that I do not travel, or I would be able to visit one of your communities. If one of your members is in this region, please feel free to call on us, the door is open. If you wish to see me it can perhaps be arranged if you write ahead of time. But my visits are quite limited and usually I have more than I strictly should. In a case like this an exception can always be made.

Emmy Arnold's retelling of the Bruderhof story is also very moving in its simplicity. I am sure you must know Dorothy Day of the *Catholic Worker*; their spirit too is like yours.

A special word for the beautiful book *Children in Community*. This is a very special success, with all the modesty of its production, it is certainly an outstanding picture book, one that is really much more than it appears to be. (So many ambitious and pretentious projects in this line are actually far less than they want to be or claim to be.) Here there is a kind of intangible and indefinable spiritual "plus" that surely comes from the Lord Himself. Such a wonderful quality. The texts are marvelous and the pictures a real joy. I shall never get tired of this book, and the other monks and I will continue to enjoy it as long as we live, I hope. It will remain a deep bond with you.

I am sure we have analogous problems and joys. Wherever there is a special religious group there is danger of a ghetto spirit, of excessive self-concern, and as a result a kind of futile fighting with ourselves about ideals and intangibles. This is right in a way, but it also tends to get in the way of our real aims. For the ideal is right in the real, and the end is already in the means, if the means are right. The means are right insofar as they are honest and faithful. Let me assure you that your "rightness" and your faithfulness are evident in these books. Never fear, your joy has eternal foundations. So let us praise Jesus together and let us never fear to love all, for in love surrender is victory.

I will send you some of our own books and some of the papers that are put out here in the novitiate. Please give my warm fraternal affection to all your community and let us be united in prayer and hope together.

To Father Godfrey Diekmann, O.S.B.

Father Diekmann, an American Benedictine liturgist of St. John's Abbey, Collegeville, was well known for his many labors in liturgical renewal as editor of Worship. *In recent years, he has championed the cause of full ministry of women in the Church.*

July 15, 1964

Thanks very much for your notes on the Einsiedeln meeting. I had already heard from Dom Leclercq that I am numbered among the elect consultors and that I owe this honor to you. It is a pleasure to accept, and I hope I can be of use. I really want to, and it is so important that we do all we can to keep the monastic movement in this country making sense and progressing in the right direction. I don't know how cramped and hindered I am going to be in my responses and efforts to work with you. How official is this? Is it an offshoot of some Council Commission? If so, then I suppose the authority it has will lend a certain strength to requests for cooperation on my part, and the Superiors here will be less recalcitrant about granting the necessary minimum of freedom of action and movement.

One thing I think is going to be very important is the preservation of a sane and broad-minded spirit of unity in diversity with lots of sober flexibility in adaptations, so that there will not be a few rigid norms laid down which all must meet, but that, especially during the interim of experimentation, there will be a certain amount of choice left open. It seems to me that it would be a great mistake to present the step into vernacular as *necessarily* a complete abandonment of Latin for everyone. I think that it should be optional. I think three options could be envisaged.

1) Houses with one vernacular choir for all.
2) Houses with a Latin office and a vernacular office (as we have now).
3) Houses with Latin only (these may not be in existence much longer, maybe).

Then I would say there should be a certain latitude permitting men to change from one to the other temporarily or permanently.

It seems to me that a kind of wise planned pluralism, brought about by collaboration among all the monastic Orders in America, could result in a much more efficient and sane monastic life for everyone, without too much useless reduplication and conflict. There could be some regrouping, for instance, and communities could fall into one or other of the following patterns:

1) Active communities with vernacular liturgy and emphasis on pastoral liturgical apostolate.
2) Semi-active communities (with teaching) (or retreats, etc.).
3) Enclosed cenobitic communities with more elaborate liturgy.
4) Enclosed cenobitic communities with very simple liturgy and perhaps retaining Latin?
5) Eremitical groups with rudimentary liturgy (Latin?).
6) Eremitical groups with missionary witness.

and so on. I for one would like to see one Ordo monasticus, united for the purpose of hashing out common problems, divided into traditional families with their own observances, differing in accidentals, essentially one. I would also think it most important that each community retain a great measure of autonomy under its own abbot, in matters of observance, cult, etc.

To Dame Hildelith Cumming

July 22, 1964

Today two books arrived, beautifully bound: the *Spiritual Anker* and the *Treatise on Discretion*. Thanks very much indeed. I will read them and take good care of them and send them back safely. Meanwhile I have received others, some time ago, and I don't remember having acknowledged them. I am very ashamed of myself.

What I received was *Dame Margaret Gascoigne* which is excellent, and I have noted some excerpts that could be used. These will come to you when I have also thought of others from the other mss. Then there is the Catholic Record Society material, as well as Dame Barbara Constable's *Considerations for Priests*. These are very good but as they are more of a compilation I do not think we can use them, do you?

I look forward to reading the new Baker material. But by the way, I think you said you sent part of his Commentary on the Rule. I never received this. Did something go wrong? I had better check again with the secretary in Rev. Father's office to make sure it never came. Things have a way of getting into a corner or onto a shelf there, and one never knows what happened to them . . .

I am going along with a couple of other things, especially working up my notes on Celtic monasticism, which I am going to take with the novices soon, I hope. There is really marvelous material there, and so neglected. Since the days of Bede when everyone wanted to make quite sure that they were on the right side in the Easter and Tonsure questions, the Irish tradition has been a bit neglected in England. But it is really splendid. I am working on the "Legendary Voyage of Brendan," which is really a symbolic tract on the monastic life (though not a deliberate and forced allegory). There is much there. There are wonderful old poems by the Irish hermits too. That would be a lovely excuse for some printing.

What else? I had the pleasure of meeting someone I have much admired, old D. T. Suzuki, the great authority on Zen Buddhism, now in his nineties, and a Japanese Zen Master in the old style, in some ways. It was a joy to speak with him, especially as he really seemed to consider me a sort of favorite disciple and said I really understood Zen very well. He was most kind and encouraging. We had been corresponding and sending things back and forth. Do pray for him, because as a matter of fact he is himself deeply "Christian" in a natural sort of way. I am sure he is very close to truth.

For the rest, we are in rather poor shape here in this country. The race question gets more troublesome every day, with awful riots, etc. A very explosive situation, now beyond remedy in any deep sense. Then there is this frightful business in Viet Nam. I am certain that many people in this country really want a war there; I mean a full-scale one, which of course will be simply the U.S. against Red China. It is absurd, and there is no real justification for it. I do not see how it can meet any of the requirements of the just war that Catholic moral theology demands. It is just a disgraceful and crude venture in power politics, justified by emotional clichés in the public press and by a certain vague superstitiousness in the people, thinking they are being attacked by the Communist monster, etc. It seems to me that the aggressiveness is quite marked on both sides, perhaps chiefly on ours. The worst of it is that the war cannot do a bit of good to our "cause" whatever it is. It will certainly serve to bring the Chinese into solid unity under the Communists, and will get most of the non-white people in the world more angry with us than they are already. It is a disastrous thing. I hope you will pray for it somehow to be settled without this violence, but I wonder if it is possible? The one who will profit most is of course Russia.

I shall send back Dame Barbara's *Considerations* and hope they will reach you safely. Everyone likes *The Solitary Life* immensely and all are struck by the beauty of the printing . . .

To Father Callistus (Jorge) Peterson, O.C.S.O.

A monk of Gethsemani studying in Rome, Father Callistus wrote Merton about the laybrother question. He later became a member of the foundation in Chile.

August 4, 1964

Everyone who comes back from Rome keeps saying, "Write to those poor devils over there, even if it is only three lines." Your letter has been waiting for an answer, and it has a few concrete questions in it, which give a reason for writing. Normally it is hard to find how one could squeeze anything for a letter out of the situation here, when you probably know a great deal more about what is going on in the house than I do.

You ask me about the vexed problem of those poor brothers. As if I knew something about it. The whole situation seems to me to be very ambiguous indeed and much more than it ought to be. But I am told that we are in a special situation, that there is no brothers' problem here. Well, if there isn't, or wasn't, we are creating one.

First of all, principle: this is what seems to me to be the one simple basic principle about the brothers: they were created so that they would have a different life from the choir, in the sense that they would not be bound by all the same responsibilities as the choir, and would be free to work and operate outside the enclosure in granges, which was forbidden the choir. They were not bound to choir, and in order to keep them from getting involved in the complexities of the choir life they were not supposed to get educated. The whole purpose of all this was to keep them off the hook, and able to live their own form of life, very simple, humble, laborious, and untrammelled by special obligations.

Second: matter of fact. The best vocations who have come here as brothers have come looking for something other than the choir. They do not want the choir, or very little of it, and are happy with their life of work, simplicity, humility, without the burden of obligations that go with the choir. There are others, less good, who worry about whether they ought not to be in choir, etc. I speak of the ones I have in the novitiate. Others, professed, may not fit this description.

Third: question of procedure. In order to put the brothers on the same juridical basis as the choir and give them the same advantages and privileges (which is necessary, we all agree), there is a movement which seems to want to give them at the same time the same *obligations* as the choir. This amounts to the abolition of the brothers' life. Some, seeing this, have reacted very strongly, in panic.

Fourth: suggestion. It seems to me that the Church is now in a position to give the brothers the same privileges and advantages as the choir, without changing the form of their life and without adding new obligations which are alien to it. If we will avoid problems and indeed the ruin of many very good vocations (to the brothers) we should concentrate on giving the brothers a completely equal juridical status, without involving them necessarily in the same schedule and obligations as the choir. They should not become choir monks. But it is possible that it would be very desirable to have brothers and choir all together once a day at a conventual Mass, to emphasize unity, etc. Or twice: Lauds (Mass) and Vespers or Compline.

Doubtless there are others who do not think along these lines. I hope I may be permitted to express these thoughts in all simplicity without being thought wild. They seem to me to represent the simple and obvious spirit of the Order.

I reflect often on the stage we are going through, with the hopes and desires that are felt here and there, and the fears also. This is rather a difficult and also perhaps interesting time to be living in. But as to my part in it, I am gradually becoming more and more skeptical of my ability to really get into it. I just have no clear idea of what is going on, and I certainly mistrust my own opinions of Cistercianism, seeing that I am in no real sense a Cistercian at all. So the conclusion is that I think I am going to have less and less to say on such topics as monastic reform and the monastic life, etc., etc., because, in the first place, even though what I say may be reasonable (and that is not guaranteed) it may just arouse a lot of false hopes, and create an unjustified interest or expectation of something or other. I think we have to be very careful of the area of expectations. What there is to expect . . . well, we have the past to guide us in this regard.

Thus let this be the burden of my thoughts and their conclusion: I see clearer than ever that I am not a monk, still less a Cistercian monk, and that I have no business making statements that directly affect the conduct of the Cistercian life (except to try to help my novices live without going nuts immediately. I leave them to go nuts when they get in the juniorate). With this unpleasant clarity I expect to try to live for a few more years, hoping that I will not go nuts myself. This, I think, is about the best I can hope for. It sums up the total of my expectations for the immediate future. If on top of this the Lord sees fit in His mercy to admit me to a non-monastic corner of heaven, among the beatniks and pacifists and other maniacs, I will be exceedingly grateful. Doubtless there will be a few pseudo-hermits among them and we will all sit around and look at each other and wonder how we made it. Up above will be the monks, with a clearer view of their own status and a more profound capacity to appreciate the meaning of status and the value of having one.

Well, Father, for news of the community: the place is hot.

To Father M. Placid, O.C.S.O.

This monk of the Southern Star Cistercian monastery in New Zealand wrote to Merton in regard to monastic formation.

August 5, 1964

About your questions: first I suppose the best thing I could do for the "second novitiate" question is describe what the "monastic formation" group does here. After the novitiate, these young monks who are not priests have no formal classes, go to communion daily at the High Mass, do not have to serve Mass; hence have a fairly long period after night office for lectio, have three mornings off during work time to study monastic subjects and have a few conferences a week, but are working more towards no formal classes in monastic subjects but individual contacts with a Master who will guide their reading, etc.

In the case of priests, this is what I would suggest. They should of course be free from all responsibilities, if possible. At least from all large jobs. Perhaps be given some extra time for reading and reflection, and then they could devote themselves to study and thought on an aspect of the life that interests them, Scripture, Fathers, etc., or just deepen their own spiritual life, perhaps with consultations with a spiritual Father each week, something more than just confession.

A great deal depends in fact on the spirit of the house and what actually is done there. If they have not read basic books like Cassian and other monastic classics like the *Apothegmata*, then they should do this; and perhaps get more into St. Bernard, William of St. Thierry, etc.

It seems to me that it would be practical for those who are interested to have one day a month completely free for solitude, reading and thought, perhaps apart from the community in a hermitage set aside for that purpose. This works very well in places where it is done. I also think that the idea of each one making his retreat privately is good. The amount of solitude could vary. Some in our monasteries are not interested in solitude and can't stand it. But they could have a different work schedule and so on. I must admit that the potted organized retreat that happens each year is an affliction. It helps only those who imagine for some reason that it is a diversion.

Dechanet's book is safe and useful, but I don't think it is being used in our Order for two reasons: nowhere to go, and monks usually too tired or don't have time. I think it recommends itself for officers of the monastery and people who get less than the normal amount of exercise.

I favor the Prayer of Jesus only in cases where it comes rather spontaneously and I do not think that our monks ought to make a deliberate project out of it with a great deal of concentrated introversion. This will do more harm than good. But the prayer is good on and off, when needed and when one feels it is helpful.

I hope your monastery in New Zealand will prosper and be a center of true monastic life and prayer. New Zealand is where my father came from and I have lots of relatives there; it is a kind of homeland in a way. So naturally I feel rather more interested in your Abbey than I would for instance in the Australian one.

To Father Hans Urs von Balthasar

August 7, 1964

Thank you for your kind letter. What you said concerning your theology of "Kabod" very much pleases me, especially the day after the Transfiguration! You are absolutely right, and I am anxious to read your work, although I do not know German very well. I have no trouble with some things such as Kittel's *Wordbook*, so perhaps I would be able to understand with a little more attention. This would be a good occasion to learn. At any rate, may I ask you to send me anything you can?

As for the poems, do as you wish: for my part, I think that a volume of selected poems along with *Titans* (but minus the essay on Herakleitos, perhaps), plus the "Letter to Cuadra," would make a nice little book. I am not sure if another editor is already interested in them, but in any case, as far as the commercial aspect is concerned, you can check with my agent in Munich: Dagmar Henne, at the Hoffman Agency, Seestrasse 6. I think though that everything is free [uncommitted], both the poems and *Titans*. I leave you the rights on anything that you can use, in German, as regards the poems.

I am very pleased that you like all this. I am very much in agreement with you on the importance of poetry as being, ever so often, the locus of Theophany! I am acquainted especially with some Latin American poets, as I told you. One can find in them very significant things, even if they are obscure. There is a kind of religious night, an anguish very deep but simple with Vallejo—a Peruvian Indian. He was a bit communist, but for him it was not a tag to distinguish between "believer" or "unbeliever" (which is what people on either side get all worked up about). Rather, what one finds in him is simply a very pure awareness of God, very simple and without grand articulation. And no fuss or bother. It is these very people to whom we can listen with profit. Vallejo is certainly, in a very obscure way, a prophet of our time and our hemisphere. A witness of our misery and confusion. He is the Incas' version of Baudelaire, and so simple. I have also started to read a Portuguese of the same type, Pessoa. He also describes the dark night.

I failed to mention to you that the book of yours which says the most to me has always been the one on St. Maximus. I seem to find these themes again and again, and even more so in your more recent work.

To Sister Mary Luke Tobin, S.L.

Sister Mary Luke Tobin, former Superior General of the Sisters of Loretto, was the only American woman to attend Vatican II, as an observer. She was an inexhaustible source of news from the Council, which Merton greatly appreciated.

August 15, 1964

I don't know if you have gone to Rome yet, but in any case someone will know what to do about the following suggestion. Next January our community retreat is to be preached by Fr. Illtud Evans, O.P., editor of *Blackfriars*, in England. He needs to give a few talks around here to round out his travelling expenses and so on. He will be free for talks in this area January 15, 16 and 17. I thought you would like to have him. He is good in several areas, particularly Palestine, also sacred art, also juvenile delinquents, prison reform, and probably a lot of other things. There is plenty of variety . . .

It is a long time since I have had an opportunity to chat, and much has been going on: mostly in the order of work, about which there is not much to be said. It has to be done and that's that. I finally managed to get the book on race and peace cleared and it is coming out this fall, God willing. It is called *Seeds of Destruction*. I hope it gets out before the election. Thus I can contribute something to the fray, in which incidentally I have difficulty in seeing how I can really vote for either candidate. Certainly not for the Republican choice. As for Johnson, he is a crafty dud with no sense of foreign affairs, relying on his political know-how on Capitol Hill to get by. Neither one seems very promising.

By the way, I almost forgot: Dan Berrigan, S.J., will be down this fall, I hope. Probably around the end of October. He has been in Africa and behind the Iron Curtain and has some very interesting things to say about it all. He too needs to finance his trip, and I thought you might be interested . . .

To Nora Chadwick

August 20, 1964

It is indeed a pleasure to hear from you. I am glad that my notes on monastic themes have reached you safely and that you have enjoyed them. I feel I owe you a real debt, because through you I have really come to appreciate Celtic monasticism and have started to really open up pathways that seem to me quite promising for study, but above all for my own monastic life. I am indeed grateful for people like you and Eleanor Duckett who, outside the monastery, live with a really monastic spirit and interest. I have been praying for your Carmelite sister, may God reward her: I am sure that we can profit more by her prayers, however, than she by ours. Do please recommend me to the prayers of the Sisters at Waterbeach. I love the Carmelite spirit, I mean especially that of the first Carmelites and the *Ignea sagitta* (a rare but very moving document on the solitary life).

At present I have got into the material that is available in libraries on the Celtic monks, including Dudley Simpson's book on the Celtic Church in Scotland, Clark on St. Gall, and I am following up Grosjean's articles. I am most interested, at the moment, in the *Navigatio Brendani* on which I hope to do a little study as a monastic document: a sort of manifesto of monastic and spiritual reform emanating from the Irish milieux of Treves, etc., in the Ottonian period. It is very interesting as a treatment of the theme of the *paradisus claustralis*. The real "paradise" in the book turns out to be not so much the "lost island" (which in the end gets rather scant treatment), but the paradise of liturgy which is the island of the birds, on which they always spend the Easter season. It is a lovely book. I am reading Adomnan's life of Columba for the first time, and long to see the Hebrides, which I probably never will. So you see, you are a real inspiration. I am delighted to have a copy of your *Age of Saints* which I will keep at my elbow all the time, for I know I shall be constantly dipping into it.

Do please let me, as an expression of friendship, send a couple more things: a little untechnical essay on "Pilgrimages," and a translation of a letter of Guigo the Carthusian, and an offprint that might interest the Carmelites, when you next see them. The "Pilgrimages" and Guigo are of course for you.

To Father Norbert Gorrissen, O.C.S.O.

A Cistercian monk of the abbey of Orval in southern Belgium, Father Norbert wrote to Merton on the problems of contemporary monasticism.

August 20, 1964

Thank you for your letter and your essay. I totally agree. It is very important for us to re-examine seriously all the questions which we are up against in the area of contemporary monasticism. It is no longer enough to approach our problems as a Dom Guéranger and a Dom Marmion did (even if they were both great men). Our task is more profound in another way. You are right that we have to ask ourselves where we are and *who* we are. As master of novices I see more and more that often good, serious vocations finally become disappointed with the excessively formalistic and artificial structure of a life that is regulated by a more or less Carolingian conception of monasticism.

First of all, we should see that the structures which sufficed from the ninth until the nineteenth century need to be adapted and even renewed in a very serious way. It's a whole way of looking at things that we have to transform. I am persuaded that young people here in America would no longer be able to stick it out in the mental atmosphere which existed at Gethsemani when I entered here. It is an atmosphere that I myself could accept without too much difficulty, but already now it no longer exists. We are in the process of evolving in a not very reasonable way toward something hazy and confused, while trying to "hold on to" the order and discipline which gave us a precise identity in the past. So what we need now is a true conception of man in our times, a conception of the role of the Church in the world, and a more simple and perhaps more primitive conception of monasticism, which would at the same time preserve an *openness* to the world that is wholly essential, without getting all wrapped up in dreams of activity. It is very delicate, and we cannot succeed if we think that we already know everything essential for answering these questions and that all we need to do is change our point of view a little so as to become more "modern."

You have some very good ideas in your essay, and I believe that it will be profitable to all of us if we can do this work together, while thinking of questions such as: the essence of the monastic vocation, openness to the world, solitude, poverty, work, prayer, etc., in the new setting. But it seems to me that we need to create something that is properly monastic and not a kind of adaptation to what the Little Brothers have done, for example. It is not enough for us to arrange things so we can survive in today's world. We need a real renewal of monastic *life*, not of the official organization and spirituality of the different Orders. For this renewal we need an atmosphere of courage and liberty where it would be permitted not to cling desperately to structures of the past; and we need—let's admit it—real spiritual Fathers.

To Dom Jean Leclercq

August 28, 1964

I am very sorry you have had to have so much trouble with this "Monk in the Diaspora" article. Dom Ignace [Gillet, the Abbot General] was more opposed to it than I had expected, but I suppose I should have realized that he would have felt insulted.

The best thing seemed to me to simply make a few simple corrections and emendations in the part of the text which we both have. I am doing this and sending it to you. You can make the changes in any way you wish, with all freedom. As to the part which you have and I do not, that is to say the very beginning and the last few pages about the Russians, I leave you to make any emendation corresponding to the kind of changes I have made. In particular I recognize that I was not too clear about the "diaspora" which tends to be ambiguous because it is in a state of "becoming," but it seems to me that it certainly exists in Africa, Asia, etc. But anyway, that probably needs softening. I note that the General did not like the Carmels of Periggeux, but I will leave them anyway. I think they have their message. They come with invisible Magi from the diaspora.

Dom Ignace also mentioned a possible prefatory note by you which would explain that Anglo-Saxon writers (I am really more a Celt than an Anglo-Saxon) are given to irony even when they are serious. I don't know if you think this should be done, but perhaps a note of some sort might prepare the sober reader for a jolt.

I will write to Fr. Charles about the *Collectanea*. I already wrote a small article on the subject. I think it fulfills a very necessary function, with the Chronique, etc., but the articles are often below par. Perhaps the best thing would be to get more articles from good writers outside the Order while others are learning how to do it. But I would think it a pity if it were suppressed. *Monastic Studies* is in trouble in this country. As everything is veiled in secrecy, or at least in ambiguity, I am not quite sure what is going on but the future looks bleak. We cannot count on an American monastic magazine yet, in this Order. And the Benedictines still do not provide what is needed.

In October we are having a meeting of Abbots here. I have to speak on the mentality of modern youth and their capacity to fit into the monastic life: or of the monastic life to accept them. It is a complex subject, probably different in different countries. Here I think that youths who are psychologically insecure and lost are placed in an ascetic machine designed for men of strong character and powerful egos. The result is not too wonderful. We suppress them when we ought to try to educate and develop them. Have you any ideas? Certainly the expedient of TV and recreation (of an artificial kind) will be worse than the sickness it is supposed to cure.

To Father Illtud Evans

August 30, 1964

I am not sure if you still need lecture engagements in this area before our retreat. Some of the people I contacted may have written to you. Loretto will be delighted to have you talk on sacred art. Bellarmine College is also interested. If you still want to go there will you write to Prof. Jude Dougherty? This is a silly way to do it, but it is what they suggested to me. St. Meinrad may or may not have written.

Casting prudence to the winds, I am talking to the novices these days about art. What it gets down to in reality is talking about the necessity for imagination in the Christian life, and in any life. Casting art to the winds, I wrote an article on art and prudence for the *New Catholic Encyclopedia*. They got at me very late (maybe someone died), for the thing is almost about to appear and they have been at it for years. It sounds awful. But the man now doing art, Fr. Roman Verostko, seems good.

To Sister Mary Luke Tobin

September 3, 1964

Thanks for your letter of August 20th. And first of all, I would like very much to see you before you go to Rome. I have asked Fr. Abbot for permission to talk with you if you come over here, and so this has been granted . . . Monday, the 14th, and Wednesday, the 16th, will be certainly good times, as far as I can see. Anytime in the afternoon that is convenient with you will be all right for me, up to about five o'clock. By five I am usually tied up with direction, or some other business.

Actually the Freedom Songs have not been set to music. I wrote them for a Negro singer who wants to use them in a concert, and I think he is trying to get some musician with a name . . . He tried Aaron Copland without success. I don't think he has much chance of lining anyone up. A friend of mine in New York may also be interested in getting someone to try it. But I personally doubt if anyone will take on the job of doing all eight of them, as they will probably not be easy to set to music anyway. As far as I am concerned, if Sister Jeremy wants to try one or other of them, that is fine. It may turn out to be just the sort of thing we need. I am thinking in terms of the blues-type Gospel-singing melody.

At the moment I don't have poison ivy. But I now realize that I have acquired a sensitivity to it which I did not have before, and that is not an acquisition that I like. It means I have to be careful about where I go in the woods. I hope I can outgrow this . . .

To Dom Ignace Gillet

September 3, 1964

I am writing this brief word to assure you that I received your letter with the copy of the one you sent to Dom Leclercq. I have made the changes necessary to nuance . . . "The Monk and the Diaspora" without reworking it, however. About ten major corrections, including the suppression of several lines which were perhaps not those which amused you most, have perhaps made this article less offensive. It is true, unfortunately, that when I write, I do not think at all about the reactions of the French reader, who may be very different from an American or English reader. You are well aware that I did not want to appear to be a rebel or an irreverent critic of the authorities, and I very much regret if I have hurt you, Most Reverend Father. I thought that the positive side of the article was quite pronounced enough to establish how much I love monasticism as it is and where I find myself. It is not a question of dissatisfaction, but to look at what might very well happen . . .

To Dom Damasus Winzen

September 8, 1964

It was most kind of you to write your letter of St. Louis' Day and of course I was delighted to learn that I had been on your diptychs that day. I certainly value the friendship and the prayers of Mount Saviour, and you know the respect I have always had for your community and its spirit.

So it is good to feel united to you in the bonds of the Spirit Who has called us into the desert—in which our wanderings or mine at least may seem, at times, hazardous and without aim. I will certainly remember you on the 14th, a day of monastic beginnings since it is the beginning of a season of "our own," the monastic fast. Not that we fast terribly here anymore and I for my part have a special diet so that the flesh may not glory in asceticism. I wish it could glory in humility as St. Benedict would like.

Certainly you at Mount Saviour and Dom Leo at Weston have the advantage, the inestimable advantage, of being on your own and not hemmed in by the demands and pretenses of a big institutional structure. I see more and more that though this has advantages, it is the rigidity and centralization of our Order that account for some of our most difficult problems, perhaps the chief of which is the refusal of the human dimension not so much in favor of strictness as in favor of organization. There are so many things that are meaningless and are immovable for purely abstract reasons. It is true that in the other houses there is a beginning of movement, but it is of a nature to make me comparatively glad of our inertia. The other houses are beginning to go in bizarre directions, circling about mindlessly in a way that one suspects of being aimed at distraction. Still, I am perhaps not in a position to judge. We are supposed to be having a big meeting here, Abbots and Novice Masters, but I am not expecting too much of it. Though the mere fact of talking together is important. There may even be some communication. Or is this too much to hope for?

Yes, I completely agree that what this country so badly needs and seeks is a personal and "pneumatic" monasticism: to receive the Holy Spirit in the life of the community under a common Father who is truly *pneumatikos* and then to obey the Spirit with the guidance of the Father Abbas and the encouragement of the brethren. The great problem remains that of a system and a way of life that tends to extinguish the Spirit. It all comes to that. One feels everywhere that monks are stifled, and the open window approach of Pope John has not really caught on with the Cistercians, except in places where they are breaking down whole sides of the building (while still not opening the window) . . .

In the end I suppose it turns out that I have been called to be a monk and have somehow become one (of a sort) contrary to all the blueprints. In the end, that is an aspect of the desert *peregrinatio*. But I admit it would be much more comforting to be able to agree with everyone else on all these things. In any event I see no hope whatever of a unity of *doctrina* here. It is just too much to be hoped for and I stopped even thinking of it years ago. One has to be realistic about some things: and this is a community set in fragmentation. I have more in common with friends in China and India than I have with some of the members of my monastic community. It is a rather awful thing to say. And probably means little anyway.

To Dame Hildelith Cumming

September 9, 1964

Here is the prayer of Cassiodorus I mentioned in my last letter. I send also the Latin in case you are interested, but my mind remains quite open to suggestion—whether to use both Latin and English or only English. I am sure this can make an interesting little book. How does it strike you?

September 10, 1964

Your letter came today after I had sent off my note yesterday. I am sending back the "blurb" which is fine; though "crisp" is not my favorite word. Still it applies, and I wonder what one would say instead? Would it be pushing things too far to call his prose "chaste"? I am interested in your essay; must write more about that. The Achel experiment has already gone under and I think it was a little off the beam for us. Besides it got altogether too much publicity. This question of aggiornamento is a thorny one and we must be careful with it. The basic thing for us is to be genuine monks and to push our monasticity forward into practice rather than compromising it. That is a bad sentence. I forget if I sent . . . "The Monk in the Diaspora" but I am doing so now. More later. God bless you always.

To Dom Ignace Gillet

September 11, 1964

I thank you very much, and with all my heart, for your good letter of September 2nd. I am very happy to be able to speak frankly to you, all the more since I see that we are fundamentally in agreement. And also I believe I can reassure you that the impressions given by the article and my other letter represent my ideas inexactly. Since you are willing, I will try to put on paper a few more concise thoughts, though at the same time I feel that I will not succeed perfectly, quite the contrary. Let us say, rather, that I will begin to explain, by telling you filially my position regarding modern monasticism, the changes that are being made, that should be made, and the formation of the young. Thus, it is as a monk and a son of the Church that I will try to say, before God and to a representative of Christ and of the Church, what I have in my heart. May the Blessed Virgin help me. (I am not sure how much you know English. It is not very easy for me to say clearly what I want to say on something so important, in French.)

1) *Monasticism*: I am, by the grace of God, a monk. A monk of the twentieth century, with his difficulties, which nevertheless are not those of the "young." I am completely convinced of the value of monasticism,

and of *traditional* monasticism. (The thing is to understand the "tradition.") I am even more convinced of the role of monasticism in today's world. A prophetic and even charismatic role. I dare to pronounce these terrible words. The monk is a child of God, an instrument of God. Which means that he is poorer than the others, more stripped, less "strong" and not at all a strong-minded person. His life remains hidden in God, mysterious, stripped, but it's a life which should be happy and full because it is a life in the truth and in simplicity, a life before God, with God, in God. Monastic life should be a sign of God in the world, a sign of love, of the truth of the Gospel, a sign of the poor and simple Christ, a brother to the world also but not of this world.

(I am speaking about the monastic ideal, while not being an ideal monk, quite the contrary. I know that I am a poor monk, maladjusted, with necessary indulgences, with a nervous system which plays tricks on me. I am not capable of being a monk who is simply "edifying." I think that I am not a scandalous monk, either, although some might and do think so.)

2) *Changes*: In principle, the whole of the changes and monastic renewal should be judged by the monastic life's function of being a true life in God, in Christ. But this is still very general. So let us see a few examples. Here I cannot be complete, but by speaking about a few examples, I will try at least to give an indication of my thought.

I wonder if we are not making changes without rhyme or reason, for lack of a clear and comprehensive vision of our goal. For example: wooden spoons. I, too, like them. We still have them here and I am glad. You speak about silence. That's true. And also, wood is something simple and honest, even beautiful. So, in principle, wooden spoons seem to me to be in the monastic truth. But, in principle, the monk should himself *make* his wooden spoon. (I mean a craftsman of the monastery should make them.) Where are we to purchase them in America? If the monks make their own wooden spoons, it's even better. It's the truth. But if they buy them and pay dearly for them . . . But again, if they buy them, as perhaps we could, from some primitive evangelical community, as there are here and there in this country, then there is another aspect of monastic truth. You see that it is very difficult to say in one word whether or not we should change: now, this is what seems to me to be a practical conclusion. The Order as such should not make such wholesale changes for everyone. There are too many such details in our observances, *for all the countries*, when the situations are very different. Think of Africa!! Our customs should be very, very simple, very general, and the local Superior should know how to apply them in the "monastic truth" of his place. And the visitor could give him good advice. Especially, let us not, under the pretext of "aggiornamento," adopt categorically the customs of the country, if they are customs contrary to the monastic spirit. In the U.S. we must be very careful on this point. There is great danger here of dropping beautiful things that we (Americans, Superiors and subjects) do not understand, to adopt what is typical of a materialistic society, etc.

Much is said here about Latin and Gregorian chant: things to be "suppressed" because we do not "understand" them. Well, this is a very serious point. I believe that, as you say, many young people more easily admit that they are dissatisfied with the Gregorian chant and the Latin, because they are made to believe this. I know very well that in our monasteries in America there is a real movement, an agitation, for this and for still other things. People are *pushed* into thinking that they are dissatisfied with the Latin, the Gregorian chant, the status of laybrother, the liturgy as we have it, when in reality that is not the case at all. For a long time it was said here that "the brothers" in general wanted to change habit, come to choir, change their status, etc. But it was only *a few* brothers who, moreover, were not always the best ones but who got more agitated and had more to say, and who tried to persuade the others to go with them, etc. You know these stories quite well by now.

But this is what I think about the Latin and the chant: They are masterpieces, which offer us an irreplaceable monastic and Christian experience. They have a force, an energy, a depth without equal. All the proposed English offices are very much impoverished in comparison— besides, it is not at all impossible to make such things understood and appreciated. Generally I succeeded quite well in this, in the novitiate, with some exceptions, naturally, who did not understand well. But I must add something more serious. As you know, I have many friends in the world who are artists, poets, authors, editors, etc. Now they are well able to appreciate our chant and even our Latin. But they are all, without exception, scandalized and grieved when I tell them that probably this Office, this Mass will no longer be here in ten years. And that is the worst. The monks cannot understand this treasure they possess, and they throw it out to look for something else, when seculars, who for the most part are not even Christians, are able to love this incomparable art.

I do not think that *every monastery* has to keep it, but there should be one monastery or several which would do it here. I would like it to be ours . . .

To Dom Placid Jordan, O.S.B.

Dom Placid Jordan, a German Benedictine monk of Beuron Abbey, was stationed in Rome during the time of Vatican II.

September 12, 1964

Fr. Pachomius of Erlach writes that he has heard from you, and that while he has translated a short version of "The Monk in the Diaspora," you have consulted him about translating the whole thing. If you see fit,

I think it would be better to translate the whole thing or else, as a compromise, a slightly longer version (with the material on the Russians) which Dom Leclercq has translated into French.

However, my Abbot General, disturbed by some parts of this article, has requested that I soften some of the expressions, and I have done this. The changes have been sent to Dom Leclercq, and if you ask him he will communicate them to you. I hope this is not terribly complicated, but I am grateful for your kindness and interest . . .

To Dom Ignace Gillet

September 24, 1964

I have just received a very important letter from Japan, and I want to inform you of its contents, putting before you as my Father General a question which seems to be urgent enough for me and even in a sense for the Church.

This letter is from Fr. Heinrich Dumoulin, S.J., a German and a great authority on the relations between Christianity and Buddhism, on which I wrote an article. He is in contact with all the most notable Zen scholars in Japan. I too have done some corresponding with Dr. Suzuki, a real doyen among all these scholars.

This Father Dumoulin has just visited our monastery in Hokkaido where he spoke to Dom Alexis Noda and to Dom James (present Superior of the Lighthouse? I don't know). He also spoke to the bishop of Hokkaido. Now all of these and also the Jesuit confrères of Father Dumoulin, who work with him, completely agree that there would be a very great usefulness for me and for this work if I were to come for several months to Japan. He says: "Personally I feel that this project could be extremely profitable for both sides, i.e., it would give you an opportunity to acquire a working knowledge of Japan (and the Far East), very useful if not indispensable for your writing on Oriental mysticism, and at the same time the possibilities of uniting Eastern and Western spirituality could be discussed thoroughly and perhaps even tested in a preliminary way." He adds: "Fr. Thomas assured me that Father Abbot and the community of Tobetsu would be happy to have you in their midst." Is the Lighthouse referred to, or a Benedictine monastery? I do not know.

I know that this decision finally depends on Dom James, and I am going to speak to him about it at once. But I know that, while approving in his heart the usefulness of the project, he might fear to allow such a journey. So I address myself to you, Most Reverend Father, for I think ultimately that you will have between the two of you to make this very important decision. I tell you in all simplicity that this suggestion (which is not from me, I didn't even dream of it!) appears to be very important, and that I think it my duty to offer myself quite willingly to answer a call which seems to me to come from God, if you and Dom James allow me to go there. It seems to me that my life and my labor have been preparing me for years. (You don't know how much I study Oriental spirituality and especially Zen. Those who are well up on it tell me that I am not on the wrong way and that I understand Zen well.)

If this project does not appear to you to be impermissible, I would propose the following suggestion: this permission could be considered as analogous to a leave from the monastery to study in Rome. Our Fathers here go to Rome, and visit monasteries in Europe for the very notable good which results for our houses and for their confrères. I might, in this case, go to our monastery in Japan, live in our monasteries and convents, and perhaps with these Jesuits from time to time (not for long) at Sophia University. So I could do the studies and make the necessary contacts. I would be on leave as Father Master next year, for example, and start after the annual retreat in January, for a year. Since I would ordinarily be in one of our monasteries, it would be no problem, would it? The question would not be of a special leave, but only of a fairly ordinary leave, except that the journey would be long. I could also stop at Lan Tao [Hong Kong], which would be important, too. And I know Dom Paulinus well; he would be delighted to have me.

I must add that for this work it is very important that I learn Japanese and (classical) Chinese and that is why I would need a little time. It seems to me that a year would be the minimum.

There we are, Most Reverend Father. I submit this to you with all the simplicity of a son. This project is already welcomed by a bishop, two superiors of our Order, and those learned Fathers. I also know that my Buddhist friends will be delighted. Thinking of the awful relations which exist between our two religions in Viet Nam, I think that before God I must offer myself as a fraternal and friendly envoy to bring to these people a testimony of Christian comprehension and love. With all my heart and with all my soul I would like to make this offering to God as a fruit of my vocation. Besides I am not thinking of an active tour, but of a contemplative and very serious study (austere and even crucifying sometimes) of certain thousand-year-old disciplines very important for the contemplative life. There is a very great good at stake for my soul and for my monastic life.

So it is as a monk and not as a pseudo-Jesuit that I dare to make this unusual proposal. I leave the rest to you and to Dom James. Maybe he will write you, and no doubt you will know how to tell him what God will inspire you: I hope in any case that the possible fears of Dom James will not disconcert you altogether . . .

To Abbot James Fox

[undated—September, 1964]

About yesterday's talk: certainly I am very happy that we were able to consider together the possibility of the "hermitage." It is something worth taking seriously and I am very happy that you look at it in that light. With God's help we can go ahead and I think some day we will be very glad that this plan was undertaken. This is the most important thing in my mind at the moment, because I believe it is something quite crucial in my own life. Hence I want to do all I can to make it a practicable and successful undertaking, with you and those who will take part. So I was glad that it came up and I consider it one of the most encouraging and important developments that have taken place between us in years. Many, many thanks.

The Japan project is of course a matter of secondary importance, and I know you realize I am not blindly attached to it, or even terribly involved in the idea. But it does seem to me to be one of those unexpected providential opportunities that look so strange that they can be missed because there is no precedent for them. It seems to me that it is just because this is so unique, so unexpected, and so close to the heart of my own vocation that it seems to me to be important. *Timeo Jesum transeuntem et non revertentem* [I fear lest Jesus pass and not return]. My own feeling is that this is something that could have a completely decisive effect on my life, and could be an altogether unusual grace. That is why I do ask you to please consider it objectively, and apart from your own personal repugnance to the idea. I certainly don't relish being out of the monastery and taking a long trip. But I don't think the dangers are so great. I have such a distaste for the world and its cities that I would not be physically capable of roaming around in it. I could not take it. But instead I would be in communities of our Order and in Zen monasteries or centers, which are most unworldly, I assure you. There is no unworldliness to match it in our life. That is why I think it would be very wrong to regard this as a jaunt in "the world." Quite the contrary. Except for inevitable travelling. But planes go fast.

Here is a suggestion. In case you are concerned about my ability to take this trip in a psychologically mature and beneficial manner, I think Jim Wygal [Louisville psychiatrist friend] will back me up on that. He knows nothing whatever of the project, of course. It might be interesting to call him up and get his spontaneous reaction and his judgment. If you think it worthwhile, it might be an idea.

At any rate, between you and Dom Ignace and all who are interested in the project, I trust that God's will will come clear and I am leaving it all to Him, without any care or concern. He will do what is best, through His chosen instruments.

To Father Columba Halsey, O.S.B.

Father Columba Halsey was a Benedictine monk of St. Maur's Monastery at South Union, Kentucky, established originally as an interracial monastery on the site of a Shaker village.

September 27, 1964

Probably the best thing for you to do would be to get in contact with the men of our monastery in Georgia who are editing a little mimeographed sheet called *Monastic Worship*. Just write to the Fr. Abbot, Our Lady of the Holy Ghost, Conyers, Ga. They would be glad to send it. I think there have been two issues so far. All the current issues are aired there. The Georgia monastery represents a position more "advanced" than that of the other houses of our Order in this country so you cannot judge the whole Order by them. Also a great deal is said in the sheet that is mere surmise or devout hope. But on the whole I think it is the best source of information.

Here, we have nothing unusual. Brothers' office in the vernacular of course, and some prayer vigils for the brothers on some of the big feasts, with readings, silent prayer, psalmody and so on, all leading up to the Eucharist. In the choir everything is more or less as it has been, except that the conventual Mass is at an altar facing the choir now. There is much talk in the Order about vernacular for everyone, choir and brothers, but there is little agreement on the subject. Obviously the idea itself has many desirable points, but it also raises great problems. I think people are more concentrated on the desirable points and inclined to overlook the problems.

To my mind the "vexing question of the brothers" is both more urgent and more perilous than that of liturgy. Experience here (we now have the brothers and choir together in one novitiate) shows definitely that the brothers' vocation is a very special and very living reality. People definitely come here looking for the simple brothers' life, and they find that it is really better than that of the choir. There is strong and articulate preference for the brothers' life on the part of many here. At the same time, there is another type of brother that is dissatisfied with the brothers' life and looks toward the priesthood, etc. But I have seen several change from the choir to the brothers and find it an immense improvement. My belief is that the brothers' life as we have it, or can have it, here, is more genuinely monastic and fills a more real need than the life of the choir, and I think it would be absolutely fatal for us to do anything that would radically alter the nature of that life, interfering with the timetable for instance by bundling them all into choir for all of the hours (conventual Mass for all, yes, that is needed).

To Father Hans Urs von Balthasar

September 27, 1964

The wonderful package of books has arrived, and I am reading the first volume of *Herrlichkeit*, not without a little difficulty, but I think I am getting most of it. At any rate there are parts that make me very happy, even though I have to read slowly and can only do a few pages a day. Really I am most grateful, as this is exactly what I have been looking for: a truly contemplative theology, for which we have been starved for so many centuries (though of course there have been little intervals of refreshment and light with people like Scheeben). I think I am going to enjoy your second volume even more. I am so grateful to you for daring to launch out into this *fruitio* [enjoyment] and *intellectus* [understanding]. How can there really be any other theology? Actually, I see that the attraction of things like Buddhism today resides in the "hidden" sapiential quality which is absent from our purely "scientific" theology and Scripture study. Underneath all the apparent ambiguities of Buddhism about suffering (they do in some cases seek to avoid it) there is actually a deep wisdom and *admiratio* [wonder] at the mystery of truth and love which is attained only when suffering is fully accepted and faced. I think that the reality of Buddhism is missed when this deeply delicate *admiratio* and wonder is missed at the heart of it. It is also amazingly humorous. In this I think that what one encounters is what Pope John spoke of: the remnant of the "primitive revelation." And this remnant can be detected really by one note beyond all others, I think precisely its sapiential beauty and wonder, as when Buddha held up a flower and smiled, and his disciple understood the whole thing. And how right you are about Origen and how well you use his inexhaustible mine of riches. I am most grateful.

Recently I have made the discovery of St. Ephrem, who is magnificent. I hope soon that he will be all accessible to those of us who do not know Syriac, etc. The documents of Celtic monasticism have absorbed me too, as I have been preparing a course on this for the novices. It is becoming a real avocation with me. I can think of nowhere in the West where monastic culture was so drenched in brilliant color and form, with such dazzled love of God's beauty . . .

To Brother C.

Brother C., a Cistercian from another U.S. monastery, wrote Merton about his desire for a more solitary life.

September 27, 1964

It was good to hear from you, and I think I have a fairly clear memory of your visit, though it was long ago and I see so many people that they all merge into a blur. But your letter is a good one and I will try to answer it as best I can, simply and to the point.

1) It has to be admitted that the monastic life as we have it in the houses of our Order now leaves much to be desired. There are great possibilities, and great problems. We have been blessed, and many good vocations have come to us, but in very many cases they have been frustrated rather than developed. I think our life as it is now is geared to a certain type of active monastic vocation (active in the sense of keeping busy with work and active forms of prayer within the cloister), but it does not favor those who may be called to development in other lines. There is however beginning to be a development of studies, liturgy and so on. But this development is no help to those who need silence, solitude and a great deepening of their life of prayer. In other words, we Cistercians are all right at promoting a respectable and somewhat energetic *vita activa* [active life], but we do little or nothing for the real contemplative life except more or less stay enclosed and steer clear of parish work. That is purely negative and without much serious significance.

2) The consequence is that problems arise: those who want a more primitive, poorer, simpler, or a more solitary, hidden, contemplative form of life and who need to deepen their life of prayer (non-liturgically) cannot find room to develop among us. Their desire may be genuine and it may be to some extent fictitious. Superiors have tended to regard all such desires with suspicion, on the basis of the fact that there have been so many eccentrics and neurotics. At the same time even a genuine vocation to a more contemplative life can be made to appear and to act neurotic by a certain type of frustration of his legitimate needs. I think however that in the Order people are beginning to see that this need is not imaginary, and that it is really serious. Also it may come to be recognized that we have an obligation either to do something about these people within the Order or leave them free to go elsewhere. It is *possible* that a form of hermit life may come to be permitted in dependence on a house of our Order. One can promise nothing.

3) In your case, I would say that Fr. Minard's group [Oxford, North Carolina] might offer the best solution, if you are ready to take it. The element of risk is not something to worry about. If they are only a *Pia unio* [pious union], perhaps all the better. They will be freer to solve problems without red tape. But you have to be mature enough to take this kind of thing.

As to my own case, obviously I am in such a position that I must seek a solution within the Order itself. I think such a solution is vaguely possible some day, in some form. I certainly have more solitude at present than most people in the Order, and I intend to take advantage of it. It is not "perfectly satisfactory" but it is a gift for which I am grateful and I have long ago given up looking for the "perfectly satisfactory," still less for what conforms to somebody or other's ideal pattern . . . The ability to accept paradoxical and untidy solutions has a great deal to do with the solitary life, which is necessarily unpatterned and existential. But if you do come to live as a hermit somewhere, be ready for a grim time and don't expect some of the consolations that you are leaving behind. Our communities have their disadvantages but also their advantages, and one may come to regret having to do without them . . .

To Dom Jean Leclercq

September 28, 1964

Dom Paulus Gordon is publishing a German translation of "The Monk in the Diaspora" in *Erbe und Auftrag*. Would you please communicate to him whatever changes were made in the French translation so that his version will also meet the requirements of our Abbot General?

There are many things to tell you but this must be a brief letter. The North American Abbots and Novice Masters are meeting here next week. A good idea, but I think it will be rather a confused and frustrating experience. I wish you were here to contribute a little light and guidance. There seems to be a lot of confusion and some animosity over issues like whether the priest should forgo his private Mass and go to communion at the conventual Mass, etc. I think our chief problem is the problem of the brothers. Here at Gethsemani the brothers seem to realize that they have a better monastic life than the choir, and they are very anxious to preserve the relative simplicity, freedom, and informality of their life. Some who pass from the choir to the brothers in the novitiate are impressed with a greater sense of authenticity and spiritual peace in the brothers' life here.

I have at last a faint hope that we might actually attempt to face the hermit question here. This is very confidential. But I am glad to say that in a recent conversation Father Abbot showed himself very open and understanding on this subject. This, it seems to me, is very encouraging. I hope it may be possible to do something and to plan something not only for myself but for others. If this turns out to be so, I think that it will constitute one of the most significant and far-reaching developments in American monasticism. Please don't discuss this with anyone yet, not even the Gethsemani men in Rome. But I would greatly appreciate your prayers. Of course, if an occasion comes to speak confidentially to Dom Ignace on the subject, I would appreciate very much your help with him! . . .

To Father Callistus (Jorge) Peterson

October, 1964

. . . The cervical disc is no fun but thank God it is getting better. It is in good enough shape for me to function partially. Up until a few days ago I could hardly type with my left hand, but now it is getting so that I can "use a typewriter" (let's call it that) without getting too much pain and having to stop. There are limits however. I still have to be in traction, and the doctor says I must take more of it than I have been lately. He says the most I can expect is to get most of my work in the novitiate done, and that is about it. If I can get to some offices, fine, but I mustn't expect too much yet. He does not think that I will get back in perfect shape ever, as this is a long-standing injury that has finally come out. So I am through fighting forest fires and cutting down trees, I am afraid. And there are going to be a lot of things I must not lift. Of course no Yoga, at least none that affects the back of the neck that way.

Traction isn't as bad as it sounds, because it does relieve the pressure on the nerves and consequently decreases the pain. I can't sleep at night in traction however, and in fact I don't do too well even out of it.

The weather is fine, the novices are excellent. I have Bro. Denis doing a review of David Knowles' new book for *Monastic Studies*, and he is going to be good. Bro. Basil did a fine article which will be in *Collectanea*. You men at Rome had better think of getting into this kind of thing sometime. You could review books, at least when you get back. Fr. Chrysogonus should have been writing for *Collectanea* long ago. Tell him so from me!

I was interested in your Belgian Prior friend. I have never found it terribly hard to pray in choir, except when I was so far out of my mind as to accept the job of sub-cantor years ago. It seems to me that the secret of prayer in choir is knowing psalmody, which is the basic form of monastic prayer. If one prays the psalms, if they *sapiunt in corde* [savor in the heart], as Bernard says, then what else does one want? Periods of silence? Well, fine. But we have long periods of silence in the conventual Mass. Because people cannot pray, they say, during these periods of silence, then they must be filled up with singing or something else. So be it. But if that is the case, why start breaking up the office with periods of silence because people can't pray during the vocal prayers??? I think these are matters for each community to handle individually, according to the local needs, spirit, background, etc. Here it seems to me that a lot of our changes are sort of hit and miss: we adopt things that sound good in other places, more or less haphazardly, without any serious consideration for what they might mean *here*.

But I am all for silent prayer in the office and in the liturgy and I think that to eliminate it altogether on the ground that no one is "doing anything", and therefore not participating, would be a disastrous misunderstanding of the liturgy and a total loss of the kind of spirit the Fathers (especially Greek) had in regard to liturgical prayer.

To Dom Ignace Gillet

October 18, 1964

The meeting of the Abbots and Novice Masters was really profitable for all. I will not give you any details, since the Rev. Fathers themselves will already have written to you. I spoke very little about the subject of my last letter [hermitage], but I think that in general the Abbots are conscious of the problem and that they will speak of it at the General Chapter. So I will merely give you my more precise thoughts after reviewing your letter and mine with its notorious "appendix."

1) I agree completely that the problem of the "eremitical life" in the Order should be resolved, without harming the essence of the Cistercian life, and while safeguarding as much as possible the contemplative and cenobitic life, and especially without creating a division in the Order. So I am giving up the project of a sort of special eremitical foundation for America. It's not practical and it's dangerous for the spirit of the Order, and even for its unity.

2) But it seems to me that we must take into account a fact which is, at least for us, unimpeachable and irreversible. At Gethsemani, we keep enclosure, there are very few trips, there is no "activity" in the pastoral sense, silence is insisted upon very much, etc. We should be a model monastery from the point of view of silence, contemplation, etc. But it is not possible. The din of the machines, the activity of the monastery itself, the rhythm of the life we lead necessitates a certain adaptation which would not go beyond the bounds of the cenobitic life: because to have real silence and real peace, one must nevertheless be able to go aside a bit, either in the neighboring wood or further. And here it is accepted and well understood. It does not harm the spirit of the community at all, it was approved by Dom Gabriel and our Father Immediate, Dom Colomban. So from that point of view there is no problem: and even for some, like the Father Abbot and certain officers, it is understood that a retreat day with some time apart is very useful for these persons and for the community, which profits indirectly from this. I do not regard this as an "eremitical" adaptation, but on the contrary as a new form of cenobitic solitude proper to our situation. I assure you that after more than fifteen years of experience with this type of solitude in our life itself, for me and for the others, including the novices (who do not have any retreat day, but who take advantage of the long feast days), it's a real grace. Our life of prayer depends on it.

3) On the question of aspiring "eremitic" vocations:

a) There is a problem. Some monks truly believe that they are called to solitude. In my own case (I must tell you if you do not know) on several occasions I humbly asked permission to at least go to see and consult the Carthusians and the Camaldolese who, after letters I had written, had invited me to come see them. Not only was permission categorically refused, but later, when I had practically received an affirmative answer from the Sacred Congregation to go to a Benedictine Superior who was offering me a hermitage, my Superiors blocked everything in a way that, I must tell you frankly, I still consider very arbitrary and even unjust.

b) Well then, must we believe that the Cistercian life by its very nature inexorably excludes the eremitical or semi-eremitical life within the context of the Order itself? It is true that in the twelfth century our Fathers permitted this solution only with difficulty. But they still permitted it exceptionally. There are Cistercian hermits in our menology. It seems to me that it is a fruit of the true cenobitic life and not a contradiction. On the contrary, monastic tradition tells us that the cenobitic life should, at least in certain cases, bear this fruit. Let us admit that this may remain very exceptional, and that the important thing is to extol cenobitic life and asceticism and not attract the monks' attention too much to this solitude.

c) Many of these self-styled "hermits" (I am speaking of those who clamor for this special permission) have no vocation, and are even eccentrics and free-thinkers, perhaps without any monastic vocation. So be it. But must we conclude that *all* are in the same case, even a monk who has lived obediently for ten or twenty years in the cenobium? He (I am not speaking of myself, because I know I am not an exemplary cenobite), doesn't he really have a right to *try* his vocation? But, to do this, must he transfer to the Carthusians or the Camaldolese?

4) *Proposed solution*:

a) Without making statutes which would make a fuss in the Order, no doubt the Abbots could study the question discreetly and admit in practice that an Abbot, *if he wishes*, could give an experienced monk some solitude, first temporarily, then in the end perhaps permanently, on the grounds of the Abbey or in dependence on it, at least "to see," to test this aspiration to solitude and see if it is, or is not, an authentic solution.

b) The important thing would be to establish prudent but not arbitrary supervision over these experiments. For example: the Abbot should consult his council. The monk who desires this solitude should be professed for ten years. The Father Immediate should also approve. The hermit monk could earn his living by doing some work for his monastery, work compatible with his solitary life. He would begin with temporary solitude, for example in Lent. Etc. If he saw that he did not have a true hermit vocation, he might nevertheless benefit from a relative or temporary solitude: for example Lent each year, etc. All of this is, I believe, in the authentic monastic tradition. Instead of harming the Order it would do a lot of good and would witness to the true monastic life in our communities. But I admit that some community might not be able to withstand such an experiment without serious damage. The Abbot and his council would have to judge this prudently. I believe that here this kind of experiment would be fruitful. Anyway, the question could be studied.

c) I will speak to you about my own personal case on a separate sheet. You may use all I say here on this question in general, as you wish.

d) I know that Dom James, who is certainly an experienced and prudent Abbot, is in agreement with my ideas on this point.

To Dom Jean Leclercq

October 22, 1964

Many thanks for your most recent letter, and your news. It is all right if "The Monk in the Diaspora" goes into *Collectanea*, except that I think that most of those in the Order who are interested have read it, though perhaps not in French, and perhaps also the French-speaking Abbots will only be disconcerted. However, do whatever you think best. I was thinking of writing up the notes of my talk to the Abbots' meeting into an article and perhaps that would go well in the *Collectanea*, though it will also disconcert many. I enclose the notes. They are a bit naive and oversimplified as they stand, but I could put in nuances, and will make quite a few additions.

The Abbots' meeting was lively and I think everyone was satisfied or at least glad that the meeting took place. It was also profitable to have the novice masters involved, and I think it is really most important for the novice masters in our Order to get around and get experience of other houses. Unfortunately, it seems that my Father Abbot refuses to let me travel. He even insisted that the only way a novice masters' meeting could be held with me in it was for it to be held *here* . . . In general the other Abbots think this quite amusing. I must admit that it seems to me quite odd, and I can't say I am flattered to have my Abbot give the impression that he does not trust me . . .

There was a quite general openness and sympathy among the Abbots toward a "solution" to the question of solitude within our Order. At least a relative solution in which the concept of temporary solitude would be admitted as proper to us. There is I think a quite reasonable concern lest the genuine cenobitic idea be injured, and I personally am as convinced as anyone of the importance of the cenobitic life since without it normally there can be no basis for further solitude. The hermit will be the exception, the cenobite will be normal, and it is important I think to present the extension into solitude as a normal and legitimate prolongation of what begins in the cenobium, and temporary solitude as a dimension of the *cenobitic* life itself. Thus the rare case of the complete hermit will later on come to be accepted with less difficulty. My own temporary solitude gets to be more and more extended, for which I am glad.

Your *Otia* came yesterday and I began it immediately. It is just what I am looking for. A splendid book.

To Jaime Andrade

October 25, 1964

It was good to get your letter and to hear of your new work. The mosaics in relief seem to me to be a very exciting development, full of life, and a very original idea. The photographs you sent gave at least an impression of what must be a very splendid display. How I would like to see them some day. But that does not seem very likely.

The books on Ecuadorian folklore are very fine and I am delighted to have them. That kind of material means a great deal to me. It is perhaps more important in many ways than works of prominent writers. Though in the case of Latin American countries I think that the poets and novelists always have a great deal that is important to say. Thanks in any case for these fine books . . .

Your statue here has attracted a lot of interest and comment and one novice master in another monastery said he would be interested in having a statue something like it for his place. I do not know precisely what he has in mind, but I presume a statue of the Virgin and Child somewhat similar to the one you did for me, though I am sure you would want to rethink it in terms of the new ideas you may have now. I should be very interested to know how the project comes out . . .

To Father Columba Halsey

October 29, 1964

Many thanks for your good letter. I mean to send along mimeographs of what I had to say at the meeting of the Abbots here, and that will explain much of what I cannot say here, for lack of time. It was a good meeting, I think. The "Diaspora" article seems to be getting around in Europe. I would say rather that the Benedictines are divided concerning it, some being apparently rather for it as you are. So I am glad of that.

Yes, there is work being done on a monastic *ratio studiorum* [program of studies]. There have been copies of documents and projects around here but I have not read them yet. It is all in an initial stage as far as I know. There is of course a lot of work being done on Canon Law and that came up at our meeting here. In fact there is a commission meeting on this at Spencer with the Benedictine *periti* who are working at the same thing.

On monastic theology: Dom Leclercq mentioned lately that he thought Von Balthasar was the one who came closest to a monastic theology in our day. I very much agree. I am reading Von Balthasar's new book, *Word and Revelation*, which is excellent.

We have problems everywhere, and I think it is necessary to expect the real progress of monasticism from ourselves as well as from our institutions. I think there is a temptation to think that we can change ourselves by changing the institution. But it is also true that no amount of change in the institution will matter if we do not grow and change ourselves. And I think the crucial thing in all this reform is the deepening of *faith* in the individual monk. This will mean to a great extent placing his hopes and expectations in God and not in men, in the Holy Spirit and not in laws. Though laws can and must be under the guidance of the Spirit.

To Dame Marcella Van Bruyn

October 29, 1964

How many letters do I owe you? I blush to think of it. Please forgive me. (I have just been preparing a conference on a monastic text of Abbot Isaias, in which great stress is laid on acknowledging one's faults and saying *ignosce*.) I am really sorry. I have been much too busy for a monk. It is true that I can handle a fair amount of activity in peace, by God's grace, but it still is not right, and it would be much better if there were more proportion in my life. I hope that one day there will be, and the hope seems less vain than it once was, as there are chances of more solitude. Do please pray that the attitude on this in the Order will develop in the right direction, as it seems to be about to do. It is so absurd to live in a community that is always too busy, and being always too busy oneself. Especially when there is a chance of doing something about it . . .

The meeting of American Abbots took up a lot of my time and thought. It was only for a few days, but required weeks of preparation and then for some time after it one is still picking up the pieces. I think it was good, though I am congenitally suspicious of meetings and never expect anything from them. At any rate it was exhausting.

Of course the question of people leaving was always there. I agree of course that if a professed is really miserable, he or she should go so as not to affect the others, according to the Rule. But it is a pity that so many manage to make themselves so miserable that they then have to leave when, given a little more maturity and a somewhat better understanding in the community, they might see their way to staying. This is a mysterious question though. At any rate I am sending notes of the things I was asked to talk about.

Incidentally, I dared to speak up for Latin in the Abbots' meeting, and met with a great outcry, except that one little Canadian Abbot (French Canadian from up among the Acadians in New Brunswick) agreed with me and was delighted to find that the trend toward the vernacular was not unanimous. There is however a great demand for vernacular in office and Mass in our Order, at least in the American houses. I think it is very foolish in a way, because it seems to me to be thoughtless and based on an insufficient and flighty assessment of the Latin. People have just never bothered to see its value. I for one will not be happy with an English office . . . I hope a few will keep to the Latin; I know Solesmes will and I presume *you* will.

Do pray for the solitary business I spoke of. There is at least a hope that we may be able to spend several days at a time alone, though I am not sure of this. It would be a godsend. It is all rather confidential however, so please do not let it get out of Stanbrook, and perhaps not too much around the community. I already have a hermitage where I can spend considerable time, days at least. It makes a very great difference. It is about a quarter of a mile from the monastery, hidden in woods and with a very good view, quite quiet and eminently suitable for permanent living. Water for drinking has to be brought from the monastery. I have a lamp and not electricity and of course everything is quite primitive.

I have been reading St. Ephrem wherever I can get access to bits and pieces of his work, and he is very fine. I also sent Sister Hildelith a prayer of Cassiodorus which I am hoping she will print and she already has some good ideas . . .

Now I must stop. My fiftieth year has been going well, I think. I have had a lot of bother with my skin, due to some mysterious cause. And various other irritating things to deal with, which I suppose is all to the good. In perils from censors, in perils from agents, in perils from publishers, in perils from the Abbot General, a night and a day in an abyss of fan mail . . .

To Sister Mary Luke Tobin

All Saints [November 1], 1964

It was not really a surprise to me that you were chosen as observer from the better half of the human race, hitherto represented exclusively at the [Vatican] Council by the Blessed Mother, I suppose. But in any case I congratulate you warmly, and the more so because the honor done to you redounds upon us your friends and neighbors. It is all the more clear than ever that if the Church wants to get the best out of America she has to look to Kentucky.

One reason why I have not done this before is that I was hoping to get your Rome address. But Dan [Walsh] let me down and forgot to ask for it, and then sent a message to Loretto which somebody probably forgot to deliver. So I will send this to Loretto along with the copies of my talk, in the hope they will be forwarded. The talk went over all right, and there was very little discussion which means probably that they were left in such bewilderment that they did not know where to start. I am sending the talk along with a copy of a longer version which I discarded as too radical, and which is being circulated in mimeo but is not for publication. (This one is called "Identity Crisis and Monastic Vocation.")

What I hear of the Council sounds exciting in the main, but we are far behind with our news here. I know Schema 13 is being debated at present and I know that there was a very good passage on nuclear war written into the schema, but I don't know any more than that. I think the questions of Revelation and Collegiality seem to have been settled satisfactorily, from what I hear. As for you, I am sure you are getting all kinds of good ideas and information. By the way, Giorgio La Pira, the famous mayor of Florence, was here, and I spoke of you. He would very much like to have you call upon him in Florence when you can, and I think that would be worthwhile. He is a dynamic and devout man, and was here for a whirlwind visit that impressed everyone he met.

Everyone is agreed that the monastic Orders need some attention of their own in Canon Law, so that we will not be lumped together with other religious whose lives are oriented differently from ours. I hope that people in Rome are aware of this difference. If they are not, it will probably not be from lack of effort on the part of our higher Superiors to make things clear. The trends seem to be good in the main but there is still a lot of confusion it seems to me. I think our main job is to broaden out and leave more room for development, not to soften the life up but to make it more intelligent and broader-minded toward everything. Some day when you are sitting around with just nothing to do (I am sure that happens often) you might pay a visit to our Abbot General. I am sure he would like to meet you. More practical perhaps: if you see him around at the Council, maybe you could manage to bump into him and say you are a friend of ours here, etc. His name is Dom Ignace Gillet, and I think he speaks some English, but your French is probably better than his English anyway . . .

To Dame Hildelith Cumming

November 11, 1964

The cards arrived today and they are simply splendid. Thank you ever so much, and thanks also to those who worked so lovingly on them. Each is perfect in its own right. What a rarity to have such things in our time. I feel richer than the rich.

Your ideas about Cassiodorus have all seemed very good and doubt-less you have thought of other aspects of the project. I leave it all to you.

The Abbots' meeting went off well. I think there are stirrings of life and certainly there are good desires. I still have not had time to take up the interesting questions you have raised. I am mailing you a mimeograph of something along the lines of what I had to say, though it is a little stronger (!) than what I put forth before the Reverend Fathers. I will also include an old bit on Chinese thought, which we have run off afresh.

To Dom Ignace Gillet

November 25, 1964

I have just received your letter of the 20th and I thank you for it. You took the time to answer me at some length, when the time perhaps cost you dearly. Thank you.

First, on the question of Japan, I will speak to Dom James about it this evening, and I assure you that I will accept his decision with much good will, without afterthought. It was proposed to me, and I believed that I should submit it to my Superiors. This is what I did, but without much desire for a long trip. I am seeking only God's will and I tell you frankly that my emotions are completely neutral.

You remarked that this neutrality is not usual with me, because it seemed to be lacking in some of the remarks in my letter of October 18th. I spoke with perhaps too much vivacity in it, and I regret it. You reprove me, and I thank you for that. But especially I thank you for telling me what happened. At last it is a bit clear. I can tell you frankly, Most Reverend Father, that with young people (and I am no longer one of those) it is much simpler to be plain and frank and to tell them everything, or at least everything they can be told. If they sometimes give the impression of being a bit disagreeable, isn't it because people act towards them in a way which causes them to think that they want to deceive them in one way or another? Certainly they could beware of their judgment, but . . . that is how they judge anyway. I am telling you this because you asked me to tell you what I thought about the present problems of the Order. That is one, I think.

To Father Illtud Evans

The English Dominican, Illtud Evans, was asked to preach the annual retreat at Gethsemani in 1965. He wrote to Merton asking his advice as to the best approach.

December 7, 1964

Well, I always wanted to write a novel, and I know it is a truism that what you want in youth you get in middle age. So without having written *Elected Silence* [*The Seven Storey Mountain*] as a novel, I am enjoying the reputation of it as a novel. Thus I eat my cake and have it. Feels a little like Zen.

Besides I have been reading Ionesco and am surprised at nothing. I think Ionesco is fine. He has cured me of Sartre and helped with Brecht.

You have not only wanted to ask suggestions, you have asked them, and I have failed to live up to my good intention of replying. All I can say is this: we have suffered a plague of those retreat masters who insist on giving the old hashed-up routine. Almost anything different from the routine will be welcome. Actually, I think myself anything that will help toward the idea of renewal will be helpful to us. Renewal is in everybody's minds. There is on one hand a lot of fake enthusiasm and a lot of naive hope, a stirring of projects, with every simple professed monk writing a new liturgy of his own choice. On the other hand, there is a great deal of resentment and artful political guile to frustrate progress while seeming to be in favor of it. I think that what is needed in this situation is a retreat that will get people focussed on the great realities of the Gospel and of life, and the reality of the position of the monk, so that we will not simply let go one set of fantasies in order to attach ourselves to another. As to the fact that we are contemplatives, well, I suppose that by that the Abbot means he will be furious with you if as a result of one or other of your talks someone comes up and declares that he wants to go out into the parishes and convert the millions. But this I think is no problem. I wouldn't even give it a thought.

Anyway I hope we can have a quiet afternoon at the hermitage when you are here. As a matter of fact anything you can say to encourage specifically monastic renewal will probably be a help. Spirit of the desert, etc., etc. It turns out actually that I have a fair chance of living in the hermitage for good, after perhaps another year. I am already half in it, even sleep there, and am there most of the day sometimes but of course have to be in the novitiate most of the time on ordinary days.

Have I yet told you how excellent the *New Blackfriars* is? Looks, content, everything, very fine indeed. Congratulations. I am glad you are using *Religion and Race*. Mother Luke at Loretto was our American woman observer. You will like her—I hope you will meet her there. She is just back from Rome and I hope to have a word with her and find out some new and curious affairs. But seriously I thought the interventions on Nuclear War were not too wonderful, except for Msgr. Ancel and who was the other? Suenens? But Washington and Liverpool were scandalous, with their Pentagon line.

Now I must stop. Hope you have a good trip. Look forward to seeing you soon. God be with you. Best wishes for Christmas. I don't remember John Fisher house, all that comes through the blur in my memory is that the Red Cow must have been around there somewhere. That was more my speed *in illo tempore* [at that time].

To Father Aelred, S.S.F.

Anglican Father Aelred was stationed at St. Mary's Cottage, Oxford, at the time of this exchange.

December 8, 1964

. . . In such solitude as I have now I have been renewing my contact with Lancelot Andrewes, not as a steady diet, but his précis for the evening are very wholesome and rich, and I am quite drawn to his spirit. But also to the other and more profound spirit in the English tradition, that of Lady Julian, the *Cloud*, etc. I have an interesting ms. from a Jesuit in Japan treating the *Cloud* in its relation to Zen. In fact I also met Dr. Suzuki this summer, and this was a helpful contact indeed, because he really understands what interior simplicity is all about and really lives it. That is the important thing, because without contact with living examples, we soon get lost or give out. We need to be sustained in the interior work that we alone can do, with God's grace: but still there is need of the push that comes from others who do the same, and who can, in the briefest signals, communicate some of their direction to us.

As to whether you are right in thinking that the Catholic contemplatives know all about this and practice it, I am not sure you are not a bit optimistic. It is true that they *should*, for all the material is there. At the moment however there is a great deal of running around in circles, a lot of rather premature and ill-directed fuss in the sphere of liturgy (fine that this is changing in the parishes, but it seems to me that the monks are dashing about with a kind of fear that the parishes are thus "getting ahead" of them, and this is absurd). There are among the novices and young monks here quite a few genuine contemplative vocations (I mean to contemplative prayer) and I think they ought to survive in spite of everything. But in our monasteries there are plenty, in fact a majority, of Baker's "active livers" and they are never really at peace, always carried off into some new realm of fuss, and trying to sweep the whole place with them.

Under separate cover I am sending you some more notes, some of them dealing with monastic renewal, and these are more or less confidential, especially those so marked. But of course one of the essays was published in *Blackfriars*. It has been the object, or target, of considerable comment.

To Nora Chadwick

December 17, 1964

Many thanks for your last letter, which I must have received some time ago. I have been rather busy this fall with some meetings and so on, concerning monastic reform and "adaptation," all the result of the Council or at any rate part of the same development in the Church. I am so glad you liked the Pilgrimage article. It has been printed in a fuller form, with all the proper footnotes, and you are mentioned there. So I am sending you the little magazine that has this complete and annotated version. You may find in it a few more ideas. I enjoyed writing it, and am much indebted to your most recent book.

I also received a charming letter from the Carmelites of Waterbeach. I hope to write to them and send them some more of the little mimeographed pieces we do here in the novitiate. In fact, I think you might be slightly interested in a couple of them, on monastic topics, which I will send along to you by sea mail. One of them is merely a set of notes, but I suppose they can be followed.

In a recent book of mine I have had occasion to use a couple of quotations from Henry Chadwick's translation of the *Contra Celsus*, published by the Cambridge Press. I am afraid I do not have all my Chadwicks identified and properly placed, but I wonder if I am guessing correctly when I suppose that he is your husband? If he is, then it will be easy for me to make my formal request for permission to use the quotations, amounting to some fifteen or twenty lines, not more . . .

To Sister Mary Luke Tobin

December 21, 1964

It was great having you here, and we all enjoyed the talk very much. And profited by it too. Thank you for coming. The tape is being played, though it does not do justice to our meeting.

Recently some abstract drawings of mine were exhibited in Louisville at Catherine Spalding College, with a certain amount of success. They are now being asked for in New Orleans. If they are going to start moving around, I thought the reasonable thing would be to organize the trip so that they can proceed from one place to another in a logical sort of way. Hence I want to find out what possibilities there might be for an exhibit at Webster Groves?? I don't know if any of the Sisters went in to see it. If they did, they can give you some idea of it. The enclosed notes may suggest something. I assure you the drawings are entirely abstract. A few were sold (I am using the proceeds for money towards a scholarship fund for a Negro girl at Catherine Spalding). They are not the popular type of thing and may scandalize some. Still people seem to like them. What do you suggest about Webster Groves? When they get back I could lend them to you for Loretto if the Sisters were brave enough to face them.

Please let me know what you think about this, and I will meditate on the results . . .

To Mother Angela Collins

December 26, 1964

. . . I don't think there is much chance of my formally taking on a regular direction assignment by mail. I do not have any of these and

Father Abbot is so negative about the question that there is no point in my asking him about it. If you do so, you will only get a sweet but frustrating answer. But I have no objection to your asking if you want to. I just don't think there is any point to it. On the other hand, I would say in practice that if once in a while you send me a letter sealed and marked "conscience matter" he will most probably let it through, though there is no telling whether eventually he might send one back and tell you not to send any more. That can happen.

It is true that with the things you are contemplating, you do need sound advice. The Passionists have been giving you this, probably. But since they are moving to St. Meinrad's that brings further problems.

Regarding the proposals you make in your notes, I think they are mostly sound, but I do not know enough about the actual situation in the Order to be able to tell you exactly what to do. I would surmise that the idea of letting nuns get out to study and so on might meet with difficulties. Yet it is very important to bring the Carmelites up to date and into touch with realities. This problem exists everywhere. I am not sure that going out to study would provide an adequate answer at least at the moment. Rather I would say it would be a question of making sure that they have a better and more general formation before they enter, and then after that perhaps having some speakers come in once in a while. But it is a very delicate question. Perhaps the Carmelites might have a sort of house of studies so to speak where they could go for a few months for special courses and seminars, always remaining in the cloister. For instance in close connection with a Carmelite Friars' house of studies, say, at Washington. But that would take a lot of planning and hard work.

As to a desert for nuns: I would say that one of the main factors would be the number of mature and well-balanced nuns in the American and Canadian Carmels (English-speaking) and the serious need for and capacity to profit by such a house. It seems to me to be a vicious circle: the way the nuns are formed keeps them childish and deprives them of a mature perspective, and thus they are unable to take advantage of the measures that would help mature them and deepen them, and the answer of Superiors gets back to "keeping order" by preserving a stable but unsatisfactory setup just as it is. In all Orders, especially contemplative, we face the same dilemma: growth and development are needed, but the moment one loosens up a little, the whole structure begins to collapse. I see it in our own Order. Communities are breaking up, Abbots resign right and left, monks leave to start new foundations on their own lines (and get nowhere) and the higher Superiors panic, not knowing what to do next.

The best thing I can suggest is to encourage you to study the "desert" idea, discuss it with capable and intelligent people. *Don't* discuss it with people who are frightened of the slightest change, find out the possibilities of actual realization in the Order. The important thing is that the nuns who have some sense and some good forward-looking ideas should be allowed to communicate with "experts" and knowledgeable people, even with one another. Gradually with this interchange of ideas the project can grow in a sound way. With lack of communication, each one is isolated, fails to see the problems, projects are framed in an unrealistic way and are rejected immediately. So I would say that your first problem is one of communication. And that is not going to be easy, as is shown by the fact that you will hardly be able to communicate with someone like me. However, I urge you, when you have something definite and clear, to try sending me a conscience matter letter and I will advise you if I can. On the other hand I should imagine that your Fr. Albert, for instance, could be a great help in such matters.

I think that even if a desert is formed (which is unlikely) without this basis of intelligent and open communication, it will not be practical. A desert merely isolated and directed "from above" by people with narrow and fearful ideas will be stale from the start. It has to be alive and realistic. This requires open perspectives. And study. For a start, I recommend that you get hold of a book called *The Call of the Desert* by Peter Anson (I forget who publishes it, Helicon perhaps). This book surveys the whole field of the hermit life, and gives references to plenty of books about it. You should be acquainted with the literature, at least to some extent. But be careful not to let it just stir up your imagination and feelings. You have an objective job of studying to do, and you must keep it objective. There are problems to be recognized, historic solutions to be considered, matters of past legislation to be noted down for reference, and so on. Without this knowledge, any project that is drawn up will be merely an essay in imagination.

When you are further along with the idea, you can write to Dom Jacques Winandy, Merville, British Columbia. He has a group of hermits there and is strongly supported by the Bishop of Vancouver who made an intervention in the Council (written) about the need for recognizing the hermit life in the Church. Dom W. can give you sound advice and maybe if you get that Bishop behind you, you will be in good shape to develop a practical "desert" project that your Superiors will take seriously—*some day*. Not next year or the year after. But I think it is something that must come eventually.

I shall certainly keep you in my prayers. I am sleeping at the hermitage, as I think I told you, and spending often whole days and nights there, taking some of my meals there. There is no question in my mind that this is the solution, and it works very well. Most of the "big problems" and objections that are always being put forward just do not exist. At least when one is supported by a large well-established community. But I think that, of course, a hermit community on its own would have many more problems . . .

III.

The Later Solitary Years
1965-1968

I have at last the complete sense of having found my monastic vocation. At least in my own mind, I am convinced that I have now found the place which God had destined for me when He called me to the monastic life, and that if before this I was always to some extent unsatisfied and looking for "more," it was simply because this was needed to complete what God had given me before.

THOMAS MERTON
IN A LETTER TO ANDRÉ LOUF,
APRIL 26, 1965

To Mother Coakley, R.S.C.J.

Mother Coakley, a Religious of the Sacred Heart, was Novice Mistress at this time.

January 3, 1965

Thank you and your novices again for the gift of honey, which came as a very welcome reminder of our union in the Lord and our one quest that His will may be perfectly fulfilled in us. The gift fills all the requirements of the "eulogiae" mentioned in the *Rule of St. Benedict,* and which one meets here and there in early monastic history. When the Spanish nun Etheria made her pilgrimage to the east in the late fourth century, and climbed Sinai no less, the hermits living there offered her "eulogiae" of fruits from their garden in the oasis. So you see we are in a good and ancient tradition. The honey from your apiary is then not just something which tastes very good (and it does) but it also takes on almost the nature of a sacramental, not only from a blessing but from the charity of Christ which it signifies.

What can I send you in return? I am putting some more of our recent papers in an envelope, hoping that something therein might be of service to someone there, always of course contingent on your own judgment. I suppose that we here are a rather more radical novitiate than most, in some respects, so I cannot judge others by our perhaps scandalous standards. But I will send you what I have. Some of the material has found its way into magazines and perhaps you have already seen it.

Let us then continue united in prayer and faith, and realize more and more the truth and mercy of God in our lives. For we are called above all to be signs of His mercy in the world, and our fidelity will in its turn be a small sign to others of His fidelity, not that our fidelity has any value of itself, but it enables Him to give us richer blessings and to manifest Himself in doing good to us who are nothing.

To Father Peter Minard, O.S.B.

Father Peter Minard, a French Benedictine monk, founded a small contemplative Benedictine monastery at Oxford, North Carolina, which later was transferred to the Cistercians. He died on June 10, 1988.

January 9, 1965

Thank you for your good letter of November 14th. Perhaps you were wondering if I received it. I did. And I agree that it would have been very good to speak to you. I hope we will yet meet and converse about monasticism. Your foundation in North Carolina sounds very fine, and I think of you often, keeping you in my prayers. There is no question that there are very intense aspirations both for the small cenobium, such as you are starting, and the hermit group of Dom Winandy. The fact that free and open discussion of this is still not tolerated, and that people here, for example, fear to let me meet and speak to others like yourself and Dom Winandy, gives some indication of the extent of the crisis in the accepted and well-organized monasteries. I would say that there has developed an enormous crisis of doubt in the big monasteries, and the crisis is being met with measures that are inadequate to solve the real problem. The real problem is the insecurity, the doubt, the fear of error and loss (in the sense of a fear that one may have spent one's entire life in futility and sham), which is devouring so many of the young monks. Simply to repeat the well-worn official declarations that the life is not a loss, and that it is fruitful, actually does not help, but keeps the doubts very much alive. Why would one be constantly replying to implied arguments and attacks if they were not real, and perhaps totally right?

Very simple and basic facts of the monastic life, such as work in direct contact with nature, solitude in a primitive setting, etc., will provide realities which alone can offset the mental doubts that plague the young monk. The problem is in the mind. As long as the monastic life is too mental and too juridical, and too abstract, it will breed doubt by the very fact that it foments a certain kind of thought. No matter what one may do with the liturgy, no matter what one may do with observances, or work, or anything else, as long as the monk is encouraged to constantly reflect on himself and be aware of himself in his "role" as monk, he is going to be encouraged to question that role, and his vocation, and its validity. Perhaps the less we are aware of ourselves as monks, the better chance we have of being real monks.

I know that this applies to solitude. By the grace of God and thanks to the crisis, I am getting much more than I ever had, and am better off at present than most of the Camaldolese and Carthusians, though I am not in the hermitage all the time. [That would come in August of the same year.] But when I am, I have a much better setup than they have. I still have to spend part of the day, most days, in the monastery. Gradually I think that we are going to start a real hermit group in connection with the monastery, because otherwise we will lose all our best men to Dom Winandy's place.

I have found a great deal of understanding among Baptists. The students of the Southern Baptist seminary in Louisville are very interested in the monastery and I have had many interesting talks with them. There is a general climate of sympathy and many of them are interested in mental prayer and contemplation (for want of better categories), which hitherto have been almost unknown among them. There is among Protestants in general a new aspiration toward solitary *oratio*. They are perhaps a bit confused by the post-Tridentine Catholic methods, but in reality it is the monastic formula which attracts them. The idea of *lectio, oratio, contemplatio* [reading, prayer, contemplation] is in fact quite congenial to them, minus the Latin.

I don't know why you think, on the basis of "Monk in the Diaspora," I might not agree with your foundation. The point I have tried to make about monks in the diaspora is precisely that they should not aim at anything other than being monks *sine addito* [without additions, such as parishes and schools], but that if they do this they are likely to find themselves with a small amount of direct and unplanned apostolic radiation. There is bound to be fruitfulness where there is real life. Well, I certainly retain a genuine confidence in the reality of the relevance of monasticism in our time, but perhaps it has ceased to be a confidence in monastic plans and organizations. Perhaps the temptation of monks is to think more of "monasticism" and "liturgy" and "works" (or "contemplation") than of God. I find in the novices a serious lack of the fear of the Lord, and instead of that a great deal of human insecurity which one might term "identity crisis."

You may or may not know that there is in Missouri a project of a monastery that would have a mixed community of Catholics and non-Catholics, but I do not know how it is getting along. Nothing has been started; it is only a project, and in fact it is being started by a secular priest, not a monk, so this is something of a drawback monastically, but as far as his juridical status is concerned it might be easier. He works directly under his bishop.

To Father Illtud Evans

February 8, 1965

Thanks for your letter from Pittsburgh. I am glad everything went well there. I will keep your sodalists in mind and in prayer, and will consider myself an honorary member since I have a life sentence and hope to be confined to solitary eventually.

Here are the pictures you did not want me to take. I think it is not bad, the slightly enlarged one.

I will try to do something for your people in California: when is their issue on "Contemplation" supposed to come out? I am buried under assignments at the moment. For some reason or other, all deadlines seem to fall in March and April. And I have a manuscript to clean up for publication too, and proofs coming and so on.

Reviews on the new book [*Seeds of Destruction*] come in and I am beginning to think it is my most non-understood book. The essay on race is not according to the liberal party line at all, and people read it, get miffed and then don't read the rest. It goes over better with those who have been hitherto uncommitted in any way. Few good comments on the peace section, but reviewers who have actually read that bit seem to find it fairly good. On the whole I think it is making some sort of impression.

I got a good letter from Hans von Balthasar in which he takes a rather guarded position on the current explosion of liberalism in theology, and I think he is right. In the last year or two the thing seems to be running away with itself into directionless excitement. I wonder if we are not soon going to find ourselves, especially in America, involved in an enormous and exhausting pointlessness, in which everybody has something to shout about and nothing is comprehensible except the one thing: what we already have needs to be thrown overboard at once. The sheep who think they were foolish to stand around quietly are now proud of themselves for running madly in some direction or other. But it does not make them any the less sheep . . .

To Father Godfrey Diekmann

February 13, 1965

For some time I have been aware that your very interesting and important ecumenical conference on the spiritual life was going to take place. I knew Douglas Steere was involved in the plans and that he very much counted on my being present. From the first I tried to indicate that this would hardly be possible. Although I recognize that it is a very important meeting, and though in my own personal opinion it is certainly important and unusual enough to justify an exception to our very rigid rules regarding travel, the decision is unfortunately not in my hands.

If it were up to me, I would of course feel that it was almost a matter of obligation, in view of the Council and the present needs of the Church, for me to accept this invitation. Also I would suppose that in such a case, rather than harming my own spiritual life or my monastic vocation, I would personally profit by the experience and would come back with the capacity to live as a better monk. But these are only my own views, and I am afraid that they count for nothing in this particular case.

I tried to present the matter in as favorable a light as possible, but had no success: Father Abbot handed down an immediate and final refusal, as usual. There was no room left for reasoning on the point. Our Father Abbot here considers that it is highly disedifying for a monk to travel at all, for any reason. While it would be disedifying for any other monk to do so, in my case it would amount to a scandal of major proportions. It does not seem quite that way to me, of course, as I have retained at least a vestige of confidence in my ability to be outside a monastery without immediately causing some kind of cataclysm. However, it is certainly true that if I go to one or two meetings, it becomes increasingly difficult to refuse other invitations. Also it is true that by the end of the summer I may be in a somewhat different position, as I am hoping to be relieved of my job as novice master in order to prepare an experiment in greater solitude. I was not under the impression that by August the situation would be such that attendance at your meeting would prove an absolute obstacle.

Needless to say this is a great disappointment to me. I feel that I would gain very much indeed by participation in the Institute. But such is not to be the case, I fear. If you want to write to Father Abbot about it, you can. He has his answer all ready, though. I suppose it would just be best to forget about it. I do hope however that Dom Leclercq will be able to stop by this way (Fr. Haring would be most welcome too). Please give my best regards and my sincere regrets to Douglas Steere . . .

To Father Charles Dumont

February 14, 1965

Certainly the magazine is a good venture and it must continue and it must improve. I know what you mean about needing support; I will try to give you what I can, at least moral support.

It is good to know that the "chroniques" on Islam and so on will get printed, even though not monastic. I have Schuon on Islam and the book on Hallaj, both of which I have been waiting to read, not certain whether you would be expecting a "chronique" on them. Can we decide more or less definitely one way or the other whether I should produce another chronique on non-Christian spiritualities for this year? If so I will gladly go ahead with it, and I have some interesting material which is close to monasticism even though as the Koran or rather some Hadith asserts: "There is no monasticism in Islam." Actually I think Dom Leclercq has written on this subject. Do you by any chance have his essay? It was published I think at Toumliline. If you like I can write myself because I need another study on the same thing published in Morocco (Brunel, *Le*

Monachisme Errant dans l'Islam, Institut des Hautes Etudes Marocaines, 1955). I could write for both at the same time unless you have them on hand.

Naturally I look forward to the "new" *Collectanea.* God bless you for your work on it. I know that anything of this kind can be accomplished only under constant discouragement and opposition, and nothing good is done without the Cross and grace.

To Father Ronald Roloff

February 27, 1965

. . . I am especially anxious to hear more about your little Council, with schemata on all monastic topics. Do you have any final drafts and conclusions? I have to do a study on the whole question of monastic aggiornamento and this would be very valuable to me, though of course I would use it very discreetly and would not mention St. John's, unless I am specifically told that St. John's would be glad to be mentioned. The study will be part of a symposium got up by Bellarmine College and someone will probably publish it.

I think that the businesslike way in which your community has gone about this is a very valid and sensible application of St. Benedict's ideas on consulting the community. Of course the whole question of obedience is urgent. At least the idea one can have of it. There is no question that the young ones coming in now are absolutely not interested in an artificial and trumped-up concept of obedience for obedience's sake, as an end in itself. They are most allergic to anything that is even faintly scented with monastic sterility: the round and round the mulberry bush act of passing responsibility and so forth.

In such a context work for work's sake becomes poison too. I certainly am no advocate of "keeping them busy." That is one of the banes of monastic work: when one feels that the job has been dreamed up to make sure that you are not idle. But I do think, and I am more and more convinced of it, that in our situation here a really valid and productive manual labor is of essential importance. The monk has to make his living, and if he can make it by work that also makes him physically tired, that is all the better. I mean the good kind of tired, not just nervous exhaustion. Though of course that cannot be avoided always, in our day. And to try to sidestep it would be an evasion of the cross which everyone else has to carry. But from every point of view I think that the Cistercian has to be a man who works the land and takes a wise and effective care of the natural resources (forest, etc.) which God has given into his charge. This is the kind of work that, for us, helps the "identity" problem to get solved and also takes care of most of the others too. Stability is much more reasonable and Christian when one has grown roots in the soil of his monastery by work and concern, and when one has been participating in the productive endeavors of the community, sharing in work and in the fruits of work. The business of keeping the monk feeling useless, a non-entity, and so on (Trappist style) is fatal today, and it is just not *true* either. Of course there is no question that the jobs of officers are important and very helpful, but the average monk will not be an officer and should not feel that only those who are in office have an identity . . .

I thoroughly agree that the problems we confront are certainly going to be with us for a long time, and I am sure neither you nor I will see the real solutions. Happy if we can just get a glimpse from Pisgah. There is no question that the whole new look of the Church is in question, and we will have to take our turn, we cannot outstrip everyone else. You are right too about learning about the new generation from the new generation. Yet one thing I find is that they are not all that different. I do think that here at least the young ones who are most excited and perhaps even upset about the question of changes or lack of changes are ones who have been "got at" by older ones with axes to grind. The most excited people in this place seem to me to be not the novices or even the young professed, but the young priests and budding officers who came in ten to fifteen years ago. They are all up in the air, because they seem to have a feeling that they missed out on something (they had a very old-fashioned novitiate training and their theology was very straitlaced and dry). The new ones are much more able to get along and take what comes without insecurity, though I have one now that is perhaps "typical" if anyone is, and cannot settle down here because, as he says, there is "too much Mickey Mouse." That about describes it . . .

To Mother Myriam Dardenne

March 6, 1965

I received your letter the other day, and certainly there is nothing I would like better than to come to Redwoods and have a talk with you. A couple of years ago I asked permission to come out there for a rest, but naturally this was refused. Dom James certainly may have good reasons for not letting anyone go from here to preach a retreat. But at the same time he is extraordinarily strict in the matter of travelling, and with no one is he more strict than with me. So by now I believe it is well known in the Order that he even refused to let me attend a meeting of novice masters unless the meeting was held here. This seems to me to be somewhat extreme, but after all one has to expect such things.

Since probably we are in about the same position with regard to travelling, and since perhaps it might be even easier for you than for me to get permission to travel, why not arrange to come here sometime, if you can? Are there any more General Chapters coming, or any other occasions which would bring you in this direction? I think that if you put this matter before Dom Ignace he *might* consider it, but I cannot offer much hope. What I want to say is that I would certainly be delighted to help you in any way I could, and it is up to you to find a way.

Actually I have had little or no news of Redwoods since you founded it and I have little idea of how things might be going. How are you getting along with the American mentality??? This is a funny country, in many ways exasperating, yet I think one has to be thankful that there is as much good in it as there is. Generally one has very little trouble with them, at least as novices. The big problems all center around their identity, I think. Once they are convinced that they are real, and that they don't have to do something at every minute to prove it to themselves, they settle down and are quite happy, except for those who must inevitably devise new plans for rebuilding everything, reforming everything and inventing five thousand new schemes for putting the Church at last in order. I find the naive approach to these things a bit irritating at times, because in reality it seems to me that the problems of the Church and of our Order are quite serious and profound. The chief problem is that of freedom of the spirit, and allowing the Christian to develop and grow, rather than keeping him in a straitjacket forever. On the other hand, of course, so many people *desire* control and though they do not even admit this, they fear freedom and want to be told what to do all the time, provided that they can sometimes have the pleasure of resisting and attracting the attention of authority. And of criticizing others who do not absolutely conform.

For my part, I ask your prayers. It looks as if we are really going to develop an eremitical project. I am already much more in the hermitage since last fall and this is excellent. At least I find it so. I sleep here, and am learning to cook also. It is a good thing I like rice . . .

To Dame Hildelith Cumming

March 9, 1965

Sorry to subject you to my handwriting but it is a quiet time and I can't type—the novices are reading, but I want to answer your letter and not let it lie around . . . Certainly let us consider the long thin book. I like the idea for this prayer. Ten inches is a good length—even a little longer if you like—maintaining the proportions you suggest. Spectrum good. Hardcover fine. Just tell Tom Burns at Burns, Oates you are doing "a book" but when he realizes it is only a few pages he will not mind.

About the paper—let us at least consider the samples. I hope we won't have *too much* color. Would you say that if we use colored paper, one ink would be sufficient? I am always willing to let myself be convinced by samples. And of course we are doing homage to the Scriptorium of Vivarium.

Our English texts of Gospel and Epistle at Mass are ridiculous. Full of trite and empty expressions. At Vespers I was thinking how fine are so many of our simple Gregorian antiphons—for example, our daily commemoration, in this season, of Our Lady—*Ave Regina Coelorum.* If these things go, the loss will be great! Pray for us . . .

To Sister V.

Sister V., a member of a contemplative order, wrote to Merton asking his advice about implementing Vatican II's decrees on updating religious communities.

March 21, 1965

. . . It is true however that the great problem and the great source of confusion is the way in which we interpret the idea of "openness to the world." This affects you and us, because in the contemplative Orders we have always been too passive about letting others tell us what ought to be done. At the moment we are accepting uncritically a lot of ideas which have been formulated for the active life and which do not fit our own situation at all. The danger is then that contemplatives will find themselves trying to imitate the active people in a tentative and confused sort of way, which will put them in the sad state of being neither what they ought to be (contemplatives) nor what they are trying to be (pseudo actives). Then there is a lot of nonsense going around under the guise of "personalism," fulfillment, etc., etc. Much of this is in reality very immature and pseudo, though it can at times borrow interesting new slogans from interesting new writers. There is nothing whatever wrong with progressive tendencies in themselves, but in our cloisters they can get a very funny and weird perspective, and God help the mixed-up people who think that this is the truth. The rigid conservatives do not help, they only make matters worse by their fear and negativism. What is necessary is for us to develop our own solutions.

The contemplative Orders, while understanding the need for discipline and austerity, and not sacrificing their truly contemplative ideal, need a greater flexibility and maturity. This would allow, for instance, on the one hand a greater opportunity for strict physical solitude, and on the other some occasional venture into dialogue with others. The important thing is to make sure that the contemplatives keep themselves free from routine active work and odd jobs that oppress and overwhelm the freedom they need to be alone with God. I mean schools and what not. It is imperative that contemplatives do not get roped into these organized "works." Anything that threatens their freedom and disengagement from routine obligations in the active life must be fought and fought hard.

There must be no confusion about this. Once the bishops get you signed up for this or that little job, you are in the rat race. And may God help us if we get ourselves imprisoned in a system of relationships that involve constant talking, contacts on a superficial level, etc.

On the other hand, I think the great problem is getting ourselves free from silly routines within our own cloistered life: the gestures and activities that used to be very much to the point, but have now become formalities which are carried out more or less as ends in themselves, without anyone really knowing why. At the same time, we must remember that a lot of these things may still have a meaning which American girls are likely not to have understood, but could be capable of understanding.

In all things we need patience, tact, prudence, willingness to wait. With us, sweeping reforms are not a matter of immediate and urgent necessity. We can take our time, though many will not be willing to do this. But at least, let us try to see clearly where we are going and measure the statements made by others, Cardinal Bea for example, in terms of our *own* life. I have a letter from the Cardinal which states clearly that all he wrote was intended *only* for nuns in the active life and diminishes in nothing his respect for the contemplative life in which "being" is more important than "doing."

To Dame Marcella Van Bruyn

March 28, 1965

Many thanks for your letter. I want to say that I said Mass for you and Stanbrook on the 12th and appreciate your prayers for me on the 19th. On that day they had concelebration here for the second time, and I decided I had better get into it, celebrate the anniversary and so on. I did. It has its points. I certainly do not agree with all the enthusiastic nonsense that is said about everything that is new because it is new. Concelebration as we have it here now is quite imperfect and out of shape. There are inevitable flaws in it, and interminable waits, blundering around, and so on. Obviously, until it can get properly organized, it is going to be a somewhat ponderous affair with many gross stupidities about it. Imagine the collection of chasubles for instance, with every priest all vested up to the eyebrows. Eventually I think all this will be simplified and straightened out. The principle is good, and I stick by that: the expression of unity and charity and oneness in the priesthood and sacrifice of Christ is very clear, and will be clearer when it is all simplified. But I am not going to get into this more often than would be decent for me, I mean more often than I can sincerely say I mean, all things considered. I have already abstained from the one on the Annunciation, expect one on Holy Thursday, the obvious day to be in on it, and then perhaps . . . we'll see. There is some reserve here about it, and half the priests are being rather stolid about getting involved. Our other monasteries however are off in a cloud of dust. I liked your splendid card of James Stevens (whom I have not much read).

The fiftieth birthday was peaceful, and things have been going smoothly. I am mostly intent on getting as much of the hermitage as I can and getting all the experience I can. I see that though I am by no means the ideal hermit, it is definitely the thing for me. For the first time in my life, I feel I am really getting down to bedrock and getting to grips with what matters. At the moment I am seeing how one gets along in and out of a hermitage with a bad cold. Actually, as long as I stay up there, it is better. But I have to come down to the monastery, do my jobs, talk and so on, and get into the rooms heated by radiators: I go back feeling worse. There is a lot of rain and flu about. The solitary life is by no means a matter of sitting around and going into nirvana. There is quite a lot to be done, keeping the place clean, getting in wood before it rains again, etc. It is certainly never dull, I can swear to that!

I must close now and give a conference of sorts to the novices—my voice has gone . . .

To Father Brendan Connelly

April 3, 1965

Thanks for your notes on the "Jesuit Spirit." From what I know, which is not much, I would agree with you. Except that what you list as an "achieving" Christocentrism I would, from my own remote viewpoint, add a special modality which I have always associated with the S.J.: not expendability, exactly, but a special vocation to be "at the disposal" of the Order, the Church, and to achieve as part of a concerted work in which one's personal achievement may mean vanishing completely into the background and giving up results in order that someone else may come out with *his* results. In other words, supernatural teamwork yet ability to free-lance as a commando, etc. This may just be my romantic notion of the Jesuits. But it is tied up with what I think was Ignatius' sense of his men as chosen instruments of the divine will. To be a flexibile instrument in the hand of God is a great and sometimes terrible vocation. I think you people have that sense much more than anyone else in the Church. It is certainly not the Benedictine concept of obedience, but it can obviously manifest itself anywhere that there are men and Christians. We are all in some way instruments. And we all have to be virtuosos at taking a back seat when necessary, way back. The prayer life of a flexible instrument cannot be well ordered. It has to be terribly free. And utterly responsive to a darkly, dimly understood command. I think that really rejoins what you say about "indifference" . . .

To Mother Angela Collins

April 3, 1965

Well, anyway, congratulations on the new post [Prioress of the Savannah Carmel]! I am sure it is in some way or other providential. It is Our Lord's way of moving you where He wants you, and in the end His will doubtless will bring you to solitude in a way you have not planned: but meanwhile the thing is to accept His will in perfect trust and self-forgetfulness, without concern and care, and go ahead with hope in His wisdom. It is quite possible that He wants to use you for the good of Carmel in the ways that are most urgent at the moment, and perhaps put you in a position where you can plan the kind of solutions you have hoped for.

I had already heard about the St. Louis meeting from the Cleveland Carmel. I am very glad you are going. They certainly do not give you much time to say anything. Five minutes is just nothing. I don't think there is much point in me going over the paper; I just suggest that you emphasize the importance of this for the real objective of Carmel, and take into account the fact that so much is said today about action and "Incarnational witness," etc., that even in the contemplative Orders people are tending to doubt the basic value of their most essential traits. I had a letter from Cardinal Bea assuring me that what he was saying for active nuns should not be taken to imply essential changes in the *contemplative* life. He said contemplatives should continue to be what they are. This does not mean staying where they are, if they are in a rut. But returning to a more perfect living realization of the essential contemplative tradition. This last part is my comment, not Bea.

The solitary life is certainly not an idle one. I am quite busy when in the hermitage. At the moment I have found there is an excellent spring nearby but it is choked up, and the woods between the cottage and there are all grown up with vines and brush, which makes a fine fire hazard too. All this has to be cleared out and the spring opened up. And I can't count on the help of the novices, as they are taken up with work in the monastery. I have electricity now, though, and that is a big help. I am down in the monastery for six or eight hours a day, not more. It looks as if I ought to be able to move in completely at the end of the year, when Rev. Father has more or less assured me he will let me out of the novice master's job.

One reason why he is so much in favor of solitude all of a sudden is that I am constantly being asked to get in on meetings such as the one you are going to. He wants in the worst way to prevent me from doing so, and we have had to refuse several already. Or he has refused them for me. In one case, they even wanted to have the meeting here and he forbade it. Because probably I would meet some very interesting people who are active in the hermit movement. One man you should know is Dom Jacques Winandy, who has now established his (men) hermits at Courtenay, British Columbia (address: R.R.2). If anyone can help with the idea of women being hermits, he can. When you get to Savannah, you could contact him.

To Dom Colomban Bissey

April 7, 1965

You were very kind this morning and I am very sorry to have caused you some annoyance by being the occasion of hard words that you spoke to Fr. So-and-so in my regard. I know that I do not need to offer you any explanation, but in any case, in order to be fully open and very clearly so, I will consign these few words to paper for you.

1) As regards my health: The condition of my spine is quite a serious matter, because it affects the use of my left hand, and when things go badly, I cannot very well use it to type on the typewriter, etc. Above all it is necessary to avoid a delicate operation which perhaps will not be successful.

As to the refectory, I absolutely cannot digest the milk dishes and so it is much more convenient for the brothers to let me eat in the infirmary instead of having to bring eggs, etc., into the common refectory. This is well known in the community, and if this good Father has seen a problem in this, it is perhaps due to a lack of good will, I don't know. As to the (private) room, it is well known that I absolutely cannot sleep when I am in the common dormitory and I even have quite a bit of insomnia in the private room. I agree that this is a sign of nervousness which perhaps indicates a lack of mortification and control.

2) With all that, it is true that by making a greater effort I could arrange to be at the night office, but I have rather thought that it is by these means that God offers me a little solitude with more time for meditation, etc., more silence, and I accept this possibility at the cost of a certain danger of making certain people murmur. I do not say that in this way I am more in the truth than if I tried hard to do otherwise so as not to offend them and get into a jam that would make me more nervous and tense. It is a choice which I believe I must make under the Eye of God, and Dom James allows it. There you are. I am responsible before God and if He wants me to act otherwise, I shall do so. There is the danger of disedifying the novices perhaps, and if I believed that they absolutely did not understand what I was doing, I would make any kind of sacrifice in order to edify them (but not merely to justify myself in their eyes). I believe on the contrary that they understand well enough that I have valid reasons.

If Dom James means that I am absent from night office in accordance with the doctor's orders, that is perfectly true, as is also for the case of the refectory and the infirmary.

So here you are, Reverend Father. I explain myself with simplicity and I hope that I will not cause you any further unpleasantness.

To an English Carmelite Prioress

April 22, 1965

Ever since last November when you kindly took the trouble to write me your long and interesting letter, supplemented by that of Sister Subprioress, I have wanted to send you at least a word of acknowledgment. Of course I have been relying on your full understanding of my plight as a too active contemplative, with far too many letters to write. But charity remains the fulfillment of all the law, and I cannot let you go without a sign of life even at this late date.

I am afraid that when I was in Cambridge I was not thinking in terms of convents, alas, and I was not aware that you were in the Chesterton Road, though I used to go to a cinema down that way, and further out my Italian tutor had his house, so I must often have passed you. And no doubt the prayers and sacrifices of the Sisters must have secretly brought me many graces. I am happy to be in touch with Cambridge through Mrs. Chadwick, for whom I have the greatest admiration, as well as through Blackfriars, where Fr. Illtud Evans is a good friend of mine. I am also in touch with Clare, my old college. And now your convent at Waterbeach. I am not sure I remember Waterbeach, but I think I must have gone through it. Is it on the way to Ely?

It will always be a pleasure for me to send you any of the papers and things we use here in the novitiate. I will pop a little package of them into the mail this morning and I hope they will reach you eventually by surface mail. Perhaps through these few poor pieces of work we may maintain a fraternal bond in the love of our common vocation and of Our Risen Saviour.

Let us certainly be united in prayer in these days of change. I think you are probably less affected by some of the more violent movements than we are. It is going to be a real struggle to see that valuable, perhaps even essential elements of the contemplative life are not thoughtlessly discarded in some quarters. But on the other hand, a simply static conservatism is obviously not going to do any good either. May the Holy Spirit guide us all in making changes that will effect a genuine renewal, and not simply let us plunge madly into the latest fashions which are sometimes quite superficial . . .

To Father Charles Dumont

April 25, 1965

Thanks for your letter and also for the new *Collectanea* and for the offprints of my article . . . You mention my coming to Europe. As Dom James has himself just taken off on the plane, I can speak freely. Certainly I would be happy to come to Europe at least once before I die, and I think I would profit greatly by doing so. There are many things I would want to see and study, and personally I feel that my Superiors would not be acting irresponsibly if they saw fit to permit this. On the other hand, I must tell you frankly that this is a subject on which Dom James has what almost amounts to an obsession. He is very, very rigid in the matter of "sorties" but he is almost pathological about it in my case, though I can get to Louisville to see the doctor all right. But any mention of a long trip, especially to Europe, makes him almost physically sick. He is in fact something of a joke to the other Abbots in America because he refuses even to let me go to another monastery to attend a meeting of novice masters for instance. The meeting had to be held here, and he seems to have insisted that I would not go to another meeting elsewhere, in fact blocking the very possibility of such a meeting indefinitely because of the fact that I might be expected to go to it. It seems incredible, but it is true. Hence, to get me to Europe for some task for the good of the Order would almost require a special statute of the General Chapter, or at least a strong personal intervention of Dom Ignace. Dom James would never, never permit it on his own, no matter for what reason.

At the same time, of course, my own feelings on the subject are not unmixed. You mention your good nuns. Exactly. The last thing in the world I would want would be a tour of convents and monasteries, giving conferences and causing a great fuss. If in fact I ever went to Europe, I would want to stay away from most monasteries of the Order for that very reason, and very quietly go to visit the places and people that I could see without raising any fuss. Hence if in the future it does become really necessary for me to come over there for some reason or other, I would want to do it in such a way that I could be of service without drawing attention to my presence in Europe; I would want to stay away from Rome and from most monasteries of our Order (exception made for Mont-des-Cats, for example) but there are some things that I would like to do in England and Ireland and perhaps France. However, there is no point in planning on it . . .

To Dom André Louf, O.C.S.O.

Dom André Louf was born in Belgium in 1929, entered the Cistercian abbey of Sainte-Marie-du-Mont (Mont-des-Cats), and in 1963 became Abbot. He has written and lectured widely on the contemplative life and prayer.

April 26, 1965

I want to thank you for your very fine letter, so encouraging and so positive, about my notes on the eremitical renewal. And as a sign of confidence and friendship, I thought I would share with you the beginnings of the experiment which Dom James has already permitted here— of course it is still within certain limits and doubtless he would not want to be embarrassed by having it discussed as yet. But certainly, as your letter indicates, a really providential movement of the Holy Spirit in our Order has quite unexpectedly opened things up so that an eremitical life really seems possible for Cistercians. If so, that is certainly one of the greatest graces the Order has received since it began.

In this question of solitude, no amount of theory can substitute for a grain of practice. That is why I write this letter, because already in my life there is a mustard seed of it, and I would like to say what I think of this very small taste of experience in the field of solitude, even though it is limited and relative as yet.

It is known that I have had a hermitage for nearly five years. It began somewhat ambiguously as a place for meetings with non-Catholic retreatants apart from the monastery, in a quiet setting, etc., and a place in which I was permitted to spend the afternoons. Since then, the visits of retreatants have stopped; I have spent more than the afternoons, as much free time as I could get in fact, and finally since last October I have been sleeping here, saying the night office here, taking frustulum or mixt, sometimes supper, going down for work in the novitiate and usually for Prime, Tierce, High Mass, Sext, dinner and perhaps some of the afternoon offices, unless I am completely free, in which case I may return to the hermitage after dinner and not come down again until the following morning at Prime. So you see that at least some solitude is here. What of the fruits?

First of all I can say that for me the experience has been wonderful, and it has dissipated any doubts I may have had about my own need for and happiness in solitude. I have at last the complete sense of having found my monastic vocation. At least in my own mind, I am convinced that I have now found the place which God had destined for me when He called me to the monastic life, and that if before this I was always to some extent unsatisfied and looking for "more," it was simply because this was needed to complete what God had given me before.

Second, there is a sense that this is a complete, inexplicable gift of

God to me, without reference to any merit of mine. Frankly I have not been a perfect cenobite and I am by no means a perfect hermit. From the objective point of view one might say that there is a great deal to be desired in my "preparation" and "aptitude" for this kind of life. I am by no means the ideal type of the one called to solitude. But I am not worried by this, since God can do what He wants, and if He wants me here He can see that I make such use of this opportunity as will be pleasing to Him. And in fact I am very happy and busy with Him all the time I am here, though of course I have work to do, manual labor, cutting grass, splitting wood in winter, sweeping, etc., and even some writing (which would scandalize some people) but I try to take three hours a day at least for simple meditative prayer, and in addition to that I have another three hours of *lectio divina* or study when I am here for a good part of the day. When I am here permanently (which I hope will be soon), I hope to spend more time on the Psalter and so on.

This is of course known in the community and on the whole it is quite well accepted, by choir and brothers alike. The cellarer, who is quite critical of the fantasies of the monks, is benign and positive in his attitude toward the hermitage, which he considers quite reasonable in my case, and I have no trouble getting cooperation from the brothers in getting food, or in electrical installation. (I have electric light; I think it is necessary and it is very cheap, about three and a half dollars a month, which includes electric cooking.) The novices of course know it, and there has been no difficulty with the novitiate, as I have an undermaster who is willing to spend a lot of time there so as to be available when I am away. But the novices seem to be very content to be alone themselves reading and praying, and some seem willing to wait patiently for the number of years that may be required so that they may perhaps ultimately have a chance to try some solitude. I would say there is one who is serious about this and who would quite probably make a go of it in fifteen years or so. (I expect to be relieved of all jobs at the end of this year.)

There have been some difficulties, but nothing very great. It is cold in the winter, and one does not have the comforts of the community. But I prefer this. I have also had some sickness here, but find that I got along all right, though quite ill, and when it became bad I was put in the infirmary and recovered quickly. In a word, sickness is no greater problem here than in the monastery. There has been very little *cafard* [in the dumps, the blues]. In fact, much less than in the community, for me!!! But some moments of purification and profound emptiness and loneliness, not so much loneliness for people as metaphysical emptiness and sense of the nothingness of myself and even in some sense of life and of "everything." There are times of purely sickening void. But there is never any feeling that one could or should escape this by returning to the distractions of the community. Quite the contrary, one sees there is no escape except in God Himself who in some way presents Himself as this Void. The Void is then its own fullness. And in fact it generally turns to great light and freedom and joy, much more than anything I ever knew in the monastery. I have never had so true a sense of the nearness of God and of His care for me, yet always in a more inexplicable and less "sensible" manner than in the monastery.

In fact I can say that there is really no special problem at all in the hermit life as far as I now know it. True, I like to go to the conventual Mass in particular, and I would like very much to continue this contact with the community. I certainly feel great love for my brothers and it is a really strong consolation to see them and be with them. It is a very great joy to remain dependent on the community and to feel that I will never have to sever my bonds with my monastic family. I consider this *most important*. It is almost the most important thing about the vocation to solitude for a monk, I believe. The grace of belonging permanently to one's monastic family is irreplaceable. My only slight difficulty is the fear that Dom James will want to organize something more formal and more permanent, perhaps a small "laura," further from the monastery, and that I might have to leave the situation which is now completely perfect for something much less perfect for me and much more "organized." But of course I will do whatever he wants and will trust in God. Actually, it seems to me that if I can only be here all the time, going down to conventual Mass several times a week, and for the rest living on my own as I have been, it is all I could possibly seek or need.

To Father Francis Derivaux, O.C.S.O.

Father Francis Derivaux, a monk of Gethsemani, was studying monastic theology in Rome at this time at Sant'Anselmo.

April 26, 1965

Peace and joy in the Risen Saviour. I enjoyed your recent letter read in the refectory and wanted to get after you about your St. Bernard studies. I think that a version of your study on St. Bernard, about 12 typewritten pages, would make an excellent article for the *Collectanea*. Why don't you write it up, not in a big rush, but when convenient? It would be much appreciated, I'm sure. Just one suggestion I would offer, as regards the terminology. On this "real self" business. I am not sure I am right but you seem to make a division between "real self" and "true self" which could be confusing. If you are using "real self" for our actual everyday exterior self, then I think the most convenient term would be "empirical self," which is used by psychologists et al. who get involved in this sort of thing.

I got a nice letter from Joe Chatham, who is still flourishing *aliquo modo*, and who came out with a fine statement on race, etc., in the South.

What is needed is Southern white leadership in this mess, and until we get it, there will be nothing but confusion and hatred. There will be that anyway. I wonder what will really come of all this. Selma was a real breakthrough though, in many respects, especially for the Church.

I must say Fr. Gerard Majella looks most rakish in a beret, and seems to like this form of headgear. He is being brainwashed by French influence, I can see that . . .

To Mother Mary Margaret

April 29, 1965

It has been a long time since we corresponded about the possibility of my doing a little ecumenical meditation especially for you. I hope you did not think I had forgotten about it, or given up the idea. However, as you may imagine, I do have a fair amount of work and so it was necessary for me to wait until the meditation took shape peacefully, in its own time. I would hardly want to send you a few mad ideas dashed off on the spur of the moment. Of course I realize that the pages I am enclosing are not really adequate, and hence I will rely on you to edit it in a way that befits your needs. Do feel free to ask any changes you like. I have used the Moffatt translation for the quotations from the Psalms, but if you would rather take the King James I would perhaps prefer it, but I do not have a copy of that version here. Personally I am not one of those who likes an indiscriminate modernizing of the Scripture text. In the prayer I have composed for the end of the meditation I have used the modern "You" instead of the traditional "Thou" but actually would perhaps prefer the latter if you do. I leave these minor considerations entirely to you. The meditation is yours to do with as you please.

Roman Catholics are going through all kinds of changes, some needful, others apparently arbitrary and perhaps ill-considered on the practical level (I refer not of course to the Council but to the various local applications). Hence we do need prayers. And I can tell you, as I tell all my Anglican friends, I hope that you will have the sense to maintain traditions that we are now eagerly throwing overboard (Latin, Gregorian Chant, etc., in monastic communities) . . .

To Dom Jean Leclercq

May 11, 1965

. . . Above all I want to thank you for your generous defense in the German article. It is gradually dawning on me that there must have been more discussion and criticism of me than I had imagined. Perhaps it is just as well that I did not know about all of it . . . In any case, reading your remarks was a salutary experience, in the first place because your frankness and goodness in taking up what must be in some quarters a quite unpopular cause, gives me a sense of the charity and concern of the Church even for the least of her children. But in any case you are noted for defending unpopular causes. Actually of course there must be many ways of looking at the "case." In many respects my life and work are certainly very equivocal. If anyone wants to measure me by "normal" standards, it will be easy to find that I fail to meet the requirements— like everybody else, because in the long run, what are normal standards, and who meets them, except superficially? Then, too, I am certainly a *Geheimnis* [mystery] even to myself. And I have ceased to expect anything else. Nor do I have any secret hope left of making complete sense out of my existence, which must remain paradoxical. Thus in the end I must do what everyone else does and fall back on the mercy of God and try, as far as I can, not to fail Him in His loving will for me. Certainly if I tried to please everyone, I would fail Him, and if I am to please Him I must inevitably displease a lot of very earnest and well-meaning people. And I intend to continue doing this without scruple.

The inner contradictions of the Dom Calati people are in any case rather amusing. *They* are the hermits and monks who have precipitated themselves with open arms toward the world. They blame me because I have refused to do this and have instead tried to get back into the desert. Yet the *real* source of their objection and anger is that, after all, the world is listening to me rather than to them. Which is really very funny indeed. And I don't think that I am entirely in contradiction with myself because I have consistently held that a monk can speak *from the desert*, since there is no other place from which he has a better claim to be heard. Oh well, it is all ninety percent nonsense anyway, but I am grateful for your Christian charity and for your encouragement, because there are certainly times when I can use it.

You know of course that Dom James is now at the General Chapter. In inviting you to come in September (or whenever you can) to give a couple of talks to the novices and juniors, I am not in a position to do so fully officially yet, but I am sure that (though he will not be very happy about it) Dom James will not refuse me the permission and will support me in the invitation. I will make it fully official when he returns, so I hope you can plan to come.

It will be really quite useful for you to come in many ways, for us. There is a project now of a more elaborate kind of hermit establishment (on which the Abbot himself is suddenly quite keen as he foresees the possibility of six-year terms for Abbots), in a valley about five miles away from here. A kind of laura might be set up there, possibly. This is all very nice, and taking the idea in itself I would have no objections. However, there are the following considerations:

1) The Abbot's plan for this is disconcerting. He wants the hermits

to live there in *trailers*. Do you get the picture? This means bright modern little machines for living with all possible comforts, etc., etc. Not only do I find myself incapable of accepting it, but my friends think it is very funny.

2) I have considerable reservations about being in a group with other people, even though only four or five. It has distinct disadvantages and means less solitude than I would have and do have where I now am in the hermitage (which is ideal for my own purposes).

3) I am very much afraid that this "colony" will turn out to be over-organized and that in the end we will end up with Dom James running it like a little abbey, and everyone under his thumb not able to move or breathe without doing so in the way that he would like. I know he is my Abbot, but I am very much afraid that I have never honestly been able to deal with him as with a "spiritual father" and it would be impossible for me to do so sincerely.

4) My suggestion to him is that he should make his foundation in Norway and concentrate on that for the time being. That he should let me give up the novices and live all the time in the hermitage where I now am for part of the time in any case. That he put a temporary hermitage in the valley where he wants his "colony" to be and let different monks go out there for a few days at a time to see how they like it. Later, when all have more experience, we can think of something more definite. And I hope it will *not* be elaborate.

I thought I would let you in on all this while I had a chance to do so.

Problems in the various houses of our Order in this country continue and I have the feeling that some of the biggest ones have yet to be faced.

To Father William McNamara, O.C.D.

Father McNamara is a Carmelite priest who developed a number of hermitages in the United States and Canada following the Carmelite eremitical ideal. He has written many books and articles on the contemplative life.

May 12, 1965

It was good to hear from you, and to receive your literature on SLIA [Spiritual Life Institute of America]. The new developments look impressive and I must say I think you have a very good thing going, and it is wonderful that so many have been able to avail themselves of the opportunity to be hermits in the desert. Actually I must say that I am grateful to you in more ways than one, because the fact that so many Trappists have gone to you, to Dom Winandy and others has finally made the Order wake up, and I think there is now a very serious chance that hermitages will be officially permitted within the Order itself. So you see what a little leaven will do. Keep it up, for there is much more to be done.

Actually I have not had a chance to go over the literature carefully because I handed most of it to a man who might be interested in coming down there, a former Naval officer from a Polaris submarine who was not able to make it here . . . I highly recommend him, and I think he could be of help to you. He is not necessarily a hermit type, but very serious about the interior life. He does of course need formation.

You ask for suggestions: this one is very general and to be taken with a grain of salt. I am all for the development of the "whole man," for a humanistic approach in the right sense of the word. At the same time I think one must be careful not to state this as if it implied a lessening of genuine ascetic effort. The point is that where the ascetic life is serious there is a genuine all-round development of the whole man, and there can be also a real flowering of human, intellectual, cultural values. Today there is so much dilettantism in these matters, I am sure you must know it better than I: for perhaps the LSD boys have been after you already. I do not envy you the struggle with confusion that must result from dealing with *all* the people who claim to have an interest in prayer and mysticism today. So many of them are simply deranged, or ready to become so with a little encouragement. Hence I would say you will probably very soon find, if you have not found already, that the ancient monastic policy of being reserved and not too encouraging to newcomers and enthusiasts is imperative. Test the spirits (I am sure you do) and let the welcome on the mat be a little dim perhaps. There will be a lot of complaints, but firmness will eventually be respected. From what I hear of all the new ventures, Camaldolese, etc., I think this seems to be one of the most necessary measures . . . I am living in my own hermitage much more this year, with hopes of being there permanently soon. Keep this in your prayers and naturally I pray for SLIA.

To Nora Chadwick

June 2, 1965

First I want to acknowledge the booklet on St. Columba, which I read with great pleasure, since he is one of my favorite saints. In fact, his feast day will be next week. I have been planning to offer my Mass on that day for you, and will also include Eleanor Duckett who just sent me a very nice note written in the Cambridge Library, where she plucked a very delightful monastic paragraph from a document from Gembloux. I was very happy with it. Such writing and thought from the "dark ages" reminds us that people then had a great deal more depth than we, in our complacency as twentieth century men, often give them credit for. In fact, to put it bluntly, I think they had more depth and more capacity to think than the average man of our time. When one looks at the "world" around us, one wonders at the term "dark ages." What is, then, required to make ages "light"?

You did indeed mention in your earlier letters to me the fact that your sister had died as a nun in the Waterbeach Carmel, and I have since that time prayed for her, though I am sure her prayers for me will be more valuable than mine for her. I am glad, too, that you liked the finished version of "Pilgrimage" in *Cithara*. Perhaps it will come out in book form with some other essays. I must try to find you one other you might like, on "Virginity and Humanism"—all very familiar material, mostly about Jerome, and rather like the essay Prof. Duckett sent me recently . . .

Certainly I agree with you about Cassian. Ever since I had him as a Lenten book in the novitiate, I have kept close to him, and of course use him constantly with the novices. I have done a little work on St. Anselm lately, however, and though he is quite a different sort of person I am quite fond of him too. I have a long essay on his "argument" coming out. I think it is not appreciated.

The possibility of real eremitical life in our monastic Order is now settled, and I hope myself to be among the first to undertake it. In fact I am already half in it now, in the traditional form of the hermitage in the woods close to the monastery. But I still have to come back to the monastery several days during the week to carry on my work. Next year perhaps I will be relieved of this. So do ask Our Lord to give me the grace needed to carry out this venture in the true spirit of the ancient monks, and with all their faith and simplicity. I know you have a real appreciation of the eremitical spirit, from your long familiarity with so many texts about them, so I do not hesitate to speak to you about it.

To Mother Mary Margaret

June 10, 1965

Many thanks for your kind letter of May 19th. By all means make use of the name of the author, in any way you see fit, in printing the meditation. I am glad that you found the text suitable, and I felt that you would like that approach. Certainly we must be convinced that since God has mercifully called us by a way of simplicity and prayer, He will make our lives very fruitful provided we trust Him and gladly accept the grace of our special calling. And I know you all realize there, as we do here, what a consoling and rewarding path it is, even though it is often seemingly bleak. What could be better than to find ourselves always close to Our Lord in silent faith and in humble liturgical praise?

Even though the Church officially and publicly encourages monks to retain the Latin liturgy, I am afraid that there are very many communities, perhaps the majority in this country, which are seeking the vernacular at any price. They are of course free to ask for this concession, and I am sure that many will perhaps regret it after they have lost what they had. But this is an irreversible trend, I think, at least in the U.S. For my own part, as I have hopes of a more solitary life, and they seem about to be realized, I think that at least I will be able to keep the old Latin office *privatim* . . .

To Dame Marcella Van Bruyn

June 16, 1965

First, since you mention the prospectus at the top of your letter, I will say "yes" to the offer now, in case I forget at the end. I would like to see that, as something to keep up my hopes for the book. They have certainly waited a long time, but that is the way things go in monasteries anywhere.

As to your questions:

1) I think that the most sensible and desirable thing for one who has a genuine vocation to monastic solitude, in touch with a community, is to really be in solitude. In confidence, I have hopes that after this year I will be permanently in the hermitage. I sleep there now and spend days at a time there when I can, but am almost always there for at least twelve hours out of the twenty-four and usually more than that. I hope next year to come down perhaps for conventual Mass at first, and for one meal, as this will simplify the problem of cooking and washing dishes.

2) I hope gradually to give up writing. I don't plan to cut it off all of a sudden, because I know myself well enough to realize that this activity is helpful to me and in no way interferes with a genuine life of prayer. It has always been a help, the writing part. The publication [problems are] a little more distracting. But I think eventually the writing will die out by itself. I can see now that I would soon begin to lose interest. But I will probably always write a few little things like meditations or poems, on the spur of the moment.

As to correspondence, that too will gradually work itself out, I hope. At the moment I have a great load of it, with all kinds of letters from strangers, people wanting direction and so on. Most of it I cannot answer, and I do not try. Next year I would want to cut it down to just proportions. It seems to me, though that "just proportions" includes keeping up a *monastic* correspondence, within reason. Obviously not a continued barrage, but occasional necessary letters on points of some interest. Your question would be a case in point . . .

3) I would obviously give up the novice mastership and other offices, and I have already spoken of renouncing active and passive voice in the Chapter. I suppose I might have to continue voting, but I firmly intend to refuse all offices, above all that of Abbot, should they ever become so

far afflicted as to elect me. Naturally I would not be involved in monastery politics.

4) Secular reading: that covers a wide area. Personally I would perhaps want to keep a bit in touch with philosophy, poetry, art, a little. Again, it would be a gradual affair. I don't think that I am called of set purpose to make a sweeping renunciation of all interest in what is being written and said outside, but on the contrary, I think that it is relevant to me. I don't think a monk can absolutely cut himself off from the really urgent secular problems and ideas, and still be realistic.

5) As things are now, I say the night office in the hermitage, and on many days I am there for None and Vespers. I say Compline there too. I would plan to come to conventual Mass, I think, not more than that, except perhaps Sunday Vespers. Much depends on what they do to the liturgy. If they go over to the vernacular then I doubt if I will find it so attractive. I may just come down for feast day Masses (and might even continue to concelebrate once in a while). At the moment I have an Ambrosian Gradual and Vesperale in the hermitage and am finding some perfectly lovely things which I add to my own office up there. I say the office silently of course, but I sing a few Ambrosian things, and they are quite a lift.

There is certainly every hope that there will be hermitages here that people can go to for a day or two. This plan is, as Americans say, "in the works." I am sure that some vocations will be saved, and I agree that the thing we need to keep vocations is not to make silly concessions and play around with recreation, TV and what not, but to make the monastic life fully serious and solid, as it should be. The problem is to distinguish between real seriousness and the pettifogging regularism that puts exaggerated emphasis on trivial externals and the letter of outdated usages, thus preventing a real return to the essence of the life, which is in solitude, silence, contemplative prayer, reflection, time to penetrate the word of God and listen to His voice, etc., etc. And of course with all this there is absolutely essential humility, compunction, self-stripping and "self-naughting," which people seem to get away from, with their hopes of "self-expression," though I suppose in a way this is a need too, but has to be rightly understood.

It turns out that the skin trouble on my hands is due to sensitivity to sunlight, not to poison ivy. I have no doubt that strain may play a part in it, but actually the important thing is to keep the sun off the skin. As long as I wear gloves outdoors I have no trouble. I suppose it will go away gradually.

My big hope now is that I will definitely be able to move completely to the hermitage at the latest after January 1. Do keep that in your prayers. I think often of you and Stanbrook, and feel such agreement with all of you in your tradition so strongly marked by Dom Augustine [Baker] and Dame Gertrude [More]. Hold to all the good that you have, and to your own spirit of solitude . . .

To Dom Jean Leclercq

July 5, 1965

Many thanks for the offprints on African Monasticism and for your letter from Togo. I am convinced, by both of them, that the purity of the life there must be something very inspiring. Of course God will bless them more than other countries insofar as they are much poorer, much more dependent on Him, much closer to the nature He has made. I do not mean to imply by this that technology has something bad about it, but nevertheless I think that in the big and prosperous nations the problems of monasticism will be otherwise complex. To begin with I am becoming more and more convinced that true simplicity, in the depths of the heart, is almost impossible for an American or a European. Certainly they may be subjectively sincere and mean well, but the fact that they come from a society that divides man from the very start and fills him with conflicts and doubts must mean something. I am impressed by the fact that what aggiornamento has meant here has been doubt. And that is perhaps healthy, or healthier than the old rigid refusal to admit even the possibility of anything being questioned. Now that everything is questioned, and should be questioned, too many are realizing that there is nothing in the monastic life that they consider worth holding on to. And if that is the case, all right. We do not have to try to persuade them that they are subjectively wrong. But I still think we are perhaps here too ready to think that after all we can prove them all wrong by a few adjustments. Anyway, there is a profound distrust, and if it finally leads to monks becoming Christians and having faith at last, then God's will be glorified by it.

I am delighted that your African essay will be in *Monastic Studies*. It reads like Cassian.

About your coming here: Fr. Abbot said that in September much of the time the diocesan priests will be on retreat and that is not a good time for visits. But the last week in September is all right, and so I extend to you the official invitation to come and speak to the novices at the end of September or early in October at your convenience.

Yes, I was a bit surprised that the General Chapter even officially and publicly admitted that a Cistercian could become a hermit without the Order collapsing. It seems definite that I will be able to do this, and I am in fact spending most of my time in the hermitage: but it is uncertain as yet when Fr. Abbot will let me give up the job of master of novices. I am sending to Clervaux a study on symbolism you might like. It was written for a magazine published by Hindu followers of Ramana Maharishi.

To Sister Mary Luke Tobin

July 7, 1965

It was nice to see some Loretto bonnets up in the balcony at Mass today. But that is not what I am writing about . . .

Here is a piece I have written on the supposition that . . . changes in Schema 13, art. 25, on the question of war, were in favor of the bomb. I am not sure whether my information was correct. Do you have the new proposed text? Do you think the article is out of line? I have other copies if you want them ["Open Letter to the American Bishops on Schema XIII"].

You might enjoy (?) the poem ["A Devout Meditation on Eichmann"]. It deals roughly (very roughly) with everything and is perhaps not totally edifying, so it is not intended for general circulation (though I hope it will be published). I mean it is not refectory reading.

Have you read Karl Stern's new book, *The Flight from Woman?* I think it is on the whole very good, and I think you would like it. But you are not the ones who need it . . .

To Sister J.

July 13, 1965

Ever since I published my first book, there has been an almost unlimited choice of rumors about me, each one sillier than the one before it. As I have no clue as to which of these rumors you refer to, it would be hard for me to make it understandable. Especially since I don't understand them myself.

I am at Gethsemani and it is my firm intention, with God's grace, to remain here. I assure you that I have no plan to leave here, and do not expect to have any such plan unless they finally decide that they have had all they can stand and throw me out. I intend, for my own part, to continue following what has been my vocation from the start, and to seek God in a solitary and contemplative life. That is my only ambition. And I intend to do it here.

May I please ask you to tell your friends that rumors about me are nonsense and are not to be believed? . . .

To Father Hans Urs von Balthasar

July 17, 1965

Thanks very much for the two new little books you sent. Your *Rechenschaft* looks particularly intriguing, and I am delighted to have a bibliography of your work. My German is so slow that it takes me time to get down to something like this, but I hope to soon.

Meanwhile I am sending you a couple of new poems. I thought of you especially when getting out the one on Origen, and hope you will like it. It ought perhaps to be in Dr. Gisi's collection, so I send you two copies. Will you please pass one of them on to her? The other poem is heavy with irony that comes through mostly in the intonation, and I suppose it is hardly translatable. I am in contact with a Chilean poet who writes devastating satires in this vein. Finally I also send you some notes I hope to publish on Schema 13. There is reason to fear that the American bishops, or some of them, are trying to slip some approval of nuclear weapons into the Schema. Do you know anything about this?

To Sister Mary Luke Tobin

July 18, 1965

I have just received the final ok about moving into the hermitage, which will be sometime next month. On the 23rd of this month I have a Hindu visitor, but as far as I know I am clear on the 24th, if Fr. Abbot says ok. I could be out for a short visit with your two Canons from Louvain, whose book (Canon Gelluy's) I know. It would be good to see you also: I don't know what the future will hold in store as regards visits, but I imagine they will be very limited, though perhaps not absolutely, so there has to be some necessary and human contact, and there will be matters of importance that may arise.

The notes on Schema 13 have gone out to a few bishops but I am not making a great project out of it. If *Commonweal* prints it, all right.

Last night's storm was a great experience in the hermitage. The place got "hit" but of course it was immediately grounded. Yet one definitely felt something. I felt as if a wave of static electricity came out of my feet, if that makes any sense. Or perhaps this was a religious experience? I doubt it. But the great thing was seeing the whole valley lit up by continuous flashes of lightning. The hills really seemed to jump and dance like young lambs, as in the psalms. It was splendid . . .

Pray for me to be a real good hermit and listen to the word of God and respond like a man. That is what it really involves. Simply to stand on one's feet before one's Father and reply to Him in the Spirit. Of course this is very much a Church activity. Anyway I will be down to concelebrate habitually and this will add an interesting and lively dimension: maybe I'll be one of the first hermits with that kind of a setup, at least since the very early days.

(That business about replying to the Father in the Spirit may sound like big talk but I don't mean it that way. "In the Spirit" in any context I know, of solitude, means flat on your face. How one can stand on one's own feet and be flat on one's face at the same time is a mystery I will have to try to work out by living it. Maybe Yoga is the answer, but don't report this to Fr. Abbot. I have no intention of trying to solve it that way.)

To Dame Hildelith Cumming

August 23, 1965

Unfortunately I have misplaced your last letter, but I know what the main point was and I hasten to answer it. Please, I beg you, do not let us change the plans for Cassiodorus in any way. Please do not interrupt your schedule and turn everything upside down, and above all let us in no way change the design of the book, for what matters most is quality and truth. This idea of rushing to get it out for Christmas is simply silly, but it gives you some idea of how things are in America: already in the middle of summer people are getting themselves involved in the simply incredible ritual of the Christmas rush. You would hardly believe the extent of this ailment in our country . . . I assure you that I myself knew nothing whatever of the idea until a day or two ago, when I was shown the letter from the Secretary of Publications. And of course for my part I never in the world thought of this in terms of a Christmas card.

Incidentally, the parting word of Father Abbot sending me to the hermitage was that I was to write a new postulants' guide and have printed copies ready—in time for Christmas, naturally. I am still pondering on the mystery of how to deal with printers while living in the woods. But it will solve itself one of these days. Such things always do.

As to life in the hermitage, it is beyond all expectations: for the first time I really know and experience all that I came to the monastery for. So true is it that in some cases the full fruit of a vocation matures late or even not at all if special conditions are not envisaged. It is however truly characteristic of the monastic life in the best sense that it *does* envisage and provide for special conditions. That must surely be an element in any real aggiornamento . . .

To Dom Jacques Winandy

August 30, 1965

It was a joy to receive your letter some time ago, and I am sorry that at that time it was already too late to make use of your remarks in order to significantly alter the article on eremitism which had already been taken and was being set up in type by the *Collectanea*. Naturally the article is very incomplete and lacks nuances as it stands. However, I hope it will be of some use. At the same time I am more and more skeptical of the value of anything looking like an "eremitical movement" within our Order. Perhaps however the thought that all possibilities are not closed may help wake up something of the dormant and rather despairing spirits of our monks.

Certainly I think the worst thing at present about our conventional cenobitism is that, in the conservative monasteries, all possibilities are simply closed and all original growth and development are simply forbidden, and all initiatives discouraged: but in the ones that are opening up, the possibilities are suddenly so irresponsible and so baseless that one sees people running around in all directions with no real sense of what they are seeking. I am afraid that in many cases this takes the form of a supposed eremitical vocation, and doubtless you have discovered that all these are not very positive . . .

For my own part I am glad to say that I have been relieved of my job as novice master and am living in the hermitage. I am very grateful to be able to do so, to taste the life in its special character, its emptiness, silence and purifying force. And I have very rapidly discovered that what I am seeking is not eremitism or spirituality or contemplation but simply God. Also that He lets Himself be sought in order to be found, and that all the realities that have been proposed about the desert are real indeed, and not illusion, except that in my case if I think too much about "desert" and "eremitism" it does become a bit of a delusion. It is much simpler just to be an ordinary Christian who is living alone, as it happens. But certainly this ability to expand and move in emptiness, out of the rather confining and limited structure of the community, is an enormous blessing. I am grateful to God every moment for it, and will not spoil it by imagining that my life is in any way special, for that does indeed poison everything.

I have no program but I find that in fact this living in the "shadow of the community" is a very simple and practical formula, though it might be that I would like your setup even better. There is certainly a large amount of struggle and ambiguity involved in remaining overshadowed by the "spirit" of the community . . .

To Father Brendan Connelly

September 7, 1965

. . . Yes, there was some material on the bomb in that pile. I did not write anything about Herman Kahn, in spite of the interest, I might almost say amusement, with which I read his rather gruesome proposals. There is such a contrast between the bland innocence of his tone and the horror of the ideas that the result is a kind of macabre humor, I am afraid. I am sending along a copy of another text on the subject that might well be filed. It was not published or submitted for publication, was a talk given to some Protestant ministers interested in the morality of nuclear war in 1963. I thought you would like to have it.

Meanwhile I am getting back to work on the Celtic monks and am preparing a series of talks on them. I remember the Irish collection you have there and I think you are the one best equipped to help me out. Here are a few of the things that would be most valuable to me at the moment:

> *The Rule of Tallaght*, edited by Gwynn, Hermanathena XLIV, 2nd Suppl. Vol., Dublin, 1927.
>
> *Ireland and Medieval Europe*, by Robin Flower, Proceedings of British Acad. XIII, 1929.
>
> *Early Irish Monastic Schools*, H. Graham, Dublin, 1923.
>
> *The Early Monastic Schools of Ireland*, W. G. Hanson, Cambridge, 1927.
>
> *Irish Teachers*, Turner (this is all the reference I have).
>
> *Early Irish Missionaries and St. Vergil of Salzburg*, J. Ryan, Dublin, 1924.

And an article: "Origins of Irish Nature Poetry," G. Murphy, *Studies*, XX, 1931. Especially this: *Monastery of Tallaght* by Gwynn and Purton (?), PRIA, XXIX, 1911.

Any texts of early Irish monastic rules would be a great help, if you let me know which you may have.

I know you like to be bothered, so I won't apologize. Especially as this is a fascinating subject that has not been treated nearly enough in this country. Maybe some day a book will come out of it . . .

To Dom Jean Leclercq

September 18, 1965

Your two packages of papers have arrived from Collegeville and they are in the hands of our guest master until you arrive. Please let us know the exact date, when you have decided. We are all looking forward to your visit. I have now been replaced in the novitiate by Fr. Baldwin (whom you may have met in Rome) but he is eagerly expecting your talks to the novices. I have received permission to retire to the hermitage and have been there over a month now. It is working out very well. I go down once a day for Mass and dinner; the rest of the time I am here alone, and later, I hope to be alone all the time. For the time being it is difficult to get Fr. Abbot to allow me to say Mass here.

For the first time in twenty-five years I feel that I am leading a really "monastic" life. All that I had hoped to find in solitude is really here, and more. At the same time I can see that one cannot trifle with solitude as one can with the common life. It requires great energy and attention, but of course without constant grace it would be useless to expect these.

Hence I would very much appreciate your prayers. But in any case it is good to have this silence and peace, and to be able to get down to the *unum necessarium* [one thing necessary].

It is a great pity I was not able to be at Collegeville. Some people think there is a conflict between solitude and rare, exceptional meetings of this kind. I do not. I think they go together, and I am not of the opinion that the hermit is supposed to be so superior to all others that he cannot profit by humbly listening to what they have to say and learning from them. In fact I am afraid that there is an element of unconscious pharisaism in our exceptional zeal for separation from the world here. But the principle does remain, and if God wills solitude for me I take it entirely on His terms. If He wants it to be absolute, that is fine. I am glad at any rate that you thought of saying a word on my behalf. I feel very ashamed for not having been able to come, especially because of this implication of "superiority" which is so silly.

Thanks especially for your offprints on the hermit life. I wish I had had them when I was writing my article, which from the bibliographical point of view is very incomplete.

I look forward to seeing you, though I suppose Fr. Abbot will make a lot of difficulties because I am a "hermit now and not supposed to see people," etc. He is delighted with this aspect of it, and in fact I am convinced that the reason why he allowed me to come so quickly (for at first he was making me wait until the end of the year) was precisely so that he would have a firm reason for denying all permission to go to the meeting of the editors of the *Collectanea*. *Omnia cooperantur in bonum* [all things work together for good].

I do hope to see you. If necessary, just come up to the hermitage; I think you know how to find it, or someone can tell you. But normally I will come down and see you in the guest house . . .

To Father Charles Dumont

September 18, 1965

Thanks for your good letter of the 14th. About "The Council and Monasticism" having appeared in a book in this country, it will also appear in England in *New Blackfriars* this fall. In the version sent to *Blackfriars* I made certain changes and I believe I actually left out the parts that Dom Samson objects to. In any case I would want you to use their version. Please write to the editor, *Blackfriars*, Cambridge, England. I do not know the name of the new one: they just changed.

You understand of course that when you receive mimeographed articles from me here, unless I say so explicitly, I am not offering you what they call "first serial rights." In other words you are always welcome to print what you want as long as you realize that unless I have written it especially for you, it has been sent to and published by some other magazine first. I forget what articles I sent you, but I am sure they are all published elsewhere. If sometime you could let me know what you are using, it would refresh my memory.

I am still not too clear about how the double edition is supposed to work. As for *Murder in the Cathedral*, give me a bit of time and I will look it up in the library. Actually as I remember it the problem of Thomas à Becket is whether or not one is allowed to *seek* martyrdom. The problem is "doing the right thing for the wrong reason." Here in the case of action and contemplation I think it is the heart of the problem. I do not think that it is valid and Christian to adopt a set a priori principles that *one will renounce all apostolic activity* regardless of circumstances, because that in effect is telling God you know His business better than He does. It is normal when one matures in the monastic life for certain contacts to become an obligation of charity. To simply say: "because I am a monk I am absolutely bound to enclosure and must never go to any ecumenical dialogues, must never attend any conferences, must never speak to anyone who has a spiritual problem," etc., is simply an evasion of God's will. It is imposing on God conditions. The true attitude, it seems to me, is to adopt a strict policy of separation from the world which nevertheless can admit of obvious exceptions, and then pursue the course of judging by *discretio spirituum* [discernment of spirits]. The way we do it here and the way I at first approached it, when I was a young professed, is that there are no exceptions to be even imagined once one has adopted what is theoretically the best. This is simply un-Christian as well as unreasonable.

When I first came here, and up until about ordination, I was a very hard-line *strictioris observantiae* Trappist. After ordination, I had enough sicknesses and problems to learn a wiser way of being a monk and I think I have learned by experience that the absolutist viewpoint is—as you know and as any real monk knows—often just an excuse for self-love and defiance of God. More and more I see that there is *nothing* but submission to God, as directly and as inscrutably as He may will it.

The solitary life is really all that I had been hoping, but it has its difficulties too. It is a real desert for the heart, *Deo gratias*, and physically there are problems of snakes, hornets and all sorts of unpleasant things: one lives in a community of animals and insects in which no rule is violated with impunity. Pray for me; I am poorer than when you last heard from me, and will probably be most indigent when you next hear from me.

To Dom Jacques Winandy

September 21, 1965

Thanks for your very good letter and for your observations which are to me precious as a confirmation of what I thought was God's will.

The more I appreciate the grace of solitude, the more I see its depth and its pure gratuity. I am convinced that for me the fullness of the monastic vocation would be impossible without this dimension of complete solitude . . .

As for your *idée bizarre*: well, I must admit it was a surprise. No doubt your humility dictated it, and I cannot agree entirely with you. I am sure the Lord will provide in His own way for the lack that may arise out of difficulties of language. At the moment I am, for my own part, delighted to be free from the responsibility of directing others and to get down to the business of caring for my own soul and delivering it from the habits of trifling and evasion which it has accumulated while dealing too much with others. However, I am sure that I want nothing but to be totally open to the Holy Spirit and completely *disponible* [available]. But as far as I can see, there is no indication that God wills me anywhere but in my present situation. As a matter of fact I am going to take good care to not push myself in any way into a kind of colony of hermits, and end up with too much talking and nonsense. There is a vague possibility that we may have one here some day, but I think more and more that it is not for us, or for me, a good idea. However, situations often change drastically overnight. It is certain that if I did not have the facilities I have here, I would want to be with you. It would be a very fine thing to have *you* for spiritual Father . . .

To Father Brendan Connelly

October 21, 1965

It is perfectly all right, as far as I am concerned, to lend the ms. [*The Seven Storey Mountain*] to Bellarmine College. As long as there is nothing done about publication . . . As a matter of fact I now have a couple of literary trustees or executors . . . For your reference, they are Naomi Burton at Doubleday and James Laughlin at New Directions.

Anyway I am glad you could do something to make the Bellarmine people happy. I am returning another one of the books along with some mimeo material. Three others went back the other day. Many thanks for them.

I really think I had better dig into the Irish material seriously. I learn from our monasteries in Ireland that no one there is doing much work on Celtic monasticism, and that is a pity, because there is so much and it is so fascinating. Hence, I will certainly ask for more, beginning now. From the lists you sent could I please have:

> *The Rule of Ailbe of Emly*, Eriu III, 1907, 92–105, same in Irish
> Eccl. Record, VIII, L871, 180–190.
> *Cormac's Rule*, Eriu II, 1905, 62–68.

Eimine's Rule, Eriu IV, 1908, 39–46.

Maelruain, fragment (Bergin), Eriu II, 1905, 221–225.

Mochuta (K. Meyer), *Gaelic Journal* V, 1895, 187–188.

Cartach, Irish Eccl. Record, I, 112–118 and 172–180, Irish Eccl.
Record 4, Ser. XXVII, 1910, 495–517.

Old Irish Metrical Rule, Eriu I, 191–208, and II, 58–59 (Strachan).

From your other list I give the numbers, as it has numbers: 1885—
(D'Arbois de Jubainville, *Rev. Celt.* IX); 1886—Gougaud, Irish Eccl. Rev.
5, Ser I. Also the following on Tallaght, which you have marked as being
there: 1893—Vendryes, *Rev. Celt.* XLV; 1894—Gwynn, Eriu IX; 1895—
Gwynn, Eriu VII and id. Eriu XII.

Do you have 1882 Geary, *Irish Homily on Poverty*, Cath. University
Bulletin XVIII, 1912, 266–279?

I am very interested in everything one can possibly get on Irish
monasticism. Also I am interested in Suibhne, and the story of Suibhne
Geilt. A reference I have to this is O'Keefe, in Irish Texts Society, XII,
1913.

Do you have Robin Flower, *The Irish Tradition?* This next is just
an inquiry; don't send it: but do you have E. Bruyne, *Etudes d'esthétique
mediévale*, Bruges, 1946? I may want it later if I can perhaps get it.

Now I think I have outdone myself in imposing on your generosity
. . . Do you have some kind of manual for learning Gaelic, just in case?
I might look it over and see how it shapes up. Since there are lots of texts
to be translated, it might be worth going into. I never thought I would
come to this . . .

To Dom Jacques Winandy

November 13, 1965

A happy feast to you and your brethren on this day sacred to the
memory of so many Benedictine hermits. I am sure we owe much to their
intercession. It is so difficult to gain access to this most beautiful of lives;
one needs much help. May they also help us to persevere in it. I am
more and more aware of what a great grace it is, and with time the depth
and beauty of the life grows on me, as also the realization that there are
many dangers and difficulties. But the Lord is always there.

We had a good time with Dom Leclercq and I had several good
conversations with him. In fact one afternoon we took him out in some
woods quite as wild as yours and we all got lost. He had much to say of
your colony and I was glad to see your picture. I have not yet dared ask
permission to grow a beard, as I continue to concelebrate with the community on Sundays and feasts and I feel the beard would not be acceptable.
Perhaps later when I have a chapel of my own, some day, I will have the
traditional beard.

You offered me your book on the Canticle of Canticles. I would be delighted to have a copy. I need material for scripture study. At present I am just reading the prophets in the Vulgate as though they were the psalter, not studying them. But I am studying other things, vg. Isaac of Stella and (do not be disedified) the poet Rilke, who is somewhat interesting. His poetic experience has analogies with spiritual experience but there are also serious differences. So also with a certain poetic solitude which he has. It is good to know of these nuances.

It is the deer-hunting season here and I will be glad when it is over, for my nearest neighbors are the deer, and this morning I saw that one of them was wounded, but I think she will be all right. How terribly saddening it is to see the cruelty of man and his insensitivity. If men needed to hunt for food here, it would be different. They hunt in order to kill . . .

To Sister Elaine M. Bane

December 24, 1965

It is Christmas Eve and the afternoon is free, so I have taken time to get a few letters in the mail. I am writing far fewer letters now, of course, but I still keep some contacts open. It is good to hear from you, and I am always interested in anything that comes from the Cloister. I think of the Cloister often and keep you in my prayers. The task of contemplative nuns today is important and difficult and the waves of change will come and unsettle many in all Orders, who cannot cope with the demand for newness. I think that we contemplatives understand better than others that renewal means the recovery of the primitive and the original, not just total innovation.

Yes, I am in the hermitage. The other rumors are all crazy, but this one is true. I have been in solitude since last August, in the woods, about ten minutes' walk from the monastery, but completely isolated, as though I were in the hills on the other side of the Alleghany river, there at Alleghany.

This has certainly been a very great grace. I rewrote the *Climate of [Monastic] Prayer* here, so that is part of the fruit of solitude I guess. The life is not easy, but I can see that for us it is the only thing. This kind of solitude is a must for me. The life is totally different from what it is in the monastery. You are completely on your own, and everything is up to you. You can't depend on anyone else to keep you going. Only God. Actually it is a very simple, comforting and consoling way to live. It is a down-to-earth existence. I have to keep busy cutting wood and so on just to keep the fire going. It is not as cold here as it is up there but it gets cold enough nevertheless and I am glad to crawl under a pile of blankets when night comes. Of course there are trials, but there is also the grace of God with which to bear them, and the assurance that all is worthwhile. You certainly see life and death in a new light, living alone. In social life, there is a great deal that has been unconsciously built in to protect man from the fear of death.

Well, I just wanted to share with you a few thoughts before Christmas and to say I will keep you all in my prayers in this season. And the best thing I can tell you is, value your contemplative vocation; prize it above everything, don't let anyone talk you out of it, and don't let anyone steer you away from solitude as long as it is God's will for you . . . Keep me in your good prayers.

To Dame B.

Dame B., writing from Montserrat in Spain, asked Merton how to go about "mental prayer," to which he replied in the following letter.

January 30, 1966

You ask about Mental Prayer. Perhaps the best thing would be to send you a mimeographed set of notes which I have. I will do this. They will take a little time by sea mail.

The basic principle for authentic interior prayer (I do not like the term "mental" prayer because it suggests that it is all in the "mind") is the same as the basis for the monastic life itself: *si revera Deum quaerit* [does the novice truly seek God]. Our interior prayer is simply the most intimate and personal way in which we seek the Face of God. Two things follow from this principle:

First, since the way we "find" the Face of God is in faith, as long as we are in this mortal life, the basis of all interior prayer is faith. And the function of faith is to purify our hearts of all that is not faith, including all imaginings and desires that have nothing to do with God and His love. On the other hand, everything willed for us by God and everything related to His love can be material for prayer if it is used by faith to seek Him. Ordinarily however we must seek Him directly, as best we can, in our interior prayer. Meditation on His words will be a great help. Because in reflecting on His words with love and faith, we open our hearts to receive secret knowledge of Him together with an increase of love.

Secondly we must seek Him and not ourselves. That is to say we must not seek some special experience or "state" but only God, and accept whatever He may will for us. In our prayer we should avoid everything that makes us uselessly examine and analyze ourselves, and simply go to Him in faith, even if it means that we have to be very patient with a form of prayer that seems dark and arid. He will teach us if we are patient and trust in Him.

I will leave further details to be answered in the notes which I will send. It is a pleasure to hear of someone from Montserrat, which is not so far from the place where I was born—on the other side of the mountains, in France . . .

To Dame Marcella Van Bruyn

February 1, 1966

Certainly I do not regard monastic letters as a distraction and I was glad to hear from you. I admit however that some of the other mail is a bit of a burden, and I have arranged so that I do not get all of it. But I thought your letter was very sensible and of course I am glad to give you my views—and perhaps a little comfort. But where does one start?

One reason why I am very glad to be away from the community—I never go to anything except an occasional concelebration—is that they have really gone ahead with the throwing out of everything that can be thrown. Prime went some time ago, but I still say it. There has been an experimental redistribution of psalms throughout the various hours to get in the ones that used to be at Prime. This means no gradual psalms at the little hours anymore (or if they appear it is only by chance). I am allowed to keep the old arrangement, and I am hoping that when we finally get the English office I will be permitted to stick to Latin and to the old way of saying it . . .

Yes, here everyone has the cowl (all solemn professed) but that is not what constitutes much of a problem because I am sure they will eventually all get rid of it. The tonsure has gone, and I don't mind that. We have really simplified quite a bit. Thank heaven all the pontificalia have more or less gone in practice if not in principle. All solemn professed now have the vote, but I think that is only right, since all have to spend the rest of their lives under the Abbot they elect. They might as well have their choice. Though I hear the life-term for Abbots may also go. You don't have that in England. I don't know what to think about it. Probably in practice it would be better to have six-year terms or something like that, and anyone who was really good could be repeatedly re-elected.

As I see it, the situation is this: I speak of the ideas prevalent at Gethsemani and I suppose we are more or less typical. Taking this monastery as a kind of pattern, I would say you find most monasteries (in this country) divided between:

1) A majority which is all for activity, expansion, or relaxation, in the case of Benedictines more and more new projects, in the case of Cistercians, much liturgy and common—what shall I call them?—goings-on of one sort or another verging on recreation. In our monasteries around the country (not here) they are more and more going in for a little tv here and there: Kennedy's funeral, then something of the Pope, and then as one might guess (I did guess it in fact a year before it happened) there

comes the need to watch a baseball game in which some "outstanding Catholic player" is involved. Isn't it hilarious? . . .

2) The minority, in some monasteries very small or nonexistent, here quite large, either wanting possibilities for solitude, even to be hermits, or wanting the small, poor, remote, experimental new foundation, of which in fact there are now quite a few. Two of the best are primitive Benedictines, and then there is Dom Winandy, resigned Benedictine Abbot of Clervaux, with his hermit community in British Columbia, mostly ex-Cistercians and Benedictines. I question the value and wisdom of some of these "small communities" that have been started by Cistercians. I know some of the men who have started them and I wonder if they really know what they are after. In some cases these communities too are very talkative and active, in fact they may at times be founded by people I rated as "majority."

The official trend in the Order is to try to hold things together with a combination of the old insistence on observance, but with the changes that have been made: as if we were the same old Order simply having a few accidental new observances. Actually the changes have gone too deep for that and I think there is going to be quite a split one of these days.

In my opinion, quite frankly, the big official ancient monasticism is in crisis. I think that the best solution for those who want the kind of thing that has been regarded as "the Benedictine life" would be to stick to something like Solesmes which will keep to Gregorian and be somewhat conservative, I believe. Perhaps some of our own French houses will do the same. But I foresee nothing but chaos in this country. Gethsemani is pretty stable so far, but anything can happen to it.

I would not venture an opinion on Stanbrook. Certainly in the spirit of the house it would have been possible to make a simple adaptation, keeping all the contemplative notes and a certain austerity, simplifying and getting rid of a lot of useless formalities. I am sure in any case that Stanbrook is one of the best places going. I suppose that in many ways you will develop as Gethsemani has, which I don't recommend, but it could be worse. In that event, what should someone like you do? I would say do not be too easily tempted to hope that there is something far better on the other side of the next hill . . .

My own position in the hermitage is really providential, because I would certainly not take gracefully to the changes in the monastery. I go down to say Mass in a chapel quite apart, in the former brothers' novitiate. It is very quiet and undisturbed, except for an occasional tractor outside. I have one meal at the monastery, to save me from my own cooking, and then return to the hermitage. I make my own breakfast and supper, but of course that is quite simple: just a question of bread and butter and something for sandwiches. In fact, since I have been on a diet for years and unable to take milk and eggs, I can have meat which really simplifies things: I often have a meat sandwich for supper and that is all I need.

No dishes to wash, nothing to cook except a pot of tea. With an open fire I have the luxury of toast.

We have had quite a bit of snow and the other night it was down to twelve below zero Fahrenheit, which was a bit brisk. But I am snug in bed and after some painful moments got the fire blazing after I got up. I admit it was a bit grim getting up: some water froze inside the hermitage near a window . . .

Really, though, everything has been going very well indeed. I like the solitude immensely for all the reasons you guessed. Never see anyone except when down at the monastery, can go for days without speaking except to say Mass, but I do have to give one conference a week to the novices and young monks still. It is only half an hour however . . .

To Dom E.

Dom E., a Dutch Cistercian, wrote to Merton about the structures of the Order and asked about monastic renewal in the United States.

February 14, 1966

. . . I have read your essay, and I must say I read it with great satisfaction. To begin with, it is very lively, intelligent, well written and human. The emphasis on "reality," which is so welcome, is supported by the approach you take. It is a very good document and I must say that it surprised me a bit: if you will understand my meaning, I had not expected much of this sort of thinking from General Chapter circles, though I know some of the young American Abbots are quite advanced (though perhaps sometimes irresponsible too). Hence it was good to see your study which is not only progressive but realistic. Though I am certainly not competent to say anything about the structure of the Order, what you say seems to me to be reasonable, and as to the spirit and life of the Order, I certainly agree with you . . .

Here at Gethsemani we have seen so many potentially good men come and make vows and then leave frustrated and defeated, one cannot go through such an experience, over a period of twenty-five years, without becoming inwardly a little negative. If I wanted to formulate reasons, I would say that I felt that it seemed that men were being consistently sacrificed for the "institution" and not even for the institution itself but for a kind of abstract institutional image: i.e. the image of the institution as "the Strict Observance par excellence" and so on. I know that many monks have not only felt but have said without hesitation that they felt this was pure pharisaism. It is a serious accusation, and I know that the genuine kindness and good intentions of Superiors show that it needs to be qualified with a more discreet judgment. Yet the accusation can be made. And I firmly believe that unless we can learn to consider the good of *men* before abstract ideas and images, or before a mere ideology of "enclosed contemplative life," our days are numbered as an institution. The number of small monastic experiments being made in this country—mostly by escapees from the "Trappists"—is significant, and yet I do not have too much confidence in these either.

I feel very fortunate that I have a margin of freedom in this hermit experiment, and I hope that I will not by lack of humility do any harm to my chances of succeeding in it. Certainly one remains a member of one's community and still subject to many of the conflicts and ambiguities which make one's brothers suffer. In terms of men, this is a good community, and they take their conflicts bravely and humanly. Pray for us and for me. I am always delighted to have some real information about what is going on in the Order, and if you feel inclined, I hope you will let me know the progress of your scheme. I shall certainly keep it, and you, and Zundert, in my prayers. The great problem in our monasteries is to achieve a greater human latitude and honesty while respecting the authentic demands of our life, and I understand that in Holland you are a little more advanced on this path than some of the rest of us. In progressive America the nineteenth century has not entirely ended, at least in some of our houses . . .

To Mother M. L. Schroen

March 17, 1966

. . . For different reasons we are prisoners of grace in one way or another. And I suppose we can both say "it is good for us to be here."

Certainly the solitary life is no joke, but I can say I have been enjoying it, and the struggle part, which is quite real, is nevertheless rewarding because it makes sense. I do not claim that it makes "explainable" sense, but it leads in a direction where I know I must go. Part of the way leads to the hospital, and next week I have to be operated on for an ancient back injury which has finally reached the point where nothing else will serve. It is not the usual slipped disk, but rather an old injury which resulted in the deterioration of a disk and now affects various nerves. Perhaps by the time you get this I will have been on the table, but I don't know. I should go up for surgery probably the 25th, which will be a very nice day to unite my Fiat to Mary's. In any event I would much appreciate your prayers . . .

Your vocation to Asia is terribly important I think. No one can say what the future holds, but certainly anything that can maintain an understanding between these continents, on a spiritual level above all, is of the greatest importance. I think often of you and of the College and all the students in your care. I have a very great love for Asian people and John Wu insists that I am really a reincarnated Chinese monk.

Whether or not I am, I love Asia and the tragic things that have happened there, and the more tragic ones that may be being prepared are not cheerful subject matter for thought. May God protect all those dear people who have so much to suffer and have such great need.

To Dame Marcella Van Bruyn

April 17, 1966

At last I have the joy of reading your fine translations of Raïssa [Maritain], and the book itself is extremely handsome. Congratulations on it! It was worth waiting for, though I am sure we would all have been happier to have it sooner. The binding is fine, but as I got the book before your letter I thought it was the Gethsemani copy and passed it on to the Library. I will get it back and give them the other. Your letter came sea-mail and I got it *only yesterday*. It did not make very good time, did it?

No—your Junior has not written, or at any rate I have not received anything. They are cutting down on my mail now—not giving me much choice in what I get or don't get, so the system can be quite arbitrary. If she wrote "conscience matter," it might stand a better chance of getting through . . .

Now I must tell you I had to go to the hospital for a serious operation on my back. I hope it has come off well but am not sure yet. It was a rather sobering experience! Had a deep effect and I hope I can cope with it all fruitfully. Pushed me a lot deeper into the desert I can tell you!

More and more I am convinced that there is much triviality under the guise of ecumenism. Good for those that can profit by it but I don't think everyone should feel obligated to get involved in every little ecumenical picnic—or to be enthusiastic about such things.

Glad about your Tibetans. We have some here in the U.S., too. They are worth knowing, much deeper and more to the point . . .

To Dom Samson (James) Wicksteed, O.C.S.O.

Dom Samson (James) Wicksteed was Abbot of Caldey Abbey on Caldey Island, Wales, and the first editor of Cistercian Studies.

May 27, 1966

Many thanks for your letter of May 15. Yes, I had heard about the English *Collectanea* [*Cistercian Studies*] and am glad to hear the first number is in press. I hope you will do well with it. There is actually a lot of interest in monastic topics among the younger generation and there might be some chance of success if your magazine is lively and discusses current issues. Of course this will not please everybody. But surely it will not be of much avail to continue giving in English little more than we have been having in French, though the *Collectanea* is all right in its way. Having said this, I suppose I am somewhat committed to trying to help as best I can. But on the other hand as you see from the enclosed copy of my letter to P. Charles [Dumont] I have been in the hospital (well, you know this from your contact with the man in Kenya) and so I am far behind with my regular work . . .

As to possible collaborators in the U.S.—what do you want, reviewers or articles? For reviews we have a bunch of students here who do well enough, our Bro. Alberic is promising, is doing some work on John of Ford. They have some writers in Georgia, a Fr. Anselm [Atkins] I believe, but I don't know how he would fit with your magazine. He is a bit "popular" in the lively sense. A Fr. Regis [Appel] at Conyers can turn out a fairly competent article or review. Fr. Charles [English] of Conyers is a good writer; you might get something out of him. His interests however are mostly literary. Our Fr. Barnabas [Reardon] studying in Rome now is a pretty smart fellow but I don't know what he can write on. You could try him out on some reviews. Our Fr. Gerard [Bryan] at Monte Cistello is doing something on St. Bernard and Teilhard de Chardin; you might ask what it is . . . A Fr. Denis from Snowmass who is now a hermit at Christ of the Desert, Abiquiu, New Mexico, is a good man and might do something for you. I am afraid however I am not in touch with the houses of the Order in this country and cannot give you much information. Our Bro. Patrick [Hart] now in Rome is really very good and is developing an interest in Celtic monasticism. He has done a couple of bulletins on it in past *Collectaneas*. I would keep in touch with him and perhaps let him review books in his field; he would be delighted and is quite competent . . .

To Father Gerard Bryan, O.C.S.O.

Father Gerard Bryan, a Cistercian monk of Gethsemani, was working on his doctorate in Rome on St. Bernard of Clairvaux and Teilhard de Chardin.

May 27, 1966

. . . I well understand that in Rome one does not write letters, except those which are to be immolated publicly in the refectory. You can tell Fr. Timothy that his last one was utterly massacred by Bro. Wilfrid. But it is always good to get a personal note. I am happy about your thesis and some time ago gave Fr. Innocent my last copy of the Teilhard piece to send you. He got the thing copied and mimeographed so there are more copies now. He may have sent an extra one to you, but here is one also. Just so you won't be short of copies of this outdated article. I am not going to try to publish it. Just got sat on for the effrontery of writing an article for a non-Christian magazine in France, which asked for one. The magazine is "too esoteric" and no monk should ever appear in it, etc., etc., etc. The usual. Has the Council affected us yet? I seem to have heard strange mutterings at one time or other about something called ecumenical dialogue, but of course that must be something perilous and communistic.

I am very interested in the possible parallel between Soloviev and Chardin. St. Bernard, too. Certainly St. Bernard's optimism about nature is right in there. Question is what does he say about matter. I don't remember. Perhaps traditional semi-Platonist ideas. In any case your best bet is to refer back to people like Gregory of Nyssa (have you looked at his "Creation of Man"? I don't know but what you might find some clues).

The Church here presents a spectacle that would shock you. The steeple is just about gone and the Church looks as if it was hit by hurricane Sally or something.

Hermit life suits me fine though I have had to be out of it partly, due to the operation. I got back full-time a few days ago sleeping and all. I am not a natural-born hermit, but the life does agree with me and it does put the heat on where the heat needs to be put in many ways. I don't feel it is a waste of time at all, and will probably write less as time goes on, though I do need work. Miss manual work at the moment; can't do anything that gets up a sweat, and that is needed. One needs to let off steam. I will always need to write something just to stay sane. What it will be God only knows. Right now I follow meekly a certain kind of providence which asks for this or that through editors. I have written very little this year that simply sprang from a pure idea of my own.

Talking about writing, I mentioned your thesis to Dom Samson Wicksteed (Caldey), now editor of the English double of the *Collectanea*. I can't for the life of me get straight information about what goes on with this publication on whose board I am supposed to be, but apparently it is now twins and the English version appears at Caldey, and is *not* the same as the French. You might do a rundown on your thesis for them, or help out in some other way. They need reviews too . . . Fr. Flavian is going to move in as hermit at the other end of my hill, Mt. Carmel, out in the weed patch that looks over to Lintons . . .

To Dom Inácio Accioly, O.S.B.

Dom Inácio Accioly, a Benedictine from Rio in Brazil, wrote Merton about the monastic studies program at Gethsemani.

June 13, 1966

. . . I am no longer Master of Novices and have been out of touch with the monastic formation program since I am now living as a hermit.

But I think I can say that the four years of the program have been considered generally successful. I will try to outline what took place when I was active in the program.

The two novitiates, brothers and choir, were united into one. Both classes of novices received exactly the same formation. Since then the two classes, brothers and choir, have been officially merged into one class of "monks" in the whole community. There are however two offices, one in English and one in Latin, and those who participate in the English office also usually have longer hours of work; that is to say they prolong the kind of life that was led by the brothers and which they sought when they entered the monastery, but there is no difference of habit, of status, or anything else. The Master of the Brothers has been eliminated and now there are "Deans" in the community to whom monks may go for consultation.

The postulancy was extended to six months for all postulants. They simply participated in the regular novitiate formation without anything special except for the necessary instruction in the choir books, beginnings of chant and so on.

During the novitiate, courses were given on the vows, on Cassian, on Monastic History, on Cistercian Fathers and history, on ascetic theology, Scripture and the Monastic Fathers, Liturgy, chant. All this was spread over two years. For my own part I also at the end of my period as novice master gave some talks on literature, especially the poetry of Eliot, Rilke, and other modern poets, to novices and to all those in the monastic formation program. The three-year monastic program after the novitiate concentrated on giving the young monks more time to read on their own and more freedom to penetrate deeply into the monastic life, rather than multiplying courses. However they did follow the lectures on the Monastic Fathers and Scripture. And they have also come to the ones on literature and some lectures on philosophy from a monastic viewpoint. Most of these courses and lectures have remained optional for the individual.

I am not too clear about the later course of studies. Those who wish to be simply monks have nevertheless participated to some extent in the studies of theology and philosophy with the future priests. But the study program is now long and I myself am not too sure who is going on to the priesthood and who is not. There is still much talk of revising the *ratio studiorum* for the priesthood in our Order, and all I can say is that everything is supremely indefinite.

To Brother Patrick Hart, O.C.S.O.

Brother Patrick Hart, a monk of Gethsemani, had just arrived in Rome, where he had been appointed to the staff of the Cistercian Generalate.

June 19, 1966

Thanks for your note from Monte Cistello and the quote from Maritain which in no way surprised me. He has always insisted on that aspect of things, as did Raïssa. I was above all happy to hear of your visit to him in Toulouse and the things he said there. The publication of Raïssa's *Journal* is not settled yet but people are still working on it. I hope something can be done. Jacques is supposed to be coming to this country in the fall.

I have horned in a bit on your Celtic field by asking the *Collectanea* to send me a couple of new Celtic monasticism jobs for review, one by Nora Chadwick and some Dublin professor. Not quite out yet but she says it will be out soon. You might get it to review for *Monastic Studies* or something. Or don't you have time for that over there?

Things are ok with me, except that I have bursitis in one elbow and can't get much work done. I would probably be better off if I could keep producing, but still it is not essential and one has to be patient about something, and after all one has to be emptied out and purified in some way or other before it is too late.

I wish you luck with Gaelic—wish I were young enough to tackle a new language but it probably would be Japanese or something of the sort. Someone tried to tell me you could learn Chinese in six weeks. Ha . . .

Best wishes to all the gang there. [Five monks of Gethsemani were in Rome at the Order's House of Studies at this time.]

To Dom Basílio Penido, O.S.B.

Dom Basílio Penido, Benedictine Abbot of S. Bento de Olinda in Recife, Brazil, introduced several of Merton's books in Portuguese.

June 20, 1966

. . . I have been meaning to write and thank you for writing the prefaces for books of mine in Brazil: it is really most generous of you to take from your valuable time as Abbot in order to do this and I certainly do not think I deserve it. I admire your charity and am deeply grateful for it.

I could write you much about the steps that have been taken in this monastery to adapt to the needs of modern vocations, but I think that by now things are pretty much the same everywhere. Successful amalgamation of the brothers and choir, concelebration, etc., etc., and a good monastic formation program. I don't think we have done anything that would be new to you. The state of things is peaceful and alive, and we are now taking over a foundation of another Cistercian monastery in Chile. Thus Gethsemani will be in South America at last.

About my hermit experience so far: I have not written much about it directly and probably will not. I will send an offprint of an article about the hermit question but you may have seen this. Actually, I have been sleeping in the hermitage for a year and a half, and have been living in it all the time (not having a job in the monastery) for nearly a year. The most obvious thing I can say about it is that it is the kind of life I have always wanted, it is what I came to the monastery for, and I am very content in it. I do not pretend to be an ideal hermit, since I am after all quite an active person and I need to keep working, writing, studying, thinking and so on. But since I manage to get along quite well with all this, I don't care if theoretically my life is open to criticism for not being one of one hundred percent pure contemplation. The rhythm of the life is totally different from that of the community and though one has a great deal of time, one "does" a great deal less.

There is less concentration and pressure and one has fewer "results" to show for one's activity. For instance, though I could read all day if I wanted to, I probably read somewhat less in terms of quantity than I did in the community. I say all my offices alone, and only go down to con- celebrate on Sundays or big feasts. I go down and say Mass in a chapel on weekdays and take two meals at the monastery now (dinner and supper) because I do not have water at the hermitage and cannot wash too many dishes, etc. Drinking water has to be carried up by hand. As I recently had a back operation, one of the brothers helps me kindly with this chore. Since this operation I cannot do much manual work and that is something I miss. I think it is necessary to use the muscles and get up a sweat. This is a big help and keeps one more peaceful. However the life is very peaceful and thoughtful, quite empty; many would be bored or go crazy but I am never bored with it. One has to struggle with illusions and deceptions, of course, but really one has to do that anywhere . . .

The hermit experiment is being looked at with a certain favor now in some monasteries, but I think there will inevitably be disappointments if too much is expected. Probably the best and most practical thing is a limited and relative solitude accessible to those who need it: for instance a day a week, or a couple of days a month, or perhaps a week of solitude in the year. Also it is to be taken into account that some genuine hermits are also somewhat eccentric in the eyes of others—the two things are compatible, and one has to consider the effect in the community if monks have trained themselves to consider a hermitage as a reward for perfec- tion. It is always better for monks to think in terms of the individual need of each person. Traditionally some were allowed solitude because they were in some way *weak*. For me it is a blessing because I had lost all ability to sleep in community, for instance. And I am much more relaxed just living according to my own tempo with plenty of time to think.

To Nora Chadwick

June 20, 1966

It was a great pleasure to receive your letter of May 28th, and I am glad to hear that you are getting so much work done, and that you and Prof. [Myles] Dillon have done a book in which you treat Celtic monasticism. I hope I will be able to review it for the magazine of our Order. Though I am not an expert in Celtic matters, I hope I will be competent to write a good appreciation. Actually, my task in the magazine of the Order (the so-called *Collectanea* [*Cisterciensia*]) is now to report on non-Christian forms of monasticism and spirituality: especially Buddhism and Islam, and it is very interesting. I am in contact with a few good people in the field, I mean people who are not simply scholars but also experienced in their various traditions. I find the contacts quite fruitful.

The day after tomorrow, the 22nd, will be the day assigned in our calendar to a commemoration of St. Paulinus. Since he is your favorite saint and certainly one of mine too, I shall offer my Mass on that day for you, and will include Eleanor Duckett also. This at least a hermit can do to show his friendship and to bring gifts from God to his friends.

Actually, I go down to the monastery every day for Mass and dinner, as I do not have water here and cannot do much dish washing. So the simplest thing is to eat one meal or two down in the community which is a little over a quarter of a mile away. I write few letters, but have time for much reading, meditation, study. I find it hard to get much writing work done, as one tends to lose interest in *accomplishing* things, though I still have to do articles on various things, perhaps too many of them worldly. But the whole question of relations with "the world" is in ferment today and it has to be treated even, and perhaps especially, by a hermit. However I shall not plague you with my conclusions, but will rather send you a little study I have done on "The Cell" which I think you will enjoy.

It is always a joy to have news of you and of your work, and I am always eager to see anything new you write about the Celtic monks or those of Gaul. The life of solitude is certainly a beautiful and peaceful one, not without its trials and difficulties, but on the whole I see that it is the best life there is. At least for me . . .

To Mother M.

June 24, 1966

Do you remember that some time ago you sent me a book of Ira Progoff, *The Symbolic and the Real*, and asked me to comment on it for one of your friends? I have no idea how long ago it was, but at the time I said I would write a comment if and when I got around to reading the book. Well, I am reading it now. So here is my comment, for what it is worth, and very late in the day too.

Essentially I agree with your own idea. The principles given in the book are excellent. This is a very good approach, especially all he says about the negative and diagnostic type of analysis which just binds people more firmly to their obsessions. His idea of a positive therapy which loosens up the flow of psychic and living dynamism is fine. On this score the book is very worthwhile. The application of the principles is good too. The only problem I have is with the relative banality of the symbols of his patients, which seem to me to be rather a letdown. I have noticed this before with the Jungian approach. Exciting theories, and then stupid mandalas by the patients. It is true perhaps that they cannot connect with traditional archetypal material, but it would certainly be a good thing if they could. It is much richer than what these patients are digging out . . .

To Dom Jean Leclercq

July 7, 1966

Thanks for your good card from Africa. I have sent some mimeographs and books to the monks of Hanga, and hope they will be able to get something out of them. I am always delighted to be of use if I can, and thus justify my miserable existence. Actually it is not miserable at all and I am getting more and more roots in solitude, so that the hermitage is to me the only conceivable kind of life. I do not claim that I am an ideal hermit, but then neither was I an ideal cenobite. I will probably cause less scandal being hidden in the woods, hence everything points to the fact that I am where I belong. But it is really an excellent life. Time takes on a completely different quality and one really lives, even though nothing apparently happens at all. The direction is all vertical, and that is what matters, though at the same time one is not conscious of it.

Fr. Flavian is having a hermitage built for himself and I think he will do well in it. This does not however mean that Dom James is entirely friendly to hermits, but at any rate he tolerates them.

After four months of unremitting and strenuously applied effort, I managed to get hold of a copy of the December *Worship* for April. It seems to have been both banned and burned around here. But I certainly appreciate your article and the fact that you included me in such a litany of monastic boat-rockers. Many thanks. I wrote you a note about this to Rome but got the wrong number on the Via di Torre Rossa and the thing came back. It must be 21: right?

I very much like your article in the recent *Collectanea* on the future role of contemplatives. In fact it is true that already in the U.S. the problem of leisure is crucial: there is no work for more and more of the youth. I am afraid the solution in the minds of some people is to put them in the army and send them to Vietnam. An active response. I am giving talks to the monks now on technology, Marxism, etc., etc., and their implications for us . . .

July 21, 1966

Thanks for your two recent notes. I will certainly do what I can to help Fr. Aelred Squire to get his book attended to in New York. The best I can do is recommend that it be read sympathetically by various publishers. However my first suggestion is this: you yourself have been published by Farrar, Straus and Giroux, 19 Union Square West. You will pass through New York in a few weeks. Why not call on Mr. Robert Giroux, one of the partners and a good friend of mine: say I suggested it, and talk to him personally? He would then take an interest and I think he would be disposed to take the book seriously. Though I do not normally accept to write prefaces these days I could probably manage an exception in this case (for a "saint of the Order," etc., etc.). If Farrar, Straus and Giroux does not accept the book, then I could try it on Doubleday, another big publisher. I think the Catholic publishers in this country would not respond . . .

I am having some books and papers sent to the nuns in Uganda, very gladly.

The summer has been pretty hot, but not bad. One thing I miss is that I cannot do much manual work; I have a bad arm and my back is still affected by the operation I had in March. I am glad to hear Fr. Aelred Squire is a hermit; I did not know that. I hope he will pray for me—and I will also remember him. I am afraid I like the solitary life very much indeed and enjoy every moment of it . . .

To Father Aelred Squire, O.P.

Father Aelred Squire, an English Dominican, was living the eremitical life in Norway as well as writing books. He later joined the Camaldolese hermits at Big Sur, California.

August 29, 1966

Many thanks for your kind and amusing letter: I did not remember you as a critic, but then I have had so many critics that it is hard to keep track of them all. And in any case the books deserved it. I would say the same about most of them myself now that I am, I hope, wiser. Or at least older.

I waited until Dom Leclercq came here before answering your letter, because I did not know exactly what was being done about your book. I understand that it is on the way here. I have already written to my publisher about it and they are interested, so when it comes I will read it and send it on to them, and we can get to the question of the preface later . . .

A visit from Dom Leclercq is always stimulating. He left us this morning and I am sure we are all the better for having seen and heard him. He has great hopes for significant change.

For my own part I have no need of further changes—except in myself. The life I have now is quite a good simple formula: I am about ten minutes' walk from the monastery and have no obligations except to give a talk once a week. I say Mass and take a meal a day at the monastery, or two now that I am still recovering from an operation. This saves cooking and dish washing. I am only responsible for breakfast and that is easy. I will indeed pray for you, and ask you to pray for me. I am making a sort of profession on September 8th. A formal commitment to remain a hermit, not a matter of vows but as far as I am concerned it is meant to be definitive . . . [See Appendix II for this document.]

To Dame Marcella Van Bruyn

[undated—August, 1966]
. . . The hunters around here are wild shots. Lightning strikes trees all around the hermitage. The other day I came within a foot of stepping on a copperhead (a poisonous snake, which I had to kill). I am not trying to make my life sound romantic, but I do think I have a good chance of making a quick exit and not lying around in bed interminably. I hope so at any rate. But I am very pleased about the "commitment" [a private vow to remain always a hermit] and being a proper hermit for good. I am angry at *Jubilee* for putting that picture of the hermitage in. The place was built for meetings with ministers, away from the monastery, hence the useless chairs. I just gave four away to another monk who is building a hermitage and will move into it this month . . . Really the life is fine; it is what I came here for, and I now realize why I felt so frustrated with the nonsense in the community about all these silly things that they get so excited about. Of course you are right to wonder about the changes: I am delighted to be out of all that and to be able to settle things in a good way for prayer and leave them that way. I still say the old office (the community dropped Prime and rearranged all the psalms). I am going to keep the office in Latin *usque ad mortem*. I read the Vulgate for my *lectio divina*. I am horribly conservative in these respects. Otherwise I am using some Zen Buddhism, etc. . . .

By the way I am reviewing the collected poems of Edwin Muir, and incidentally reading his autobiography along with them. He is quite remarkable. If you do not know him, you should. Not exactly Christian in a very formal sense, yet very Biblical too and soaked in a sense of myth, a very fine poet. A bit like Blake, a bit like Rilke. Eliot liked him . . .

I saw that my little French poem got printed in *La Table Ronde*. Jacques [Maritain] must have sent it to them. Well, I will stop now. God bless you. Pray for me and my "commitment." I hope to make it Sept. 8th, Ladyday. Pray that I may really get further and further into this. I know it is for me, and hope I will really correspond with the grace that has been given . . .

To Father Hans Urs von Balthasar

September 12, 1966

Many thanks for your letter. It is already three months ago that you wrote. I am sure that your very able translator, Fr. Alberic, will have mentioned to you several points which touch on his work. I am hoping that your book on Barth will be translated here. As for me, I have just published an article on St. Anselm where I speak much of Barth. It seems to me that, of all those who have been discussing Anselm these past few years, Barth and the Orthodox P. Evdokimov have appreciated him the best. (I have not yet read what you have to say of him. I have resigned myself to reading through *Herrlichkeit* in French.)

You have made a fine choice among my poor poems. Thank you. I only hope that the book will be worthwhile. I am very grateful for the concern you have shown for the project by writing an introduction.

Yes, I feel it is very important for us other monks to show gratitude towards a theologian such as you, who are, after all, more contemplative and more "monastic." These are the beacons that are the most helpful to us, and not arguments or novelties. As monks, we ought to live "with eyes open to the deifying light."

I am sending you in a separate envelope a small article on present-day Buddhism. I have met a Vietnamese Buddhist monk whom I love very much. To me he is a true brother . . .

To Abbot Anthony Chassagne

September 21, 1966

Instead of taking your questions in order and strictly as they are (since I am not on the scene at Mepkin), I will start with the question of the *number* who ought to be allowed to make an experiment in the hermit life at any one time. First of all, I think there is a real danger of the experiment getting out of hand and becoming disproportionate, and this would be very much to the disadvantage of the experiment itself. In a small community like yours I think two hermits would be more than enough for the time being, that is to say two who live all the time in solitude. For the others, who might want to have more solitude, I would say that several might be permitted to have a day or two or three or even a week at a time. But two "hermits in residence" I think would be plenty *chez vous* . . . It must be clear that the permission to be a hermit in the shadow of one of our monasteries must always be considered unusual and exceptional. If on the other hand it comes to be regarded as "normal" to have a sort of laura of hermits attached to the cenobium, then I think that objections based on a threat to the essence of our life might be justified. I by no means think that there should be hermits attached to all our monasteries.

It seems to me that one of the chief reasons for permitting hermits within the confines of our monastery properties is to see that too many do not leave the Order to join hermit groups. But still it should be rather normal for people to do this . . . My first point is that it is eminently desirable to prevent too wide an expansion of the hermit experiment and to take as a principle that the hermit in our Order will remain rare and exceptional, that one for a house would be normally the most, perhaps two, or three at a big place. Here there will always be exceptional conditions, I suppose. So if here we were to have four, it would be not out of the way. If however a laura is formed near here (as I once proposed) I think it would not be a good idea. I think the hermits should live alone and apart, not in a group, and that they should depend directly on the community, not have a minor Superior of their own. In other words I think they should never come to form a group within the Order, or a community within the community.

At the same time I would say that in our Order *temporary* solitude could be much more encouraged. Retreats of one day, or several days, could be quite normal for those who would benefit by them. A sort of common hermitage where people would take turns on retreat could become a normal feature of our life without endangering its essence. Such at least is my opinion.

In my opinion too much enthusiasm for the hermit experiment could wreck it at the beginning. Also I think the Order should take a good long time before coming to any formal decision about this one way or the other. Time is most important. And also I think that in the end decisions should rest with the local Superiors advised by their private councils. Even if in the Order as a whole it is decided that hermit vocations within the Order should be "discouraged" (which would be a bad decision surely), then I still think the local Superior should have the right to permit hermit experiments nonetheless, rather than letting men go to join other Orders or groups. But in any case I think there should never again be the real abuse of *forcing* those who ask to try out the solitary life to remain within our communities by fair means or foul. This is not only an injustice but it also harms our life and has a generally bad effect . . .

Now for some more personal reactions and random suggestions or observations:

1) In my own personal case I must frankly say that the permission to live alone has been the solution to all my problems. You yourself have been aware in the past of my struggle, and in case it is useful for you to speak of it I authorize you to use anything you may remember about it, whether it was confessional matter or not. I am perfectly happy in the hermitage, with the feeling that this is what I came to Gethsemani for. I have no longer the slightest desire to leave and go elsewhere. . . .

2) At Gethsemani my impression is that the community as a whole has accepted the hermits with good grace and positive approbation along with charity, sympathy and even a certain joy. Maybe they are glad to get rid of us, but joking aside I think most people are "edified," not in the sense that we are very edifying hermits, but in the sense that everyone feels there is *hope* for broader scope for individual vocations now. In other words we are a sign of hope that personal spiritual needs will be respected more than they have been in the past. We are a sign of hope that rigidity and arbitrary uniformity are perhaps now a thing of the past. This is important, and I believe that if the hermit experiment were arbitrarily squashed it would be a real scandal and it would unsettle many who themselves have no attraction to solitude. It would once again bring up the old sense of confinement and hopelessness . . . Some of us certainly had it!!

3) After one year of "novitiate," I have been allowed to make my "commitment." It is not a vow because personally I don't believe in multiplying vows. I have however committed myself to live in solitude until death as far as health may permit. When I get more decrepit than I already am, I presume an infirmary room will fill the bill. Rev. Father has also indicated that this commitment constitutes a kind of "protection" against a future Superior getting unreasonable about it. On the other hand I would say, myself, that if the next Abbot should want to stop the hermit life here, I would feel bound by my commitment to go elsewhere, with permission of course. But I think also it would constitute a kind of claim on the permission being granted, presuming it is reasonable and not obviously unjust and wild. However I think a period of probation of five years would not be a bad idea in some cases.

4) In practice and considering each hermit as an individual (which he will most definitely prove to be), I would say that Superiors must not be astounded if their hermits seem in some things almost eccentric. Each hermit is bound to be something of a nut. *Crede experto* [Believe one who has experienced this]. And the hermit life leaves one open to errors and risks. But this is perfectly normal. The hermit may make mistakes but that is his privilege; he should be allowed to learn for himself, not instantly cramped and confined with restrictions. One reservation however: he *must definitely mind his own business*. I would say without equivocation, any hermit who really disturbs and unsettles the community, by interfering in its affairs unduly and importunely, must be slapped

down at once, in the interests of the hermit life itself. On the other hand a hermit who in the management of his own solitary life makes a few mistakes or does foolish things (as long as they are not grave scandals at least) should be left to work out his solutions (with proper help) and not immediately have all the laws thrown at him at once. The purpose of the hermit life is to let a monk with the help of God's grace swim for himself in the stormy sea. It is good for him, and it is just what he needs.

The blessing of God is on our Order, I think, in its efforts at renewal, and surely if we give the benefit of the doubt to the potential solitaries, the Holy Spirit will take care of all, hermits and cenobites alike. I would hate to see a prematurely frightened and negative reaction!

To Father Tarcisius (James) Conner

October 1, 1966

Thanks for letting me see the conference by Fr. [Ladislaus] Orsy. It is as you say very good and should be made known. I hope you will keep me in mind when you run across anything like this. In reading through, I thought I would comment on one point that I think he leaves undeveloped.

This is his concept of the meaning of *animae sibi commissae*, "souls entrusted to the superior." This certainly requires much more clarification than he gives it. In fact he seems to accept it in a sense that would imply that the religious remains not only in a state of minority and tutelage but even in a sort of sub-personal condition. He only makes it worse by assuring us that here the "soul" means in fact "the whole person." As a matter of fact I do not think it does. I think that here the word "soul" is to be interpreted quite loosely as meaning something like "the interests of the soul" or the "interests of the person" or "the conditions under which the person lives and develops." In other words here I think we absolutely need a clear distinction between the person in its existential mystery and what is exterior to it, related to it, surrounds it.

It seems to me quite dangerous to suggest that the *entire person* of the religious is "held in trusteeship" (he does not use the phrase but it follows logically from the use of the concept) by a Superior. This reduces itself to a notion almost equivalent to slavery, certainly stronger than that of minority. Parents do not hold the persons of their children in trust. One can be a trustee for the interests and property of another, but never for a person himself. The concept used here implied that the person is an object, a piece of property owned by God and managed by the Superior as trustee. But it seems to me that even God does not claim complete *ownership* over the person in its radical freedom.

Not to develop this inordinately, a line for better understanding of this concept would be it seems to me this: the person is not the property of anyone. If God entrusts the person as person to anyone, it is to Christ and to the person himself, and here the term "trust" is not to be understood in the material sense of a piece of property, but in the broader sense of the person's own interests. Thus the person is entrusted to Christ and Christ makes Himself responsible for that person's salvation. The Superior can never be strictly responsible for the salvation of anyone other than himself (St. Benedict has to be interpreted in this light). The person is also responsible for his own salvation.

The Superior is a trustee in the sense that he is responsible for ensuring certain conditions which are propitious for the person of the religious to save his soul and find God while also carrying out his work for the Church. But even then he is not responsible simply and directly to God. From a certain point of view he is responsible *to the religious* (that is where the idea of service comes in). Just as a trustee for my property is responsible to me for my property, so the Superior as trustee to whom I entrust my spiritual and material needs and interests is responsible to me for these. (Obviously if I have any sense I will let him run things; presumably that is what he is there for: that is his service.)

But to leave it at that would be misleading. The responsibility of the Superior is to the *community* and it is through the community that he fulfills his responsibility to the individual and to God.

Some other points that also suggest themselves for further investigation: Is it rather naive to speak of the will of God [existing] "prior to . . ." something else that makes it known? Certainly it is most important to make clear that the Superior is not a machine who fabricates decrees of the divine will by his own fiat. But on the other hand this "prior to . . ." is strangely misleading and needs clarification. It is perhaps a relic of an old conception that looks pretty strange in a new context.

Hence the inadequacy of a conception of the will of God as the object of a communal treasure-hunt by Superior and subjects. This is good, mind you, but the way it is said leads to great ambiguities.

What he says on trust is excellent. It is the only way to get real obedience from religious. It puts the responsibility on *them* and they will usually accept it.

Later when he talks of personal uniqueness he seems to underestimate the reality of the person: he places personality in the psychological order whereas the person is a *metaphysical* concept. A person is not constituted by the sum total of his individual gifts.

However, what he says about respect for the "person" even on this level is most important practically.

To cut this short (my back hurts if I try to read sideways, watching the text from the viewpoint of a typist) I would say this conference is excellent in all its practical suggestions, but that some of the ontological and theological ideas, especially about the person, are antiquated and hence leave the way open to abusive interpretations. This is bound to be quite common in an age of transition, when people are left straddling the old and the new as they get even further and further apart . . .

To Father Callistus (Jorge) Peterson

After completing his studies in Rome, Father Callistus was sent to the foundation in Chile, where he was for a time Prior of the community.

October 4, 1966

Your card from Lima came today, just after we had buried Bro. Paul, and a few minutes after I read it I discovered a group of monks kneeling in the grass under the little tree by the greenhouse, and they were praying around Fr. Stephen who had just dropped dead. He was on his way back from his garden; it was just before dinner. They took his body into the post office and dressed him there and Fr. Flavian and I watched by the body for a while, before they took it up to the temporary Church. Another funeral tomorrow. Two in two days. The old order changeth. It will certainly be strange around here with so many old-timers gone, not to mention those who have gone or will go south to Chile soon.

I hear you had a pretty wild party with the Carmelites in Guayaquil. Hope you enjoyed the trip. You will find S.A. religious, especially Carmelites, very conservative indeed. They are all bound up in the old Spanish colonial spirit.

Today, feast of St. Francis, I am reading a book you would like and ought to have there: *Motivos de San Francisco* by the Chilean poetess Gabriela Mistral. She is one you must know about if you want to cut any ice in Chile. A very fine Catholic poet, dead now, but very well worth reading. This particular book is poetic prose, very beautiful. St. Francis has a way of inspiring good books.

It is getting colder now and Bro. Martin de Porres was up to see about giving me a gas-heater for the hermitage. Fr. Flavian has his going now and also has his electric line in. I am not able to chop much wood but I am burning up that stuff you all brought up from Fr. Idesbald's cubbyhole last summer. It goes fast.

I hope to be publishing in a quite good new Venezuelan magazine called *Zona Franca*. You perhaps ought to know about it. I don't know if it gets around down there (address: Apt. 8349, Caracas).

I can't think of much else that is important, but you can't prove anything by me around here. It just happened that I was there when Fr. Stephen died. Usually I am not on any spot, but up in the woods with the squirrels . . .

To Dame Hildelith Cumming

October 24, 1966

I think I must now remember not to call you Dame, is that right? Personally I rather liked it. I am returning the proofs as fast as I can, and will try to answer your questions.

Title page: I suppose it could be: *A Prayer of Cassiodorus*—translated by Thomas Merton. Or do you want to add on the title page the fact that the prayer comes from the *De Anima?* You will also want to put the name of the press and the date, no? I leave the details to you . . .

The queries of the proofreader have all been checked with the critical text I used. That text is in *Traditio* xvi, 1960. If you have it there maybe she would like to go through that text once. Otherwise I would not bother. I may have missed something however. The critical text seems to be worse Latin than Migne.

Please don't bother making a new device with O.C.S.O. I find that the censors of the Order themselves are using OCR and probably even the *curia ordinis*. So . . . In any case I never use any letters at all after my name (I think it Jesuitical). I think we do not need a new device, unless of course the book requires one anyway. But OCR would be perfectly all right . . .

Senator—yes, you can play it up if you like. Cassiodorus himself was probably vain about it. I leave you to judge about Oratio, but I think it might look well. Then Prayer for the English. On the other hand, will the page look nicer without? The initial letters may carry it. I don't know. You know how it is going to look. From the point of view of the text, it makes no difference really.

Sr. Marcella will be glad to hear Jacques Maritain was here recently, and we had a fine time for a day or two. Raïssa's *Journal* has finally found a publisher in this country and will get a large printing in paperback. I am supposed to do a preface.

The Stanbrook Books were at the University of Kentucky but it was not possible for me to get over there. I would not have been able to get permission just for a visit to the library, and the doctors I go to are in Louisville; otherwise I could have combined it with a visit to the doctor for a bursitis shot . . .

To Father Callistus (Jorge) Peterson

November 5, 1966

I suppose you all heard about our snowy All Souls' Day. One of the deepest snows I have ever seen around here. The next couple of days were beautiful. Today it is a dirty day with rain getting rid of the old snow.

Just want to take up a couple of points from your letter, for which many thanks. Certainly I know [Pablo] Neruda, and he is I think a better poet than Gabriela Mistral, when at his best. Anyone who wants to really understand South America needs to have read his *Residence on Earth*. This is available in English too, and I can perhaps get it for you if you like. His more recent stuff is written on whiskey and is Communist Party propaganda of little value. Still you might get to know Neruda one of these days.

The magazine *Zona Franca* is chiefly literary. It has some of the best and latest European stuff in Spanish translation. Maybe a bit too secular for you all. But it looks worthwhile. I will see how it goes when I see the issue that has my stuff in. It would probably be a good way of keeping up with culture and ideas on a world level.

Now about your hermit. Though I have no mandate to judge, I would say that this idea of going to Sweden seems to me to be very unfortunate indeed. I have kept track of his vocation, and it seems to me that now he has what he has always sought, and what he believed to be God's will for him. And he is in really good conditions, I should think. I would definitely regard his idea of moving as a temptation. But what worries me is this: he can of course do what he wants with his own life, but what he does will have a grave effect on the rest of us, because it will register in the mind of the Order and influence the thinking about hermits in the Order. If as soon as someone gets permission to be a hermit in the Order in rather unusual circumstances, he then leaves and goes elsewhere, it will have a very adverse effect. All those who are against hermits will immediately say "I told you so!" Moreover, the whole point of permitting hermits in our Order is in a way to safeguard stability, that is to say, to make it unnecessary for a man to leave the Order . . . No one should be a hermit within the Order unless he firmly intends to stay. I agree, the hermit life should have a certain unpredictability about it, but let's face our present problem . . . I do hope, then, that he will think of the rest of us and please, please not do anything rash until our own case is more secure.

I definitely feel now that anyone who gets an exceptional permission to be a hermit in the shadow of one of our monasteries should, if it works ok, consider himself bound to stability and make a point of that unless some very, very clear indication of God's will shows otherwise. The indication should be clear enough so that even Superiors would be able to see it. God knows, even Generals. And General Chapters.

To Brother Patrick Hart

November 16, 1966

Many thanks for the beautiful little Péguy book which arrived some time ago; also for your card, the previous letter, and the good word of the Padre. At the time I got it I was going into the hospital for the usual gut X-rays. Everything as usual, i.e. not bad but not perfect. May have to have another back operation, but I hope to keep away from it as long as I can. Actually however things are going ok, very peaceful out in the woods at any rate. Fr. Flavian seems happy too. Rev. Fr. still in Chile. I won't attempt to give you any community news, as you probably have more than I.

What is happening to the *Collectanea?* One gets the impression that it has folded up. It might as well. They have a stack of old reviews and "Bulletins" of mine going back a couple of years by now. I haven't heard any more noise out of Patrick [Catry] of Mont-des-Cats who used to keep after everyone for the Bulletins. Maybe the whole thing is quietly disintegrating. I suspect *Cistercian Studies* is in difficulties. Have you any inside dope on this? Where is their second number? It should have been out a long time ago. You will be pleased to hear that we have decided to drop [Marie] Tadié [Merton's French translator and agent]. She was such a nuisance to everybody, right on up to [Abbot General] Dom Ignace . . . But she did say in a letter to Dom Ignace, in so many words, either give me complete control over all [Merton's] writings in France, even magazines, or else let's drop the whole thing. I told Dom James to write ok, we drop the whole thing. Bro. Simeon says a missile whizzed by on the way to Chile in reply to that one. I haven't seen the lethal contents of the warhead yet.

You people who have changed your names (no complaints, yours was an improvement [Simon to Patrick]) will be interested to know that in the present Chinese "cultural revolution" everything and everyone is changing names: "Collaborate Joyously Avenue" turns into "Hate with Frenzy Boulevard," but the one I like best is a young Communist girl who changed her name from "Fragrant Celery" to "Look Up to Mao." As a lover of the plant kingdom, I think I will change my name to Fragrant Celery in order to keep the name alive and look up to the plants . . .

To Mother Coakley

November 16, 1966

Many thanks for the honey and for the news of your centenary. I did celebrate with you, and you can celebrate with me today which is the anniversary of my Baptism. It is good to know the One Spirit who works in us all and in all the Church—and all the Orders. And it is good to know that He has perhaps a little more freedom to be unexpected— though no matter how hard we tried we never really managed to make Him act otherwise.

The hermit life seems to agree with me. I have forgotten all the problems I may have had before and have almost too much peace. But I am not complaining. The life is not easy, but it certainly is a joy and I feel very spoiled—and very free. There is so much that goes on and takes up time and is purely and simply nonsense: and one is well out of it. True, I am not bad at dreaming up nonsense of my own, but somehow it all seems to turn out fruitful, even when it has crazy aspects.

I just wanted to share a word with you and the novices. For the rest let us be united in prayer and joy. God is so much greater than all our thoughts and acts and problems and the best thing we can do is forget ourselves entirely in Him and go along where He wishes. For me an acre of woods seems a wonderful exchange for the entire world and I would never want to trade back. In fact I was allowed to make a profession of a sort on Sept. 8th. Not exactly formal vows but a commitment to the solitary life. So let's keep praying that we will all get lost in His love. And this may help us bring more love into a world that needs it.

To Dom Jean Leclercq

November 18, 1966

Yesterday your *Chances de la Spiritualité Occidentale* arrived and I want to thank you very much for it. Though I have seen most of the articles, in fact all of them, in one form or other, it will be a pleasure to go through them all together. But of course I must above all thank you for pages 28–31, clearer to me in French than they were in the German version. Thanks for having the courage to defend someone that most people apparently don't know what to make of. That is an element of my solitude, but I do not grudge you bringing me this kind of welcome company. The desert is never absolute, or should not be! Seriously, it is a consolation to find oneself after all part of the Catholic Church and not excommunicated without appeal as Dom Calati and others would apparently want me to be. Many thanks for your charity and, I think, your objectivity too. It helps me to evaluate my own life and my own position in the Church. I am also very grateful to P. Von Balthasar for his generous introduction, or rather postface, to the little selection of my poems. The selection was good, the translations seem to me to be very well done, and I am happy with the whole book. With you and him behind me I can feel a little more confidence—not that I have yet made myself notable for a lack of it. Perhaps I have always had too much.

Reflection on my critics once again: of course they have no trouble at all finding faults in me since I have frankly discussed my own faults in public. An *ad personam* argument is not too difficult under such circumstances. I would however like to see them meet me on my own ground. Let them write spiritual journals as frank as mine and see if they will meet the test of publication. I do not fear this kind of competition because I know it will never exist, or not in the camp of these amiable integrists.

However, I have continued to produce such and another volume is on its way to you—with its faults and perhaps its merits. I trust the charity of my friends to find the merits. The book, *Conjectures of a Guilty Bystander*, is off to you today. I have an alternative title for it: "The Subjunctives of a Guilty Bartender." It is not however a "spiritual journal" anymore. There is not much that can be called "spiritual" in it. This will of course cause more comment. Those who were irritated because I published a spiritual journal (like Dom Sortais who is no longer there to complain) will now be more irritated because this one is not spiritual. The children in the marketplace.

Jacques Maritain was here in October and we had a fine visit. He is very much a hermit now, and his latest book has added a hermit voice to the contemporary harmony (or disharmony). *Le Paysan de la Garonne* is I think very fine. I think you would like it. I have heard from your friend Dom Gregory in Tanzania and will write to him soon. Also we had a true Sufi master from Algeria here. A most remarkable person. It was like meeting a Desert Father or someone out of the Bible. He invited me to come and talk to his disciples in Algeria but I told him this would be quite impossible. Yet I would love to talk to them in fact, and also to see some monasteries in Africa. But I suppose that will never be allowed. No matter. The woods are all I need.

To Father Charles Dumont

November 25, 1966

I was certainly very relieved to hear from you. I had worried about your health and was wondering what had happened to the *Collectanea*. As to *Cistercian Studies* I have seen only the first number but it looked quite good to me. I think it has very good possibilities and I think that now it has begun as a completely separate kind of magazine and is not associated in anyone's mind with the *Collectanea*, it ought to continue as such.

You ask me what should be done to help make this new magazine known. I assure you I haven't the faintest idea of such things. I imagine the thing to do would be to get the *Cistercian Studies* known in academic circles and particularly to libraries in England and the U.S. Probably this would call for a discreet campaign, sending out free numbers and a circular letter along with them: but I know nothing about all this and I do not pretend that I could help in any way. I am sure however that Dom Samson is doing a good job and will continue to do so, and he will know better than I what ought to be done. Besides, he can go around and see people and that too is quite necessary.

I have nothing on St. Aelred but I suppose you know Fr. Aelred Squire, O.P., who is living as a hermit in Luxembourg or Belgium (at

St. Vith, Belgium, in fact). [Pfarrhaus, Herresbach] has done a book on Aelred. He could let you have part of that or write an article for you I am sure.

On my piece about psychedelic spirituality, much has happened since that was written and I think I ought to add to it, at least a note. I will think about that and send on the extra material when I have it. Before the New Year, right?

About the article on the "Desert Fathers and Spiritual Fatherhood," etc., better go slow on translating it. I have had an enormous amount of trouble with my agent-translator, Marie Tadié, who is, to tell the truth, trying to get a more and more exclusive control over everything of mine published in French: she has caused enormous complications with the poor magazine *Hermès* that first obtained this article from me as a gift. She may perhaps translate it into French without our authority and sell it somewhere. She is acting quite impossibly in many respects and becoming a terrible nuisance to everyone from Dom Ignace on down . . .

I am glad to hear about the commission for the revision of the Constitutions. If I get any ideas I will let you know. As a matter of fact, living in the woods, I find I have a quite different perspective and probably if I had any ideas at all on this subject they would be useless. But if something does occur to me I will suggest it. My present thought is: if the Constitutions could be kept down to two pages it would be fine . . .

To Mother Angela Collins

December 1, 1966

. . . I must admit that the real solitary life is a whole lot better than solitude of desire or intention. It does make an enormous difference. One changes considerably, just being out in the woods, watching the sun rise and go down, and listening to the night noises of the forest. I am really having a harder and harder time getting down to work: but I know what you mean, I won't give up writing. I can't; I have too many odd jobs I have to do all the time. But I just have no desire whatever to get down to another book, though I finished a crazy book of poems recently. That's different. And I don't really want to write much about "spiritual things" either. That least of all, in fact. I have gradually developed a sort of nausea for talking about it. Except when I really have to. The words sound too empty and trivial. Not that I am immersed in something marvelous: I just live and don't feel like spinning out a lot of words about life or God or prayer. I feel in fact immensely poor and fallible but don't worry about it. Just live. Still, I suppose a lot of stuff does get turned out: do you receive the mimeographed material that they send out? I might as well send you a copy of the new book—*Conjectures*—hoping you don't have it already. I will send it along with this. A Christmas present.

Thanks for the Masses: I did of course say the one for you on Nov. 24. I hope there were many blessings for all of you on the great feast. And thanks for the one for my own intentions. I need it. Since the operation things have been rougher—yet better—than before. I can't do much manual labor and I rather miss that. But I go for walks instead. Have a gas-heater now instead of wood fires, though I have a little wood around and light a fire for a while to make toast and burn trash . . .

By now you are in Baltimore: I hope you profit by it. There is every reason why you *should* get out and go to things of this sort. It is most necessary. On the other hand there is a lot of loose talk around about religious and "the world," and one must distinguish between the good and the bad. When it amounts to a sheer capitulation to all the chaos and stupidity of worldly life, then there is no advantage whatever in being "open"—though one must have sympathy and understand. But in the end, Carmel is there to be a sign of hope to people who are crushed at the thought that the emptiness and vanity of worldly life may be "all there is." No, there is more, and there is good reason for leaving the world to find that more. No one should be guilty about doing so. So the great thing is to keep the real values of Carmel and the contemplative life, and go out to help strengthen that life by acquiring necessary information and contacts: no more . . . Far be it from me to cheat Sister R. out of a trip if she would profit by it. Still, she might get the same value out of something else somewhere else. Miami? I've been there. It's a dump. And about as far from Carmel as one could get. Also I know from experience with chant around here, it is all much less permanent than it appears to be. We have been through one thing after another here, worked on this and then on that, and then dropped all of it to start from scratch on something else. Many in the community have been soured against all of it by this continual whipping up of new enthusiasms over something that will be dropped in six months—for the next big enthusiasm . . .

To Father I.

Father I., an American Benedictine monk, wrote to Merton about the uselessness of the monastic life, to which Merton responded frankly.

December 5, 1966

. . . Doubts about the validity of monasticism are not new. They go back to the beginning. Some of the arguments were dealt with (not politely) by Jerome. There has always been and there always will be a conviction in certain minds that the monastic life is useless. Well, it *is.* It is not meant to serve some practical purpose. It is not "for" something other than itself. On the other hand, the assertion that "reality" is to be found in secular life only is patently foolish: but people will continue to make it. And in the same breath they will lament the fact that they have no time for anything, that they are always nervous and frustrated, that people get on their nerves, that the Negroes are creeping up on them, and so forth. The world has its dignities and heroisms and its servitudes: and for many people life in the world is little more than the latter. The monk should have the courage and patience to keep his life going as a sign of freedom and of peace: he should be in his own way open to the world, and he should even to some extent be able to share some of the advantages of his life with people in the world who seek a little silence and peace to restore their perspectives. The monk can also in his own way be effectively concerned with worldly problems: more effectively for the fact that he is *not* immersed in them up to his neck.

You are perfectly right that a lot of the talk against the monastic life and for more activity and commitment is simply a rush to get on the bandwagon: and monks of all people ought to realize how silly that can be, and how utterly unreal.

In this time of change there is necessarily going to be a great deal of critical talk, and some people will be most generous in pointing out the faults of others. It is easy at such a time to go around trying to find out (as the old Rabbis used to say) who it is who is preventing the Messiah from appearing. People who are insecure are usually quite aggressive towards others, and there is much insecurity today. It may mask as charity, but is not quite that. Still, it may be well meant, and there may even be something to it. The thing is to be tolerant and patient ourselves and open to new ideas insofar as they have any value: but one can't swallow all the current absurdities. Jacques Maritain has a good new book, which many will not like, discussing some of these things very frankly: *Le Paysan de la Garonne* [*The Peasant of the Garonne* in the English edition].

To Father G.

This Italian priest, who chose Merton as the subject of his doctoral dissertation, wrote to Merton asking for biographical information.

January 7, 1967

I have received your letter of December 26. Unfortunately I do not have any biographical material to send you. A few minor articles have appeared here and there with references to the subject, but nothing of any real importance, and in any case I do not read most of these things, and when I do I do not keep them. Hence I am afraid I have nothing to send. As a gesture of good will, I will enclose a brief curriculum vitae and a list of writings.

As to bibliography: one was published ten years ago but it is of course out of date. However it is possible that a copy of this may be found in the library of the General's Curia of our Order: Monte Cistello, Via Laurentina 471, Rome. I am sure the librarian there might help you better than I.

Some useful remarks on your subject have been made by Dom Jean Leclercq, O.S.B., in his book *Chances de la Spiritualité Occidentale*, pp. 28–31. Also by P. Hans Urs von Balthasar in his postface to his German edition of some selected poems of mine. The book is called *Grazias Haus* and was published by Joannes Verlag, Einsiedeln, Switzerland, last year.

Since I am your subject, I hope I may be forgiven for expressing some sentiments of my own on the subject. I am only fifty-two years old and I rather wonder if your subject can be adequately treated when I am as yet only "nel mezzo del cammin' di nostra vita". However, since I have written autobiographical books, I suppose I must regard myself as culpable for such results. But I would only remark that like every other Christian I am still occupied with the great affair of saving my sinful soul, in which grace and "psychology" are sometimes in rather intense conflict. I am certainly aware of the fact that my life is not necessarily a history of fidelity to grace. Like every other Christian, I can only admit my failures and beg the Lord to have mercy on me. I would like to say that I have never intended to claim another position than this. If certain readers have taken an exaggerated and perhaps distorted view of some of my books, it may be due to my faults as a writer. If in trying to give God thanks for His mercies I have sometimes helped others to do the same in their own lives, I am glad. But I still need the prayers and the compassion of my fellow Christians. I hope you will make clear in your thesis that this is my attitude and my conviction . . .

To Nora Chadwick

January 10, 1967

Last year you mentioned in a letter that you and Prof. Dillon were doing a book on Celtic Christianity in which there would be material on monasticism. I have been hoping to review this for the magazine of our Order, the *Collectanea*, but so far they say they have had no reaction from the publisher. Do you think you could intercede and make sure that they send me a copy? I have reviewed the Loyer book which you mentioned also, and to my untutored eye it seemed quite good. I thought he tied in Celtic monasticism with pre-Christian tendencies in a rather interesting way.

My time has been going along quietly and I suppose rather busily. I always seem to have plenty of work. The weather has not been too bad and we have had only very few days of extreme cold. The woods are as nice as ever, but this year I see far fewer deer.

To Father Matthew Fox, O.P.

Father Matthew Fox, an American Dominican whose books on creation-centered spirituality have become popular in recent years, wrote to Merton about graduate studies. According to Fox, this letter convinced his Superiors to send him to Paris.

January 23, 1967

I'll do my best to answer your questions. Unfortunately I am not too well informed as to what is available academically in this country. The first place that comes to my mind is the Institut Catholique in Paris. However I know that you ought to be able to get good comparative religion courses at places like Columbia and Harvard. My line is Buddhism more than Hinduism and I know there have been good Buddhist teachers at both these places.

For information I suggest you also write Dom Aelred Graham at Portsmouth Priory, Rhode Island, who is pretty well up on all this. If you get a chance, by all means go to India. You could spend some time at the Ashram of Dom Bede Griffiths in Kerala (Kurisumala Ashram, Vaghamon P.O., Peermade, S. India). He too will provide information I am sure. There are plenty of Yoga schools in India, like the Yoga Vedanta Academy at Rishikesh, somewhere in the north. I don't know the exact address.

Nearer home, in Montreal, there is the R. M. Bucke Memorial Society, at McGill University, specializing in comparative spirituality. They might be the most helpful at this point.

Your general direction seems good: but where is Mystical and Ascetical Theology on your program? I don't think History of Spirituality covers it well enough. Maybe you include it in moral. If I can dig up a set of notes for the course I gave in "Mystical and Ascetical Theology," I'll send it along. Admittedly, one has to start all that from scratch. The Tanquerey approach just won't do. My own stuff is out of date after five or six years.

You can do a great deal by reading the right books. The Bucke Society can keep you in touch with the new literature.

I am glad you are going to work on spiritual theology. The prejudice in some Catholic quarters against mysticism is a bit strange, when outside the Church there is such an intense and ill regulated hunger for and curiosity about spiritual experience (what with LSD and all that). I do think we are lying down on the job when we leave others to investigate mysticism while we concentrate on more "practical" things. What people want of us, after all, is the way to God.

I wish you luck in your search. Pray for me here in the woods. I feel very fortunate to have found what I was looking for. I keep you in my prayers. God be with you in everything.

To Abbot Edward McCorkell, O.C.S.O.

Abbot Edward McCorkell was the Superior of Holy Cross Abbey, Berryville, Virginia, at this time.

February 17, 1967

I do not think there should be a sweeping judgment made that would *exclude* all possibility of art work in a monastery. Artistic work is not of its very nature inimical to the life of prayer. It can be used properly and there are monasteries where it is used to very good effect, without undue aestheticism.

Here as in other such things it seems to me that one must judge according to the individual case. Two things must be considered: the individual and the community. It is possible that a person may help the community by creative work. It is possible too that he may help his own monastic life by such work. But if he is obviously going about it in the wrong way, if he is clearly using it as an evasion from other more important responsibilities, then he should not be encouraged to practice his art. This seems to be St. Benedict's idea too. Even if a person can make use of artistic talent without harm, he may nevertheless have to do something else in his work time to contribute to the livelihood of the community: but in such a case he might prudently devote a little free time to his art work.

Experience has shown, I think, that merely letting problem-children resort to art as an "outlet" is no good at all. It does not work. From your letter, I would judge that the person in question might be one such, but I have only one side of the case. However, I would be inclined to say that the Abbot General will be on your side. It is true that modern vocations do have a greater subjective need to feel that they are doing something constructive and "creative." Hence they should not be unduly or arbitrarily frustrated just to slap them down. But they must be detached and obedient in the practice of their art . . .

To Dom Jean Leclercq

February 17, 1967

. . . Your proposed Asian journey sounds fascinating. I hope you will see Dom Bede Griffiths—and please give him my warm regards. I am doing some writing for *Gandhi Marg* in New Delhi these days, but you will probably not run into them.

I thought I had sent some books to your monastery in Sweden. I am sure I did, but I will send more things to make sure. On the other hand it is one thing to send books from here and quite another to have them arrive. One never knows what happens to mail.

Your "little St. Bernard" is perhaps one of the most attractive and lively of introductions. Above all, I am glad to hear that you will say something in the Review of the S. Congregation on eremitism. I was glad to see the little *Lettre de Liguge*, but I did not think any of the hermits really said anything important. Still it was a touching and simple thing and a consolation to find others felt pretty much the same.

With Rome as it is, renewal will always be a slow struggle. The whole conception of authority all down the line is not favorable to a really spontaneous renewal, but we can be glad that things are as good as they are and not worse. The dead concepts will continue for a while to usurp the place belonging to life, but I do not think it will really matter much— except that some monasteries may finally be closed down. Perhaps that will be for the better.

I will see that the Swedish monastery gets some books and papers. Keep me in your good prayers: let us all hope we can manage to be at the same time obedient and free. It is not easy. But God is faithful, and that is my only hope.

To Sister K.

Sister K., an active Religious, wrote to Merton about social concern and renewal in her community.

March 10, 1967

Yes, I think Dorothy Day is there as an example of what it means to take Christianity seriously in the twentieth century. In our religious life, we have managed over the years to develop a kind of system that neutralizes a really radical fervor and channels it into little gestures and substitutes for real Christian action and love. This is all harmless no doubt but it is also a bit futile, and people realize it. However, we have to start from where we are, and respond to grace as we are, within our own communities and we have to take one step at a time. The main thing is to be ready to refuse nothing when the call really comes, and to be open to each little thing, each new opportunity to make our life more real and less of a systematic and mechanical routine. But we have to be patient and not demand instant sweeping results. You ought to know how much frustration and how many obstacles there are in a life like that of Dorothy Day, and at times the Catholic Worker seems to get nowhere at all: yet the sincerity is there.

Not one of us can just pick up and walk out and from then on live the Sermon on the Mount literally: yet we should want to try as much as we can to live in that spirit. There is no question that the Christian spirit is truly a spirit on non-violence and love, and Christians who support a war like the one in Vietnam are no doubt in good faith, but they are far from realizing what they are really doing, or what the war really means.

Let us all pray for one another that we may give Our Lord what He asks of us, as best we can, and each will do a little toward the renewal of the whole Body.

To Dom John Morson, O.C.S.O.

Dom John Morson, a monk of Mount St. Bernard's Abbey at Leicester, England, was at the time of this letter the Definitor for the Region of the Isles (England, Scotland, Ireland, and Wales) at the Abbot General's headquarters in Rome, and also a contributor to Cistercian Studies, *the English-language journal of the Order. He completed his doctoral studies on Guerric of Igny, one of the four "Cistercian Evangelists."*

March 29, 1967

Your letter was dated the 27th of February and postmarked the 28th, and yet I did not receive it until the other day, Holy Thursday or Good Friday. I was simply not able to write up my notes for you over the Easter Weekend, and have hurriedly done so now, aware that they are not satisfactory at all [see *Cistercian Studies*, Vol. 3/3, pp. 247–252]. I am very sorry not to have got them to you "within a week" of the time you anticipated I would receive your letter. Sometimes mail, especially important mail, has very strange things happen to it here. I do not attempt to say how or why your letter was delayed, and I know that often the postal service itself is unaccountable. So too is our front office. In any case, the letter was delayed nearly a month, and my notes, besides being in themselves of little worth, are now probably too late to be of any service to you. I am very sorry indeed.

In these notes I have not done anything to outline a theological curriculum, but simply talked around that subject, trying to bring out aspects of the monastic life which I think are largely ignored. These reflections will probably just irritate a lot of the Abbots anyway. I present them for what they are worth, as a sort of personal effort. The Order will doubtless want to take a different view of things, and at best my suggestions might stimulate a little thought on some points. If that is still possible, then I will feel that I have not entirely let you down . . .

To Dame Hildelith Cumming

April 28, 1967

(I have no idea now whether I should call you "Dame" or merely "Sister" but since you have been called Dame before it is at least sure.)

Forgive me waiting to thank you for the Cassiodorus books. They are all here now, and a wonderful success the book turned out to be, as a work of art. The cover is magnificent; I love the paper; the type is fine, and everything about it is perfect. The only thing I lament is that there were so many blank pages and I have a secret obsession about filling them, but I would not dare, of course, even to write great long messages on them. It is a most lovely book and I am more grateful than I can say for all your work and thought that have gone into it. I hope it is much liked.

One of the reasons why I have been so slow to write, besides the usual one that I have far more letters than I can intelligently handle, is that I also have a bad arm which has not been improved by an operation in Lent, and so that slows me down too. I write letters when I can, and try to keep up with things as best I can. I am not getting as much work done as I would like, but again I suppose we are all obsessed with work. But the weather has been so lovely that it is a consolation. We got a lot of wind down here when they were having tornadoes in Illinois, but otherwise it has been a beautiful spring so far.

I am secretly rather glad that I am out of the mainstream of the changes that are being made (though my own change to the hermitage is naturally rather a significant one in itself). Not because I am bothered by changes but because they are all necessarily a bit equivocal. It seems to me that just enough changes are being made to unsettle things without making things really better. In other words, much of the real value of the old is lost and nothing very new is gained. Still, I think a lot of people find life more livable and human in the monastery here: there is more time, and that is a blessing. More freedom to roam about in the woods, etc. I do think though that a lot of the frenzy for new legislation is unfortunate. Well, we shall see. There is so much more in it all than meets the eye.

I keep your priest friend in my prayers and all your intentions. I do look forward to hearing news from Stanbrook. There is an Anglican nun I know who translated some Isaac of Stella and can't find a publisher. I did an introduction for her. I wonder if some of it would not appeal to you as a possibility for a book? Doubtless it would have to be just my essay and a couple of sermons of Isaac, a small book. I can send you my part of it if you are interested.

To Father John Eudes Bamberger, O.C.S.O.

Father John Eudes Bamberger, a monk of Gethsemani at this time, was infirmarian for the community and involved in the screening of vocations to the life. Later he was elected Abbot of Genesee Abbey at Piffard, New York.

May 4, 1967, Ascension

Through the devious workings of Providence I have now fallen into the hands of a new doctor who persecutes my allergies with an entirely medieval frenzy. I am on a ruthless new diet which works, it seems, if only because of the effect upon my awestruck imagination. I have to see him again next Tuesday when all the traces of any kind of milk or cow-like effluence have been purged from my humors. (I will need to go in at eight a.m. if possible.)

The purpose of my present note is this: since allergy suddenly appears to me in all its fantastic incoherence as an object of fruitful and amusing study, I would like to read up on the current myths about it. Can you give me any reading material, any articles from medical digests, or other stuff that comes your way? It occurs to me, after reading that book of Foucault on madness, that doctors are in reality creative artists with a remarkable flair for improvisation on people's backs, elbows, guts, etc. Since I am now a museum of such creative enterprises I feel that my self-understanding would be improved if, through appropriate reading, I could come to see myself as I am: a masterpiece of medical camp.

Seriously, I'd appreciate something to read that would let me in on the mysterious thinking about allergies that is presently current.

[undated]

Thanks for the tip about Reitzenstein and recluses. To what source is this found and do we have it here?

About the levitating postulant. He is a good and interesting person. I will not speculate as to whether his experience is mystical or simply valid in a deep spiritual way. I do not question its validity in this sense. Yet, though I do not oppose his entering, I am sceptical of his vocation to this kind of life. I do not know him well enough to know whether he has the special humdrum qualities that will counterbalance his gifts and enable him to bear up under the particular strain that he is going to feel here and which he does not anticipate. If he has these qualities, he will be ok. Nothing he said proves that he has them, but nothing disproves it either. But I think he is vulnerable and that the rigidity, etc., of the place will seriously affect him. He may be able to stick it out, but whether he will grow or not is another matter. He may just get ulcers . . .

To Dom John Morson

May 4, 1967

Thanks for your letter, and I am glad that my notes on the theological training of monks were not too late or utterly useless. Certainly if there were question of publication the last sentence should be omitted, and also I would probably want to go over the text and polish it up a bit.

Be sure of my prayers, such as they are, in this time of preparation for the General Chapter. I myself am quite remote from all that is going on and I hasten to add that I am glad of my position. Indeed I fervently hope that the General Chapter will continue to approve and support the few of us who have had the grace and privilege of a greater solitude. To me it has brought the full meaning of my own monastic vocation and the solution of most of my problems. Do please pray that I may correspond worthily . . .

To Mother Peter of the Holy Face, O.C.D.

Mother Peter was Prioress of the Louisville Carmel at this time. Preparations were being made for Dan Walsh's ordination and first Mass.

May 10, 1967

Of course as far as I am concerned I want very much to keep in the background, but I cannot do anything about the curiosity and love with which people want to see Dan [Walsh]. Hence I would offer this as a solution to the difficulty: perhaps in a discreet way tell people when Dan is to celebrate there and don't let on to anyone that I will be there. Then I'll just be there and they can be surprised if they like, but I was really hoping that we would have had the place rather quietly to ourselves and you—inside the cloister would have been so perfect. However, I'll take whatever comes.

In one word: I hope to remain as much in the background as I possibly can, but it is unavoidable that it will be at least slightly "public" in the end. Let us be united in prayer for Dan and for one another in these holy days and may the Holy Spirit bring us all kinds of light and grace to grow in God's love as a result of sharing in Dan's great day.

To Mother O.

May 31, 1967

As regards the question of enclosure for contemplative nuns: certainly the principle is important, and the *purpose* is important. You should guarantee for yourself the peace and tranquillity in which your hearts can be open to the slightest call of grace without useless distractions. But this surely does not require grilles and other medieval showpieces which are mostly for psychological effect. For modern women, the prison mentality is not much help. You should feel yourselves free from the noise and useless bustle of an over-loaded life. This means that you should preserve the spirit of solitude and avoid useless contacts with the outside. But where charity comes in, as in the case of allowing other nuns to make retreats with you, I would say that you almost had an obligation to share with a few others the advantages that enclosure creates for you. Silence is the greatest luxury in the world today, and it is a true alms for contemplatives to give others a share in what they have.

On the other hand, insofar as the coming and going of strangers and perhaps the increase of talking might be concerned, it would be well if some of the sisters could have personal opportunities for greater solitude from time to time, as a compensation.

As regards an "authority" who would be helpful, I can recommend Archbishop George Flahiff of Winnipeg, who wants to help contemplative religious. The Trappist Abbot of Our Lady of the Genesee, Piffard, N.Y., is fairly near you and might be helpful. I don't know him too well but he seems a nice person. Incidentally, I would say also that contemplative nuns need a certain amount of *useful* contact, that is to say, to talk with others sharing the same ideals and the same problems, to perhaps attend conferences (at least Superiors, novice mistresses, etc.) and to learn more of what needs to be known today. This can be done without real danger to the spirit of enclosure.

To Mother Angela Collins

June 14, 1967

I hope by now you have the tape I made; I asked the nuns of Loretto to make a copy and send it on to you. On the other hand I am sure it is not quite what you wanted. But at least it is something. If I get a chance, I will try to do something more useful. Also the Carmel in Louisville copied another talk that I did for them, and that might be more up your alley. It is too bad you were not there when Dan Walsh and I concelebrated. And we had a nice talk with the community afterwards. So I hope those two tapes will at least be a sign of life and some indication that I want to help insofar as I can.

Have met the new Archbishop that Louisville stole from Savannah. I like him very much. He seems like a genuinely open and good man who really honestly does want to advance a little, and is very well disposed toward helping the monks open up too . . .

When Dan was ordained, I had a little more social life than I am used to. But I have been able to get back to the woods and get work done: finished a short book before the worst of the hot weather gets here, and hope to spend more time in reading and prayer now. In the real hot weather it is pretty rough trying to type with the sweat pouring down into your eyes, and one can't really compose well under such conditions. (Though I've had a crack at it in the past.)

How are you getting along? I hope the problems you have there are not beyond handling. I know it is certainly true that in many contemplative

communities, and active ones too, religious have been deliberately encouraged to stay on a kind of kindergarten level, and sometimes they are
just out of contact with reality. This is tragic, especially when there does
not seem to be much hope of doing much about it as things are going.
However, I do believe that in our Order as a whole there is much desire
to get moving, though Dom J. usually presents a picture that hides many
of these aspects. The General Chapter is over, and I'm not sure what has
gone on there, but apparently as a whole it was progressive. I keep you
in my own prayers; pray for me too. I like the woods better than ever,
but really need to work harder at the prayer side of things. One tends to
just "live," and it is fun.

To Father Paul Bourne

June 23, 1967

Here is the ms. of a book of poems—or rather a mosaic of poetry
and poetic prose, which New Directions wants to bring out next spring.
It is experimental, hence far out, and—well, Fr. Shane has gone to his
reward but he'd never have passed this. I think however it is in reality
very tame indeed. Anyway, here it is for the usual processing. I hope the
General isn't going to pull any funny stuff about censoring when he is
here. We expect him in July. By the way there is in the current *Jubilee*
an article on a brother from Cîteaux which I didn't bother to send you,
but I don't think it was necessary. I do hope we don't get back into that
old bind of going over everything for every magazine—as they still do in
France.

No comments on the General Chapter. I don't feel that I have the
real perspective anyhow. I just cannot say that I think this Order is going
anywhere whatever. Maybe we can comfortably die out without undue
disgrace and without everyone leaving first. Let's hope so. This does not
represent my considered opinion; I have no considered opinion, and I
am too suspicious of being, perhaps, had. But progress in my language
also includes something in the nature of challenge. If there is no challenge,
we aren't going to have anyone around . . .

June 30, 1967

Thanks for your kind letter. I do hope we can reach some kind of
real openness in the Order as regards things like censorship—and a lot
of others too. It is pointless to try to keep up this farce of rigid control
and over-control of every gnat-swallowing contortion we go through. But
we have a French General. My feeling nowadays is to just go ahead as
much as one can and wait until they feel they *have* to object. I am not
going to try to get diocesan censorship for "Cables"—I gave that up on
the poetry etc. books four or five books ago. It's absurd to send a book

like that to Spellman's boys, and distract them from moneymaking activities.

Of course I agree with you: all the monastic institutions are in trouble, we in our own way and the Benedictines in theirs—including the primitives. And all the other Orders. I have plenty of hopes for monasticism itself, but not for the institution. The sense of disillusionment and frustration one gets around the community is too strong: and one feels that they can't be kidded and jollied along anymore. There is just not enough real substance left. Except of course for those who know what they want and are more or less able to work at it on their own. I am convinced that a lot of the playing around with new gimmicks only shows up the futility of it all, even to those who claim to be happiest about it.

It certainly is a grave shame that there cannot be more open contact and mutual stimulation, and more opportunity to really get down to work on what needs to be done. As to the need for real monasticism, I couldn't agree more: and it will rise out of nowhere, or out of strange places. The appetite for it shows up in all sorts of queer things, including the hippie movement. It would be nice if we were doing something to meet that need, but we aren't: so I guess we'll have to make the best of it.

To Father Benjamin Clark, O.C.S.O.

Father Benjamin Clark, a monk of Mepkin Abbey, Moncks Corner, South Carolina, was one of the censors of the Order at this time. Originally he entered Gethsemani in 1942, so he was in the novitiate with Merton. He was later sent to Mepkin at the time of its founding in 1949.

June 30, 1967

Thanks for the return of the ms. Yes, you are right that the publisher takes care of style, spelling and all those details. I don't know quite what the book is going to do: it has to be a paperback original, because I don't want too many collections of essays one on top of the other in hardback. And this kind of stuff quickly gets out of date, with a few wars like the Israeli-Arab one breaking out in between the appearance of the original essays and the appearance of the book. I don't think Alliluyeva will be forgotten immediately. (Kosygin incidentally announced that she was really mentally unbalanced: typical.) Still, the one thing I have read of hers is not well written: terribly effusive and gushing. She needs a good editor to give her the business and get her style tightened up.

You are right of course about [Lyndon] Johnson: an operator and something of an opportunist (let's be nice and say "pragmatist"). But I don't quite know where he is going to take us. The war on poverty is just about a dead letter now, and the war in Asia is getting pretty close to the point where there is likely to be some *real* trouble. I believe that the next five or ten years are going to be pretty rough. The Near East situation is no joke at all. Well, I'm no Walter Lippmann, but it doesn't take a pro to see that things look a bit dark on the horizon. The relative helplessness of man to keep his own affairs straight becomes more and more obvious. I guess we all see that even as individuals . . .

To Dom Jean Leclercq

July 18, 1967

I have just finished reading your collection of letters on your Asian journey. Quite an experience! This is a memorable document and it could form the nucleus of a most interesting book. I hope that something more will come of it. How about working it up into a book using the material in the letters as a basis for a more amplified treatment—before the details slip out of your memory? And with more development of your monastic ideas. I am sure Bob Giroux, at Farrar, Straus and Giroux, would be very interested.

You give a very clear and forceful impression of the Church's situation and problems there. And I was glad that the picture of monasticism was, in the main, hopeful. I will be happy to help in any way by sending books to anyone who can use them. Keep me informed, and I will send things. The picture you give of Vietnam was very depressing in a way (though the monks looked good). I am glad you are coming to this country at the end of the summer and hope to see you.

It was comforting to note that all the places where you found some reality and life of prayer were places that had at least some remote connection with Cîteaux (as, for example, the foundations of La Pierre-qui-Vire) and I am glad the Trappists of Indonesia were good. Of Kurisumala I had long had a very good impression, but I was happy to learn of the others. As to the corruption that American civilization is bringing with it—that is a source of more and more sorrow to me. One feels this corruption even here, in spite of all the good there still is in the country and in this monastery. Yet there is a stink of decay, not the decay of oldness, the enfeeblement of something past its prime: but rather a splendid cancerous fullness that shines with a kind of health, a richness and a flowering of something overgrown, overdeveloped, and lacking in basic intelligence, above all in living wisdom. Here in the monastery we have a sense of struggling with futility even in the midst of great opportunity. There is now being introduced an elaborate game of dialogue in which the monastery will be divided into groups like communist cells in which everyone will discuss how to discuss, and when they have finished that will discuss possible changes; thus changes will be put off indefinitely, in the name of "discussion." It will take time to organize the cells and to make sure that they are properly indoctrinated, that they have the suitable frame of mind . . . etc.

My own life goes well. I have finally obtained permission to say Mass at the hermitage, though I will also sometimes say Mass at the monastery and occasionally concelebrate.

I hope you will come down here. Let me know and I will send the "official" invitation. I'd like you if possible to meet a woman theologian who has some strong ideas about monasticism having "lost its soul" (she is a radical eschatologist and works with Negroes) and it would be great if we could have a little discussion on this. She hopes to be here around the end of August.

To Father Charles Dumont

July 19, 1967

I would have wanted to write more on psychedelics but there is just no end to it. There are mountains of literature on it, much of it coming from the underground and really quite interesting. The psychedelic movement among the young has a sort of strange eschatological innocence, at once beautiful and pathetic, and also open to the chance of terrible damage. It is a kind of mass movement of hope and desperation like the movements that swept Europe in the late Middle Ages. A very portentous thing, and the *Collectanea* would be foolish not to take note of it. All I can send is an addition to the introductory note. It will suffice to set the two other reports in their context and bring people more or less up to date . . .

I am really rather glad to hear you have dropped off the official "team" of Constitution revisers. I think it would be bad for you to have to go through the interminable discussions and struggles to arrive at a new official formulation which may turn out to be quite useless. I want to say quite frankly that I think the chances of a really worthwhile restatement on the official level is just about impossible. I think that the best they can do is perhaps pull things together a bit, temporarily, and keep everything from going to pieces. But this is not worth the struggle of people with good minds. It is a routine job and that is all. Personally I am not getting involved in any such thing. When the questionnaire was handed around last year, I could see at once that it was hopeless and did not waste my time answering it . . . I can see no point whatever in trying to help formulate new laws or reformulating old ones, myself. That is not the business of a hermit. I want to be quite frank about this. I have seen too many people exhaust themselves doing good hard work to try to reform something, vg. liturgy, and then have the whole thing collapse around them in a few months . . . I am working in a quite different area now, that of literary criticism, where something constructive is still quite possible . . .

I am terribly sorry to hear of your continued sickness, and glad that you are once again better. But take care of yourself. The labors of Sisyphus will do you no good. Keep up the good work with the *Collectanea*; we are all grateful to you for that.

To Father M. Basil Pennington, O.C.S.O.

Father Basil Pennington, a monk of St. Joseph's Abbey, Spencer, had done studies in Canon Law in Rome and was on a commission for updating our Constitutions at this writing.

July 25, 1967

Thanks for your letter and for the interesting enclosures. I am awed by the work you people are doing on the Constitutions—and hope that something good will come of it in due time for us all.

The article on Conversatio Morum appeared in Dom Samson's *Cistercian Studies*. But there may also still be stencils around and I will have someone get more copies to you. If you still want 150 (and if there is not some way Dom Samson himself could offprint them maybe?) our mimeograph man (Bro. Martin [Michael] Casagram) could send more.

I am having him send a few copies of a new piece on "Openness and Cloister." There are other things around if I can dig them up.

I am not in a position to do these things into French, but you can get someone else to, of course, any time you like.

Sure, I'll gladly keep your work in my prayers, such as they are, and hope that the Order can come up with something that will correspond to the desires of the ones who will be its future majority and also to the demands of a real monastic life. I do feel pretty much out of touch with all this, however, where I now am [in the hermitage].

To Sister Elaine M. Bane

July 31, 1967

Thanks for your kind letter of the 17th. I will ask someone to send on some more copies of "Identity Crisis" if we have them. They may have to be run off from the stencils. I am enclosing a new one which you will probably receive in due course on the mailing list . . .

It is absolutely essential for contemplative communities to get into some kind of dialogue with one another about their problems. One of the things I can and will do: I can make tapes and circulate them. I do not unfortunately have time to do a great deal of this, but I might make one for you if you like. To make this easier for me, why don't you send me some questions and topics. Do you have a tape recorder? Mine is a Sony, and is stereo, which means that the tapes have to be played back on a quarter-track recorder (not half-track, that blurs the tracks) . . .

Sister Luke of the Loretto Motherhouse has some tapes I made for her novices and one for the Superiors of her congregation, and she might be willing to lend or send you copies of these. Sr. M. Luke, Loretto Motherhouse, Nerinx, Ky. Their problems may be different from yours but the tapes might be useful for sisters from active communities on retreat there. I think a tape library would be a good thing for the retiro. But you would need tapes fitted for your special needs.

Life in the hermitage is fine. I am now saying Mass up here and like it very much. Sometimes I still go down to concelebrate with the community or to say Mass down at the monastery. But Mass in the hermitage is what fits my life best. I do keep up with events to some extent. I do not see how one can simply shut out the world: it would be utterly unreal to do so today, at least for one in my position. And the time is really one of crisis for the country. It is literally possible that violence might sometimes take on the look of civil war in some of our cities, and there is really no reasonable solution in sight. Our country needs prayer and intercession—and penance . . .

To Father P.

August 13, 1967
. . . One of the things I had been meaning to ask you about was the Carmelite Desert. Of course I am very interested in this sort of thing. In fact sometime I'd like to discuss some of the problems of the renewal of contemplative orders in this country, and especially the problems of women contemplatives. I have a real feeling that some kind of intelligent and concerted action is needed to keep them from getting swept away by the waves in all directions at once. In general I don't think the clergy and hierarchy in this country have much awareness of what the contemplative life is all about, or what it is good for. And the nuns are probably too passive and unsure of themselves to be able to speak up for their own interests intelligently. The thing that bothers me is that there is a very real desire for contemplative experience in this country, mostly among non-Catholics, and Catholics are too dense to be aware of the fact that if we don't wake up, the need for contemplation will seek satisfaction everywhere but among Catholics. In other words, a strong, intelligent movement of renewal in the contemplative Orders and mixed Orders would be very desirable . . .

To Colman McCarthy

Colman McCarthy, a former monk of Holy Spirit Abbey, Conyers, Georgia, is a writer for The Washington Post *and other publications. His article "Renewal Crisis Hits Trappists" aroused considerable controversy.*

August 15, 1967

Thanks for your letter. Sounds interesting. I gladly contribute what ideas I can, and here they are. Use what you like or can. Under separate cover I'll send a couple of recent papers that are not in print, and you can draw on them too if you like [for an article that subsequently appeared in the *National Catholic Reporter*, December 13, 1967].

1. There is real hope for monasticism in the overall world picture: I find such hope in African monasticism, in things like the Indian ashram of Dom Bede Griffiths, in the Protestant monasticism of Taize, in the Little Brothers and the less known, more monastic Brothers of the Virgin of the Poor. But as to the established monastic institutions in America I would not say that I was exactly "hopeful." Some of them seem doomed to complete inertia. Others—like Gethsemani, Conyers, et al.—are trying to be progressive but are caught in a bind that makes real originality and creative solutions seemingly impossible. They are committed to the organizational approach, hence to building the institutional image before all else. They are not exactly bad or decadent, but in their decent prosperity, their commitment to permanent security, to their established position, their traditional place of dignity in the Church, they are bound to a certain inevitable rigidity and conservatism, no matter how hard they try to appear progressive. They thought that changes like a vernacular liturgy were revolutionary, and already in less than two years they have discovered that they were not even especially significant. Recent changes in observance will make the life more tolerable but not more meaningful. These monastic institutions have to a great extent failed in their promise to give their postulants deeply meaningful and creative lives. People are now looking elsewhere. These big Cistercian and Benedictine monasteries may survive, but they have no real future unless they show themselves suddenly capable of really radical change.

2. The misfortune of established monasticism, in America as elsewhere, is that for over a thousand years it has been solidly and completely identified with what Carl Amery calls "milieu Catholicism" and which he analyzed in Germany. Milieu Catholicism is Catholicism which is so completely committed to a social and cultural established milieu that when there arises a choice between the Gospel and the milieu, the choice is not even visible. The milieu wins every time, automatically. In such a situation there may perhaps be saints and even prophetic individuals. But the institution will strive in every way either to suppress them or to

absorb them. Instead of exercising a prophetic and iconoclastic function in the world, instead of being a dynamic and eschatological sign, such monasticism is occupied entirely in constructing a respectable and venerable image of itself, and thus ensuring its own survival as a dignified and established institution.

3. Can the younger generation in these monasteries really make a dent in the prevailing conservatism? Is the progressivism of the young really in accord with the monastic charism? Or is it merely another version of secular apostolic witness? These are questions I cannot answer. I know there is a real ferment going on in these monasteries. Unfortunately, there is a lot of ambiguity about basic values. For instance the term "contemplative life," already in some ways suspect theologically today, is used more and more negatively as the "non-active" life. In other words "contemplation" is reduced to its juridical significance: cloister and attendance in choir. The term "contemplative life" is being used defensively as an excuse to keep monks in the monastery, to keep them out of contact with the problems and needs of the world, in short to keep them out of dialogue with the world. This is disastrous. Such a use of the term will bring complete discredit on the real value of contemplation. In a clumsy attempt to protect the monastic life, this negativism will only sterilize it and guarantee its demise.

4. What am I doing personally? Without going into details, I can say I am to a great extent living on the margin of life at Gethsemani and concentrating on my own personal task, my own personal development and my contacts with people in my own fields, such as (a) poets and other writers and artists; (b) Buddhists, Hindus, Sufis and people interested in the mystical dimension of religion, whether Christian or other. These contacts remain however very limited. I had a very interesting invitation to go to Japan and visit the chief Zen centers there but permission to go was categorically refused. My Superiors, in a state of almost catatonic shock, said: "But this would be absolutely contrary to the contemplative life." Comment on this is not necessary. The invitation emanated incidentally from a Jesuit who is a consultor on the Commission for Non-Christian Religions, from a Japanese Bishop and from a Superior of the Order in Japan.

I think that ought to cover the waterfront OK. Any further questions? Feel free to ask. I'd be very interested in seeing the article, incidentally. Good luck, best wishes, God be with you.

P.S. Please for the love of God take care not to represent me in any way as a spokesman for the Order; I am anything but. I think that ought to be obvious enough, and surely you know it if you were in Georgia!! Where is Fr. Charles [Jack] English these days? Still in the Bahamas?

To Dom Jacques Winandy

August 19, 1967

. . . Thanks for giving your consideration to the needs of J.B., whom I do not know personally but who has written to me. The question of women hermits is one that seems to become increasingly actual. Sometime I would like to discuss it with you more in detail.

I am sending you the full text of the article on "Christian Solitude." It is good to realize that you like it. Certainly I leave you to consider what you think best about its publication in French. Perhaps it is too outspoken for *Collectanea*. An idea that occurs to me is this: why not get the Editions du Cerf to do a volume of essays like this by several collaborators, yourself, Dom Leclercq, and so on: various aspects of the solitary revival of today. It is time for such a book. This essay might fit in under the rubric "Monastic Hermits."

The article will also be sent to Bishop de Roo and I will show it to Dom Leclercq when he comes here next month. Dom L. has written some remarkable letters on his monastic journey in the East. They will make a book of great interest . . .

To Father Timothy Kelly and Brother Patrick Hart

Father Timothy Kelly, O.C.S.O., has been a monk of Gethsemani since 1958, and had been a novice under Merton. After studies in Rome, he was appointed Novice Master, and in 1973 was elected Abbot of Gethsemani.

August 23, 1967

I guess it is ok to answer you both with a single letter. Your letters came about the same time and I don't imagine the thing about the message of contemplatives is so secret. Anyway I hurriedly dashed off something for the Abbot of Frattocchie, but I am sure he will not like it much and will have regretted that I was ever asked to write anything. That day I was rather depressed about things in general, as we sometimes are, no? Anyway I said that I wondered if we contemplatives had anything to say to the world that could be dignified by the name of "message." I thought of the story of the "safe" Southern Negro who was asked to give a message from the Negroes of the South to the world during a racial crisis: supposedly a message that everything was ok. When he saw that he was on the air, he grabbed the microphone and yelled "HELP!" I won't say I felt exactly like that, but things are not all that simple with us. Anyway the next day I tried to add more material that was a little more positive. Here things are not what one would call disastrous, but one gets the feeling that the fort is being held for the time being and that there will be an inevitable collapse some time or other. In such circumstances I wish some kind of real action were possible, but it isn't. So, ok. God will take care of us no doubt. Fr. Bartholomew is about to celebrate St. Bartholomew's Day by leaving. I like the woods very much indeed and feel it is what I came here for anyway.

As you know we have another hermit. It pays to get tough sometimes if it means the management will be glad to get rid of you: but on the other hand two years of moral theology is an awful price to pay.

The Church, as far as I am concerned, looks very good. It is a nice, clean, peaceful, well-lighted place of worship. I am not crazy about the altar, which is either Aztec or Druidical, I am not sure which, but anyway is designed for bloody and possibly human sacrifice. The sacrifice of the heart, removed with an obsidian knife and offered to the Sun God. I hope that is not in the new liturgical books. The thing I most dislike is the throne: it is awful. As grim as the old Chapter Room throne, Dom Edmond's, remember?

All joking aside, I think that there is absolutely only one hope for Gethsemani: for those of us who have some brains to hang together (hang is a badly chosen word but it may be all too true) and try to salvage the reality of what we came here for, by hook or by crook, and to keep things going. The most Dom James can and will ever do will be to hold things together as they are and implicitly prevent any real change . . .

I am really not depressed but very cheerful, comparatively, today. You ought to hear me when I'm gloomy. Best love to all of you. *Orate pro me.* Oops, sorry: Pray for me.

To Father Filiberto Guala, O.C.S.O.

Father Filiberto Guala, a Cistercian monk of Frattocchie, near Rome, had been a personal friend of Archbishop Montini as a college student and later when he became Paul VI. The Holy Father had summoned Filiberto and his Abbot, Francis Decroix, to Castel Gandolfo to discuss the possibility of a "Message of Contemplatives" to be written by Thomas Merton, among others, and presented at the Synod of Bishops the Pope was planning.

August 29, 1967

This is just to tell you that I began working on the "message" [see letters to Abbot Francis Decroix in Volume I of the Merton letters: *The Hidden Ground of Love*] the other day and got a fair amount done, about half. But unfortunately I got a severe attack of influenza which has laid me up for two days. I am now recovering . . . Perhaps my difficulty in beginning the work was due to the fact that this sickness was already developing without my knowing it. In any case I feel better now and I hope to finish the work soon. It will then have to be typed, and I hope to mail it to you early next week. It should then reach you before September 8th.

I have not been able to look up and check Scripture references or to dig up quotations, but perhaps someone else will be able to spend an hour or two with a concordance, and others will think of quotations from the Fathers, etc., that may be to the point.

The full beauty of the Holy Father's idea did not become clear to me until I had begun working on this text.

To Brother Patrick Hart

September 1, 1967

I forgot Fr. Timothy wasn't there. Maybe you sent the letter on to him. Meanwhile I have finished the "message" and sent a copy to P. Filiberto [Guala]. The work was done throughout a bad case of flu: in and out of bed, making innumerable pots of tea, lamenting my destiny. The result is doubtless a complete calamity but anyway I got it finished and done with and now they can make theology out of it, if they can. Or just junk it and write something better.

Now will you do me a favor? I very much need an article by Paul Ricoeur, published in *Archivio di Filosofia*, Rome, 1963, nn. 1–2. The title of the article is "Symbole et Temporalité." Probably runs in two issues and doubtless the simplest would be to get the store to send them both (rather than fussing with Xerox). I'd be much obliged.

Sunday big opening of new Church, complete with air-conditioning and two organs . . .

To Father Basil DePinto, O.S.B.

Father Basil DePinto, a former monk of Gethsemani, had transferred to Mount Saviour Monastery, New York, while still in temporary profession. He has since made his stability at Mount Saviour and also does some teaching and counseling at St. Mary's College in California.

September 1, 1967

Thanks for your note; very gratifying because I would certainly hate to see *Monastic Studies* go under. It was one of the best monastic magazines (is) and the handsomest. So I hasten to send you this ms. which I have been too lazy to peddle. It was written for a non-Christian magazine in France and publication in it was prohibited by the most un-ecumenical censors of our Order in France, since the magazine was "heretical." Not the article (I hope).

It is so long that most magazines would not take it, I think, so I have just let it sit: but *Monastic Studies* has handled things this long in the past. I hope this will settle the question for both of us.

Thanks, too, for your offprint sent some time ago. Too long ago for detailed comment: though I'd mention in passing, *d'un air rêveur* [like a dreamer], that in any case whether a Christian is or is not under the Law is at least optional. That is to say whether he elects to be judged by it . . . (Galatians). Don't mind me. I'm all for good works, provided one is not in fancy justified thereby.

I do keep your community in my prayers. Pray for me, too. I am pretty much out of Gethsemani now, and glad of it to tell you the truth. Pray for Gethsemani—and its three hermits.

To Father Filiberto Guala

September 6, 1967

First of all, thank you for the moving witness of G. Ermiglia, a very fine document. Unfortunately it arrived after I had sent my "message" which simply followed the points of the outline.

Your cablegram of Sept. 4 reached me only today—by mail . . . I hastened to ask the Abbot's secretary to have a cable sent to you in reply, but I am not sure whether it was sent. In any case, you must feel perfectly free to edit the text just as you see fit . . .

I have not discussed this message very fully with my Abbot, but I get the impression that he is a little annoyed that such a message should be coming from the men in the ranks and not from the Superiors. I have no doubt he will make efforts to have some ideas of his own included in it, but as I have not discussed the matter with him I do not know what he will do. But I doubt that his ideas will be of much value for the purpose for which the message is intended.

I hope the message will progress in the best possible way and reach a form that will really be significant. G. Ermiglia certainly represents so many "worldly" people who are anxious to see *authentic* human and religious values expressed in the world, in the place of merely formal and official pronouncements which do not touch the heart of the ordinary person. He is very right, above all, in saying frankly that no one is interested in hearing contemplatives advertise their own virtues, the strictness of their lives, and their long hours of prayer.

Keep in touch. I hope that later we can discuss some of these matters and their implications in greater detail. The contemplative orders are in a rather critical condition today. I am glad G. Ermiglia ran into a good and wholesome monastic experience at Mont-des-Cats.

To Sister Miriam Benedict, O.S.B.

Sister Miriam Benedict, a Benedictine nun of Regina Laudis, Bethlehem, Connecticut, was one of several in that community who corresponded with Merton.

September 16, 1967

This is really a sort of round robin reply to all the various letters and notes, including a letter from Sr. Mildred, as well as the notes of your two novices and the note of Mother Benedict. First, to Sr. Mildred about Fr. Clifford Stevens: the trouble with him is that he is an Air Force chaplain and that means that anything I have written on war or remotely like that becomes not only unacceptable but invisible as far as he is concerned. And the invisibility extends to everything else in that neighborhood, therefore to everything I write these days.

I'd like very much to hear the songs of Janis Ian. Can I borrow it, or better, can you put it on tape? (I have a quarter-track Sony, which in fact is stereo; don't be scandalized.) While I am on that subject I have made tapes for various people and you might be able to get copies from them. I am just finishing one for the Carmel of Savannah and I guess they'd send you a copy eventually if you asked them . . . Also another one could be had from Sr. Elaine M. Bane . . . You might enjoy parts of them at least. I don't *sing* however.

The hippie movement is a sort of pathetic children's crusade-cum-monastic-movement; the joy is touching but under it all is a kind of despair that makes one sad. In the *National Catholic Reporter* the other day there was a picture of a hippie child on page one for whom, we were told, the whole world was just one big flower. But the poor little thing had vacant eyes like an idiot. One big flower!!! Tell that one in Vietnam. Or in Harlem.

On *Seeds of Destruction*, Sr. David, I have added a thing or two in this enclosed piece, "The Hot Summer of '67." Do you all know the magazine *Katallagete*? It will be in that. A radical Christian Southern magazine. I'll send a copy herewith also.

Really I think that we who have sought our identity in the monastery and found it in the Cross of Christ (there is no otherwhere) must be strong to defend our freedom against every wind of doctrine and the fashions of people who run in all directions and want us to run with them: we have our own way to go, a way of freedom and hiddenness and non-production, and we need to appreciate the peculiar joys and hazards of life in the desert, the paradise-wilderness, the loneliness and love which is our own special way. It is good to hear from the other pilgrims behind the hills of sand over there . . .

To Father Illtud Evans

September 19, 1967

Many thanks for your letter of the 11th. Glad to hear of you as always. I was invited to the Toronto thing and would have enjoyed meeting you there (might not have met in that mob). However Fr. Abbot was inexorable, and in fact did not even pass the invitation on to me. I only heard about it indirectly.

Yes, I'd heard about *The Sunday Visitor*. What will become of American Catholicism if [it] becomes a decent paper? Surely this is the end! Good Catlicks will have to read *The Wanderer*. Or the double zero or whatever it is that the right-wingers are starting. I am really happy to hear that you have a hand in it.

On the other hand: you get me at the worst possible time. In a mood of repentance for the triviality of a misspent existence, seeing the sands in the hourglass running out, contemplating the eternal years and the futility of writing some of the stuff I have written: and above all coming at last to grips with the awful insidious vice of writing prefaces and brief articles for newspapers . . . If I said yes to your invitation, it would be like an AA ending his Gethsemani retreat by walking into the nearest Bardstown dive.

Seriously, I can't do it now. I have a book to work on and have not been doing it. Have to refuse little bits and pieces of things now and get down to business or I'll never write anything serious. Not that the Sunday Visigoth is not serious, but you know what I mean.

If I once get my conscience clear by finishing a book I haven't even started, I may do an occasional piece for you in the future. Come again with a reminder this time next year and perhaps I will be in a better position then—at least for one or two articles . . .

Sorry I could not see Patrick Quinn, but it has been a bit crowded (that is part of the same problem). However don't let that deter you from stopping by when you are in this part of the country.

To Father Aelred Squire

September 25, 1967

I am sorry I have taken so long to answer your letter. Obviously it stirs me deeply, because I can read between the lines and see how mixed your feelings must be. First, however, let me dispose of the obvious worries: Naomi is surely not offended about anything. Maybe she has written you by now, but probably the whole thing is just a matter of sheer desperation and not being able to do anything with a medieval book in this country—unless it is some sort of hoax, a novel or something masking as biography. For my own part, I have not heard from Dom Samson [Wicksteed, Abbot of Caldey Abbey] either. In fact here we count ourselves lucky if we get *Cistercian Studies* at all, even when we have subscribed to it. This is not Dom S.'s fault, and as to his correspondence, since he is head of our committee for revision of the Constitutions, I think he must be about at his wits' end.

The real thing about being a hermit is of course that a hermit is outside all categories whatever. The hermit who succeeds, or thinks he can succeed, in simply having a recognizable niche—a nest of his own that everyone can account for and understand—may well be lacking an essential element of solitude. The hermit life is a kind of walking on water, in which one no longer can account for anything but one knows that one has not drowned and that this is to nobody's credit but God's . . .

I agree that solitude is a really essential element in the religious life. One does have to cut loose and float away without ties, in one way or other, and those who try to get away from that aspect of it today are deceiving themselves. Perhaps there could be a less stark, less inhuman kind of loneliness in some communities, however . . .

My chief complaint about the hermit life is that a twenty-four-hour day is not long enough to do what one would like to do. Really, didn't you find it slowed you down? I find I simply do not have the power to go on doing many things. I have to stop and vegetate. Eventually I may take root and turn into a plant. Certainly I am going to do much less work, I mean of the "productive" kind, publishable work. But I never know what kind of plan is going to come out. Everything is just what you don't expect.

Do by all means keep in touch. I hope your new place [hermitage in Norway] will be as good as any other, if not better. Pray for me, please (we may have an abbatial election here and I may have to go through the tiresome business of refusing—if anyone is fool enough to vote for me) . . .

To Father Filiberto Guala

October 13, 1967

Many thanks for the copy of *Epoca* which arrived last evening. A very fine interview with the Holy Father, and a good magazine. I am sending the revised version of my original piece, with a new title, and tied in (I hope properly) with the "Message." It may or may not be suitable for *Epoca*, and may need more editing. I am perfectly willing to have you and Mons. Macchi make all the final practical decisions on what may be necessary in view of publication. Mons. Macchi may want to make some changes to bring the article more in line with the mind of the Holy Father. My only wish was to do this to please the Holy Father and to render him this small service, hence it is "his" article to do with as he pleases. I seek only to represent what I hope to be his mind and the mind of the Church, perhaps in my own language and with my own peculiar viewpoint.

Also, as I am not a very good theologian, perhaps this article should be read over by someone. The one who springs to mind is my friend Archbishop Paul Philippe and the Congregation of the Doctrine of Faith: he would be sympathetic and would know what would be best. Would it be possible to have someone like him look it over?

The "Message" itself turned out to be excellent and I was very glad that it was so much better than the material I sent, while at the same time making some of the points I had tried to make. I am glad Dom Porion was involved. He is a person for whom I have the very highest respect, and there is no one I would rather see in collaboration on such a message. How did it turn out, was it well received by the Bishops?

I am honored to have had some part in all this and only hope that this final version is satisfactory. If for any reason you and Mons. Macchi feel that publication would be inadvisable, I leave the decision entirely in your hands and will gladly accept anything you say.

To Brother Patrick Hart

October 14, 1967

Well, it is Yom Kippur, the Day of Atonement, and I had better do some atoning by writing a few letters and trying to catch up. Many thanks for the book with the Ricoeur article. The whole thing will probably turn out to be useful, but the Ricoeur piece is important. Thanks for your good article on the Celts in the latest *Cistercian Studies*. A very nice job. That is such fine material anyway. Thanks above all for the Irish tea. It is excellent, better than anything I have managed to lay hands on so far.

I wonder how the Message finally panned out. I saw the final copy, and thought that was very good indeed. The man from Mont-des-Cats [M. Gérard Dubois] and Dom Porion certainly turned it out nicely: after all it was a tricky job, to give a message like that to Bishops. I have rewritten my own piece in the possibility that Mons. Macchi might want to place it somewhere, and I think that is what is desired. Hope I don't raise an uproar. I am in an ideal position to please nobody. But there is nothing too new about that, after all.

You doubtless have heard some of the rumors. One thing is certain. Dom James' hermitage is under construction. Perhaps as a place of retreat for days of recollection? He is off on a junket around various daughter-houses. Then the Abbots' meeting. I don't know much other house news. Things seem quiet enough . . .

To Father R.

November 6, 1967

I have not yet seen Rosemary Haughton's article that you refer to but perhaps the point about my approval of Dom Lemercier needs clarification. I wrote in praise of his monastery as a small progressive Benedictine foundation, before the matter of the group analysis came up. From what I know of the experiment, I would give it less unreserved praise, but still in general I think it justified. I do feel that perhaps he went overboard on it. As you know, the whole group is now excommunicated, which I also think very extreme. It is a sad business.

Group analysis is a perfectly legitimate and practical thing in religious communities and I think it can be carried on in the spirit of dialogue that has been recommended in these Post-Conciliar years. But I do not think that everyone in the community should be required to participate in it.

If you can find a group of religious willing to engage in analysis together, with a qualified psychiatrist, I would say the experiment would be well worth trying . . .

To Sister Mary Luke Tobin

November 8, 1967

Plans have finally matured for the contemplative Superiors to come down here, but as it is a very small group (twelve) I managed to get clearance for them to occupy our Ladies' Guest House. We will not have to resort to your hospitality unless there are suddenly six or seven more. In which case I will issue an urgent appeal.

We hope to have the talks here and you are of course invited. I do not intend to do a lot of formal lecturing but only make a few informal points at each session, to get a discussion rolling. There will be morning and afternoon sessions on Dec. 5 and 6, and a morning session on the 7th. On the 4th they want to get together among themselves and get acquainted and I will go up to meet them in the afternoon. I'll let you know later about the times. Probably something like 8:30 to 11 a.m. and 1:30 to 3:30 p.m. . . . .

To Dom Jean Leclercq

November 10, 1967

Sorry to have been silent so long. I have been over my ears in letters, etc., and cannot handle it. I was sorry when Dom James said you had written him that you were ill and needed an operation. I hope you are better. It was a pity you could not get to this country. But I hope we will see you next time.

Thanks for your interest in the "Message of Contemplatives": I thought it had fallen completely flat. I have heard absolutely nothing about it. I am sending a copy of the draft I wrote when requested to do so . . . I don't know what books of mine would correspond to what was said there, except that those ideas crop up everywhere in what I write. Especially however *New Seeds of Contemplation* (which corrects the errors of perspective in the earlier version) says a lot of what I have been trying to say. Also *The New Man*. The material is also in *The Ascent to Truth* but that (from my point of view) was an "unnatural" book. I was trying to be academic or a theologian or something, and that is not what I am.

At the moment I am writing more and more poetry and studies that deal with primitive religions.

I am very interested to hear of the big meeting in Asia. In a way I wish I could be there. Yet I am coming to a kind of inner decision on this question, in case I may need it later. Dom James is retiring here—to the immense relief of everyone!—and it is likely that the next man will be much more liberal in regard to going out to conferences and so forth. I get innumerable invitations which I have to refuse. My decision is that since I am a hermit I shall continue to do so. That is to say that I will not appear anywhere in public or semi-public, anyhow. Do you agree that this is a good decision for me? I think it is best that I stay out of the mainstream of things and mind my own business . . . In other words, Dom James has succeeded in his policy of insulation and I will not get involved in monastic affairs. It seems that his greatest fear for me has always been that I might go around monasteries talking and spreading "dangerous" ideas. I think that now, however, my "dangerous" ideas are not needed and are even a bit old-fashioned.

Keep well, peace and joy! I keep you in my prayers. Pray for me and for all of us here, as we approach our turning-point.

To Sister Elaine M. Bane

November 14, 1967

Thanks for the letter and the points for discussion. Some of them are really first-rate. All are interesting. My plan is to concentrate entirely on the basic question of ends and means, and not to get too much carried away with details of observance. The big question is to make up our minds what we are really trying to do.

It might be worthwhile if I proposed two enigmatic questions for the Sisters to think over as they prepare for this meeting.

1) Suppose that tomorrow all religious communities were dissolved

by law and you had to go elsewhere: what would you do? Would the life you took on be very different from your present life or would it be essentially the same? (In other words, would it make a difference?)

2) Why?

About the two who wish to bring companions, that's ok; we have room. If they *all* bring companions however we just won't be able to find a room big enough for the conferences. That is our one problem. (In a pinch I suppose we'd go to Loretto but that would be confusing and a bother to everyone.)

Certainly the love and grace of Christ are calling us together for His work, and I think it will be very fruitful. We do need much light but I am very confident that the cooperation and freedom and openness that seem promised will do wonders for us. We will all learn and all get grace to face the unexpected. It is exhilarating, isn't it?

P.S. One technical business point about the tapes—we'll discuss this further. The literary rights on this material and any commercial rights in any medium are controlled by a Trust that I am setting up to handle rights on all my unpublished material . . . This organization (three friends of mine, publishers) has been made necessary because there are so many collections of writings, manuscripts, etc., in various colleges. All routine permissions will be handled by this "Trust."

To Sister Mary Luke Tobin

December 2, 1967

I really appreciate the kindness of the Sisters in going to Louisville to pick up my gang of cloistered retreatants and giving them hospitality over there for the day. When you bring them over—well, they will be here by the time this letter gets to you anyhow, but they'd go straight to the Ladies' Guest House up on the hillside. I think some of them may want to go to Loretto again Thursday afternoon when we finish up here (last session Thursday a.m.). They have probably contacted you directly about that. Anyhow, you are most helpful. Cooperation around here is slightly cool. I am not quite sure whether the atmosphere is for or against, but there has been a slight amount of sobbing and foot-dragging and remarks about "Of course, you can do this only ONCE you know!" Well, we'll worry about that some other time . . .

To Mother Angela Collins

December 2, 1967

This morning I said Mass for you and the Savannah Carmel in the hermitage. I wanted to write before doing so but didn't have a chance (have had a couple of long sessions with dentists in Lexington which meant all-day trips). I prayed especially for Sr. J., but I am not surprised really. Reverend Father has been in the hospital, and is retiring now. He will have a hermitage in a place six miles away across the valley. It is a fine spot on top of a hill and the brothers are putting up a whiz of a little house for him: it will be fine all round except he will depend very much on whoever brings him his supplies. No one else could depend on that kind of service! I'd like a place like that if I could have my own jeep and take care of myself but I doubt if they'd allow it. I'm better within walking distance of the monastery where I can go get things if I need them. Rev. Fr. had a small operation which turned out quite big when they began looking for cancer, but they didn't find any. Which is a good thing and we are all grateful. The election will be in January. Pray hard we'll get the best possible man for the job. Everyone knows I intend to refuse so I don't expect anyone to vote for me: I'd be the worst possible man anyway. And having been out for nearly three years I'd hardly be able to live in the community again. And certainly would never want to go back under any circumstances (unless I was falling apart and had to be in the infirmary. Even then I'd rather be up here, unless it was necessary for someone to be right there all the time) . . .

Please pray especially for this meeting which will be going on when you get this letter. It could be very useful. I'll try to inculcate respect for those who want solitary lives and silence, not to get everyone lined up in the active parade . . .

December 5, 1967

I was just about to mail the enclosed when I got your special delivery letter. What a shame there was such a misunderstanding. I particularly wanted you to be here, but I remember getting a letter from you indicating that you probably would not be able to come. I then assumed that you had told Sr. Elaine M. Bane that you would not be coming. She told me that most of the Carmelites invited would not come because of the General's impending visitation, and that two who were coming were doing so at some risk. I had left the organization of it all to her, as the meeting was a kind of substitute for a planned meeting of an association of contemplative Superiors which had been killed by the late delegate, Vagnozzi. She was one of the moving spirits in that. So it is really her party though I particularly mentioned you as someone I'd suggest inviting. I am sure she would have been delighted to have you, but must have got the impression, in the context of other Carmelite refusals, that you really could not come.

All I can say is that I will do my best to make up to you, and will take this as an occasion to plan another meeting here, smaller, and you will definitely be invited. Maybe we could think of five or six Carmelites, and you could pick them. But much will depend on the new Abbot here and we'll have to wait to see how he turns out. The meeting began yesterday; they are a good group, and I think it will prove very fruitful. I do wish you were here. It would make it even better, and you belong with this group: you'd like them!

To Sister N.

December 10, 1967

Denise Levertov was here today, and in fact she left only a couple of hours ago. She presumed it would be all right to show me your letter, and I do want to say that I don't see any reason why you should have to go through that much nonsense. The Church does not consist entirely of bourgeois squares, however much some of them might want to make it appear so. And one should not have to go through all that fuss over a few simple and obvious rights. I don't know what you want to do about it, but certainly there are other possibilities.

For one, there is the simple possibility of changing to a congregation that understands this kind of thing better. Sister Luke, the General of the Sisters of Loretto, an observer at the Vatican Council, is near here and a very good friend of mine. I know that if you felt like changing over to her congregation you would certainly feel at home with them. They are most alive and open. Also, incidentally, as I was telling Denise, Sister Luke and I are beginning to think up ideas for a kind of small contemplative community for women in the woods near here. I haven't any guarantee that anything will come of it and anyway I know that that is not your particular problem. But evidently you could use something more freewheeling than you have and this would certainly be that.

Also you don't have to be so terribly alone out there: have you any contact with the Dominican Fathers at Oakland and Berkeley? My friend Fr. Illtud Evans would probably be of some help and I certainly suggest that you get in touch with him. I believe however that he is temporarily away from there now. (I don't have the address of the new Berkeley House right at hand but I'm sure you can find it. Otherwise St. Albert's, Oakland, ought to get him.)

I won't write much at this point, except to say that I think you are right and you should not feel too depressed by what you have had to go through. Perhaps it is not as fruitless as it may seem. I am sure you have made some of them think. You can't obviously make them agree with you. You don't have to beat your head against the wall trying to do so. They owe it to you to let you go elsewhere if you can't see eye to eye with them. There might be other angles to remember in presenting the case, if that is what you would like. I'd suggest getting in contact with Sr. Luke and trying to talk with her sometime, before you go any further. Cheer up. Things are not as black as they may seem. Don't expect other people to understand you. Some of us do, and that is about the best one can hope for, all of us! It is a lonely business, and we won't be as effective as we'd like, but we forget that God has all things in His hand and that we don't know what is happening, or what the judgment will be. I have a feeling it will be more swift than we anticipate. Then, of course, there will be other problems.

To His Brethren at Gethsemani

This humorous letter, addressed to his fellow monks in order to forestall his candidacy in the forthcoming (January) Abbatial election, bears the caption: "My Campaign Platform for Non-Abbot and Permanent Keeper of Present Doghouse."

[mid-December, 1967]

I realize that you are for the most part sane enough not to vote for a dope like me, but since there seems to be still a certain amount of confusion in some minds, I hope you will excuse me for referring to such an indelicate matter. It may be worthwhile to set down in unmistakably clear terms exactly what my position is. Just in case anyone is interested.

1. More than ten years ago I made a private vow never to accept an Abbatial election. This vow was approved by Dom James and the Abbot General, Dom Gabriel Sortais, both of whom accepted it with evident relief as a sign of the Lord's mercy and of His continued determination to protect the Order from disaster. I consider myself permanently bound by this vow and believe that under no circumstances should I consent to a dispensation.

2. My reasons:

a) My vocation is to the solitary life plus a certain amount of writing. Indications have long since made it morally certain that this is what our Lord asks of me. To accept the Abbatial office and dignity would be an infidelity to my true calling.

b) I would be completely incapable of assuming the duties of a Superior, since I am in no sense an administrator, still less a business man. Nor am I equipped to spend the rest of my life arguing about complete trivialities with one hundred and twenty slightly confused and anxiety-ridden monks. The responsibility of presiding over anything larger than a small chicken coop is beyond my mental, moral and physical capacities.

c) Even if I did once cherish a few ideas about possibilities of monastic development, these have by now become foggy and indistinct, due to the encroachments of age and mental deterioration. In any case I always knew that *nothing* I might be interested in could be accomplished in a large, well-established and highly official institution.

d) Since I have been a constant and unfailing disedification to the community for twenty-six years, it is obvious that anyone voting for me would have to be in a dubious condition spiritually. You would probably be voting for me on the grounds that I would grant you plenty of beer. Well, I would, but it takes more than that to make a good Abbot.

e) I cannot think of any single thing connected with the office of Abbot that makes any real sense to me in the context of my own life.

3. Consequently—in all seriousness—I feel obligated in conscience to do everything in my power to prevent this happening and to refuse it if it happens. I cannot under any circumstances agree that I should accept an election as Abbot. My vow and my solitary life are the divine will for me.

4. I apologize once again for putting something like this on paper, but it would be even more embarrassing to have to talk about it *viva voce*. And of course I do realize that the matter is not that urgent: few would be tempted to waste their votes on me in any case. If you threw the paper away without reading it, you missed nothing. If you got this far without feeling physically indisposed, pray for me. Otherwise, see Fr. Eudes [resident psychiatrist-monk]—and pray for me anyhow. *Tu autem Domine miserere nobis* (note conservative trend!).

To Sister Elaine M. Bane

December 21, 1967

. . . I really think we ought to keep the tapes of our conferences to ourselves. Just those who came and their communities. I don't think it would mean so much to others and besides I think it would be much smarter to keep the whole thing more confidential. I am very much afraid that someone who might not understand or get the context of it all might denounce us to some official and get the whole thing stopped. At the moment prospects for next year are very good, and apparently Dom James told Mrs. Gannon that this would be an annual event . . . By the way, pray please for Leo Gannon: he woke up the other day and found that he had lost the sight of his left eye, due to a blood clot. It was too late for medical intervention to be any good . . .

I'd like to write to all those who were here and have written back, but I doubt if I can make it or even send cards. I'll see. I am really swamped and a lot of the stuff is the kind of thing that needs at least a bare acknowledgement.

Don't take that article in the *National Catholic Reporter* too seriously by the way—if you saw it. I mean the Colman McCarthy one. It is very slanted. I don't think half these people really know what they are talking about. He is another one who is completely hung up on the active-contemplative division, and who thinks that the way to solve it is to put all the weight on the "active." Utterly stupid. He seems to think I think so too . . .

To Mother A.

The article that appeared in the National Catholic Reporter *by Colman McCarthy caused considerable reaction among Merton's correspondents. His response was typical, sharing the blame with the author.*

December 23, 1967

Just a quick response. Colman McCarthy's article was extremely slanted, I thought, and I got slanted along with him by the way he quoted me. Actually, I agree with him to some extent about the failure of the contemplative orders up to a point. I don't think they are really contemplative; they have emphasized externals more than anything; they have been rigid rather than disciplined, etc. They have not formed contemplatives. Yet there are contemplatives around, in spite of everything.

But I don't think Colman McCarthy has a clue as to what it is all about. He knows that the official Trappist life isn't working, and that's correct. But he has no idea of what a real contemplative life might possibly be. And his notions of the apostolic life seem pretty sketchy too.

About seeing the fruits of one's work: in a real contemplative life one can get along without it. In a pressured and enclosed life, people are keyed up by the ambiguities and in fact driven to expect results (better liturgy, etc.). This causes a lot of trouble. In a life of organized frustration you can't expect people to understand what it means to be completely indifferent to results—because they know rightly and instinctively that their frustration is unhealthy and that something needs to be done about it.

Don't worry about that article: it was mostly Sound and Fury, on a basis of objective truth. I felt sorry for my Abbot, but he has been noble about it. Not a murmur. Anyway, he's retiring . . .

To Mother Angela Collins

December 26, 1967

This is not an adequate answer, just the essentials. What I have been thinking of planning is a small meeting with three or four Carmelites (you pick them) and a couple of Benedictines like Mother Benedicta of Regina Laudis and maybe one of her nuns, perhaps our Mother Myriam out in California, but I think I might wait some more for her.

I'd like to keep silent during Lent if I can, so let's make it after Easter, and Easter week is all right: make it a three-day job. So if you want to, you can start planning on four Carmelites (three besides yourself) who will make it a good meeting. Any time right after Easter is good for me, but let's make it definite fairly soon.

You are right about the bishops but I just don't have time to build up a strong position that way. I have too much other stuff to do. If you want to consolidate things with bishops you know like McDonough, by all means do so. I hope to see him sometime and put in a good word. But anyway the meeting was really charismatic and everyone obviously felt it.

Pray for our election. Anything can happen . . . I have definitely scuttled my own ship by announcements that I would never accept. I hope a really good man gets it . . .

To Father Felix Donahue

Father Felix Donahue and four other monks of Gethsemani were at Monte Cistello in Rome, and were granted an indult to vote by proxy in the forthcoming Abbatial election at Gethsemani. Besides Father Felix, there were Fathers Timothy Kelly, Linus Doerner, Barnabas Reardon, and Brother Patrick Hart, some of whom were inclined to vote for Father Louis.

December 26, 1967

Your letter came through today and I am making sure that my answer gets out. I checked with Victor today—only one I saw, and he had not received your letter. He is checking with Raphael and I will follow up with the others. Obviously, however, your letters are not getting through.

Just in case my letter to Barnabas did not get out the other day, I wrote to him saying that I could not possibly handle Abbot and had moreover scuttled the ship for real by an announcement and by the enclosed document . . . My own feeling is that at the moment Flavian is absolutely the one solid candidate, the only guy around here who can make sense out of the situation . . . Flavian is the only candidate likely to get it who also has a mind of his own and won't be dominated by someone else—certainly not by Dom James. Flavian's year as hermit has done him a great deal of good. He is intent on the right things, means to get in all kinds of good people like Winandy to promote something alive, and I honestly think he can make a monastery out of the place. I can also see to some extent working with him and getting something grooving. Not that this is a sales talk, but I just think he is the one possibility that makes real sense . . . And I still think Tim has no chance, but none, this round. His turn comes next . . . [Father Timothy Kelly was elected Abbot in the 1973 election.]

To Father Filiberto Guala

December 28, 1967

Thanks for your kind letter with the greetings and news of the articles. I am praying—a little late!—for La Pira [mayor of Florence, Italy, and a mutual friend]. Your letter reached me only yesterday. I hope everything has gone well.

As to the articles, I am grateful and confused at all the trouble that is being taken for them. I hope that in due time "The Contemplative and the Atheist" may appear in the right place and will do good. I was not surprised that it was too "special" for *Epoca*. It would have been a marvel otherwise. There is no rush at all; whatever comes of it will be all right, and many, many thanks.

Back in November a group of Quakers interested in peace in Vietnam approached me about forming part of an unofficial delegation of American religious men to meet and talk with representatives of the Vietcong. I think this would have been a most important chance to try to do something but Dom James would not even hear of it! Whatever God wants, I can easily accept. But one would like to try to do something concrete. In an exceptional case one wonders if it might not be better to go out, discreetly. Would this not be more truly in accord with the unusual nature of the monk's vocation and place in the Church? I wonder.

Dom James, as you know, is retiring. Please pray for our election which will be about January 15th. I do not feel that I could accept it if they elected me, and as this is known, I do not expect to get many votes.

With my very best wishes to La Pira, and to all of you, for a good and holy and joyful New Year, in the Lord.

To Mother Henry, O.P.

Mother Henry, a cloistered Dominican nun, was stationed at the monastery of the Infant Jesus in Lufkin, Texas, at the time of this writing. She was one of the group of contemplative Superiors who attended the retreat at Gethsemani in 1967.

January 3, 1968

Thanks for your card and the pictures. You have a handsome place there. Maybe if our next Abbot dislikes hermits and throws me out, I'll come looking for sanctuary in a corner of your woods.

The real purpose of this letter is this: I believe you are the one who has the Meerloo manuscript on silence? If so, may I please have it back for a while? I have need of it temporarily—I want to reproduce some parts of it, and can return it afterwards if you still need it.

I still remember with joy the fruitful days we all spent together here. No doubt Sr. Elaine M. Bane is sending on copies of the taped remarks I made after the retreat. Hope to see you all again this year.

Do please ask your community to pray for us here and for our election, and for various questions of my own. The monks of our foundation in Chile seem to want me down there. I don't know what will come of that, or what to decide myself if the decision is up to me . . .

To Mother Angela Collins

January 3, 1968

My letter went out just when yours came in. Making this one necessary—and making me realize I shouldn't have enclosed the dittograph in my letter. You are right, it was not humble. But still I think it was a good thing it got out and I saw the different reactions. Those who knew me well liked it. Those who didn't got into orbit fast. Anyway it didn't get around too much. One thing is certain: I don't expect any votes after THAT one!

Purpose of our getting together: the old word "edification" would do if old words like "edification" were still understood. Simply to help our spiritual and contemplative lives by a kind of informal common retreat with discussion of problems and possibilities. To get to know one another, to find out what is cooking in the contemplative Orders. Under no circumstances should anyone get the impression of something official. "Retreat" would be the best word to use. I am certainly not trying to organize anything whatever. That's for the Superiors themselves when the time comes. But of course that can be discussed . . .

To Father Felix Donahue

This was the first letter Merton wrote following the Abbatial election at Gethsemani.

January 13, 1968

. . . Fortunately, Fr. Flavian was way out in front from the start— already by the second ballot he nearly had it, needed only three more votes. He took it in a big sweep on the third ballot.

I was very surprised that it went so fast . . . Despite of the fact that I had insulted the community to make them desist, I got a few votes (which I guess switched to Flavian). But I do think he will be a very good Abbot. I think we can really groove now (in the right kind of way). Also I really think that the showing of Fr. Timothy was a very good thing. I felt that when his score was announced, it made an impression, and this will be remembered. We also incidentally passed by an overwhelming majority the proposition that the Abbot should not be for life (provided the General Chapter approves). That was the big sign of hope that occurred last evening and prepared us to expect a good result today.

For all of you in Rome I can say frankly that I am most encouraged by the events of the day here. The spirit has been excellent and I feel the community is solidly behind Fr. Flavian and that he will be a broad-minded and unpolitical Abbot, not attached to power but interested in the monastic life and in the problems of people—but not in nonsense projects. In other words what I am saying to you all is: hope! It looks as good as it possibly could look in such circumstances, and your prayer has been answered to a great extent. The future will be better than the past (unless of course something goes wrong with the whole blame country which it certainly might). But as far as Gethsemani is concerned, we can truly thank God, I think. It could have been very bad, and it turned out to have been quite good.

To Dom Jean Leclercq

Merton does not conceal his excitement over the election of Abbot Flavian Burns when writing to his friend Dom Jean Leclercq in imitation of the pontifical manner of announcing a new Pope: "I announce with great joy: we have an Abbot."

January 14, 1968

Annuntio tibi gaudium magnum: habemus abbatem—I waited for the election before replying to your letter. Fr. Flavian is our new Abbot. Certainly the best man we have for the job at the moment. He is certainly also the one who will most understand the AIM [Inter Monastic Aid] meeting and I think that eventually he will consent to my going. I am most anxious to attend the meeting and believe it will be very fruitful. Certainly I am convinced that it is very important for me to meet some Eastern monks and also see some of our own Christian monasteries out there. I pray that this may be realized, though I fear that Thailand may be involved in war by December! Not sure though. There is always hope that some glimmer of sanity will still prevail in Washington.

Unfortunately if a letter of invitation has already reached Dom James, who remained in charge until the last minute and is still here as "advisor," then he will have sent a negative reply. I have heard nothing of course. I suggest you write personally to Fr. Flavian about it perhaps.

The election was only yesterday and has not yet been confirmed but I suppose it will be by the time I get this letter mailed.

As soon as I get a chance to talk over matters with Dom Flavian I shall make the following proposal: that I should be allowed to make one discreet and fruitful monastic journey each year, lasting about a month or six weeks, visiting monasteries of other religious and traditions and also some of our own. This one to the AIM conference would be the one for 1968. What do you think? Such journeys would always be kept quiet and there would be no "public" talks or anything like that. I feel this would be something quite necessary at the present stage of my vocation, don't you? I mean not only for myself but for others, as this sharing is essential. If you agree, perhaps you might mention it to him . . .

To Father Basil DePinto

January 22, 1968

We have had two of those three books read here in the refectory and they are ok, but they are past and I can't warm up interest myself. Boros sounds interesting and I might read that one day in conjunction with his book on death which I have: but I am not inclined to review it at the moment.

I do propose a review of what seems to me a most important book which most people will not run across easily. It is by a Persian psychoanalyst who is also a specialist in Sufi mysticism. The book is *Final Integration in the Adult Personality*, and I am reading it now. It could be of decisive importance for some of us in monastic renewal. If you give me the green light I'll do a review article.

Fr. Eudes does some reviewing. Our Fr. Matthew [Kelty] (subprior) would also be a good one; I'd like to see him get into this. Chrysogonus is ultra-busy composing ten liturgies a day, so he can't do anything else.

I would be especially interested in something like D. Chitty's edition and English translation of Barsanuphius and John in the *Patrologia Orientalis . . .* Or something special in *Sources Chrétiennes*.

You know perhaps that our new Abbot is Fr. Flavian. A fellow hermit. I am very happy to have him. I am sure it will mean real newness of life. Why don't you all invite him up there and ask that he bring me along?

To Mother Angela Collins

January 22, 1968

My Mass on Sunday the 14th was for your meeting. I hope it went well. I more than prayed for you during the week—I got a real nasty attack of flu which gave me a couple of particularly bad days. I hope they were not marred by impatience and were valuable for you in the Lord's sight. I had medicine, etc., here so I just stayed in the hermitage. Or rather, it would have been better if I could have stayed completely. But I did have to go out a couple of times with a high fever and that slowed down recuperation. Still, I prefer not to be in a hot infirmary.

One very important thing before I forget: I must unfortunately change the date of our possible meeting. It will not be possible to have it Easter week or during April at all. I am not sure of May, but certainly would think safer to put it off toward end of May. How about as a preparation for Pentecost? Three days or so between the 26th and 31st of May? Could you manage that?

Finally, I deeply appreciate the prayers for the election. It went beautifully. A most peaceful and charitable event, everyone quiet and happy, and in a very short time the best candidate was elected. He is Fr. Flavian, former Prior, also a hermit for a year. He has good monastic ideas, is young, is taking on the job seriously and hopefully, and has everyone behind him. I am sure that the prayers of so many holy people did much to earn us this great grace . . .

To Mother Mary Francis Clare McLaughlin, O.C.S.

The Prioress of the New Orleans Poor Clares, Mother Francis Clare was responsible for the "Shalom" sign at the door of Merton's hermitage.

January 28, 1968

Thanks so much for the "Shalom" sign, which now hangs by my door. One of the first to be greeted by it was a Benedictine from Jerusalem who was suitably impressed.

We have a very good new Abbot. Your prayers have been very much appreciated in this regard. In fact he is one of the other hermits. And is open to meetings like the one we had in December. So I think the future is hopeful.

Dom James is still with us. I was out and took a look at his trailer, which is all ready for him as a temporary dwelling till his hilltop retreat is finished. It is in a hidden cozy spot, but there is quite a lot of mud on the way to it . . .

To Father Julian Rochford, O.S.B.

Father Rochford, a monk of the Benedictine abbey of Ampleforth, in York, England, had written Merton about the action-contemplation problem in monastic communities.

February 1, 1968

I think your letter reflects a very sound and reasonable working out of the action-contemplation problem in the concrete. Such a working out is really a matter for the individual, in the sense that in practice we all have to reach some kind of dynamic balance, no matter what our theoretical program might be.

For my own part I have tended to be more and more diffident of definitions. The elements set forth by David Knowles seem to me reasonable, and he is right that "works" should be subordinated to these other "essentials." I do think there is a place, and an important one, for so-called monasticism *sine addito* [without additions, i.e. parishes and schools], or one in which the community is not committed to furnish some kind of work other than running itself. Of course this does not escape the dilemma by any means, but simply puts it in a different form which should, ideally, be simpler. But in fact it causes a different kind of self-searching—and the Cistercians in the U.S. are quite deep in this at the moment. (I don't know if you see the *National Catholic Reporter* in which there has been some noisy and not always relevant discussion.)

In the long run, it seems to me that the monastic life is ordered to the radical transformation of the one called to it, in and through his common life with his brothers in Christ: the most complete metanoia (*conversatio morum*) ideally ending in complete openness to the Spirit of Love and complete surrender to that Spirit. Which of course could mean all kinds of things: eremitical solitude, pilgrim life, preaching to people of utterly different faiths (or dialogue with same!), works of mercy . . .

I am only paraphrasing David Knowles when I say that a school, or whatever other work the community is engaged in, should be seen as furthering this kind of life and not become a systematic impediment to it. But that also applies to anything—from the liturgical movement to cheese factories and breweries. And perhaps in the end when this has been said, nothing much has been said anyway. The contemporary approach seems to me much sounder than the old one because it leaves much more scope for dealing with unpredictable details.

To Father J.

Father J., a Cistercian monk from another U.S. monastery, wrote to Merton about introducing Eastern methods of prayer.

February 14, 1968

Actually I am getting a lot of questions about the discipline thing so I guess the best thing I can do is mimeograph some notes, but they won't be anything very new.

Actually, what I am thinking of is a mixture of traditional monastic ascesis and some interesting ideas on psychoanalysis which have been thought up by existentialist analysts like Victor Frankl and a Persian who knows a lot about Sufism and is also an analyst. I hope to do a review of a book of his soon in *Monastic Studies*. Also Zen.

I do think the one thing we need in the whole movement for a new monasticism is people with experience—not just old grads of the Trappist college of hard knocks. It takes a bit of working for, and yet as you say when one has worked hard for it he still knows he can only wait on grace. And it is pretty hard to tell people what to do. If I were more able to get around I would really like to visit some of the places where this is done systematically—meditation centers in Burma, Tibetan monasteries blossoming out in England, New Jersey and God knows where, the Zen center in the mountains behind Monterey and so on. But what I think is important is not so much the sitting around cross-legged as the realization of what kind of breakthrough we might expect if we do open ourselves up a bit and are willing to push, be dragged, or something. And of course a lot of the pseudo-Asian stuff is sheer fantasy and perhaps also trickery.

R. H. Zaehner is good on comparative mysticism. Arberry on Sufism I like. A lot of the books on Zen are worthwhile. For example, Alan Watts' "Psychotherapy East and West," while not being anything special, has some useful ideas in it (he is not always very deep though). Victor Frankl's books are I think a must, even though they are not specifically about spiritual guidance . . .

To Sister Elaine M. Bane

February 16, 1968

Thanks for the list of the people who are getting the tapes. In a while I hope to send you a rather unusual one, on "Cargo Movements." Something one hears nothing about, and new in many ways. You'll see. It may be quite stimulating for some. And perplex others.

What I really want to write about: would you like to come down here for a small meeting toward the end of May, in the week before Pentecost? Like May 27th to 30th? I am only inviting a few, the Carmelite Prioress of Savannah who couldn't come in December and who will pick a couple of Carmelites. Then you and maybe the Benedictine Prioress of Regina Laudis. Not for any big business, but a get-together and a conference and since the woods are prettier then we might sit around under the trees. Let me know if you can make it. I'm keeping this down to seven or eight at the most as we can't hope to have the whole guest house at such a time.

One other thing I have been meaning to ask: could someone, sometime (no hurry at all) jot down a very brief résumé of the tapes of our meeting last December. Just a page or page and a half to a side so that I can recall in general what we covered. I don't want to be going over the same ground again. Though that is inevitable to some extent.

I made a tape for the Louisville Carmel, in case you might want a copy from them. I'm sure they'd be glad to provide . . .

To Dom Willibrord Van Dijk, O.C.S.O.

Dom Willibrord Van Dijk (1903–1989) had been Abbot of the Dutch Cistercian Abbey of Tilburg from 1945 to 1966, when he resigned. He was the founder of the monastery at Rawa Seneng in Indonesia in 1945, and was interested in Merton's promised retreat following Bangkok.

February 24, 1968

Several months ago I received a warm and excellent letter from you, and ever since then I have been trying to send an adequate reply. I have hesitated because Indonesia's problems are so remote from my own experience here. Yet I have always been greatly drawn to more understanding of Asian religions and culture and hence to consider the question of Christian monasticism in Asia.

And now, as you may know, there has arisen a providential opportunity for me to come to Asia—provided I can get the permission of my hesitant new Superior, for I have been invited as a *"peritus"* (!!) (I wonder where my *peritia* [expertness] lies? Only in talking) to a meeting of AIM in Bangkok this December. To me it would be an invaluable opportunity to learn rather than to teach or to explain or clarify anything. But I would certainly do what I could for others. To that end, I would love to visit your monastery [in Indonesia] on the way out or on the way home. I could stay long enough to give a few talks if you so desire (do they speak English? I also speak French).

But there is as yet a problem. My new Father Abbot hesitates to send me, fearing that this will give him a bad reputation with the other Abbots. I believe he really is afraid of our former Abbot, Dom James, who is still living near this monastery and might cause trouble. But as Dom Leclercq has said: Fr. Flavian is the Abbot and he should just go ahead and send me. Fr. Flavian therefore has frankly told me that he would like some strong letters from various people, urging my presence at the AIM meeting, and then he would be able to say that they convinced him it was God's will and for the good of the Church. He is in principle in favor of my going.

May I ask you, in all simplicity, if you think my presence there would be welcome or useful, would you please write to our new Abbot, Fr. (Dom) Flavian (he does not like to use "Dom") and urge him to send me to the meeting? And also extend an invitation (if you think it wise) for me to come to Rawa Seneng for a few days. Then this might help him to decide to let me go. All very complicated, but he has just been elected and does not yet feel sure of himself. He is young and will I think turn into a very good abbot.

Rev. Father, let me say in all brotherly frankness: I would like to meet you and share some ideas. I need to learn from you and your community. I need a much broader and more vital perspective on the problems of monasticism than I can obtain here in this very prosperous community—or in the hermitage where I live. The balance between openness and solitude, between silence and speaking the word, is a delicate one and in our Order we have simply fled from the problem altogether by locking ourselves up.

I wonder if Bangkok will be in a war by December? In any case, even if the meeting is not held, I hope some day to visit you. I also have family in New Zealand whom I have never seen, and this could be combined with a stop in Indonesia. And as I say I would like to meet you.

To Sister J.

Sister J., a member of an active religious order, wrote Merton about their experiments with living as a smaller group within a larger community.

March 4, 1968

. . . I am interested to hear of the experiment of "living in groups of five." It would be fun to talk to your group, but unfortunately I cannot. Some time ago I had indeed thought it might be possible to occasionally receive small groups here. But as soon as this information began to get around, there were so many requests that I saw I would be swamped. Hence I was forced to say no to everybody.

The idea of community really needs reviving: it has got lost in the idea of institution. Community and person are correlative. No community without persons; no persons without community. Too organized an institutional life tends to stifle both community and personality. Primacy tends to be given to an organizational task. Community is an end in itself, not a means to carry out tasks. Community is ordered to life, as a good in its own right. It is life-centered, person-centered. Hence we should not be too anxious about "getting anywhere" with community, except that community itself should "be" and celebrate itself in love. Probably one of the things about it is that it is too simple. We have forgotten how to be that simple. But I am glad your generation is finding out about it again, and maybe the rest of us can learn from you.

To Mother Neri, R.S.C.J.

Mother Neri, a Religious of the Sacred Heart, was Mistress of Novices at the time of this exchange at the convent of the Sacred Heart in Albany, New York.

March 6, 1968

. . . Yes, I am glad to get acquainted and to continue the "tradition" of friendship and union between our communities. I do often think of and pray for your novices. One of them has written me a couple of letters. I know it must be hard to be a novice today, for in the novitiate it is after all a help to assume that everything is stable and permanent and that one does not have to make it over while one learns. In the long run, the basic thing is faith and prayer however one may look at it, because without these there is no real love: love does not have deep enough roots without them. If one has a deeper and hidden stability in these things, then the externals can change as much as you like. But a novice does not usually have that stability which comes from experience, and sometimes bitter experience.

But of course each has his (her) own special grace and outlook, and today the great thing is to trust these things to produce unexpected fruits.

Dan Walsh is more energetic now than he ever was, and does more. We are expecting Mother Sullivan [Scripture scholar] down in these parts next Saturday. It will be a pleasure to meet her. Do you ever hear from Mother Schroen? I feel guilty about not writing to her for so long, but I am so overwhelmed with letters that I simply cannot make it. But I think of her and pray for her and rely on her prayers—as I do on yours and on those of the novices.

To Dom Jean Leclercq

March 9, 1968

I am afraid I cannot yet give any definite answer on the Bangkok project. Fr. Flavian has not said no, but he has not said yes. He is quite timid and noncommittal about it. I do not think in the first place he has any realization of the importance of this meeting and he regards the whole affair purely as a matter of making a "concession" to some supposed instinct for activism. He says he is willing to make this "concession" provided that he has enough pressure put on him from persons in positions of importance or authority. If Abbot de Floris wrote to him, and if someone else of importance (including yourself) wrote direct to him urging strongly that I be present, he would probably consent. It is also important that someone in the Order write to him. I have written to Dom Willibrord at Rawa Seneng to put a little heat on. This puts the problem as simply as I can formulate it at the moment . . .

I have a very great problem about staying in America (U.S.A.) and thus to some extent remaining identified with a society which I believe to be under the judgment of God and in some sense under a curse for the crimes of the Vietnam war. On the other hand, I do not see how leaving the country can be fully honest either. I have asked to be sent to our foundation in Chile, and this was refused. But it would not be a real solution. I might also go to the very small monastic foundation of a former novice of mine in Nicaragua. I could be a hermit there. But this too might be equivocal. I hope to speak to you about all this sometime. Perhaps if this society is under judgment, I too should remain and sustain myself the judgment of everyone else, since I am after all not that much different from the others. The question of sin is a great one today—I mean collective guilt for crimes against humanity.

What you say of Thien An breaks my heart. I think of those poor monks, to whom I felt close, and to whom I had written not so many months ago. I shall certainly pray for them very earnestly, especially in the Eucharist. They too were destroyed by my country, in its eagerness to "save them from communism"!!!

If I get any definite decision from Fr. Flavian, I will write to you about it.

To Mother Myriam Dardenne

March 12, 1968

I am happy to say that with the improved situation here I have been able to obtain permission to come out and see you and spend some time with you in discussing our common aspirations and problems in the contemplative life. However, it will not be possible right away. I suggest that the best time might be in the middle of June, or after that. If the 17th of June is a good date, I could fly out then and spend six or seven days with you—or whatever you like. If you cannot have me there at that time, will you please suggest other dates after that? I could also come earlier, for instance about May 10th, but as I have a lot of work to finish I think it would be better to put the trip off until later.

Please let me know if June 17th is all right, and also give me some idea of some of the things you would like to discuss. For my own part, as I have been doing some work on Zen and Sufism, I think it might be useful to include some talks on them. Needless to say, I hope to profit a little by the solitude and quiet of the Redwoods to make a quasi-retreat myself, while at the same time sharing whatever I can with you.

To Father D.

Father D., a young diocesan priest, wrote to Merton about his difficulties in relating to his new ministry.

March 14, 1968

. . . First of all, I can readily understand that you feel like a fish out of water as an assistant in a parish. I am sure I would too. Certainly the life is probably not at all suitable for you. I can understand that you would feel discouragement about it and think of laicization. But go slow. Before you take that step, would it not be well to explore other possibilities? After all, it does seem that you have a priestly vocation and that you can live happily as a priest provided you find the right place. Since you are after all not in perfect health, I think your bishop would be willing to fit you into some marginal or even experimental position. Why not talk this out thoroughly with J.C.? Couldn't you be a sort of "underground priest" in lay clothes, saying Mass in private homes among people you are at ease with, and perhaps also serving some tiny community, some convent, and helping out with shut-ins, people who are forgotten, who suffer, etc.? In other words it seems to me that in this Post-Conciliar period you might be called to a kind of hidden service in the sort of unofficial and informal life you desire. In short, be like a layman, live like a layman, but do some priestly work or service along with it.

I don't see that you have to stop being a priest just because the routine machinery of parish organization is bugging you. All the more reason to get out of the ordinary patterns and yet to be a priest nevertheless, and work in a quiet, relaxed relationship with people you can relate to without too much difficulty. After all, you are always going to have to relate to people. See your priesthood not as a role or an office, but as just part of your own life and your own relation to other persons. You can bring them Christ in some quiet way, and perhaps you will find yourself reaching people that the Church would not otherwise contact. J.C. can certainly help you implement all this, and if your Bishop doesn't go for the idea we might work out something in this diocese. The new Archbishop here is good and open . . .

To Father Filiberto Guala

March 20, 1968

. . . I am interested to hear that there will be a "commentary" on the message, though I do feel that it is so simple that really no commentary is required. You ask me for some information: and I find that I am not in a position to be of much help.

1) I have not seen to what extent the message was spread around in this country. I assume it was printed in the Catholic press. I have heard absolutely *no* comment on it one way or the other. I have received no reaction of any kind. If such reaction was communicated to Dom James, it never reached me. I do not know if the message was read in the community here. It may have been read before Compline. It was not read in the refectory. I have heard no comment on the message even in this community. I have not seen any manifestation of interest in the message on the part of anyone in the community from Dom James on down, except that Dom James did express considerable interest in a

statement in my draft, about hermits and the necessity for such. He agreed with that. This may sound shocking, this lack of reaction, but on the other hand I may not have been informed. All I am saying is that no reaction reached me. The only really articulate reaction in Europe came to me from Dom Leclercq. He seems to have liked the message.

2) I thought the message was a very clear statement, useful for Catholics themselves. I presume that the Bishops accepted it fairly well—though I really have not heard much except for the letter Card. Suenens sent to the *Collectanea.* I think that the message gave the Bishops a much needed sign of life and concern on the part of contemplatives. It counteracted the conservatism and lack of involvement on the part of some contemplatives who do not seem to understand the world at all or even want to do so. However, I do not think the message was strong enough to reach American Catholics or to counteract the very strong anti-contemplative trend in American Catholicism at the present moment. (Did you see the recent controversy in the *National Catholic Reporter?*)

3) My original draft was oriented to the Bishops but also to the "world" and to the unbeliever. My intention was to bear witness to a common ground—a kind of existential searching which is implicit in the *experience* of struggle in which all modern men, believers included, must *examine* the integrity of their own inner motives for believing (as opposed to the apologetic and reasonable conscious motives). Is our "faith" really in "good faith" or is it an evasion, a falsification of experience? But the message seemed to me to take a really different position in this regard. It was a position of distance and withdrawal from the unbeliever, *telling* him once again to believe: but telling him in a more moderate and sympathetic way. However, the general tenor of the message was: "because we believe, then others ought to believe also." "Others should imitate us: we can assure them, on the basis of our experience, that it is worthwhile." In other words, there was no question of joining the unbeliever as a brother and of examining, together with him, the grounds of our experience: still less the idea that there might be a *common ground* between us.

4) I wonder if Giovanni Ermiglia is not being too kind to the monks when he says we are "not compromised." I think historically we are just as much compromised as everyone else. Consider, for instance, how the Cistercians of the early 13th century were officially enlisted in the struggle to put down the Cathari, and the difference between the Cistercian approach to this problem and the Dominican approach which was more charismatic. I think that the monastic institution is so deeply involved in a historic establishment that it can only with the greatest difficulty see the necessity and the possibility of a truly monastic dialogue with the non-Christian and the non-believer.

5) I am certainly willing to discuss the question with Giovanni Ermiglia later on—at the present I have a lot of work I must finish. Perhaps

the best way to begin would be to send a couple of things in which I have already discussed some of these problems, for instance some recent articles on Camus which are not yet known in Italy. And a new essay that is just being typed. Incidentally, did anything ever happen with the article "The Contemplative and the Atheist"? Frankly, I am afraid that if a frank discussion between me and Ermiglia were published in Italy it would cause scandal. I do not want to get involved in any seemingly "official" dialogue. I would much rather make it clear that anything I say is spontaneous, informal and personal. Also there is the problem that what can be said frankly in America must be said with much more caution in Italy. I may add that I have some trouble with some of the more conservative members of this community—for instance, in my opposition to the Vietnam war, *a fortiori* in matters of theology which might seem to them daring.

I think the best thing I can do would be to send along some of the recent things I have said along these lines. If Giovanni Ermiglia wishes to join my other friends (I have many other "unbelieving" friends with whom I am in frank and open contact) who discuss these things, that is splendid. We might exchange a few informal letters (though I am a bad correspondent, since I have an enormous amount of mail), and forget about publication until later, if the need for it became manifest.

But I am quite reluctant to get up and make formal announcements and appeals, as though in the name of the Church, to "unbelievers." I would rather quietly discuss with them, as my friends, what we have in common, on a personal and informal basis, and let these ideas also appear in my current work. I do not wish in any way to take up a position that would appear apologetic, because I think such a position is for me quite fruitless . . .

A friend of La Pira's wrote to invite me to do an interview on atomic war for Italian TV but of course I had to refuse. I believe that it would be wrong and unwise to get involved in anything so public, and in any case Dom James was so opposed to this, and has communicated his feelings to his successor. I think we should steer clear of TV. However, I thought you would be interested to hear of this. Also, one other thing: I have been invited to a meeting of the AIM (meeting of monastic Superiors of Asia) in Bangkok, but I doubt if my Fr. Abbot will consent to my going. If you happen to think of this topic sometime when you are with the Holy Father's secretary, you might ask his opinion. I think Fr. Abbot would be very willing for me to go if he thought that Rome was strongly in favor. (I think Monte Cistello [the Trappist headquarters in Rome] would *not* be in favor, and please don't let them know of it!!)

This has been a frank letter. I hope there is nothing in it to offend! I remain united with you and your good friends in warm fraternal affection. Please give my best regards to Giovanni E.

To Abbot Flavian Burns

March 30, 1968

This letter is a good one and a strong one. What strikes me most is the point about Rawa Seneng: that this might conceivably be a sign of God's will, since it is an important matter. I'm only saying how it strikes me. As to Tilburg and the rest of the houses in Holland, that's another matter. They have lots of people to talk to them.

About Bangkok, as I said I am in the dark. I don't know what I think about it. I think the meeting might be a waste of time, but I just don't know.

I honestly think I should go to Rawa Seneng, and that it is important. It's one of those deep convictions that one can't explain.

As to the General Chapter—ugh. However I leave that entirely in your hands. I trust your judgment and if you think that is what ought to be done I'll accept it in faith. If that is the case, I'd say best for me to go to Rawa Seneng *first*, then come to France and either Tilburg or not—and get home fast trying to evade all the other consequences. If I were at the GC and it were known I were going to Rawa Seneng after, there might be more and more invitations, or talk or etc. If I had been there and had to get home . . . might be easier. And we could leave Bangkok for another decision, keeping Rawa Seneng separate from that.

If you'd like to know what I personally would prefer—"my own will"—it would be to go to Rawa Seneng and maybe to Japan (to some Zen places) and then sneak home entirely, avoiding Europe and the inevitability of going to various houses there. To me, the Trappists in Europe are of no interest whatever and there is no point in my getting involved with them. As I say, this is just "my own will" . . .

Anyway I like the way you do things, have complete confidence that you will do what is best, and assure you that I will be frank and reasonable (insofar as this is possible to me) . . . Next week Rev. Allchin, Anglican from Oxford, is coming for two days; he has been here before, very good interesting guy, works with contemplatives, knows a lot about Greek Orthodoxes, you might want to meet him?

To Mother Peter of the Holy Face

April 9, 1968

I have more than one letter from you that has been waiting for an answer. The one that most concerns me I can't find. But it seems to me you asked about penances in the refectory, etc. In my opinion the type of penances that can be considered somewhat "artificial" do not have the desired effect on modern young people, because they increase their self-consciousness and self-concern instead of helping them to forget self. The purpose of all penance after all is to deliver people from impulsions, obsessions, feelings, desires, etc., which are hindering them. One of the great problems of renewal centers on this point, because there is so much in cloistered life which did, in the past, bring peace and inner freedom and which now do just the opposite. So I'd say this could be taken as a principle which applies fairly generally today. The mere fact that something causes an intense repugnance does not mean that it is a good or fruitful penance. It must also have genuine meaning and have the effect of liberating the heart to love God more, instead of just tying it in knots.

Thanks for the résumé of the tape: it is useful for me to have on file some record of what I may have said. Naturally in making the tape itself I repeatedly said I did not expect you to agree with everything, but that I would just speak my own mind in simplicity.

I now have permission to have the Blessed Sacrament reserved in the hermitage, and hope that soon the work will be finished that will give me a fitting place for it. That will be a real grace.

To Sister M.

April 9, 1968

I am of course very much concerned about Sister J. and know how painful it must be for her. At the same time, the world is full of people in the same crisis of faith—it is standard for all of us in many ways. Is a trip all the way down here the answer? Will it do more than perhaps a letter might do? And would that help much? I don't know . . . The only way for her to grow is to get through this thing. But really she has to do it herself, because at this stage there is nothing another person can do for her except perhaps trigger something unexpectedly. I can't guarantee to do that. The best I could do is perhaps assure her that, if she could manage to see it from a slightly different angle, she would see that there is no problem because God isn't an object anyway. But that is not something you arrive at by reasoning.

My best suggestion is that if the thought of God bugs her, she should forget it. It is not that necessary to be thinking about Him. We act as if He depended on our thoughts. And then of course we get involved precisely with a God that does not exist because He depends on us thinking about Him. Surely that's a waste of time. He can take very good care of us when we are not thinking about Him.

To put it another way: if there were no God whatever, I myself would still be living exactly as I live now and doing what I am doing. If that is the case, surely the "question of the existence of God" is not all that important, is it? Maybe I am too hung up on a Pascalian gamble or something—she might have to arrive at it some other way.

If she really thinks she *has* to see me, I would not begrudge her an hour or two: but coming all the way down here is a long way to come for nothing. Words aren't going to do much at this point. If a person can accept her utter loneliness and realize it not as a lack or an impoverishment, but as a fullness and a ground of all freedom, then she can break through. But it may hurt . . .

To Father Charles Dumont

April 13, 1968

Admire the letterhead of my magazine [MONKS POND]! A copy of the magazine is on its way to you by surface mail. Poetry and Zen, almost exclusively. It is being very well received in literary circles. Monks don't quite know what to make of it, but they assume it must mean something.

As to your letter: I have a suggestion about the chronique. Our Fr. Matthew (your friend the Scrutator) can do a very nice job on something like this and has in fact already written a piece on the new Church for *Liturgical Arts* magazine. He could shorten this article and add other material. It would make a perfect chronique. Suppose I urge him to try this . . .

Dom James' hermitage is nearly finished: complete with built-in air-conditioning. It is a very posh little modernistic job, but somehow I wonder about it. With so much glass, it is like a goldfish bowl. It is also a bit impersonal and I wonder if Dom James will really like it. We are all amused at the fact that he is writing a great number of letters—perfectly normal. I do too: but he was always criticizing people who wrote letters as not being "contemplative" and he gave the rest of us a hard time. So we are entitled to smile—without malice—at his seven-page circular Easter letter.

Getting back to my own active life: one thing I can do for your ecumenical section is at least to review more books. It would be important to review the *Histoire de la Philosophie Islamique* by Nasr and Corbin (Gallimard, 1964). I have another book of Nasr I can review. If you would have someone keep a lookout for Buddhist, Islamic and other books in French and get them for me I'll do a bulletin. As to monasteries—I am not in contact with any. But what I could do is this: possibly I may be sent to the AIM meeting in Bangkok. Dom Leclercq is most anxious for me to go. If you write to Dom Flavian and urge him to send me, and also suggest that I visit some monasteries of Buddhists, etc., to write a chronique for *Collectanea*, that might provide something interesting. However, all this is very uncertain . . .

Everything very nice here now. Spring, birds, flowers. Tragic the death of Martin Luther King. An immense funeral—his body was taken to the cemetery on a simple farmer's cart drawn by mules. I think his death has said something to this country.

To Mother C.

April 14, 1968
Easter Sunday

It seems to me that in your circumstances there you have an obligation to do something like opening a clinic. I believe our Trappist monastery in Indonesia has done the same thing, and there are precedents for it in our Order in the Middle Ages—plenty of them. It would hardly be possible for you to be there contemplating God with a good conscience, knowing that people desperately needed some help from you, which you could give, and which you would be withholding in order to do honor to a *theory* of the contemplative life. We are living too much on paper these days, and according to theoretical blueprints and laws, not enough in the realm of flesh and blood realities. If Poor Clares do not wish to become involved in such things, then they should not go to countries where such poverty exists: but once they are there . . . And I think you can say that you went there in response to a call of God. Hence if He called you there He called you to help in some tangible way besides prayer. Something that you can do in close conjunction with your cloistered life should be done. Obviously if you find you are caught with a whole array of active works, then probably you would have to revise your ideas: but the thing is to do what is really necessary without getting caught up in mere activity for its own sake.

The principle behind my answer is this: it is misleading to talk so much of the *contemplative* life in a way that obscures the fact that what we need to renew is not so much the "contemplative" and enclosed and abstract dimension of our life, as the *prophetic and eschatological* witness of our silence, poverty, etc. Merely to put up walls and grates and to live in formal poverty behind them does not give such witness. The reality of silence and solitude are of course essential. But it should be in a kind of dialectic with charity and help to your neighbors there. In other words, the help you give should clearly proceed from a love that is nourished by silence and prayer; it should manifest a compassion that is rooted in an intimate awareness of the sufferings of Christ. The fact that you will see Him suffering concretely in the poor there ought to help your contemplative prayer to be deeper and more real. I don't know what else St. Clare or St. Francis could tell you! The original spirit of Franciscan eremitism was certainly in a context of occasional going out among the poor, being definitely *of* the poor, and not just a symbol of established religion and a life of devotion supported by the rich.

To Father John Eudes Bamberger

April 28, 1968

Thanks for letting me see your essay on Basil. I think you are on to something important: [it's the] first I've seen on "diathesis" and I think you are right. It is also in line with things preoccupying me—questions of religious consciousness and so on. I'd like to have an offprint when it's out; might be able to refer to it. Hope you will continue to work on this sort of thing.

P. Charles Dumont says he wants to hear from you about something, a translation into French of Evagrius: not clear what the issue is, whether he showed you the translation or wants to do so to get your opinion. Maybe what he wants is for you to write and say whether or not you'd consent to look over such a translation either to review or to give some kind of opinion for *Collectanea* . . .

I'll try by the skin of my teeth to get out three more issues of the magazine, which is very well received indeed among poets, but am not mimeographing any more of my own essays. Will you please return this when finished?

To Mother Myriam Dardenne

April 28, 1968

In just a week I hope to be with you [in California]. So now I am beginning to think a bit about what we might do. I intend to come prepared only in the sense of having a general line of thought to pursue: do not expect formal lectures or still less "sermons" (God forbid!). What I'd like to do would be to have a couple of good sessions each day, mainly dialogue, seminar, or what you will. The subject I'd like to pursue, in a general way, is "the modern religious consciousness"—which means wondering if such a thing exists, or can exist, and if so what kind of shapes does it take on? This would be against the traditional backgrounds of religious consciousness in Zen, Sufism, the 12th century Cistercians, St. Benedict, Desert Fathers, etc., etc. In other words, I am coming not with answers but with questions, and I just hope the questions won't be too disturbing. But I really think it is imperative that we monks and nuns devote ourselves to some search in this area which is ours to explore. We cannot go on living by foregone conclusions.

In the context of these discussions, there will probably be plenty of room to take up the current practical questions of renewal, etc., but I wonder if already a lot of these questions have not reached an impasse, for lack of perspective, insight, depth, background, etc. Probably this is not true among you there, because you have background. But many

American communities, it seems to me, have no background, no orientation, no perspective, and are just lost in the bushes trying to find themselves because they are not aware that anyone ever existed before them.

Well, pray that we may all have a fine profitable time, a real "happening" . . .

To Sister Mary Luke Tobin

May 1, 1968

I'm getting this back to you promptly, as I am supposed to leave for California Monday. Good idea to reproduce it—I'd like a few copies myself. Could I have twenty, maybe? I have gone over it and tried to reduce it to intelligible English, but there were some places where it was almost hopeless. I was looking for the stuff on Kafka's *The Castle*, and wondering if that was what dropped out. Maybe that was another tape, but I thought it was on this one. There must have been ten minutes of that. Too bad it got lost! Or maybe providential.

At the end of this month I have another small group of contemplative Superiors coming. They plan to arrive the 27th. We hope to work through the next three days—28th, 29th and 30th. Just a group of eight. Would you like to come over for some of the sessions, as you did last time? You would be most welcome . . .

To Abbot Flavian Burns

Redwoods
Whitethorn, Cal.
May 8, 1968

I had a good flight out—after Chicago was alone by a window and did not have to talk to anyone.

This place here is ideal. You really must come here and see for yourself. Perfect for retreat. Complete isolation and silence. And the woods are magnificent. I have the whole day to myself until Vespers, after which I work for two hours in a long conference . . . dialogue. Yesterday I was more entirely alone and in silence even than at Gethsemani for a good part of the day. It is much quieter here and much easier to go where you never see anyone.

I hope to finish the conferences Monday and then take two days of absolute solitude out by the Pacific where there is just no one at all. Hence I'll leave here on the 15th—please tell this to Bro. Hugh.

The community here is very alive, very simple, and very real. I think you'd love this place as I do. Be sure not to miss it when you come to Vina!

Have to go to Mass now. Will write later if anything new comes up. The conferences are going well.

Whitethorn, Cal.
May 14, 1968

Finished the talks to the nuns on Sunday and am now on retreat: which means the whole day in complete solitude over by the Pacific. Not a soul there, only seabirds and sheep.

This has been very good—also the days I had to myself before the official retreat—and I can see my situation in a new light. One thing is very clear: I am going to have to lead a less active life and be more solitary, less visits and contacts. I have some ideas I'll talk over, but the first thing is to try alternating periods of complete solitude with periods in which I see people, etc., on a limited basis. I'll try to take July and August for a more solitary period and see how it works.

I am quite definite and clear in my mind now about where I think I should go out. Only to things like this, which will contribute to my own monastic life while helping others. Definitely *not* as a *peritus* to big official meetings unless in a most exceptional case. But coming here has been excellent in every way.

As I forgot to bring Gethsemani stationery, could you please ask Bro. Hugh to say "No" to the two enclosed invitations? I think that would be the simplest. Sorry to be a bother. I leave here tomorrow for Christ in the Desert [monastery]. Back at Gethsemani probably next Tuesday.

To the Redwoods Community

Monastery of Christ in the Desert
Abiquiu, New Mexico
May 20, 1968

I am just leaving here to take the plane for Kentucky. This is a very isolated place in the mountains, in country full of traces of the Indians. And many Indians around too. I have most happy memories of the Redwoods and of my stay with you. It is the best place of all, and I can find nowhere to compare with the solitude on the Pacific shore. I certainly hope I will be back with you sometime. Thanks for your hospitality . . .

To Sister Cecilia, O.C.S.O.

Gethsemani
Ascension Thursday, 1968

As I did not use the tickets between Albuquerque and Santa Fe either way, I am returning them so that you can get a refund. The trip back went well, and I had three good days at Christ in the Desert. The arid land of New Mexico is impressive but I must say I prefer Redwoods. I miss the community and the Pacific, and hope to get back. Fr. Flavian has not committed himself about that, but I think it ought to work out. He has no good reason not to give me permission, so I have hopes . . .

Once again, I am most grateful for the hospitality shown me there. The days spent at Redwoods were a real joy for me. Also the care taken of me resulted in my putting on a few pounds!

To Father M. Basil Pennington

May 23, 1968

Thanks for the letter about the publication of the Cistercian Fathers in English. I would much prefer NOT to be on any editorial board of same, but I can always give advice when asked, if you see fit. But I haven't time to go over mss. and things like that. I already get an overload of that kind of stuff from publishers, budding authors and so on.

I do not have Sr. Penelope's manuscript, but I think Dom Samson (I forget his new name) has it, and he could pass it on to you to publish. I think he intends to publish it serially in CS.

Suggestions: it ought to be enough to *mimeograph* these translations. The duplicating processes we now have are perfectly adequate for this kind of thing, and can be handled with little expense. Small books can easily be put together. For formal publication, I think we should push translations of Hallier and Armand, and Aelred Squire's fine book on Aelred, still in ms. (English). Here we might make a deal with a publisher, guaranteeing to take so many copies of the edition so he won't lose out.

It might be a good idea to do a one-volume selection of the best of the Cistercian Fathers, a representative selection of Bernard, Aelred, William, Guerric, Isaac and some of the small fry, with a good introduction . . .

Honestly, I would much prefer NOT to come to the symposium. I am trying very hard to keep out of these meetings and to be a non-*peritus* on every level. Ten years ago it would have been great, but since I am living as a hermit I don't think it fits my life and really I am becoming awfully allergic to official meetings of any sort. They give me the creeps. That's probably more my fault than that of the meetings, I readily agree, but they just turn me off. I think my days of presenting papers, etc., are over—perhaps before they have begun. On the other hand I think Fr. Eudes would be glad to contribute something, and would probably be a big help in the whole venture . . .

To Father Filiberto Guala

June 4, 1968

Recently I had a meeting with some contemplative nun Superiors and an American bishop. The problems of the contemplative nuns in this country are, for many reasons, quite serious. Though in many cases materially prosperous, the communities are facing a critical situation in the near future. Under attack as "useless" and archaic, they are afraid to make significant changes because they fear that they will merely become involved in activity. At the same time they are out of contact with one another, isolated, confused, and in many cases reduced to inertia. The prospect is apparently—extinction within a generation or two. Unless of course they can meet their problem realistically.

The bishop present felt that the Holy Father could meet this need adequately by appointing a Commission of American Bishops to handle the situation, giving the nuns a chance to communicate effectively and to discuss their problems, in order to work for renewal in a way that fits the needs of the U.S.A. These needs are notably different from those of most European countries. It is a serious local problem, an urgent need of the American Church.

In order to make sure of my letter reaching the Holy Father personally, I thought I might send it to you and you might be best able to see that it gets into his own hands. If you see him, please assure him that the matter is much more important than many people, higher Superiors included, seem to realize. The nuns and the bishop at this meeting were all among those who are best informed about the situation . . .

To Father M. Basil Pennington

June 11, 1968

Not to leave your letter lying around indefinitely: it evidently crossed with mine. I'll try to settle the points that can be settled simply, now.

1) About editor in chief. This I simply cannot accept. It would be too phony. First I am not a scholar; second I am not a manager; and third I would not want to be a pure figurehead, which is all it would be. I think you can get the support you say you can get, if I am simply on the board. To be editor in chief as a mere decoy is something I would not be able to live with. Sorry.

2) I consent (with distaste) to being on the board of editors along

with the others. Why have anybody as editor in chief, if it comes to that? If not you, who are actually doing the work?

3) I am already sort of committed to P. Hallier, as I think I told him I'd do an introduction for his book if it appeared in English. But I am behind with a lot of work now, and I can't promise anything for a couple of months. Could you give me until, say, September? Meanwhile I'll look over his book again.

4) Symposium—if I don't have to give a paper, it's not so bad. OK, I'll tentatively plan on coming just to join in the discussions, but did you say February? Could you possibly have it very early in February or end of January? I anticipate some other matters. When's Lent next year, by the way? Of course I want your convenience to come first, but for me the earlier the better, and after the first week or so of February, I might not be able to make it anyway. On the other hand it is much better for me if the meeting is off my own campus, as then I can be a little more free and not tied down . . .

5) About the volume of selections—let's wait. I'll think about it. At the moment, I'd rather have as little to do with it as possible.

To Dom Bavo Vander Ham, O.C.S.O.

Dom Bavo Vander Ham (1906–1989), the Cistercian Superior of the monastery of Rawa Seneng, Indonesia, had invited Merton to give their community retreat.

June 14, 1968

Today my Father Abbot [Flavian Burns] showed me your letter of June 1st in which you kindly suggest that I give a retreat at Rawa Seneng. I am very happy to tell you that Father Abbot is willing to let me do this, and that I would like to make plans for the trip at the end of the year.

As yet nothing has been definitely decided about my attending the meeting at Bangkok. But in any case, if I come to Indonesia, I will hope to make other stops in Asia. It seems to me that it would probably be better for me to plan to come to you *before* the time of the meeting, if that is convenient to you. If I go to the meeting I could go there from Indonesia and then go on with plenty of time open to make other stops, for instance in Japan. I forget the exact date of the meeting of Abbots, but perhaps, if you agree, I could come to Indonesia sometime around the twentieth of November. It would be good for me to take a couple of days to look at the country and the people and get familiar with the new environment if possible, so as to understand better what your problems might be.

I would like to concentrate not only on some of the basic ideas of monastic theology but also on the special problems of the monk in the modern world. I am particularly anxious to learn about Asian and Indonesian problems and to study monasticism objectively in that setting—and perhaps against the background of non-Christian contemplative traditions. Have you any suggestions? Are you in contact with Indonesian Moslems? Is the tradition of Sufism alive at all in that part of the world?

I am very moved at this opportunity to do some service to my Indonesian brothers and to learn from them. If there is anything you could send me to read that would help prepare me, I would be grateful . . .

To Sister J.M.

June 17, 1968

First, your division won't work. The only things I wrote before my conversion were juvenile pieces published in college magazines. And maybe a book review or two. None of it counts for anything.

I'd rather divide as follows: from my conversion in 1938 to my ordination in 1949—that is, up to *Seven Storey Mountain, Waters of Siloe,* etc., when I suddenly got to be well known, a best-seller, etc. Then a long period until somewhere in the early sixties, a transition period which would end somewhere around *Disputed Questions*. During the first period, after entering the monastery, I was totally isolated from all outside influences and was largely working with what I had accumulated before entering. [I drew] on the experience of the monastic life in my early days when I was quite ascetic, "first fervor" stuff, and when the life at Gethsemani was very strict. This resulted in a highly unworldly, ascetical, intransigent, somewhat apocalyptic outlook. Rigid, arbitrary separation between God and the world, etc. Most people judge me entirely by this period, either favorably or unfavorably, and do not realize that I have changed a great deal. The second period was a time when I began to open up again to the world, began reading psychoanalysis (Fromm, Horney, etc.), Zen Buddhism, existentialism and other things like that, also more literature. But the fruits of this did not really begin to appear until the third period, after *Disputed Questions*. This resulted in books like *Seeds of Destruction, Raids on the Unspeakable, Conjectures of a Guilty Bystander, Emblems of a Season of Fury, Chuang Tzu,* etc. It appears that I am now evolving further, with studies on Zen and a new kind of experimental creative drive in prose poetry, satire, etc.

Characteristic books of first period: *Secular Journal, Thirty Poems, Man in the Divided Sea, Seven Storey Mountain, Seeds of Contemplation*.

Characteristic of second: *No Man Is an Island, Sign of Jonas, Thoughts in Solitude, Silent Life, Strange Islands*.

Third period—I've mentioned them above I guess, and (I might add) important to some extent is the introduction to *Gandhi on Non-Violence*. I guess the essay on Pasternak in *Disputed Questions* might throw light on it. Also see Preface to *Thomas Merton Reader* and interview in *Motive* (reprint in *U.S. Catholic* for March [1968]).

Yes, I have a lot of critics, particularly among Catholics. These are usually people who have seen one aspect of my work which they don't like. Most of them are put off by the fact that I sound at times like a Catholic Norman Mailer. I get on better with non-Catholics, particularly the younger generation, students, hippies, etc. At the same time there is always a solid phalanx of people who seem to get a lot out of the early books up to about *Thoughts in Solitude,* and have never heard of the others. These tend to be people interested in the spiritual life and somewhat conservative in many ways. Hence the curious fact that there are by and large two Mertons: one ascetic, conservative, traditional, monastic. The other radical, independent, and somewhat akin to beats and hippies and to poets in general. Neither one of these appeals to the current pacesetters for Catholic thought and life in the U.S. today. Some of them respect me, others think I'm nuts, none of them really dig me. Which is perfectly all right. Where I fit seems to be in the sort of niche provided by the *Catholic Worker*—and outside that, well, the literary magazines whether little or otherwise. Mostly little. And New Directions, [the publishing house] where I have always been.

I guess that's about it. Looking back on my work, I wish I had never bothered to write about one-third of it—the books that tend to be (one way or the other) "popular" religion. Or "inspirational." But I'll stand by things like *Seeds of Contemplation* (as emended in *New Seeds*). *Seven Storey Mountain* is a sort of phenomenon, not all bad, not all good, and it's not something I could successfully repudiate even if I wanted to. Naturally I have reservations about it because I was young then and I've changed . . .

To Abbot Jerome Burke, O.C.S.O.

Abbot Jerome Burke was at this time the Superior of Gethsemani's foundation, Genesee Abbey, at Piffard, New York.

June 27, 1968

Thanks for your kind invitation to preach the retreat at the Genesee. Since I have always thought it was important for monastic retreats to be preached by monks where possible, I can agree with the idea in a general way . . . With regret, I must say No to your invitation. I have thought the matter out carefully. My own vocation seems to be one of meditative prayer and writing and this demands a certain privacy and quiet. I don't lay claim to being a "hermit" in any status sort of a way. But if I am to go out—which I also think is not excluded—it must be in exceptional cases and with definite limitations.

If I preach a retreat to one American house, you realize that I would instantly become vulnerable to requests from all the others and would have a hard time refusing . . . What I can do and will when occasion offers is this: if for some reason I have to be in your area, I will try to set aside a day or two to visit you and perhaps give a couple of conferences or better participate in a couple of dialogue sessions. When and how this might happen—that's another matter. I hope I won't have to be out of my woods more than a couple of times a year. But there again I will have to stick to a series of priorities. I just don't think the American houses need me that much. And there are others around who could fill the bill very nicely . . . Fr. Matthew [Kelty], sub-prior here, gives excellent monastic talks, and has been very well liked here. I think some of his stuff is on tape if you want to hear a sample . . .

To Mother Myriam Dardenne

June 29, 1968

Are you back alive? Prison? Bread and water? I have often thought much about you and prayed for you. How was the Chapter? Bearable? I hope some good came from it in some way.

I have taken the liberty of thinking and asking about a couple of things that might possibly be useful as sources of income. For one, the Georgia monks do well with stained glass. It requires very little capital and one or two are all they need to do the work. They could explain more about it and show you what to do. Frs. Methodius and Anselm at Conyers are the ones involved in this work.

Second—this is a bit worse—but I only suggest it as a vague possibility. You know that I am constantly being invited to that meeting in Monroe, Michigan. I can't go. But I thought maybe if they were so terribly anxious to talk to me, a few of them might be willing to meet at Redwoods for a small seminar. It would have the advantage of being in the kind of place I think they are looking for. I have not proposed this to anyone, though I have vaguely mentioned the possibility. If you are very much in favor, you might suggest it . . . ? It would of course explicitly involve the nuns paying for their time there and getting there in the best way they could themselves.

Third, worse still: I got an invitation from the Esalen Institute to speak in Big Sur, run a seminar, etc. I replied that I did not speak outside monasteries of our Order but suggested that a small group might meet at Redwoods. This would mean that any money paid to me would go to you (they offered me three hundred dollars). They would all get there on their own. And they would pay for accommodations.

All of this is merely suggestion and I have not involved you in any way. I made it quite clear that all would depend on the consent of all involved in it. But these are possibilities. In other words what I am saying is that once in a while, if I could do so, I could perhaps make a little money for you by giving a seminar there to a group of 15 or so. I would enjoy doing it and would hope to slip over to Needle Rock from time to time . . .

First, Fr. Flavian is quite favorable to my spending some time on the shore and I want very much to do it. Second, guess what (confidential)—I am to go to Indonesia and probably to the Bangkok meeting. I am to preach a retreat at Rawa Seneng!! On the way out I hope to see you briefly (it would be in November). No more for the moment. Do tell me the news and what you think about the above. I hope I haven't been too wild. None of it may ever be realized anyway.

To Father William McNamara

July 1, 1968

I am moved by your frank letter. I know how you feel. With such opportunities for real growth in the monastic and contemplative lives, it is certainly disappointing to run into so much that is pure fantasy and neurotic acting-out. It shows how little there has really been behind our imposing structures. But I agree that the college generation is very engaging and promising.

Many active orders of nuns are thinking of contemplative retreats. Perhaps they do not know of SLIA [Spiritual Life Institute of America]. It seems to me that instead of building a lot of new specialized houses they would do well to examine the possibilities of retreat in places that already exist. However, there too you might run into problems. It is something you could explore however.

I get so many requests to write this and that that I am no longer committing myself. If I did my time would be entirely taken up with small peripheral projects. If I ever get an idea that I think would suit *Desert Call*, I'll try to jot it down and put it in the mail . . .

To Dom Willibrord Van Dijk

July 9, 1968

I have been meaning for a long time to write to you and tell you how distressed I was to hear of your bad health. I hope that things are better now that you are relieved of your heavy responsibilities and can rest more.

One reason why I delayed is that it took a very long time for plans to finally mature. Only the other day did my Fr. Abbot finally give me full clearance to attend the regional meeting at Bangkok. He had before that given approval for a retreat at Rawa Seneng. I now hope that I may be able to get to Rawa Seneng after the meeting. I would very much appreciate any suggestions you may have to offer about what would be helpful for the monks there. As I have never been in the Orient, I need some preparation. Anything at all you can say to guide me, to suggest readings, to give addresses of people I should meet in Indonesia, etc., would be most appreciated. I do hope to spend a little time in Japan before the meeting. I am particularly interested, when in the Orient, in making some contacts with non-Christian monks, above all Buddhists, as I am quite involved in the study of comparative mysticism—or ways of "contemplation"—and in relations with Buddhists and Hindus. Also with Moslems—particularly Sufis.

It would give me joy to meet you in Tilburg, but I do not think it will be at all possible for me to return via Europe, since I have to go to California. Hence I will have to return across the Pacific, unfortunately. But surely I hope we will meet some other time . . .

To Father Roger De Ganck, O.C.S.O.

Father Roger, a Belgian Cistercian monk, was chaplain to the nuns at the Redwoods Monastery at Whitethorn, California.

July 9, 1968

Good news. First of all, Fr. Flavian has definitely granted me permission to make a retreat of two months or more on the shore out there somewhere. I would hope to do this sometime after the New Year—if possible at Bear Harbor, Needle Rock, or somewhere in that area, overlooking the ocean.

I hope to be out there briefly in October or November on my way to Asia for the regional meeting of Abbots at Bangkok. I hope I can stop at Redwoods and perhaps make tentative plans for where I would stay in the winter on my return from Asia.

Fr. Flavian hopes to come and visit you there after the election at Vina—in three weeks or so. He will talk about another and more long-range project we have been discussing: the possibility of our establishing permanently a little hermit laura for two or three out on the coast. I told him you would be most glad and helpful, and that you knew all the best places. Etterburg would also be one of the possibilities, and you may have thought of others. But of course there is no hurry about this. If I could get a place to try out what it is like for several months, we could then look into the idea of something permanent. But Fr. Flavian is most interested in the pictures I have shown him of the coast.

He is concerned about the canonical questions involved in a long-term hermit place there. It would of course be ideal if we maintained our present status and did not have to be exclaustrated.

I wrote to Mother Myriam recently, and spoke of a couple of ideas of a more active nature—possible meetings of people at Redwoods. But (in case she mentioned them to you) they are not the kind of thing I am really most interested in myself. They are however possibilities. What I am really looking for is to get away from activity and constant contacts such as I have here and settle down to a really prayerful life. In any case, I hope all is well at the Redwoods, and that Mother Myriam's experiences at the General Chapter were not too gruesome. I look forward to seeing you briefly in the fall, and being with you on my return from Asia. Please ask the prayers of the Sisters that all may go well, especially with the Asian project.

After the meeting in Bangkok I will probably be satiated with meetings for a good ten years. Will reserve some energies for the one in Africa in 1969, if I am invited, which Dom Leclercq says I will be . . .

To Mother Myriam Dardenne

July 11, 1968

The best way to reply to your letter is to enclose the letter I received from Sr. Benedicta. She knows of my idea and is eager to have a meeting at Redwoods. I think if you write to her about it she will be glad to make some kind of arrangement that would allow you to substitute it for a talk at Monroe. We might make that one of the themes of the meeting . . . ? Anyhow, the only thing for me would be the timing. I might have difficulty clearing it with Fr. Flavian before October. But in October I could make it part of the trip that is already planned. I hope to fly to Asia Nov. 1st now, so October would be best for the meeting. Around the middle of the month would be best for me. Could you please return Sr. Benedicta's letter?

Fr. Flavian will visit you, he hopes, after the Vina election. He will hire a car and drive over, in the beginning of August. He is very interested in looking over possible places, as—this transpired recently—he is perhaps thinking of something more permanent, where two or three of us might settle down in a little hermit group, about a mile or two apart. Or closer if need be. Certainly there is room for two or three spread out along the shore. I don't know what kind of arrangements he plans to make, and of course it is a long-term project anyway, far in the future. For my own part, I am looking forward to moving out to the shore on my return from Asia and getting a good taste of it. A year would not be a bad beginning . . . I don't know what the chances are.

Let us keep praying. Meanwhile, if I get a chance, I'd like to look at some of the big wilderness reservations which are east and north of Garberville. One could not of course have anything permanent there but I guess one could spend long periods in a tent. The conditions would be very primitive, but ok for summer I'd think.

It was nice that you thought I could handle a course at Louvain!! I don't know if ten years of Needle Rock would fit me for it. Actually, the more I see of solitude the less I want to teach courses in anything—

except occasionally sharing something with a small congenial group like yours, entirely *en famille*. I do earnestly hope to stop being a public figure of any sort (which is why I am having second thoughts about the Esalen Institute: but we'll see what they think).

I will be happy to share your news and ideas from Europe. And probably will have a few ideas of my own! (I have refused the editorship of the Cistercian translations and don't especially like the idea of the meeting of the board . . .)

To Father Frans Harjawiyata, O.C.S.O.

Father Frans Harjawiyata is a native-born monk of the Cistercian monastery at Rawa Seneng, Indonesia, which Merton planned to visit and give the community a retreat after Bangkok.

July 14, 1968

Thanks for your kind letter which evidently crossed with one of mine to your Superior. As that letter says, my plans have worked out so that I will go first to Japan, then to Bangkok, and after that to Indonesia, if God wills. So I am planning to meet you at Bangkok and travel with you to Rawa Seneng. I agree that it would be very good to take time to see a little of the country. Also, perhaps at Rawa Seneng or somewhere in Java I might take a couple of days for silence and retreat myself, as I will probably need it after the meeting and preaching the retreat. I am not used to going about preaching! My further plans at the moment are to go on to New Zealand where my father's family lives: there are some relatives there I have not seen for many years and this will probably be my only chance to do so. I could go there about the end of December. Thus I hope to have the joy of spending Christmas with you.

Perhaps it will be better to have the retreat after the meeting, as this will help me to understand better the situation in our Asian monasteries. In any case, I rely on your prayers to make the retreat fruitful for all of us. It will be a real joy to meet my brothers in this distant monastery and to share with you a little of the grace of our vocation to deeper union with God.

I shall obtain the Geertz book you mentioned. I had heard of it, and it is regarded as being one of the best. Thank you.

To Mother Myriam Dardenne

July 20, 1968

It does not surprise me that Jones seems about to sell his land on the shore. I got that impression last spring. I wrote to him a couple of weeks ago, or perhaps less, saying that we were interested in getting some land out there and I hoped he would keep us in mind. I have not heard from him. My feeling is that the place will be split up into small lots, and that there will be a number of houses or cabins built out there.

Mrs. Barnum may have a good solution for us. I am thinking now of the project Fr. Flavian has in mind for the future. I told him that there might be a possibility with her.

Meanwhile, for myself next winter on my return from Asia—I'll look for something when I'm out there in October. Perhaps by then it will be too late for Needle Rock, etc. Or maybe even then they will let me spend part of the winter there. It will not be hard to find a temporary place of some sort, and certainly for a brief period of a few months, perhaps a trailer on your own grounds somewhere would be a good start—back in one of those valleys that don't have roads into them, perhaps up on a hill . . .

As things are now, I plan to reach Redwoods late in October. If Sr. Benedicta wants a meeting there, sometime between the 24th and the end of the month would be best for me. I must get going November 1st. Things are shaping up well for Japan, I think.

Yes, I think the question of solitude is very important—naturally. We need a real solitude that will empty us out, help strip us of ourselves. There is a great deal of "vanity" (in the sense of Ecclesiastes) even in a social life that is serious and good. One needs periods of real silence, isolation, lostness, in order to be deeply convinced and aware that God is All. Without experience of that, our prayer life is so thin. Certainly I hope we will get a chance to talk of it—and live it. That is the one thing that preoccupies me now. The way Fr. Flavian is talking now, it is quite possible that I may move to California for good next year. I am certainly ready and anxious to do so!!! And I pray that God may show us the place He has in mind . . .

July 22, 1968

This is just to say that my constantly changing plans have changed again. I have another important invitation in Asia—and have to be in India at the time when I hoped to be at Redwoods. However I can still come by on my way out. I have to fly to Asia October 14th or 15th. I may get a couple of days with you before that . . .

The Asian trip is shaping up famously however, with India now on the top of the rest. I don't expect to travel much in India but I may meet some very interesting and helpful people—even a chance I may meet the Dalai Lama, which might mean an entree to a lot of interesting monastic centers . . . I am beginning to think that my big trouble will be getting back from Asia at all!!! But I do hope to be back by February. If Sr. Benedicta could wait until then, it would be easier to arrange a meeting with more time . . .

To Dom Jean Leclercq

July 23, 1968

Thanks for your good letter about the arrangements for Bangkok. I will be glad to give the talk on Marxism and so on. Important indeed!! I've familiarized myself pretty well with Herbert Marcuse, whose ideas are so influential in the "student revolts" of the time. I must admit that I find him closer to monasticism than many theologians. Those who question the structures of contemporary society at least look to monks for a certain distance and critical perspective. Which alas is seldom found. The vocation of the monk in the modern world, especially Marxist, is not survival but prophecy. We are all busy saving our skins . . . Do I speak in English or French?

To Dom Aelred Graham

August 3, 1968

About Japan: I had better suspend definite plans about the time until I see what happens in India. Things are still very flexible as far as I can judge, and it might be possible to stretch the trip a bit and go to Japan in the spring. I do very much want to visit little temples and monasteries out in the mountains and spend a lot of time just sitting. And the idea of meeting Fujimoto Roshi is entrancing. I look forward very much to meeting all those who have been suggested so far. I have not yet contacted anyone. It would be marvelous to have a good interpreter. If Miss Okamura could do a little of that for me, I would be most grateful. I don't dare ask her myself; I'd feel I was imposing too much. But if Elsie wants to ask her I'd be most grateful. Perhaps it would be better to wait until I am definite about the time of going to Japan, unless you and Elsie think it would be worthwhile to bring it up now, well in advance. In any case I do definitely intend to go to Japan, and if I have to make it in the winter, I'll just have to be more prudent about where I sit!

What I would appreciate at this point would be introductions and leads for Thailand. I will stop a couple of days at Bangkok, on the way to Calcutta, and then again for a week at least in December. Perhaps I could make a first contact on the way through in October, and if necessary or feasible come a little earlier than my meeting. I certainly want to function as freely as possible and without "Catholic auspices" of any sort. But it will mean raising some money for hotels. I can't go out and give some lectures to get cash. I could of course borrow on a future book. I wonder about foundation money? Probably too late at this juncture.

If Harold Talbott is living in Northern India, I should very much like to meet him. I have other possibilities for meeting the Dalai Lama but they might fall through. I am sure Mr. Talbott would have all kinds of good ideas and suggestions. I hope I won't have trouble with a visa—my passport picture unfortunately has a Roman collar . . .

Chances of my having a secretary with me are nil. I will have to make the best of it in my usual way, with notebooks here and there.

So then: I'd very much appreciate any introductions to Buddhists in Thailand and Northern India. Did you make it into Burma? This would keep me going until I know more exactly about Japan. I could inform you about that from India, and in any case will be eager to report to you on my progress along the way.

To Mother Myriam Dardenne

August 5, 1968

Wishing you all luck at Monroe—whenever it is. Will you tell Sr. Benedicta that if she wants to meet at Redwoods I'll be available there October 11 and 12 and part of 13? Will that be ok with you? I hope to get moving on the 14th on my big *pèlerinage aux sources* [pilgrimage to the sources]. To the big overflowing confused sources of humanity. It was an Asian humanity that the Word chose . . .

Ours is an Asian religion, basically. Though of course also non-Asian, beyond Asian.

I hope Fr. Flavian had a profitable visit with you. More than anything else, I hope his idea of starting something hidden and solitary out there somewhere will work out . . .

Of course, as you say, I may never get back from Asia. But don't let's talk about it!

In any event, yes, all the monastic traditions have this in common: total liberation and availability to "let go" and open up to the unspoken silence in which all is said: *qui erat et qui est et qui venturus est* [who was and who is and who shall come].

To Father M. Basil Pennington

August 14, 1968

Thanks for your recent letter. And the enclosures, questions, etc., which I can't pretend to answer right now as this is just a quick note.

Sorry I haven't yet got the Hallier preface. I have been tied up with this literary magazine I've been running—and have now closed down, so I'm through with it. Last issue finally wound up. But also I have all sorts of commitments with other magazines and have articles to finish. But will get the Hallier preface to you before mid-September.

Now here is a proposal. I have a small book which I was not planning to publish commercially for the simple reason that I have decided to avoid as far as possible any commercial publication on "monastic" topics right now. This is *The Climate of Monastic Prayer*, which people continue to ask for, and I was going to just revise it and have it mimeographed again. However, it occurs to me that it might fit in with your program and it might also make a little money for you, for the obvious extrinsic reasons!! I am sending you under separate cover a copy of the 1965 version, just to give you some idea. I am adding quite a lot and brushing it up. It is a book which people have been consistently asking for, so I don't think I am imposing anything on you. You can judge if it fits in with your program. Meanwhile I hope to finish the revision soon and send it for typing. You ought to have the completed work by the end of October.

To Father Roger De Ganck

August 20, 1968

Thanks for yours of the 17th. I have decided to drop the Esalen conference. It turns out that I may be able to stay in Asia for a longer time than I expected, and I would be foolish to tie myself down to a specific date and thus be forced to return to this country. So I am writing today to Michael Murphy that I cannot give the conference at Redwoods.

I think this is simpler for all concerned. It might be a bother for the convent, and I certainly do not want to get involved in this kind of thing myself. If I commit myself to this, it will mean destroying all hope of real solitude on the coast for me. It is much better to stay out of sight.

Fr. Flavian enjoyed his visit to Redwoods: and he mentioned the caretaker's house to me. I go along with that idea. I also think it would be unwise to buy property, and I would be glad to rent a place for a time and not get tied down in case the situation changes drastically overnight. The possibility of renting a place for a year or so would be wise. In any case, I certainly hope to have something lined up when I get back from Asia.

I am terribly sorry to hear Al's house was destroyed by arsonists. It was such a nice place. I guess that proves there are some pretty tough characters around there, just as there are here. Well, they are also poor, I guess.

I look forward to seeing you all in October—and though I know the news is out, I still hope to make my visit there relatively quiet and "unnoticed." And I hope to get a day or so on the shore!!

To Father M. Basil Pennington

September 2, 1968

I'll try to see Bob Imperato—depends on how things connect when I get down there to the monastery.

Have finished the Aelred preface and it will be typed up. You should have it by mid-September or earlier.

As regards *Climate* [*of Monastic Prayer*]—it is being typed by one of the nuns at Redwoods who is currently out in Spokane. I think she'll have it in a few weeks. An introduction would be fine—I leave you to get anyone you want or can. The only trouble is that I know myself what a drag this business of writing prefaces can be and it is hardly fair to ask people like Dom Leclercq to write them. However, I leave you to figure that out. Maybe some Protestant guy who is open to monasticism, too . . .

One thing I must say: due to circumstances I am having to drop off all these little incidental projects, prefaces here and articles there for at least six months. Therefore I can't join in the Buddhist symposium thing you sent. I will of course do what I can for you later in the way of prefaces, but really it is preposterous to be writing prefaces and articles and getting into small symposia all the time, and I really owe it to myself, to God, the Church, the monastic Order, and all and sundry to keep from getting tied up in such things. Whether I will succeed or not is another matter, but definitely I can't do anything for the next six months.

This being the case, I am pretty diffident about asking people to do prefaces for my stuff.

Fr. Flavian has a policy of keeping retreat groups down and I don't think he'd want thirty Buddhists down here. Anyhow it's too far for New York people usually.

To Mother Myriam Dardenne

September 7, 1968

Since Dom Leclercq was coming here this weekend, I waited to answer your letter. I asked him where he would be October 11; he said he was tied up in Belgium then. He will go from here to Oregon, but will leave for Europe. However he is coming back in November and can come to you then if you like. I leave the rest to you.

As to having Mike there—I leave all that to you also. Why not? Such things are good to loosen people up and break the hang-ups with too much formal method. On the other hand, artistic spontaneity is not the whole story. A little of it surely does not hurt, but will do some good. As long as people do not get the idea that it is all you need.

I'll have something to say but I don't yet know quite what. A lot depends on the actual people there and I won't know until I meet them. Corita, sure, whoever wants to come. I leave that all to you; I am simply at your service to think aloud with you.

All I can give is the little that I have, which is certainly nothing. But I can think with you in terms of my own present development and—I won't say crisis, because it is very smooth—but I am completely convinced that for some people the only thing is a solitary and "unattached" life. To simply go where the wind blows them, which is into various new deserts. With absolutely NO plans for any kind of structure, community, what to do, how to do it, but to simply seek the most desolate rock or the most abandoned island and sit there until the tourists move in, then to move on. I have NO ideal, NO program, and the last thing in the world I want is a disciple or anyone to listen or imitate. I'd rather warn everyone to do something else. For me the wind blows to Asia . . .

The Asians have this only: that for thousands of years they have worked on a very complex and complete mental discipline, which is not so much aimed at separating matter from spirit, as identifying the true self and separating it from an illusion generated by society and by imaginary appetite. At the present moment this illusion has become law, even for Christians. The talk about the goodness of the world, etc., is largely justification of the illusion, though the world is certainly "good." But all the Goodness of the World lingo seems to me to be vitiated by a Madison Avenue consumer-society approach which makes it utterly phony, and bespeaks nothing but the goodness of the market (see Erich Fromm). I don't intend to talk much about this. It is true that the yen for absolute solitude is often vitiated by pure narcissism, regression, immaturity, and is utterly sick. This does not alter the fact that there are vocations to solitude, and for these there remains only the question: when do I start? And how? Once artificial barriers are removed the question tends to answer itself.

I got a letter from Mrs. Jones. I can have Bear Harbor (to rent for a time if I want it, she says. She is eager to fix it up, etc.). On the other hand, I don't want to bind myself to return from Asia before it's necessary. I may run into some really extraordinary opportunities, as I am now in contact with the secretary of the Dalai Lama. There is much openness there and great generosity to anyone who has a really serious interest. So I probably won't be back before spring. (I have incidentally cancelled the Esalen meeting for the same reason.)

I might be at Bear Harbor for next summer, or some place else. I have no way of knowing now what will turn up. It is all too far ahead. This is all pretty much in confidence of course—I wouldn't want it to get outside your community.

Anyway, I'll try to get there a day or two early. I'll also want a little time on the shore myself, before the talks, which should be only the 11th, 12th and 13th. The 14th I fly from Eureka to San Francisco on the morning plane and the 15th to Asia. Keep praying for me. The strong prayers of Redwoods have done much for me so far! Keep them up!! And I pray for all of you too. We sometimes forget the real dimensions of our life. There must be long "dead" periods; they are necessary. But they may suddenly blossom out into unusual life, if we let them!

To Dom Jacques Winandy

September 8, 1968

Thanks for your letter: I am always glad to hear from you. But I am sorry to hear of troubles in your hermit group. I surmise, on the basis of indirect knowledge, that you must have a few characters there who are really not suited for any kind of group existence of this sort and who are simply trouble-makers. That is a great pity, for they will only make things worse. On the other hand if you leave them, that is the end of the group.

When you undertook this project of offering to people a hermit group with a minimum of structure, it was before the Council and something was urgently needed to help people to fulfill solitary vocations. Your work was epoch-making and it had a decisive effect on the rest of us because it faced our Abbots with the choice of letting us come to you or letting us be hermits within our own Order. This is still a very real choice, and your Hermits of St. John Baptist are necessary.

On the other hand I would say frankly that for some of us as individuals, for you as well as for myself, there is a better way, which is to be a hermit without disciples, simply on one's own, and without any concern to promote the eremitical life for others. At most, I would say that two or three like-minded individuals could choose to live in proximity to one another, but without any "engagement" of any kind. This would provide the maximum of flexibility! . . .

I do not want to talk more about a situation that is unfamiliar to me. It happens that I must fly from Alaska to California at the end of this month and I could break my trip at Victoria if you could come to town to see me. I don't want to make a long break in the trip, and I don't especially want to go to Courtenay and run into your companions, because the fewer people know about my whereabouts the better I like it. If you can meet me in Victoria or Vancouver, I will look into the question of a convenient flight. I would come from Anchorage on Sept. 28th (Saturday) and perhaps we could get together for a meal, and if I could briefly meet Bishop de Roo that would be fine too . . .

To Abbot Flavian Burns

Anchorage, Alaska
September 25, 1968

I am writing this in the Chancery Office while waiting to get my flight to California confirmed. It is an unfamiliar typewriter so I don't guarantee the legibility of what I am writing.

Also it is very good to be away from the typewriter for so long, with the prospect of being away from it still longer. I have had to put off going to California for a couple of days more, because I am flying all over the place up here in bush planes and getting a real good idea of what it is all about . . .

There is no question that this place is full of ideal solitude in every form. So far I have seen the Anchorage area, which is not so good—relatively crowded, big Army bases, etc. Southeast of here there is a wild coast going for thousands of miles down to Vancouver, with literally thousands of little islands, most of which would be too remote or savage to live on. But there are many which would be very practical and near some small town that could be reached by boat. Most of these small towns are themselves cut off from the outside world, have no roads anywhere and are reached by plane. The ones I have seen are small fishing villages the size of New Haven [Kentucky]. Miles from nowhere, but with a small Catholic population of a few families maybe.

I have also seen the Chugach Mountains which are extremely wild and probably too wild to live in mostly. Some of the central area which would be too cold. I am interested in the coast and expect to see a lot more of it in the next few days. The bishop and clergy here are extremely generous and encouraging and the people are simple frontier types. I think Alaska would be the best place in the U.S. for a hermitage.

Everything else is going well. I'll write again soon when I have seen more. I am in great shape (climbed a 2000-foot mountain last Sunday). The place is crawling with bears, some of which are dangerous, others not. Yesterday the bush pilot was skidding along the flanks of high mountains to find bears and mountain goats . . . I am sure that if nothing else comes up, there will be hundreds of places in Alaska and many to help us make good use of them if we wish.

To Brother Patrick Hart

Anchorage
September 26 [1968]

Thanks for the latest mail, including the New Guinea archbishop, etc. Maybe you could reply to Bp. Breitenbeck, and suggest Mother Myriam ought to attend the meeting he mentions. She would be a "must" in my opinion.

The Syracuse Library thing I sent to J. Laughlin. J. will know what to do.

I want to enclose a few postcards and notes for some of the gang with this, and may mail it from Juneau where I am flying with the bishop today—though bad weather has a lot of flights delayed or cancelled. One of the things that can easily happen here is that you wait around half a day or more and eventually get stranded in some lost fishing village for a couple of days. Hasn't happened to me yet, but maybe . . . Anyway everyone here is very nice and I have been all over the place in bush planes, really wild country and just terrific from every point of view. The mountains have got the Alps beat a mile. This is utterly unique. Lots of live volcanoes, too.

Could you please get from Fr. Eudes a supply of DONNATAL tablets and send them to me at Redwoods?

My trip to California has been delayed slightly and I will be at Santa Barbara until Oct. 4, so you can send stuff that will reach me there until that date. Then Redwoods.

This is all very fine here but I am getting impatient for India. That is the real purpose of the trip. Keep up the prayers. There are so many things involved in dialogue with Asian peoples and I really need a special charism—to say the least. And it is so important.

Give my regards to all the gang and I hope there are not too many crazy rumors. Keep telling everyone that I am a monk of Gethsemani and intend to remain one all my days—only I just happen to be out of the monastery, just as some have been absent to go to Rome, etc.

There is a lady here to whom I promised a copy of *Selected Poems.* If I remember, I'll enclose her card; I don't have it here. Oh, here is also the letter of Rev. Mr. Allchin (correct title for Anglican priest). Tell him about Basil's project to perhaps print *Climate* [*The Climate of Monastic Prayer* was published in 1969 by Cistercian Publications, and later by Herder and Herder under the title *Contemplative Prayer*]. But if he wants to mimeograph it also, he can do so, but in that case we should send him the new script which Cecilia Wilms is typing . . .

Everything and everyone just fine here. A whole new sense of Church and of community out here on the frontier. It is very striking. The charity is quite unusual—and people are still solid and simple Catholics without too many of the new complicated problems. Refreshing.

To Abbot Flavian Burns

Anchorage, Alaska
September 26, 1968

Yesterday I wrote in a big hurry on a most unfamiliar typewriter. This is still not the kind of machine I am used to, but there is more time and I can run it better . . .

1. I have now seen quite a lot of the area within a five-hundred-mile radius of Anchorage. This includes a lot of wild mountains, a mountain range bigger than the Swiss Alps, another range where the highest mountain on this continent is found, a rugged coastline with thousands of isolated bays and islands and glaciers, with a few fishing villages that can only be reached by air or by a very long boat trip. I have also seen a vast central valley with miles of nothing, millions of small lakes, canyons, etc., and a few settlements, roads, etc. This area is very cold in winter. The coastline is less cold but very rainy. In fact today I am supposed to go down to Juneau and a lot of the planes are grounded down that way because of torrential rains. However at Juneau there is an old chapel and some cabins, originally built as a retreat center by an earlier bishop and now abandoned. It may be a possibility but I think it is too near Juneau which (though not much bigger and perhaps smaller than Bardstown) is the state capital.

2. I have yet to see and explore more of those bays and islands in SE Alaska and have a hunch that near a half-breed village of fishing people called Yakutat (totally isolated) I might find a good spot. I have also to see the western part of Alaska which is vast and empty without even mountains and forests, and is a place where priests are sent when they are in disgrace as a punishment—it is so lonely. This too might be just ideal.

3. The bishop is extremely generous and good. He is very interested in having contemplatives here, and very happy that I might possibly be a hermit here. I am almost certain that I would have to at least say Mass on Sundays for a few families in some isolated place, and nothing much more than that would be involved, if I protected firmly my solitude. (Otherwise I feel he'd have me up in Anchorage giving conferences to priests and nuns.) He has meanwhile gone out of his way to get me around, chartered bush planes for me, and really I have explored the place very thoroughly (though not of course the far north).

4. My feeling at present is that Alaska is certainly the ideal place for solitude and the hermit life. In fact it is full of people who are in reality living as hermits. Men who have gone far out into the wilderness with a stack of books and who get themselves a homestead, cut wood, read, and stay away from everyone, living on moose, fish, caribou, etc. I don't plan it that way. But it gives you an idea of the character of the place. There is also an old Russian Orthodox monk who has lived for years as a hermit off Kodiak Island. In fact before him there was a Starets who is venerated as a saint, so religious hermits are nothing new here. Unfortunately I was not able to get to Kodiak and this old monk is now sick, but I hope to meet him someday before he dies.

In conclusion, though I am not in a position to decide anything yet, I believe that if nowhere else there is certainly real solitude in Alaska and that it would be very easy (in spite of obvious problems, weather, bears, and all that) to settle here. The priests and people would welcome a hermit; they are all good simple people, not yet caught up in the mess of problems which are found in the States. I think that unless something very definite comes up to change things, this would be the obvious place to settle for real solitude in the United States. Also, apart from that, I think that it is a place where God is calling some to solitude. The bishop himself is very definite about wanting contemplatives and a real contemplative life here, and would be greatly pleased to have me stay. He and everyone I have met make this very clear. I can't say with certitude that I think I am called to be a hermit here, but I do believe it is a very real possibility and that I must keep it in mind and look into it further and perhaps make a decision on my return from Asia.

As to the material problems, people are very resourceful in handling them and very cooperative with one another so that when anyone is in trouble, they will always come to his assistance by plane, etc. There is no unusual risk or danger when this is taken into consideration. As to the cold, people who have experience of different parts of the States assure me that it would not be any worse than the Genesee along the coast here, and less bad than Montana, the Dakotas, etc.

I guess that covers it so far. It has been wonderful here and I still have a lot more to see that sounds very interesting. I feel that I haven't seen the best of it yet. Last Sunday I climbed a small mountain and really had a workout. My health seems better up here and the allergies that bothered me down there are much less troublesome here. Drop me a line if you get a chance. Love to all.

Anchorage, Alaska
October 1, 1968

I thought you'd like to see some photos of one of the best places I have found. These are pictures of a lake and a bay near Cordova, Alaska—a small fishing village that can be reached only by plane. Completely isolated—already a parish priest there, so no obligation to take care of anyone—one could live five or six miles out of town and be very quiet. Of course there are a few bears, but I am told they are not grizzlies—i.e. they won't normally attack you.

I had a very frank talk with the bishop and he agreed perfectly that I would not be asked to do any parish work of any kind—the only request would be to help priests by spiritual direction if they wanted to come all the way down there to see me. It is about 300 miles or more from Anchorage.

As I said before I have made no commitments, but I do feel that I should consider seriously the many generous offers of small parcels of land or of rights to live on land, etc., that have been made. It would be folly for me not to consider Alaska as one of the best possibilities for a true solitary life and I hope I can return here when I am through in Asia.

The bishop here has been very generous and the people have been fine. They would be entranced if you wanted to send a small group but I did not encourage them to hope. You ought to see this country sometime! I fly to California tomorrow.

Redwoods [California]
October 9, 1968

I borrowed Mother Myriam's Olivetti to write out my paper for Darjeeling (they wanted it written out in advance yet!) and so now I take advantage of the fact to write a few letters also. Thanks for your note which reached me here after they had sent it on to Santa Barbara and it came back. I drove up with my friends the Ferrys and I can say without hesitation that the California coast is hopeless as regards solitude. Everywhere there is a land boom in progress and speculators are opening up new developments on every side. They can't lose, the population is increasing so fast people are going to have to build all over the place. Even at Bear Harbor which I liked so much last May, the bulldozers are active and they are opening up a lot of roads that will obviously be for housing sometime. It is just a question of time before this whole place will be spoiled.

As for Alaska, it has many advantages—yes, it is like Norway—probably the best solution would be a *small group* up there. An experimental semi-eremitical thing would be best, it seems to me, and would work very well. I am open to participate in such. The bishop is most generous and eager. I guess he has written to you. I know he will give me any manner of support, if I come up on my own. On the other hand I am not sure of it myself. I can't decide anything until I see what comes of the Asian experience. The important thing for me is not acquiring land or finding an ideal solitude but opening up the depths of my own heart. The rest is secondary.

Of course I hope to return there. I had no idea of doing otherwise, except that perhaps I thought it would be more convenient for you, if I were to live in solitude somewhere else, not to come back and then leave again. But I have no plans. Except that I don't think just permanent residence in Kentucky is the final answer for me. As a mailing address, yes . . .

As things stand now I am supposed to see the Dalai Lama in early November. Then I return to the Darjeeling area, and to Sikkim where there is an important Tibetan Buddhist center, and where I will meet some good Lamas, some of whom speak English. There will be an interpreter for the others. I also have now a definite opening for Bhutan and hope to return there after Indonesia, that is, in January. Dom Simeon wants me to "preach a retreat" at Hong Kong. I'll have to tell him I can only do so in late February, if at all. I have to be in Japan in early March. There are many, many good contacts opening up there.

I have had some advice from a very good man who knows all about the Buddhist scene—which is why I phoned Gethsemani today to get a habit. He said I'd need it, to deal with the Buddhists. Also he recommended not making hard and fast plans in advance, and remaining open to the unexpected.

I leave it to you to let me know when my absence becomes really embarrassing for you—assuming it won't do so before next summer sometime!! As to the legality of it, there is always Rawa Seneng.

As far as travelling around goes, I am bored with it already. That is not what I am looking for. When I get fed up with Buddhists, I'll let you know. I know Asia may be in many ways difficult, but I am determined to dig through the rubble and try to get through to the real springs that I think are still there. And I am convinced that they would laugh at us if they knew our monasticism. Mother Myriam has horrible tales of the liturgy meeting here, going from 7 a.m. to 11 p.m. and so on. Are these people out of their heads? What can they find to talk about at such length?

Everything is fine. Glad Dom James thinks I am now "mature." Maybe that was the result of the episode in 1966—which I am thankful (hopefully) is over. Certainly no problems of that kind yet!!

My best wishes to everyone. I fly to Asia Tuesday. Keep me in your good prayers. Bro. Lawrence has my address in Asia. Bro. Patrick seems to be handling everything real fine.

To Dom Jacques Winandy

Redwoods Monastery
October 11, 1968

It is a pity that I was not able to see you and I very much regret it. But I am sure we will meet eventually.

Mother Myriam [Dardenne] wants me to say that if you wish to get away from Vancouver any time for a change and rest, you will be most welcome here. I am very fond of this place. It is a shame California is developing so much, for there are fine solitary places all around here. And even if developments continue, there are good places in the woods near the convent which could be well protected. I am seriously thinking of the possibility of settling near here and my new Abbot would, I think, be favorable. However (perhaps I told you this) I would myself be against the idea of a hermit colony, receiving postulants and disciples. If a man wants to be a hermit, I think he should do it more or less on his own or in conjunction with one or two other well-seasoned companions whom he knows in advance (not with people for whom he would have some assumed responsibility).

Pray for me. I am going to India. I believe this is one of the greatest graces of my life and I look forward to meeting many monks of other traditions, particularly Buddhists. The experience could be invaluable. But it will need much prayer, as I am far from being adequately prepared for the encounter *in depth* that is necessary . . .

To Brother Patrick Hart

San Francisco
October 14, 1968

I am sending a couple of checks—when they are made out to Fr. Louis they are a little hard to cash because all my identifications say "Thomas Merton." Maybe the simplest thing would be just to put them in the kitty back there towards the day when I start hollering for more money. At the moment I am quite well off!

Tomorrow I take off for Bangkok. It is most thrilling. I've had a good day in San Francisco—with a Redwoods postulant! We went out to lunch at a fine seafood place on Fisherman's Wharf. She is entering in two weeks.

Tell Fr. Matthew [Kelty, the wardrobe keeper] that I am going to wear the Cistercian habit after all when I meet the Buddhist monks.

To Abbot Flavian Burns

Oberoi Grand Hotel
Calcutta
October 20, 1968

Just a word to say I am in Calcutta and the meeting is about to begin. It will be held here because there have been terrible floods in the Darjeeling area and everything is in a state of emergency there. However, I expect to get there later. Today I am having lunch with a young Tibetan Abbot who seems like a first-rate person and is of course very well versed in his tradition, etc. I hope to find out much from him and he says he can get me into Bhutan (he's a friend of the Ghesh there). So I'll be working on that—though I may not actually go there until I return from Indonesia.

Thailand was quite an experience. Though only there two days, I got right in contact with the best meditation people—and real centers of meditation are in the jungles of N.E. Thailand where the Red guerrillas are operating and I don't plan to go there. But I have got a lot of material that explains their ideas and practice. Met an Abbot of a big Buddhist monastery in Bangkok and he was the real thing—though also a busy Abbot—he has had training in the forest retreats and knows the real score. I was impressed and helped.

Calcutta is a shattering experience. I wish everybody could see it.

Incredible—and *not* beautiful really, certainly not "fun." The poverty is staggering. The filth, misery, disease, crowding, despair, overwhelms you. Cows wandering around amid the crowds, people sleeping on the sidewalk, camping in the parks, the confusion and dilapidation of everything: it is really an education. Makes you realize that you can't judge the world by America and Europe. We are Dives and they are Lazarus! The experience of being in the midst of such human misfortune really makes you think about the importance of deep prayer. For things like this, "action" in our sense of the word is helpless. Revolution would only bring madness and cruelty, but no solution. The sense that all this is there and you can do *nothing* that makes sense. (The idea of a ghetto monasticism in Calcutta is just impossible!) It has really got me shook up! The only answer is prayer and fasting. When you see so many hungry people you feel funny about eating so well!

I'll report on further developments. This is a great experience. Asia is the real works!

P.S. There have been a couple of traumatic experiences about money; one when I was charged $70 for overweight luggage at the last minute before takeoff to Bangkok. (Few days before, flew from Alaska with same load and no one said anything about it.) Then I have been grossly overcharged once, on credit card. So it goes. But all is well.

To Abbot James Fox

Calcutta, India
October 20, 1968

I have been waiting for a chance to thank you for your warm and gracious letter, which reached me after some delay, due to a mix-up. Anyway, I certainly want you to know I appreciated it, and certainly you must not feel that I failed to understand the situation. I never personally resented any of your decisions, because I knew you were following your conscience and the policies that seemed necessary then. It is also true that the new "openness" might lead to abuses and deviations. I am not responsible for what others do, but I certainly want to make sure that whatever I do is really for a spiritual goal and for the good of the Church and of monastic life.

This trip is a hard one—Asia is very different from America and Europe. I have already had a slight case of dysentery from bad water— at Mass, a quarter of a cruet of it was enough. But on the whole the journey is a real grace. I have been in contact with Buddhist monks who are really meditating. I have learned of meditation centers that have never been made known in the West. This information is invaluable and very helpful to me personally, and may have important results for all.

Today I am having a long talk with a young Tibetan Buddhist Abbot who made an heroic escape from the Communists a few years ago. He is a very fine person indeed. These contacts seem to be really blessed by God. I feel it is my duty to make the most of every chance. Perhaps eventually the experience will be profitable and will help the contemplative life in America.

Unfortunately, it has to be admitted that Americans don't really meditate, or don't go deep enough, and *never really know themselves.* Perhaps I can bring back some ideas that will change this. So many look to us for depth, and finding that it is not there, turn elsewhere.

So far every move here has been very quiet. I have avoided people who might make a fuss over me. I frequented mostly Asians and non-Catholics to whom I am not "famous." That is a blessing. I don't anticipate any "publicity" problem in Asia. We are gathered here for a meeting of various religions and I am supposed to talk on Monasticism. I trust in your good prayers.

Be sure that I have never changed in my respect for you as Abbot, and affection as Father. Our different views certainly did not affect our deep agreement on the real point of life and our vocation. I hope you are enjoying a beautiful quiet autumn out in the wild knobs.

To Brother Patrick Hart

Calcutta
October 21, 1968

I got the first package you sent here—many thanks. Thailand and India have been wonderful experiences. Utterly different in so many ways from Europe and America, in spite of Westernization. Still totally religious cultures—with plenty of good and bad mixed up together. The Thai monasteries are very thriving and there is a minority very proficient in meditation, contemplation, etc. Here in Calcutta I have met a really marvelous young Tibetan Abbot who escaped from the Reds in Tibet and now has a meditation center in Scotland. We are becoming very good friends and I expect to see a lot of him in the next month or so around various centers in the north of India, etc. Couldn't think of anyone better: he belongs to the more contemplative Tibetan tradition, speaks perfect English, and is very much in touch with what goes on. He will be a great help. Could you please send some books to his place in Scotland?

I hope this isn't too much but I think it is important to send these people books—they are all giving me things of theirs. Maybe later I will write some account of all this—but I'll wait a bit. It could make a mimeographed letter. I wouldn't want to write something to be read in refectory!! . . .

Give my regards to Phil [Stark] if you write, and to Maurice [Flood] and all.

Oberoi Grand, Calcutta
October 25, 1968

Two packets of letters today. OK to use notes on "Future of Monasticism" in the new magazine [*Monastic Exchange,* of which Brother Patrick Hart was current editor]. I have made a few corrections and additions and am returning the copy.

This week in Calcutta has been fabulous. Have met some extraordinary people—of all kinds—but made some very fruitful contacts. The Dalai Lama's sister-in-law is in the next room! Met some fine scholars and good monks—and some outlandish phonies also. Monday I go to Delhi and perhaps a quick trip to Bombay. Then after meeting the Dalai Lama, back to this side of India. The heat is like the worst part of Kentucky summer, though it is the "good" season. Have had some dysentery, etc.— but I guess life is a struggle for everyone here.

Can you write Dom Leclercq and say I am only going to Japan *after* Bangkok and he should look up Frs. Dumoulin and Lasalle at Sophia University, also Ven Shojun Bando, 13-13, 6 Chome, Higashi Neno, Taitoku, Tokyo. Best to see the people Dumoulin and Lasalle will recommend . . .

Calcutta
October 27, 1968

Thank God this silly meeting is over. I am making a sort of day of recollection and getting back my right mind before taking off for Delhi. Said Mass in the home of an American friend—with three lovely adopted Chinese children. And meditating in the hotel room—which is quiet and isolated.

Have met a very fine scholar—a Moslem authority on Sufism—and plan to meet him in Delhi and visit Sufi groups. Then I am to see the Dalai Lama on Nov. 4 (pray!). Keep sending mail to Calcutta address, until I say to stop. I'll be back this way shortly. Hope to make a few days' retreat in the mountains. City life does not agree with me! I miss the hermitage!

I am going to mail some books—they are books I consider *worth keeping,* and if they don't find a place for them in the library, they should go in the hermitage. Could you please send a (paper) copy of *Conjectures* to: The Sisters of Loreto, Loreto House, 7 Middleton Row, Calcutta. (Loreto with one "t" is correct.)

I mailed out signed documents to John Ford [lawyer in Louisville] yesterday. They should have gone airmail, but sometimes the clerks in the hotel chisel on that! Two cards enclosed for book-sendings.

To Mother Myriam Dardenne

New Delhi
October 29, 1968

India has been so far a most rewarding experience—and disconcerting also. Great poverty and misery. Yet beautiful things and people everywhere. I met a marvelous old artist who does religious paintings of a sort of folk-ikon quality. A friend will eventually bring you one of these paintings as a gift. It is, I think, very simple and lovely. Love to all . . .

To Brother Patrick Hart

New Delhi
October 29, 1968

Delhi is a big improvement over Calcutta. Better climate, nice city, and quite a few Tibetans (refugees). I am to go to the Himalayas on the 31st (by night train). Having a lot of stomach trouble: dysentery is a big problem here and I'm practically living on the medicine that is supposed to stop it. Just when you are getting better, someone offers you some food you have to accept, and it starts over again. Quite a penance! Maybe I'll be needing a big supply of Entero-vioform. Fr. Eudes can get it cheap and send some airmail—it might be more practical—but ask him if he thinks this makes sense. If it does, I'll give him an address. I haven't tried to buy it yet. Some things are very expensive here.

Can you please send mimeographs—especially Joyce, Barthes, etc., and also some monastic ones and *Monks Pond* III and IV to: Dr. Vahiduddin, 12 Cavalry Line, University Campus, Delhi, India.

I'm having lunch with the French ambassador to find out about Dom [Henri] Le Saux who is living as a hermit somewhere in the Himalayas . . .

To Mother Myriam Dardenne

Dharamsala, India
November 7, 1968

I am finishing what is more or less a week's retreat in the Himalayas—in a cottage down the mountain from the Dalai Lama's residence. It has been a marvelous week.

I have seen the Dalai Lama in two long audiences, and am to see him again tomorrow before I leave. He is a most impressive and likeable person and we have got on very well—talking about Tibetan methods of meditation, etc. Also I have met six or seven other Lamas who are reputed to be very great mystics and who are in fact very impressive. With all of them I have had really delightful and fruitful conversations (with a good interpreter) and it has been an amazing experience—like meeting monks of the time of St. Bernard. Much better than I anticipated. I have found all sorts of good directives for understanding Buddhism better. It seems to me Tibetan Buddhism is something quite special—and very interesting indeed—though some of it may appear bizarre. But the quality of these monks cannot be disputed. They are humble and profound human beings.

Tomorrow I return to Delhi, then I go to the other end of the Himalayas—for more monasteries. It has been a thrilling trip (this part of it). But also—the awful poverty and confusion of Calcutta is a shattering experience. We had two rather "shaking" experiences yesterday—two earthquakes. No damage, but real quakes!

Keep up your prayers—they are very helpful and necessary. I send you all my love. I wish you could share these experiences with me. It seems I must prolong my trip to Europe to see Tibetans who are setting up monasteries there—and other *"periti."* Please pray that this may be acceptable to my good Fr. Flavian! . . .

To Abbot Flavian Burns

Hotel Imperial
New Delhi (India)
November 9, 1968

I owe you a progress report. Not having got any mail for a couple of weeks, I don't know if there are any new things to answer. I'll pick up mail when I get back to Calcutta Monday. Sure is nice not to have a lot of kooky letters, but still, there may be things I ought to take care of. I'll see when I get back to Calcutta on the way to the eastern end of the Himalayas. I'm writing a more picturesque letter to Bro. Patrick for general consumption. [See Merton's "Asian Letter" in *The Road to Joy*, pp. 118–21.] In this I'll stick to essentials.

Just got in here this morning at five by train from the Himalayas, after a week of retreat on the mountain just below where the Dalai Lama lives—in a very primitive cottage. I had three long interviews with the Dalai Lama and met half a dozen other important Lamas living in that area, all of them representative of the Tibetan monastic tradition in various forms and at its best. With most of them I had an expert interpreter who is a Tibetan layman close to the DL for years, and also something of a mystic and an initiate into the esoteric traditions. Thus I think I have managed to get an unusually good introduction to the Tibetan scene here, and will see more of it at Darjeeling and in Sikkim. I may also be in Bhutan next week, not sure yet.

The talks with the Dalai Lama were very fine. He did a lot of off-the-record talking, very open and sincere, a very impressive person, deeply concerned about the contemplative life, and also very learned. I have seldom met anyone with whom I clicked so well and I feel that we have become good friends. He asked me a lot of questions about Western monasticism and they all had to do with "attainment" or, in other words, whether or not the monks were reaching the higher degrees of the mystical life, and what we did to help them make it. He talked a lot about Tibetan methods of *samadhi* (concentration, lower degree of contemplation in which one is working for one-pointedness), and said he had several monks working at a scientific experiment over two years in this practice and that they had attained unusual clarity of mind. This is just the elementary stuff for them. We also discussed some of the more technical stuff and he gave me some very good suggestions, so that I am going to study the philosophical groundwork which underlies both Tibetan meditation and Zen. This is Madhyamika philosophy, which is not speculative and abstract but very concrete. It fits in with the kind of sweeping purification from conceptual thought which is essential for that kind of meditation.

You will be happy to know that when we parted the DL called me a "Geyshe," which is for his group the highest praise, meaning one who is completely learned and proficient in spiritual things. Someone who was with me said the DL had never before said any such thing of a Westerner.

I guess I'll write on the back of this, to save postage. Hope it will be readable. My plans are to spend just a day here, meeting again the Tibetan Abbot I met in Calcutta. He is staying with the Canadian High Commissioner, who is interested in Buddhism and who gave some of my books to the Dalai before I saw him (but I bet he didn't read them). I also had lunch with the French ambassador last time I was here; he gave me the address of the place where Dom Le Saux O.S.B. lives as a hermit in the Himalayas, but it was too far from where I was—maybe two or three days driving. I did not try to locate it.

Monday I go to Calcutta on the way to Darjeeling (didn't get there for the meeting, floods and landslides prevented it); the meeting was in Calcutta and on the whole, looking back, it was pretty poor. But I made a couple of good friends. Incidentally a *Life* photographer was there, but I hope none of his stuff will be considered important enough to print— it wasn't.

I'll be in the Darjeeling-Sikkim area for a couple of weeks, meeting mostly Tibetans, and also studying and praying in the mountains. It is near Mt. Everest (at least Everest is visible from there). Then I go to Madras in S. India where there is a shrine of St. Thomas, supposedly the site of his martyrdom. I'll remember you at Mass there. Then to Ceylon, for the Theravada Buddhists, then to the Bangkok meeting. I am not sure of the exact date of that meeting, and have no information, but hope there will be some in Calcutta. If you or Bro. Patrick know the date and where we are supposed to meet and live, please let me know, in case no other letter has reached me.

After the meeting, then Indonesia as planned and so on through to Japan. After Japan, I believe it is necessary to make a change of plans. I was going to fly back to San Francisco via Hawaii in April or so, but the Dalai Lama suggested that I speak to some people in Europe, including a Tibetan who is setting up a monastery in Switzerland, and also this Abbot friend of mine has a meditation center in Scotland. I ought also to see Marco Pallis who is one of the great experts on Tibetan Buddhism, and another expert in Wales. I can fly from Tokyo over the N. Pole to Europe and take in Switzerland and Scotland, avoiding Cistercian monasteries as much as possible and keeping out of sight, coming back to the U.S. about the end of May. Please let me know if this is ok with you, and I can plan accordingly.

I assume that when I get back to the U.S. you would want me to come back to Gethsemani and we could plan any future steps from there. I am still keen on the idea of trying something in Alaska and I am certain of full support from the bishop there. But naturally this would have to be planned carefully with you, and in the light of whatever may come up between now and then. I often think of the hermitage at Gethsemani and of the many graces it has meant to me: but I still think that I ought to be elsewhere, though always as a member of my monastic family there. I am certainly willing to go slow and be patient about it. But let's be thinking about it and praying to know God's will.

These days in the Himalayas have been great. I am looking forward to seeing the highest mountains and other monasteries. I am glad to have started here and glad I will see the Zen people only later, as I think that will be a step beyond what is here. The Tibetan thing is very complex and deep and they have certainly attained to something extraordinary. At the same time they seem very respectful of our own contemplative tradition in the terms in which I presented it to them. One of them told me, after I had given an outline of our mysticism, that we had everything they had and even were parallel to some of their esoteric traditions (which are usually kept very secret). At the same time, Tibetan mysticism is just beginning to be known in the West and inevitably there is going to be a lot of popularization which will be quite misleading and irresponsible. I'll send you a little book of the Dalai Lama's which I think you'll enjoy. He is really a great person. You'd like him.

To Brother Patrick Hart

New Delhi
November 9, 1968

I rolled in here this a.m. at five, after a long night in a train. I took this opportunity while in Delhi to borrow a typewriter from the Canadian High Commissioner and write a few letters—also my talk for Bangkok. About Bangkok, I suddenly realized that I never got the final word about WHEN it was to be and WHERE one is to stay. If you have any idea, please let me know at once. I have in mind the general dates of Dec. 7 to 14, but I can't swear to them. I never was told where we were supposed to meet. It is quite possible that there are letters in Calcutta waiting with this information, but if you have it, please send it anyway. The Calcutta address will reach me until about Nov. 25. After that—maybe the Bangkok one, whatever that may be. If the Bangkok meeting is after Dec. 6, then up until Dec. 5 I can be reached at American Express, Singapore.

I have written a long letter with news for all [published as an appendix to *The Asian Journal of Thomas Merton*]. It should satisfy the curious at least for a little while. It can be mimeographed and sent out, and I guess not read in refectory. Send it out if you like to as big a list of my usual correspondents as you like, including of course all the nunnies, and anyone you think ought to get it.

By the way I never did see *Monks Pond* IV myself. Maybe there is a copy sitting in Calcutta, but if you can send one along where I could mull over it—and pass it on to Dom Leclercq or someone at the meeting . . .

Now I've got to get a bunch of films in the mail to John Griffin. I hope they get through; they contain all my pictures of India so far, including the Dalai Lama and others. I guess he'll send contact sheets to you, but I'll get others from him also. I better get some enlargements made of these and others, but I'll wait a bit yet. If I do, I'll have them sent there and you can keep them on file for me.

New Delhi
November 10, 1968

I typed out the notes for the Bangkok talk but didn't have carbon paper and anyhow I guess it needs to be copied, maybe mimeographed. Could you please do this first? The most important thing is to send a couple of copies as soon as possible to: Rev. P. Dom M. de Floris, AIM, Prieuré Ste. Bathilde, 7 Rue d'Issy, 92 Vanves, France.

Please explain my difficulties, being on the move in Asia and seldom able to get to a typewriter. I know he wanted a résumé in French but I was not able to do it. If I get a chance in the next week or so, I will. Then I will send it direct if I can, but once again tomorrow I will be away from a typewriter and will be in the Himalayas for a couple of weeks . . .

Anyway, the thing is for this one to take priority over the newsletter. I'll write from Calcutta when I have the mail that's there. Leaving here early tomorrow.

Calcutta
November 11, 1968

OK—thanks for all the mail here in Calcutta—I arrived this A.M. and found the USIS closed but located a guy who could get in and get my mail (Armistice Day).

About business: of course, go ahead with censorship for *Day of a Stranger*—and anything else that needs it. I forget what happened to *Geography of Lograire*—copies should be in hermitage somewhere. One copy was sent to New Directions. Try the third drawer of the bedroom file—see what's there! If none available, get a photo from New Directions, I guess!

Glad to hear the novel [*My Argument with the Gestapo*] and the poems [*Sensation Time at the Home*, which were later included in *Collected Poems*] are all ok.

Please—if no more *Monks Pond* available—try to get a complete file set of I–II–III–IV for my own purposes. Maybe Fr. Philip could bind them. The first three are in the hermitage in the little shelves (bedroom again). If at all possible, send me IV anyway, as I'd like to see it. Please send to: Mr. James George, Canadian High Commissioner, 4 Augangzeb, New Delhi, *Emblems of a Season of Fury*, *Chuang Tzu*, *Raids on the Unspeakable*, *Conjectures*. And also send him a copy of the Bangkok speech . . .

Tomorrow to the Himalayas again—long list of lamas and hermits—in view of Mt. Everest and Kanchenjunga. Will write from there . . .

> In the Himalayas
> nr. Darjeeling
> November 19, 1968

I am just finishing a few days of solitary retreat in the Himalayas. I managed to get permission to stay in a guest bungalow on a Tea Plantation and have had almost complete silence and solitude for a few days—only seeing the manager and his wife once daily, at lunch. They have provided food for the other meals, service, etc. And I have spent a good part of the time sitting on the mountainside looking at Kanchenjunga (28,000 ft.) and listening to the silence of a valley that is a couple of thousand feet deep. It has been wonderful.

Before coming here I concelebrated with a Jesuit missionary in a Mass in Nepali (needless to say, I mumbled the Canon in English). The singing and music were all in Nepali style with drums and cymbals and very beautiful, I thought. I'll try to get the S.J. Padre to send a copy of a tape he made of their singing. It does not seem I will actually go to Nepal this time (maybe January??) but I might as well be there now—only 5 or 6 miles from the border and most of the people are Nepalese . . .

About the mimeographed letter—it should go to local friends, too —ask Dan [Walsh], he knows all of them (like Jim Wygal, etc., Ron Seitz). Might as well check the *red address book* in the cupboard to the right of the fireplace. Send to people like Suzanne Butorovich, Sister Therese, Tommie O'Callaghan, my relatives, etc. I haven't heard from J. Laughlin since I've been in Asia. What goes on with the three books I sent him?

Calcutta

November 25, 1968

It is late at night and I am dropping from fatigue and ready to get to bed as early as possible, but this is the best time to answer some of the pile of mail that I met with here on flying down from Darjeeling today. I had a very bad cold up in the mountains, but still I also made a retreat in the guest bungalow of a Tea Plantation—with a view of Kanchenjunga. It was quite marvelous. Met also many new Lamas in the Darjeeling area. My contact with all of them has been excellent because I have had the good fortune to have first-rate translators. The best Lamas are extraordinary people and some of them real mystics. They have a very austere and I think effective approach to meditation and contemplation. One of them asked me to join a group of his hermits in a completely silent and solitary retreat of three years. I said I would like to try it somewhere else—on my own. (Across the road was an Indian peasant's cottage with the radio going full blast.)

Thanks for letters and all the news. Thank all those who wrote— Brothers Nivard, Matthias, Colman, etc. Not possible to get to where Brother Colman's sister is [Sister Vaune Gannon, an SND missionary in India]. I was long out of the Delhi area by the time I got the letter. But met a hospital nun from Patna—who didn't know Colman's sister but knew a lot of Nazareth nuns. Gave talks to the Jesuits in the area—very edifying people. The Jesuit scholasticate near Darjeeling is a very monastic place, and very edifying. The Jesuit brother of the great Schillebeeckx (some spelling!) is there and he is a real contemplative. Had several talks with him.

Thanks for all the stuff which has arrived safely: medicine, etc. As to queries: the article on solitude is from a magazine published at Harvard called *Contacts* or some such name. If Dom [Leclercq] had the page, he must have had the magazine. Hence, he must have the reference; I certainly don't. I'll talk about it to him. He's in India now but I don't expect to see him till Bangkok.

My Bangkok address is: AIM Meeting, c/o Missions Etrangères, 254 Silon Rd., Bangkok, Thailand. So send stuff there until Dec. 14. Then to Rawa Seneng [Trappist monastery in Indonesia where Merton was planning to go after Bangkok]. I did not have any idea of this address until the letters arrived.

As to the stuff from Editions de l'Epi, it is their problem, not ours, to clear the publication of their book with Notre Dame Press. I am not interested in this publication. It is their problem and if they want the book in its present form it is up to them to clear it [*Faith and Violence*, Notre Dame Press]. I have no way of handling it myself . . .

Please tell Dan how touched and grateful I am for his kindness. [Dan Walsh had sent a check to help out on travel expenses.] I may need it one of these fine days, as sometimes I get hit with unexpected expenses, am overcharged, or turn up overweight in luggage at the airport, etc. Anything can happen. I appreciate his thoughtfulness. Will send him a letter or card when I can. So far the money is holding out ok. Also the credit card which is a godsend in emergencies.

Thanks for *Monks Pond.* I was really happy with it. Forgot how good it really was . . . I am grateful to Phil again and to all who made it a groovy thing.

As to the presidential election, I won't comment. It could be worse . . .

Madras
November 27 [1968]

Bob Lax informs me that Emmett Williams wants some stuff of mine in an anthology of concrete poetry. Williams is on the *Monks Pond* address list. Will you please: 1) Write Williams and give him permission to use anything of mine he has or liked. 2) Send me Williams' address.

I am just about to go out and say Mass at the shrine of St. Thomas— supposedly the place of his martyrdom. Madras is a really lovely place— best city I've seen in India so far! I am going on to Ceylon—and you have my Bangkok address by now . . . After Dec. 16 it will be Rawa Seneng, at least until the end of December.

Colombo, Ceylon
December 3, 1968

I have not written before from Ceylon because of a postal strike here—and am not certain this letter will get out without delay—but there is nothing urgent. However I must say Ceylon is a really lovely place— the best I have hit so far. Have not met many Buddhists, except a couple of Buddhist hermits—both Germans—living in the jungle. One is a scholar with a nice house full of books; the other a young man in a cave, which is dry and neat and very livable. Will meet a Buddhist big wheel at University today—and off to Singapore tomorrow. Also saw the Bishop of Kandy, whom I knew before—he is anxious to have contemplatives in his diocese, and since it is in the mountains it would be ideal. I told him I didn't think Fr. Flavian wanted to make foundations, especially that far away. Of course everywhere one goes they ask for a foundation—but here it would certainly be a nice spot!! The most beautiful place in the world, all kinds of fruits and flowers. Don't go stirring people up with this idea however! I did see an Anglican ashram, very simple and poor, yet very livable. It would be easy to do it with almost no expense . . .

Singapore
December 5, 1968

I got the Singapore mail at American Express here today—including a nice newsy letter of Fr. Idesbald. Tomorrow I go on to Bangkok and to the serious business of the AIM meeting. It takes place at the Red

Cross Center there, but as you know, we are staying (so it seems) with the Paris Foreign Mission Society. Or I'll be looking for mail there.

I'll be at Rawa Seneng until the end of December and will try to write a Christmas letter somewhere along the line (for mimeographing); don't forget to send me a copy or two of Asia Letter I.

The enclosed photos aren't bad—but they aren't permanentized so may fade in a few months.

About the contracts from Fr. Basil [Pennington, for *The Climate of Monastic Prayer*, published by Cistercian Publications]—glad to see them. But I guess the normal thing is for Fr. Flavian to sign *all* contracts—no?

Money is holding out fairly well so far. I am scared of Indonesia as I have heard all kinds of tales of pickpockets there—would hate to have someone lift that credit card. It comes in handy sometimes (like I used it to load up on film here in Singapore—film is hard to get in Asia and here it is both plentiful and cheap).

Singapore is the most progressive spot in SE Asia, very alive and booming. I have been visiting with a young Chinese professor of philosophy at the University here—a young Catholic. The Chinese food here is excellent. No lamas. Glad to give that side of it a rest!

The New Yorker wants to do a profile of me and they tried to get to me through Ping Ferry. I told him to tell them politely to go to hell.

Glad the Niles songs [John Jacob Niles set twenty-three Merton poems to music for voice and piano] were appreciated in Louisville. How was the tape of the Freedom Songs? [Alexander Peloquin set this series of poems to music for mixed chorus.] In Madras I met a Negro lady from Atlanta, the education head of SCLC [Southern Christian Leadership Conference] and a friend of Martin Luther King. Very nice . . .

It is getting close to Christmas—let's keep united in prayer. I miss the quiet of the hermitage. Hope to have a little silence when I get to Rawa Seneng. Bangkok I dread—it will be all talk talk talk. Ugh!

Hope to find mail in Bangkok. Best love to all . . . I am in the famous Raffles Hotel—a sort of literary monument. Somerset Maugham and other writers about the East used to frequent it (especially the bar—which I have *not* visited).

Bangkok
December 8, 1968

I am in Bangkok—downtown at a hotel, but leaving in a few minutes for our meeting place—about 30 km. out of town. I got here two days ago, but most of the others arrive today. Dom Leclercq got in yesterday—with his usual ebullience. Main point of this is to send two tickets I did not use, in the hope there can be a refund. Bangkok has been expensive, so I think again in terms of the budget. Fortunately there will be little or no expense once the meeting gets under way tomorrow. I hope to go on to Djakarta next Sunday. Send mail please to Rawa Seneng.

No mail here yet—I wonder if perhaps I missed a package at Singapore (there was one). Not that I worry, but I want to get an answer from Fr. Flavian as it concerns a matter I wrote to him about for his judgment and clearance. Maybe something out at the Red Cross place where we're staying. (Silon Rd. is around the corner, Hq. of French Missionaries, but we are not staying there.)

I think of you all on this Feast Day [Feast of the Immaculate Conception]. Also with Christmas approaching, I feel homesick for Gethsemani. But I hope to be at least in a monastery—Rawa Seneng. Also I look forward to being at Hong Kong and maybe seeing our three volunteers there (or is it two?) [three monks from Gethsemani were helping out at the Trappist monastery in Hong Kong at this time].

No more for the moment. Best love to all,

Louie

Appendix: Two Private Vows

I. Private Vow Never to Serve as Abbot (1952)

In honor of the simplicity and humility of the Most Blessed Virgin Mary Mother of God, and for the glory of her divine Son, Jesus Christ Our Lord, I, Frater Mary Louis Merton, O.C.S.O., vow that as long as I live I will never accept any election to the office of Abbot or Titular Prior either in this monastery or in any other monastery of the Cistercian Order. Made and signed in the presence and with the full approval of my Reverend Father Abbot, the Rt. Rev. Dom Mary James Fox, in this monastery of our Lady of Gethsemani.

(*Signed*)   Fr. M. Louis Merton, O.C.S.O.
(*Countersigned*)   Fr. James Fox
                 Abbot—Gethsemani
                 October 8, 1952

II. Commitment to the Solitary Life (1966)

I, Brother M. Louis Merton, solemnly professed monk of the Abbey of Our Lady of Gethsemani, having completed a year of trial in the solitary life, hereby make my commitment to spend the rest of my life in solitude in so far as my health may permit.

Made in the presence of Rt. Rev. Dom M. James Fox, Abbot of Gethsemani, September 8th, 1966.

(*Signed*)   Fr. M. Louis Merton

Acknowledgments

Many persons have been helpful over the years in the preparation of this third volume of Thomas Merton's letters. I am deeply grateful to Reverend William H. Shannon, General Editor, and to the Trustees of the Merton Legacy Trust for inviting me to edit this volume dealing with religious renewal and spiritual direction. My own Abbot, Father Timothy Kelly, and the community of Gethsemani have been very supportive in allowing me the time and space (and even a trip to Rome and Stanbrook Abbey in England) for this task, making it a labor of love as well as an exciting adventure.

Six years ago I was permitted to visit our Curia Generalizia Archives in Rome, and I was met with wonderful cooperation from our Abbot General, Dom Ambrose Southey, and his staff. They provided copies of Thomas Merton's letters addressed to our two previous Abbots General, Dom Gabriel Sortais and Dom Ignace Gillet. Merton was not too scrupulous about keeping copies of his letters to Rome, and it was a great help to compare the letters on file in Rome with those in Kentucky. Once again I was greeted with true monastic hospitality by the Benedictine Sisters of Stanbrook Abbey, especially Abbess Elizabeth Sumner and Dame Hildelith Cumming. While I was lunching at the guest house and addressing a few words to the Stanbrook community, Dame Hildelith arranged to have copies made of over twenty Merton letters that were not filed at the Thomas Merton Studies Center Collection of Bellarmine College in Louisville.

The bulk of the letters included here were found at the largest of the Merton collections, namely, at Bellarmine College's Thomas Merton Studies Center. I am grateful above all to its director and chief of research, Dr. Robert E. Daggy, for making my innumerable work visits to the Center so enjoyable and worthwhile. He greatly expedited my work, as did his staff of student assistants, who were most generous and cooperative about copying letters for me on numberless occasions.

The earliest letters in this volume to Abbot Frederic Dunne and Abbot James Fox were discovered in the Abbey of Gethsemani Monastic Archives, and complement those on file at the Merton Center of Bellarmine College. Dom Jean

Leclercq was most gracious in placing both sides of his vast correspondence with Merton at our disposal, and even arranged to have his English-speaking secretary, Sr. Bernard Said, prepare English translations where required. Dom André Louf of Mont-des-Cats Cistercian Abbey in France brought an important Merton letter to Gethsemani at the time of the General Chapter of 1984, held in the United States for the first time. This letter of April 26, 1965, was a great defense of the solitary life.

Although most of the letters were written in English, those addressed to the two French Abbots General were in French, which Merton wrote easily. I am grateful to Father Germain Marc'hadour of the University of Angers in France for supervising the translation of the majority of these letters. Fathers Felix Donahue, Francis Kline, and Augustine Wulff of Gethsemani provided excellent translations from the French of additional letters. Sister Elizabeth Connor of St. Romuald Cistercian Abbey in Quebec and Sister Susan Van Winkle of Mount St. Mary's Abbey, Wrentham, Massachusetts, rendered accurate translations of several other letters as the work progressed. I am again indebted to Father William H. Shannon, past president of the International Merton Society, of Rochester, New York, for preparing excellent translations from the French of letters that were unearthed long after my trip to Rome.

I cannot omit a number of others who through correspondence encouraged the project, including Mother Prioress Angela Collins, Dame Hildelith Cumming, and Marcella Van Bruyn. I am grateful to the Procurator General of the Camaldolese at Frascati in Italy, Father Michael Farrell, who graciously received me during my visit to Italy and provided me with copies of Merton letters to the Camaldolese superiors over the years. Father Kilian McDonnell of St. John's Abbey, Collegeville, Minnesota, was helpful in searching their monastic archives for additional letters of Merton to members of St. John's Abbey, such as Fathers Godfrey Diekmann and Colman Barry. Sisters Mary Luke Tobin and Elaine M. Bane were present with their good advice and counsel on a number of occasions.

Finally, I must express my gratitude to Abbot Emeritus Flavian Burns and Father Felix Donahue of Gethsemani, who devoted many hours to reading the manuscript of this volume, and to Dr. Michael Downey, who offered valuable suggestions for its improvement. Likewise, I want to thank Robert Giroux, editor of this book and a Trustee of the Merton Legacy Trust, who greatly expedited the task through his gentle shepherding of the entire project. If I have forgotten anyone, please consider yourself included in this list of persons to whom I am indebted in the charity of Christ which unites us all.

B.P.H.

Index